Alfred Barry

Manifold witness for Christ

Alfred Barry

Manifold witness for Christ

ISBN/EAN: 9783743356894

Manufactured in Europe, USA, Canada, Australia, Japa

Cover: Foto ©Lupo / pixelio.de

Manufactured and distributed by brebook publishing software (www.brebook.com)

Alfred Barry

Manifold witness for Christ

THE

MANIFOLD WITNESS FOR CHRIST

PART I.
CHRISTIANITY AND NATURAL THEOLOGY

PART II.
THE POSITIVE EVIDENCES OF CHRISTIANITY

BEING

The Boyle Lectures
FOR
1877 AND 1878

By ALFRED BARRY, D.D. D.C.L.

PRINCIPAL OF KING'S COLLEGE, LONDON

CANON OF WORCESTER : CHAPLAIN IN ORDINARY TO THE QUEEN

NEW YORK
E. P. DUTTON & CO., 713 BROADWAY
1880

TO THE

RIGHT REVEREND

JOSEPH BARBER LIGHTFOOT, D.D.

LORD BISHOP OF DURHAM

THIS VOLUME IS, BY PERMISSION, DEDICATED

IN TOKEN NOT ONLY OF

HIGH PERSONAL ESTEEM AND ADMIRATION

BUT ALSO OF

A DEEP SENSE OF THE DEBT OF GRATITUDE

DUE TO ONE WHO HAS TAUGHT US BY EXAMPLE

TO UNITE CRITICAL ACCURACY WITH BREADTH OF IDEA,

FULNESS OF LEARNING WITH CLEARNESS AND BEAUTY OF EXPOSITION,

AND FEARLESS INVESTIGATION OF TRUTH

WITH FIRM CHRISTIAN FAITH.

PREFACE.

THE SUBSTANCE of this volume was delivered in the Boyle Lectures of 1877 and 1878. But the whole has been rewritten; much has been added; and in the division and evolution of the argument I have sometimes ventured, for the sake of clearness, to disregard the limitations imposed on the delivery of the fixed number of 'eight sermons annually,' laid down by the founder of the lectureship. For it has always seemed to me that what is published, as being addressed to the eye, and asking for deliberate consideration, ought to be presented in a form different from that which more properly belongs to an address through the ear to the intelligence and attention of the moment.

It should be at once stated that I have taken for granted the argument of the first course of lectures (for 1876), already published, dealing with the cumulative force of the various evidences of Natural Theology. My belief, for which I have in those lectures endeavoured to give reasons, is simply this —that the convergent force of the various lines of that natural witness for God would be absolutely irresistible, if it were not crossed on every line by the disturbing power of the mystery of evil; and that, if thoughtfully considered, even this terrible mystery only presents itself as a serious moral and speculative difficulty, capable of weakening, but in no sense of destroying, the predominant force of the great time-honoured argument of Natural Theology. Starting from that conviction, I have in these pages desired to inquire how (to adopt Butler's phrase) in this mingled 'light and darkness of Nature Christianity comes in;' and by what process it actually establishes and justifies faith in the Lord Jesus Christ, when in our own days the right to claim such faith for Him is questioned by various forms of modern thought.

It is certain, as a matter of fact, that the Christianity of the mass of men is received by inheritance and teaching, and tested first by practical experience, and then by simple study of the Gospel in itself. I contend not only that this is perfectly reasonable, but that by no other method could Christianity, in accordance with the laws of human nature and experience, hope to assert for itself anything like a universal sway. But when this natural process is challenged to justify itself by reason, it appears to me that Christian thought generally passes through the two phases which I have attempted to sketch in the first and second parts of this volume.

I. Christianity obviously presents herself as the chief representative of 'Supernatural Religion;' probably the only representative who has any chance of a hearing. The first question which suggests itself to most men on hearing her claim, is the question of the relation in which the Gospel stands to the conclusions and doubts of 'Natural Religion.' Can it do anything to strengthen the one, and to dispel the other? In answer to that question I have endeavoured to show that here, as in all other cases, the 'Supernatural is not Preternatural.' Tracing the gradual development in the Bible of the full Christian doctrine, under the pervading idea of 'Covenant with God,' I have contended that, in relation to the three fundamental points of religion, the personality of God, the spirituality of man, and the solution of the mystery of evil, Christianity accords at all points with the main principles of Natural Religion; but at the same time confirms in the calmness of absolute certitude the modest inductions of Natural Theology, and supplements them, when they are silent or speak with stammering tongue, by declarations of mystery, avowedly undiscoverable by the mere reason of man. If this contention proves to be in any degree true, I hold that it is a preparation for faith in Christ, which must in different degrees affect all minds, and which by very many men will, not unreasonably, be held sufficient to bring them to His feet. At once by analogy with the Natural, and by a power to transcend it, the Gospel will assert itself with no inconsiderable force of probability as being—what it professes to be—a supreme revelation of the God of the world and of man; and, if its positive evidences are still to be scrutinised, will claim to enter that scrutiny under a *primâ facie* presumption of truth and not of falsehood.

II. Here, however, comes in the second phase of Christian thought, the examination of these positive evidences, so often carried out in times past and present by great thinkers and critics. If (as may well be the case) an apology is needed for entering once more on a well-worn track, in which originality is impossible, I can only offer this—that at all times the inquiry should be into the natural and concrete form under which, in each age, Christian evidence presents itself; and that, while its great abstract principles remain necessarily unchanged, because unchangeable, this concrete exhibition of them is changing every day. Now it seems to me that there are two main points to which modern thought directs our chief attention. The first is the consideration of the unique combination of various powers in Christianity, considered as at once a philosophy, a moral force, and a spiritual life; for this is, I believe, to us much what the contemplation of fulfilled prophecy and present miracle was in the apostolic age. The next is the contemplation of the life and person of Christ as a whole, in the combined manifestations of power, wisdom, and love, standing out unique and unapproachable, and rightly challenging for Him an absolute faith. These I hold to be the two great points in Christian evidence as it presents itself in these days. I would especially urge that we should look at it in relation to the spirit of our own age, instead of trying to go back to the different experience and thought of days gone by; and I would also contend that, in contemplating, first, Christianity and then Christ Himself, we should contemplate them in their historic reality, discarding all abstract and artificial divisions of the subject, in which the convergent force, arising from the combination of various elements in one living whole, is absolutely lost.

For here, as in considering the witness of Natural Theology to God, the witness for Christ shows itself as a 'manifold witness;' and, even at the risk of too vague a generality of treatment, we must venture to contemplate it as a whole. It is, indeed, necessary to combat in detail special objections to the Gospel, which present themselves as practical difficulties in the way of belief. It is still more necessary to work out thoroughly and particularly this or that branch of Christian evidence, such as the evidence of miracles, or the argument from prophecy. But in doing these things there is, I think, some danger of forgetting that the whole is greater than its parts. Religious faith, like most of the strongest practical convictions of life, is wrought out in the mind by a convergence of many evidences, moral and speculative, direct and indirect; and when it fixes on any object, it looks upon it, not in the light of this or that abstract principle, but in its concrete reality as a whole. To different minds, perhaps, different branches of evidence and different aspects of the object of faith emerge into prominence. But even then others claim their place, and the witness for Christ is still a manifold witness.

III. Such I believe to be the two chief processes of Christian thought, when it is forced to estimate the evidences of Christianity. But whether we follow either or both of these, there remains one last step to be taken—the acceptance in faith of the word of Christ Himself. It is important here, as before, to recognise the relation of the Natural to the Supernatural. That the law of faith is eminently natural, and that, moreover, it is one of the greatest forces acting upon humanity, is indisputable. That the faith claimed by the Gospel is an entirely supernatural culmination of this natural law, is equally beyond question. It is well to see clearly that on the acceptance or rejection of this claim the very possibility of a vital Christianity turns, and that the profounder doctrines of the Gospel, however they may be prepared for by reason and verified by experience, still rest ultimately on faith, and on faith alone. At whatever point in our previous investigation we stop—and different men stop at various points, naturally and reasonably enough—this last process of faith must always come in to complete a true Christianity.

These are the chief points for which this volume is designed to claim attention. In the whole course of the argument I have dealt with what I may call our actual historic Christianity, not with any of those ideal reconstructions of it, which are from time to time presented to us in the name of philosophy or 'higher criticism.' For these appear to be as unreal, and as little worth fighting for, as the fanciful Gnostic theories of the early ages. A Christianity which surrenders or mythicises almost every article of the Apostles' Creed, and which practically sets aside the historical truth of the New Testament, is not one which will stand or ought to stand. Nor, again, in endeavouring to consider what are the great features of this historic Christianity, have I thought it necessary to enter into the questions —profoundly interesting and important questions—which are now being raised as to the date and authorship, the genuineness and accuracy, of certain portions of Holy Scripture, both in the Old Testament and in the New. I have dealt with the Bible as the Church has actually received it, and made it the standard of the Christian faith. And this I have ventured to do on two grounds. First, I believe that the ascendency of the negative and disintegrating criticism is on the wane; and that a sounder method of study— protesting against the arbitrary assumption of that which calls itself the 'higher criticism,' and which certainly is little apt to rest on the solid prosaic ground of external evidence—is vindicating more and more successfully the historical accuracy and genuineness of Holy Scripture as a whole. But next, in relation to such argument as that which I have attempted, it seems clear that the main points of the Creed of Christendom do not depend on the absolute authority of this or that passage or book, or the Apostolic authorship of our Gospels in their present form, or the genuineness of some controverted prophecies or Epistles. They are embodied even in the mutilated Bible which the most destructive criticism would leave us, or in 'the original documents' which it reproduces as confidently as if it had seen them. Nay, they are embodied in the very simplest record of the life of Christ, and in the actual faith of the Christianity which conquered the world. To put them aside is to create a new religion under an old name.

It only remains to add that, while it is impossible, as every one knows, to estimate how much in our present knowledge and thought is due to the teaching of others in days past,[1] yet in writing these lectures I have tried to work out the main ideas for myself, without consulting any contemporary books on the same subject, except those referred to in the notes;[2] and that although I have seldom quoted or referred to writings of sceptical or anti-Christian opinion, I have endeavoured to keep always in mind (so far as I know it) what the literature of the day shows to be the main tendencies of modern thought.

The object which I have had in view is that which I believe the founder of the Boyle Lectureship contemplated—to offer to those who are startled by loud attacks on Christianity, and bewildered by the largeness and multiplicity of

---

[1] Thus, for example, on the relation of Scripture to Natural Theology, it is difficult to estimate the debt due to the lessons taught by Professor Maurice, especially in his *Sermons on the Old Testament*.

[2] I rejoice to find that, in respect of the present force of the argument from miracles, I am much in agreement with Prebendary Row's *Bampton Lectures*, and, in reference to the Province of Faith, with Professor Wace's *Bampton Lectures*, published since this volume was written. The agreement is, however, an independent agreement.

the considerations which they open, some clue to the right method of estimating the true conditions of the great problem presented to them. In order to carry out that object with plainness and simplicity, I have abstained from any attempt at exhaustive treatment of details, and even from the addition of such notes and illustrations as might not unnaturally be suggested from time to time in the course of the argument. For I cannot but believe that when once the right method is understood, the work of examination is more than half done. The revelation of Christ, if only it be contemplated in its natural order, will prove itself victorious, as of old, over all difficulties whether of mind or of heart. Nor will this examination cease to have value when it has wrought conviction. The same study which brings out the grounds of faith to the inquiring mind will be to the believer no dead abstract inquiry, but a continual sustenance of spiritual life. Believing that the method itself is the true one—however defectively it may have been exhibited in these pages—I pray God that it may speak alike to inquirer and to believer, and to the yet larger class of those who stand midway between scepticism and belief, earnest in seeking for the religion which they feel that they need, and yet hardly knowing whether they have found what they seek.

A. B.

KING'S COLLEGE, LONDON:
July, 1880.

CONTENTS.

PART I.
CHRISTIANITY AND NATURAL THEOLOGY.

CHAPTER I.
CHRISTIANITY NATURAL AND SUPERNATURAL.

A. *The Two Aspects of Christianity—*   PAGE
Christianity as 'Natural Religion' and Christianity as supernatural,
and the relation between them 1
Christianity, in relation to Natural Theology, seen to be supernatural,
not preternatural 5
  (*a*) In the Incarnation 6
  (*b*) In the Passion 7

B. *The Supernatural not Preternatural—*
  (*a*) In relation to the physical sphere 9
  (*b*) In relation to the sphere of ordinary humanity . . 11
Christianity the supreme assertion of this law . . . 14
  (*a*) In revelation of God 14
  (*b*) In mediation for man 15

C. *The Importance of this view of Christianity—*
  (*a*) As an intrinsic evidence of truth . . 17
  (*b*) As preparatory to positive evidences 22
  ˙(*c*) In relation to the argument of Natural Theology . 22

CHAPTER II.
THE SIGNIFICANCE OF COVENANT WITH GOD.

A. *Christianity to be studied in the Bible, taken as a whole and in historic
order* 24

B. *The Idea of Covenant with God*, as bearing on—
  (*a*) The personality of God 29
  (*b*) The spirituality of man 30
  (*c*) The communion between God and man 31
Its relation to Natural Theology, speculative and moral . . . 32

C. *The Idea of Covenant with God*, as bearing on—
The mystery of evil, recognising evil and promising victory over it . 35

CHAPTER III.

GOD AND MAN IN PRIMEVAL HISTORY.

	PAGE
A. *The Introduction to Scripture History—*	
Symbolical, whether in history or parable	39
B. *The Record of Creation,* in its bearing on	
(a) Ætiology	42
(b) Teleology	43
(c) Moral Theology	44
(d) The spirituality of man	46
C. *The History of Primeval Man—*	
(a) The sacredness of work	47
(b) The power of thought	47
(c) The social nature of man	48
(d) The religious nature of man	48
D. *The Record of the Fall—*	
(a) Evil not original	50
(b) The nature of temptation	51
(c) The penalties of sin	52
(d) The promise of victory over it	53

CHAPTER IV.

THE GENERAL AND SPECIAL COVENANTS OF GOD.

A. *The Antediluvian World, the Flood, and the New Covenant*	55
B. *The General Covenant with Noah—*	
(a) The law of physical regularity	59
(b) The sacredness of human life	60
(c) The sacredness of authority	60
C. *The Special Covenant with Abraham—*	
(a) Its accordance with human nature and history	61
(b) The external and spiritual history	62
(c) The 'God of Abraham' and the 'God Almighty'	63
(d) The promise	65
(e) The slight reference to the mystery of evil	66
D. *The Mosaic Revelation—*	
The name JEHOVAH and the Theocracy	67
(a) God in history	69
(b) God in law	71
(c) The knowledge of sin in law and sacrifice	74

CHAPTER V.

THE VOICE OF GOD IN THE SOUL; THE ANSWER OF THE SOUL TO GOD.

A. *The Imperfection of the earlier Revelations,* as throwing light upon—	
(a) The slaughter of the Canaanites	81
(b) The retrogression of the period of the Judges	83

CONTENTS. [17]

PAGE

B. *The Revelation of Prophecy to the Soul by the ' Word of the Lord ' and the ' Spirit of the Lord '—*
   (*a*) Its relation to 'God in history' 85
   (*b*) Its relation to 'God in law' 88
   (*c*) Its relation to sacrifice and priesthood 89
   (*d*) Its intrinsic character 90

C. *The Answer to God—*
   (*a*) In the Psalms (spiritual) 91
   (*b*) In the Sapiential books (intellectual) 93

D. *The Knowledge thus given of—*
   (*a*) The sovereignty of God 96
   (*b*) The divine image in man 97
   (*c*) The mystery of evil 98

CHAPTER VI.

THE MESSIANIC IDEA IN THE OLD TESTAMENT.

A. *Reality and Prominence of the Messianic Idea*, as elucidating—
   (*a*) The history 103
   (*b*) The theocracy 103
   (*c*) The moral law 104
   (*d*) The sacrifice 104
   (*e*) The Psalms 105
   (*f*) The Sapiential books 106
   (*g*) The Prophecy 106
   (*h*) The character of the people 107

B. *Its Completion of the Idea of Covenant with God—*
   (*a*) As an exaltation of humanity 108
   (*b*) As a manifestation of God 111
   (*c*) As bearing on the mystery of evil 115

C. *The General Character of Old Testament Revelation—*
   (*a*) Its perfection as a grand Monotheism 119
   (*b*) Its imperfection as a Religion of Humanity 120
   (*c*) Its still greater imperfection in relation to the mystery of evil . 121

CHAPTER VII.

THE SPIRITUALITY OF MAN AND THE RESURRECTION OF CHRIST.

A. *The Resurrection the First Stage in the Preaching of Christ—*
   (*a*) As a seal of His Messiahship 124
   (*b*) As the climax of the Gospel history 125

B. *The Order of Preaching of the Resurrection—*
   (*a*) The declaration of the fact 127
   (*b*) Its significance in relation to Himself 129
   (*c*) Its significance to all mankind 132

CONTENTS.

C. *The Teaching of the Resurrection*—   PAGE
  (a) The spirituality of man 133
  (b) The immortality of man in the future 137
  (c) The nature and destiny of the body . . . 137
  (d) The revelation of God 139
  (e) The mystery of evil 142

CHAPTER VIII.

THE LAW OF MEDIATION AND THE MEDIATION OF CHRIST.

A. *The Preaching of the Mediation of Christ*, in relation to—
  (a) The Resurrection 146
  (b) The doctrine of the Cross 147

B. *The Law of Mediation in Human Life*—
  (a) Its reality as an ordinance of God . . . 148
  (b) Its dependence on unity with man . . 151
  (c) Its connection with suffering and sin 151
  (d) Its extraordinary forms 154
  (e) Its limitation in scope and nature 156

C. *The Perfect Mediation of Christ*, as Prophet, Priest, and King, as—
  (a) Redemption from the bondage of sin 159
  (b) Propitiation for the guilt of sin 161
  Its bearing on Natural Theology 163

CHAPTER IX.

THE REVELATION OF GOD IN MAN; CHRIST AS THE WORD.

A. *The Doctrine itself*, as the necessary conclusion of—
  (a) The universal royalty 166
  (b) The universal mediation 167
  Its exhibition by St. Paul and St. John 168

B. *The Origin of this Name of Christ* from—
  (a) The 'Wisdom' of the Old Testament . . 170
  (b) The 'Word' of Greek thought 171
  St. John's use of the phrase 172

C. *The Relation to Natural Theology*—
  (a) God manifest in His works 173
  (b) God manifest in man 174
  (c) The imperfection of such manifestation in the individual and the race 175
  (d) The ideal humanity of human thought 177
  (e) The ideal humanity of the Gospel 178

D. *The Climax of Christian Doctrine*, and its effect on Christian morality 179

CHAPTER X.

CONCLUSION.

A. Summary of the argument 184
B. (*a*) Its evidential force 187
   (*b*) The function of positive Christian evidences 188
   (*c*) The province of faith 188

PART II.

THE POSITIVE EVIDENCES OF CHRISTIANITY.

CHAPTER I.

THE FUNCTION AND METHOD OF CHRISTIAN EVIDENCE.

A. *The Grounds of Actual Belief—*
   (*a*) Inheritance and teaching 193
   (*b*) Practical experience 194
   (*c*) Examination of Christianity in itself 195
   (*d*) Examination of its relation to Natural Theology . . . 197
   (*e*) Examination of Christian evidences 198
   (*f*) Faith 200

B. *The Order of Christian Evidences—*
   (*a*) In the first ages, Prophecy and Miracle; in our age, History and Living Power of Christianity 203
   (*b*) Examination of the life of Christ 207
   (*c*) The relation of the province of knowledge to the province of faith 209

C. *Practical Conclusions—*
   (*a*) The right attitude towards doubts 209
   (*b*) The accordance with the spirit of our age 210

CHAPTER II.

CHRISTIANITY AS AN INTELLECTUAL SYSTEM.

The twofold problem of Being 212
A. *Individuality* in thought, will, and conscience . . . 213
   (*a*) Recognised in the Gospel 216
   (*b*) Manifested in the life of the Son of Man 217
B. *Unity* in Nature and Humanity 217
   (*a*) Recognised in the Gospel 220
   (*b*) Revelation in the life of Christ of one God the Father . 221
C. *Comparison of the Gospel with other Religions and Philosophies,* in respect of—
   (*a*) Abstract perfection 225
   (*b*) Intelligibility to all 226

CHAPTER III.

CHRISTIANITY AS A MORAL FORCE.

	PAGE
A. *The Moral Force of the Gospel a Reproduction of the Life of Christ*—	230
(a) Its relation to actual humanity	234
(b) Its relation to the power of God	234
Its characteristics	
(a) Simplicity	235
(b) Universality	236
(c) Applicability to sinners	236
(d) Permanence	237
B. *Its Recognition of Individuality*—	
(a) In the weak—the child, the woman, the poor, the slave	239
(The stress laid on purity)	243
(b) In the strong—tempering it and bringing it out in new developments of martyrdom, asceticism, chivalry	245
C. *Its Recognition of Unity*—	
Christianity essentially a fraternity of all men	248
(a) Its sanction of family unity	250
(b) Its sanction of national unity	251
(c) Its creation of Catholic unity	251
D. *Objections to Christian Morality*, on the ground of—	
(a) Selfishness	253
(b) Intolerance	254
(c) Practical failures	255

CHAPTER IV.

CHRISTIANITY AS A SPIRITUAL LIFE.

	PAGE
The two elements of spiritual life	259
A. *Self-consciousness* in the instinct of perfection, concentration of thought on self, and extenuation of evil, exhibited in—	
(a) Stoicism	264
(b) Self-culture	265
(c) Agnosticism	265
(d) Pelagianism	265
B. *Self-forgetfulness* in—	
(a) Pessimism	268
(b) Worship of the universe	268
(c) Worship of humanity	269
(d) Religious mysticism	270
C. *The Gospel harmonises both in the Life of Christ*—	
(a) The principle of faith	272
(b) The principle of spiritual life illustrated in Christian worship and practice	273

CONTENTS. [21]

CHAPTER V.

THE LIFE OF CHRIST AS SEEN BY THE WORLD.

A. *The Study of the Life of Christ—*   PAGE
   (a) Our means of knowledge 280
   (b) Necessity of study of it as a whole . . . 284

B. *The Manifestation of the Kingdom of Heaven—*
   (a) The power of His miracles 287
      1. The evidence of miracles 288
      2. The function of miracles 291
   (b) The wisdom of His teaching in tone and substance . . 296
   (c) The goodness of His life 300

C. *The Actual Stages of Faith—*
   (a) His prophetic character 302
   (b) His Messiahship 303
   (c) His spiritual royalty 303

CHAPTER VI.

THE LIFE OF CHRIST AS SEEN BY HIS DISCIPLES.

A. *The Gospel to be manifested through the Disciples—* . . 306
   (a) Their higher knowledge 308
   (b) Its imperfection leading to faith 311
   (c) Stages in its progress 312

B. *The Acknowledgment of His Messiahship—*
   (a) The argument from prophecy 314
   (b) The higher and larger knowledge of the disciples . . . 318

C. *The Acceptance of the ' Words of Eternal Life' as a conviction of faith* 320

D. *The Confession of St. Thomas—* 323
   The power of the Resurrection—
   (a) As a seal of His truth 326
   (b) As a completion of His teaching 326
   (c) As a manifestation of His nature . . . 327

E. *The Progress of Faith—*
   (a) The significance of the faith of the disciples . . . 328
   (b) The examination of its grounds 330

CHAPTER VII.

THE PROVINCE OF FAITH.

A. *The Law of Faith Natural—* 335
   (a) Its application to the individual . . . 337
   (b) Its application to the race 339
   (c) Faith in the leaders of mankind in thought, in action, in religion 340
   (d) The conception of ' inspiration ' and ' mission ' . . . 342

B. *The Phases of Faith—* PAGE
 (a) Faith in respect of what we might know 344
 (b) Faith in what we know imperfectly 344
 (c) Faith in mystery 345

C. *The Claim of Absolute Faith for Christ—*
 (a) A supernatural claim peculiar to Christianity . . . 346
 (b) His advance of it for Himself 348
 (c) The alternatives presented to us 350
 (d) Preparation and verification of faith 353
 (e) Faith and progress 354

CHAPTER VIII.
THE DOCTRINES OF FAITH.

A. *The Atonement—*
 (a) Its foundation in the word of Christ 361
 (b) The preparation of Natural Theology 363
 (c) The preparation in the Old Testament . . . 365
 (d) The verification of experience 366
 (e) The ultimate rest in faith 367

B. *The Kingdom of Christ in Glory—*
 (a) The Ascension and Session in glory, partly known, partly accepted in faith 370
 (b) The future judgment 372

C. *The Pre-Existence from Eternity—*
 (a) Implied in the Ascension and Mediation . . . 373
 (b) Set forth by the word of Christ in itself . . . 374

D. *The Doctrine of the Holy Ghost—*
 (a) In natural religion 380
 (b) In the Old Testament 381
 (c) In the word of Christ 381

E. *The Doctrine of the Holy Trinity—*
 (a) Taught implicitly, yet unmistakable 383
 (b) Prepared for in natural religion and the Old Testament . . 384
 (c) Declared by the word of Christ alone 384

CHAPTER IX.
CONCLUSION.

The Natural Method of Study—
 (a) Tradition and practical experience 388
 (b) The harmony of Christianity with natural religion . . 389
 (c) The actual power of Christianity 390
 (d) The study of the life of Christ 393
 (e) The province of faith 396

THE MANIFOLD WITNESS FOR CHRIST.

PART I.
CHRISTIANITY AND NATURAL THEOLOGY.

CHAPTER I.

CHRISTIANITY NATURAL AND SUPERNATURAL.

God, who at sundry times and in divers manners spake in time past unto the fathers by the prophets, hath in these last days spoken unto us by His Son.—Heb. i. 1, 2.

IN the great argument for Christianity, whenever we are called upon to 'give a reason for the hope that is in us,' and accordingly to analyse by reason what faith grasps as one living whole, there are two chief parts. The distinction and the connexion of these two are plainly marked in our Lord's own command, 'Believe in God; believe also in Me;' and in His declaration, 'This is the life eternal, to know Thee, the only true God, and Jesus Christ whom Thou hast sent.' *Two parts of the Christian argument.*

On the one hand, Christianity, as the one living and progressive religion of the world, is the central force of Theism. The Gospel is what Butler calls 'the republication of Natural Religion;'[1] that is—to use language more familiar to us, and more accordant with historical truth—it is the ultimate expression of all those fundamental beliefs, which, in various degrees of perfection, underlie *Christianity as the central force of Theism.*

[1] See Butler's *Analogy*, Part II. chap. i. 'On the Importance of Christianity.'

the definite tenets of the great religions of the world, and even the vaguer faiths of those who, casting off all attachment to definite religious systems, nevertheless hold firmly to the consciousness of spirituality in man, and to the acceptance of an eternal and living God.

On the other hand (as Butler has again reminded us), the Gospel claims to reveal unique and supernatural truths —'mysteries' (to use St. Paul's words) 'hidden from ages and generations, but now made manifest' in Jesus Christ—in virtue of which it refuses to be reckoned as but one of many religions, or even as the chief among many, differing from it only in degree. It cannot accept either the ancient or modern form of the 'philosophic devotion,' which unites as objects of worship 'Abraham, Orpheus, Apollonius of Tyana, and Christ,'[2] even if the pedestal assigned to its founder be somewhat higher than the rest. It claims, in the ordinary sense of the words, to be at once natural and supernatural.

<small>Christianity as supernatural.</small>

Hence, as the founder of these Lectures distinctly saw, the ground for the assertion of its unique and supernatural character must be cleared by the consideration, as against Atheism—whether it be positive or negative, whether it assume a materialistic or pantheistic form—of the foundation of the great principles of Theism. Then, and not till then, is it right in theory to go on to test those distinctive truths, on which it bases its claim to be the religion of humanity: although I cannot doubt that in practice here (as in many other cases) the concrete precedes the abstract; and that because the Gospel is accepted as a whole, and Christ is known by a true personal knowledge, therefore the mind, when it turns to speculation, is able to enter into the more philosophic aspects of the great theistic argument, or to trace one ultimate basis of truth underlying the multiform religions of the world.

<small>Both views contemplated by Boyle.</small>

I. To the former branch of this argument the lectures of 1876 were devoted. Starting with the all-important fact that by a universal consent (to which the exceptions are apparent rather than real) the faith in a personal God is in possession of the whole field of

<small>The former treated in 1876.</small>

---

[2] See Gibbon's *Decline and Fall of the Roman Empire*, chap. vi.

human thought, and recognising Natural Theology as in itself an inductive science, wrought out under two great absolute conceptions of Causation and Righteousness, I contended for three principles. First, that in this Natural Theology there are various lines, corresponding to the various faculties of man. Next, that no one of these lines ought to be treated and judged as if it existed alone. Thirdly, that, by the law of convergence, the aggregate result of these lines of evidence is infinitely greater than the mere sum of their results taken separately. Now, when on these principles we examine the lines of Natural Theology, they fall into two groups—the speculative and the moral: the first embracing the theology of the intellect and the imagination; the second the theology of the conscience and the affections; each having its own peculiar force, and the two, at once by independence and by harmony, bearing on each other. Entering on the successive consideration of these lines of thought, and combining their results, I ventured to assert that, but for one great disturbing power in the mystery of evil, their united force would be all but irresistible in deciding—what is the main issue—the great alternative between Pantheism and Theism, and leading us to a true and living God, absolute alike in being and in righteousness. But, while endeavouring to bring out the full force of Natural Theology, I also urged that according to the Christian theory Revelation itself is 'natural;' that the searching after God was never intended to stand alone; and that to the law of induction there must be added the law of faith—a faith ultimately resting on the Lord Jesus Christ.[3]

The cumulative argument of Natural Theology.

This I believe to be the right principle of estimate of the first great branch of the Christian argument. It will be my endeavour hereafter to show that the same principle should be applied also to the second part of that argument, which examines the peculiar claims of Christianity to an absolute allegiance. I believe that it is at once accordant with sound theory and true to actual fact, to hold that 'the reason,' which we are bidden to be ready ' to give' on challenge 'for the hope that is in us'

The similar argument of positive Christian Evidence.

[3] See *Boyle Lectures* for 1876, 'What is Natural Theology?' Published by S. P. C. K. 1878.

(probably implanted by other means than any formal examination of Christian evidences) must be a complex reason, made up of various elements of evidence, internal and external, direct and indirect; out of which perhaps each mind by a natural selection chooses out one or other as predominant, but of which a sound judgment on the whole question will despise none.

II. But, before passing on to any examination of this latter part of the argument, there is a consideration, which is in theory an appropriate link between the two, and in practice has certainly immense power in clearing the ground for a right appreciation of the evidences of Christianity. It is the consideration of the relation which Christianity, as a revelation, occupies towards the conclusions of Natural Theology itself. If it contradicts them, it will need strong evidence indeed to convince us of its truth. If it simply coincides with them, this coincidence may induce us to doubt whether it can claim to be a revelation supernatural and supreme. But if, on the one hand, it accepts and confirms those conclusions, and yet, on the other, goes beyond them—now turning possibilities or probabilities into certainties—now clearing up perplexities, which had hitherto appeared speculatively hopeless and morally intolerable—then there will result a strong presumption both of its truth and its necessity, which must bear very forcibly on the examination of the positive credentials of its authority.

Preliminary consideration of the relation between them.

Our first great theologian, Richard Hooker, writing not as an apologist for Christianity, but as an inquirer into the true principle of its Ecclesiastical Polity, brought out with a magnificent comprehensiveness the harmony of the 'law natural' and the 'law supernatural.'[4] He dwelt on both as correlative parts of the 'Second law eternal,' which is the expression to all God's creatures of so much as is needful or possible for them to understand of the 'First law eternal,' 'which He has set Himself to do all things by.' Now, after three centuries of change and growth, the same principle presents itself to us—under a far wider knowledge of the 'law natural,' and (as we

The harmony of the natural and supernatural.

---

[4] See Hooker's *Ecclesiastical Polity*, Book I.

trust) some growth also in the true conception of the 'law supernatural'—as the one principle which, before all others, we need to make clear in the abstract to our minds, and in practice to grasp with all the energy of our souls. We hold Christianity to be 'supernatural, not preternatural.' In relation to the conclusions of Natural Theology it occupies a position not of mere unison, still less of discord, but of true harmony. It can, we believe, prove its power over both mind and heart when it sounds absolutely alone, but its true position is as the leading note in the great symphony of truth.

III. It will be the object of the present course of Lectures to make some contribution to the exposition of this most important truth, that CHRISTIANITY IS SUPERNATURAL AND NOT PRETERNATURAL, by examining the relation in which the doctrines of Holy Scripture stand to the main conclusions and the main perplexities of Natural Theology. In the former case, I take it to hold a complementary, in the latter a supplementary position. I hold that it confirms the known and reveals the unknown. *Christianity supernatural, not preternatural,*

There are two great truths to which Natural Theology leads us, and which, as a matter of fact, have been all but inseparable in the faith of mankind. I mean the belief in a living God, having relation to us as our Creator, our Ruler, and our Father, and the consciousness of a spiritual nature in man, through which he bears the Divine likeness and is destined to an immortal life. *in respect of the light and darkness of Natural Theology.* In relation to these Christianity appears to me simply complementary to Natural Theology, taking up its converging lines of conclusion, clenching them by authority, and carrying them on to unity in God. But there is one great and terrible difficulty which, in different degrees of force, appears to bar our way on all the lines of Natural Theology. I mean the mystery of evil, whether in its slighter forms of waste, decay, suffering, or in its darker forms of sin and death as the wages of sin. In regard to this mystery of evil Natural Theology seems unable to do more than take up an attitude of sturdy passive resistance, allowing that it must weaken, but defying it to destroy, the manifold cord by which 'the great world every way is bound around the feet of God.' But Christianity here presents a far bolder front; for here it not only completes the arguments of Natural Theology, but supplements them by the enunciation of a new and transcendent doctrine. It first frankly recognises the existence of this awful mystery, and then so grapples with it in practice, as at any rate to scatter all darkness from our path of life, and to set the wings of the soul free from the burden which weighs them down. In fact, only by so doing can it present itself as a revelation, fit not only for man in his ideal nature, but for man as he actually is. No voice can really command allegiance in a world like this, except one which says, 'Come unto Me, ye that travail and are heavy laden, and I will give you rest.'

IV. This will be seen if, putting out of sight for the time the many accessory and derivative doctrines of our faith, we consider what Christianity is in that essential and distinctive idea, in which it stands out from all other forms of explicit or implicit Monotheism.

The essential idea of Christianity:

Now Christianity, so considered, is simply the 'doctrine of Christ;' and that doctrine can hardly be put forth more completely than in the remarkable passage from the Epistle to the Philippians, which unites all the freedom of enthusiastic adoration and all the clear-cut precision of a creed, in describing the manifestation of the Lord Jesus Christ in the two distinct acts of what the Church calls 'His great humility' (Phil. ii. 5-11).

The doctrine of Christ.

There is first the manifestation in the 'form of man' of One 'who, being in the form of God, thought it not robbery to be equal with God,' and who, as Son of Man, receives 'the Name above every name,' at which 'every knee shall bow.'

(a) in the Incarnation;

In this declaration of the Incarnation and of the Ascension to the right hand of God, which is its counterpart—of which ancient Christian speculation delighted to believe that they might still have been, if sin had never entered into the world—we trace most distinctly the first office of the Gospel, in its transcendent power of confirmation of the two great conclusions of Natural Theology—the belief of a living personal God, and the conviction of the spirituality of the human nature, as made in the image of God, and fit to be the means of revealing Him.

But there is next, the further declaration of the Passion, and of the Resurrection, at once its counterpart and its explanation; in which it is said that 'after He had been found in fashion as a man, He humbled Himself, and became obedient unto death, and that the death of the cross.' *(b) In the Passion.*

In this we find the second office of the Gospel, to give a practical solution of that great mystery of sin with spiritual death as its fruit, before which Natural Theology stands half amazed, and which alone has any real power to shake our faith in a living God and a spiritual humanity. It is perhaps no wonder that, above all, this truth should be considered as characteristic of the Gospel, and that accordingly the chosen emblem of Christianity should be the sign of the cross.

Now it is in these two aspects that Christianity stands out as the representative of what is called 'supernatural religion.' By universal confession, alike of its defenders and its assailants, the battle lies between it and the various systems which altogether deny the supernatural. As we survey the great religions of the world, nothing is clearer than that Christianity alone can claim to have a future, and a power to foster and direct the unceasing progress of humanity. *Christianity the representative of the supernatural in both.* Judaism it claims as its own, as simply preparatory to its own development; and, where that claim is rejected, Judaism survives, indeed, with a tenacity of life and a practical reality of religious influence which often put Christians to shame, but shows no power of so expanding as to rule the world. Mohammedanism is little else than a bastard Judaism with some slight admixture of Christianity. Against simple Paganism and degenerate Christianity it prevailed once; against gross Paganism in North Africa we hear, without surprise or regret, that it prevails now. But it is a remarkable fact—testified by all who have any knowledge of the Mohammedan world, as it exists at the present moment—that, while among the simple and ignorant classes it still lives, and powerfully moulds their life both for evil and for good, its power seems to die out at the first dawn of intellectual light, as being incompatible with science and education. It needs, again, but a single glance at the old religions of Asia—Brahminism, Buddhism, Confucianism (if, indeed, the last two deserve the name of positive religion at all)—to convince us that the doom of transitoriness, which Buddhism anticipated for itself, is coming, perhaps far sooner than is foreseen in that anticipation, upon them all. On their ruins we see at this moment in India that either Christianity, or a philosophic Deism, denying any revelation really supernatural, is destined speedily to rise.

Hence of the old directions of the founder of these Lectures one is almost practically obsolete. He charged us to defend Christianity against Atheists and simple Deists; the defence is at least as needful as ever. He charged us also to defend it against Pagans, Jews, and Mohammedans; that defence has ceased to be important, because the antagonistic power is dying or dead. When we glance at the religions of the world now, it is rather with the desire of tracing in them embodiments of the great truths of 'Natural Religion,' and perhaps of showing how far they imperfectly represent parts of the full system of Christianity itself. All who study the question from any point of view will allow that among religions Christianity prevails, and will prevail, on the principle of 'the survival of the fittest.' The battle, indeed, still remains to be fought out between those who look on the difference between Christianity and other systems to be simply one of degree, and those who hold the difference to be one of kind. It is really a battle of life and death. Although the former party constantly use the watchwords of Christian faith and doctrine, it is perfectly clear that they cannot interpret them in the old Christian sense. But this conflict will turn on examination of what Christianity claims to be, and has proved itself to be, rather than on any assault on the other religions of the world.

Maintenance against other religions obsolete.

Its supernatural character essential.

Hence Christianity must be looked upon as the representative of supernatural religion against all systems which deny it—whether philosophic Deism, or the vaguer and more atheistic theories, against which

Deism, standing alone in a cold and sterile bareness, has so much difficulty in maintaining its ground. For its supernatural character depends not on the truth of this or that miracle, on the reality of this or that instance of prophetic power; it is enshrined in the central idea, which makes Christianity what it is. Nothing can be more utterly vain than the attempt to frame a Christian system which shall be free from supernatural pretensions, and yet shall preserve any religious vitality; unless, indeed, it be the cognate idea that the sentiment and morality of the Gospel can be preserved, when all faith in its doctrinal truth has passed away.

V. This being the case, it concerns the Christian to consider very carefully what 'the supernatural' really is. *What is super- natural?*

For the word 'Natural,' by contrast with which it is necessarily determined, is used in a strange variety of senses. In the phrase 'Natural Philosophy,' Nature is the world of matter and force; in 'Natural History,' Nature is the world of organic life; if we refer to 'Natural feeling,' Nature is then the world of humanity; if we speak of 'Natural Theology,' Nature may include all these worlds taken together. If these senses were always kept distinct, the variety of use would mark only a clumsiness or poverty of expression; but all experience shows how difficult it is to prevent these various usages from mingling insensibly with each other, and accordingly how often ambiguity of phraseology proves itself to be dangerous to clearness of thought. *Variety in use of the word 'Nature.'*

Now, if we take the word 'Nature' in its various senses, and consider the method of contact of the sphere represented by each with any higher sphere of being, it will be found that the forces of that higher sphere invariably manifest themselves as 'supernatural, not preternatural.' *The super- natural not preter- natural:*

Let us take first that sense of the word 'Natural,' in which, like its less ambiguous counterpart 'Physical,' it is applied to the world of force, matter, and organic life. Even within that world there is the division —to our science as yet absolute—between the two spheres of inorganic matter and force and of organic life, to the *(a) in rela- tion to the physical sphere.*

contact of which the same law seems to apply. But, passing this by, and using 'Nature' in the wider sense of the artist or the physical philosopher, it is clear that in relation to it the attributes of humanity—the freedom of will, the contemplation of the invisible by reason, the spiritual energy of conscience—all are 'supernatural.' Whatever they are, however they may be related to the forces of Nature, they are under different laws; they bring into play forces of a different order; they are incapable of being accurately fitted into the system of physical causation; still less capable of being accounted for by it. Abstract speculation, of an imaginative rather than a scientific type, may hold that there is a hidden connexion between these two sets of forces, and may insist on believing that in some way the higher has historically been evolved from the lower. But, experimentally and practically, there is a great gulf between them. All the world of 'metaphysical' forces is here strictly 'supernatural.'

Yet these forces are never preternatural. They go beyond the series of physical forces, dealing with a sphere into which these cannot enter; they act upon and modify the physical forces within their own sphere, but they never annihilate them, or even suspend their action. Thus the action of human will, freely originated, so far as our consciousness can discern, and guided by metaphysical principles of reason and conscience, can alter within limits the form and structure of matter; it can determine the direction of force, and transform latent capacity of force into active energy. But it can never for a moment even suspend physical forces and laws; it simply mingles with them and interpenetrates them with a new and dominant energy; and we see every day with increasing clearness that the spiritual energy itself, so far as our experience goes, can work only through physical machinery in hand or brain. Hence no natural power is destroyed or paralysed, when new capacities and uses are developed by the introduction of what is in this sense a supernatural power. On the contrary, the supremacy of this latter power is not so absolute as to destroy reciprocity of influence. The physical influences unquestionably react upon the new forces thus introduced, and within limits affect their direction and their energetic action. There is a harmony established between the two kinds of force, under which their distinction is preserved, but which negatives all idea of real antagonism between them.

But let us ascend to a larger sense of the word 'Natural'—not unlike that in which it is used by Butler in the 'Analogy'—which includes not only the physical world, but also the world of humanity, so far as it falls under the ordinary laws of human nature, and is exemplified in the experience of every day. *(b) in relation to the sphere of ordinary humanity.* In contrast with the natural in this sense, it seems clear that the rare power of what we call 'genius,' which, in various forms of originative power, belongs to all the leaders of mankind, and the higher and holier inspiration which the founders or apostles of every religion claim, may fairly be called 'supernatural.' For it is an undoubted historical fact that all the great steps of human progress are originated by the few, and only tested and accepted by the many. These few see clearly a light which ordinary men cannot see, or which they see but dimly; there is a spirit in them, stirring them to deeds which none else can dare; there is an actual power over men—so great that it has often been compared to a magic spell—which we ordinary mortals cannot wield. Compared with the vision, the energy, the power of the ordinary man, their power is supernatural; viewed from the lower standpoint, it might well seem incredible. We call it commonly an inspiration; we attribute to such men a mission. The phrase is notable in its unconscious testimony to the belief in One who inspires and sends such men. But, even when this natural significance is forgotten, it indicates the presence of a supernatural force. It expresses a conviction—which certainly historical investigation supports—that, all ordinary events and natures remaining as they are, the actual course of the world's history has depended on the simple fact that, at a particular time and in a particular country, some one of these extraordinary beings has appeared.

So, when we Christians assert a peculiar revelation, made to prophet or apostle, or a peculiar inspiration, which enabled him at once to see it and to proclaim it to his fellow-men, we contend that it is only a special miraculous exemplification of a fundamental law of human life and human history. The old Alexandrine divines designated Plato as 'a Moses speaking in Attic tongue;' we read of a mediæval schoolman who looked up to Socrates as a saint, and asked his prayers; the great poet of the 'Divina Commedia' ascribed to Virgil a half-sacred character, as a messenger of God. We, looking thoughtfully on the prophets of other religions than our own, holding (with Hooker) that no religious system is 'wholly compacted of untruths,' and that no great religious enthusiasm can be destitute of some true inspiration, have learned to believe that in some special sense God may have spoken to them and in them. We do not, indeed, for a moment allow to any such prophetic utterance from without a place co-ordinate with that which belongs to the earlier stages of the Christian dispensation; for we hold that the very fact of their connexion with the supreme revelation of Christ invests them with a peculiar glory of inspiration. Nor are we afraid that, either in its own intrinsic character, or in its regenerating effects on the world, the inspiration of the prophets and apostles of the Scriptural covenant will fail to distinguish itself from these lower forms of inspiration. But, while we distinguish, we do not separate; we believe that in all 'God spake' or worked 'at sundry times and in divers manners.'

Here, once more, the same law meets us. This supernatural power is not preternatural. It takes for granted, and harmonises with itself, the natural powers of the ordinary human mind. For every great crisis in human history we need both 'the hour and the man'—the hour of natural preparation, the man of supernatural energy. The original creations of the inspired philosopher or poet are tested by what we call the 'common sense'—intellectual, æsthetic, or moral—of the whole community. The impulse of the inspired hero or saint is spread over the waters of humanity by the acceptance, the sympathy, the imitation of the mass of men. The inspired utterance of the prophet needs a preparation in the minds and hearts of his hearers, if it is to strike deep root and fructify. Not for one moment does the supernatural, in this sense of the word, supersede or suspend the natural. Yet certainly it rises far above the natural forces, and works effects which without it would never be.

It will be observed that, according to the sense in which we use the word 'Nature,' what is supernatural in one view becomes natural in another. The spiritual forces of humanity, supernatural in relation to the Nature of the physical world, are seen to belong to Nature in that truer and larger sense, in which it describes the whole visible creation in the unity of the spiritual and physical powers. The higher revelation and inspiration—supernatural, if Nature include only the ordinary course of physical and human power—we hold to be 'natural' if human history be looked at as a whole, because they are the means by which the great steps of human progress have been effected. Hence it is that, while we can use unreservedly the term 'Natural Theology' to describe the mental process, by which in various ways the ordinary human mind reaches out after God, we cannot (except under protest) accept the term 'Natural Religion' as excluding all direct and special revelation. For we believe that 'Natural Religion,' if by this we understand (as we ought to understand) the actual knowledge of a God, which, under different forms and in different degrees of purity and vividness, covers the whole world, includes what we call 'Revelation' as an ordained and principal factor in the dispensation of God. As all analogy seems to show that it should be so, so tradition on every side declares that it has been so. Coleridge declared long ago that 'Revealed Religion' was a pleonasm, for that every religion was revealed, not only in the ordinary revelation to each individual soul, but in the special revelations which are the inherited treasures of the race.

The supernatural included in a larger sense of Nature.

We trace then in all these instances the same general law. There is, as each successive sense of the word 'Natural' is reached, something beyond, which is, in relation to it, 'supernatural.' But in every case there is harmony between the two powers; and, with each fresh extension of the word 'Natural,' they invariably fall into their right places of mutual relation under a more comprehensive unity.

Now the Christian creed professes to be the complete and ultimate assertion of this law of the relation of the supernatural to the natural.

<small>Christianity the ultimate assertion of this law.</small>

For it must be obvious to anyone who considers that creed in its simplest form, that even in relation to this larger sense of the 'natural'—as including not only the ordinary and general, but also the special and exceptional, revelations of God to man—Christianity declares itself still to be emphatically 'supernatural.' For its Founder, both as the Son of God and as the Son of Man, it claims a place, differing infinitely, not in degree, but in kind, from even the highest places of those who went before Him, or who have followed Him, on earth. The distinction so forcibly drawn in the text between the mere 'prophets,' 'by whom, at sundry times and in divers manners, God spake,' and 'the Son by whom He hath spoken in the last days,' and who is 'the brightness of His glory and the express image of His person,' is a distinction which in various forms pervades the New Testament, and which accordingly has been at all times both the central idea of Christian faith, and the inmost secret of Christian life.

<small>The unique character assigned to Christ</small>

This unique and supernatural claim is put forward for Him in respect both of His revelation of God, and of His power of mediation for man.

Thus Christianity regards the revelations of God through all others as necessarily limited and imperfect; claiming no finality, but always looking onward to a larger and brighter future, and sinking all individual authority of the speaker in the thought of the truth, of which he could only declare a part. The revelation of God in Him is asserted as absolute and final, so that all others, before He came, had simply to lead up to it, and, since He came, have to be content to draw out and to apply its meaning. For these, by the nature of the case, could only 'tell of earthly things'—that is, of the imperfect manifestations on earth of the divine power; He claims to 'tell of heavenly things,' on the ground that He 'came down from heaven,' He 'ascended into heaven,' He 'is in heaven.' The constantly recurring phrase in regard to them is that 'the word of the Lord came to them,' 'the spirit of the Lord was upon

<small>(*a*) in the revelation of God;</small>

them.' But He is spoken of as being Himself 'the Word of God' and the Giver of the Spirit of God. In Him (says one Apostle) dwelt 'all the fullness of the Godhead bodily.' He (says another Apostolic writer in the text) is 'the express image of the essence of God.' 'He that hath seen me' (such are recorded as His own words) 'hath seen the Father.'

Nor is this same unique character less visibly stamped on the representation of His mediation for man. The law of mediation, by which men can affect the spiritual condition of others, even before God, is (as Butler has unanswerably shown) an universal law of human nature; and, by its operation, men can, to some extent, gain power to conquer the power of evil in others, and so save the souls of their brethren. All men have that power in some degree; the men specially inspired by God have it in supereminent degree. For it depends on the spiritual unity, which binds man to man, in virtue of which 'no man liveth and no man dieth to himself.' But in all mere men that unity with others is limited, and therefore their mediation is limited also. Without a man's will it may be able to alter the circumstances and opportunities of his life; but if it would touch the soul itself, it can reach that soul only through the avenue of consent of will. Even where it does work with success in either of these phases of action, it is bounded by limits, wider or narrower, of space and time. For Him the Gospel claims a unity with man absolutely universal and perfect, and therefore a mediation absolutely unlimited; first, in its power to anticipate the consent of man's will, and yet to alter the spiritual relations of man to God, and so to do what no power of mere man can ever do, by taking away, not the fruits of sin only, but its guilt and power; next, in its scope, as extending to all peoples, nations, and languages, and stretching down through the centuries even to the end of time.

(b) in mediation for man.

These claims are obviously supernatural in the most absolute and emphatic sense. They must involve either the greatest of truths or the worst of falsehoods. There can be no intermediate position between the acknowledgment of Him in worship, and the taking

Its harmony with all inferior powers.

up stones to cast at Him. But the same law still applies. The supernatural is not preternatural. This absolute manifestation of God, and this unlimited mediation for man, attributed to the Lord Jesus Christ, take for granted, and claim to use, all the various natural powers of which we have spoken—the physical forces, the capacities of ordinary humanity, the lower special revelations of God's truth, and the imperfect forms of mediation of man for man. Thus they allow for all the physical influences of life; on exceptional occasions and for special causes, they even make use of them by the power of miracle to subserve their own transcendent purposes. They do not supersede human reason, or coerce human will. They refuse to ignore any of the lower teachings and influences for good, whether moral, intellectual, or spiritual, whether acting within the special covenant of God or without its pale, which have lifted man above the ordinary level of human life. Christianity, as abstract in declaration of truth, and as concrete in human life, is still a complex thing, in which all the 'natural' elements of thought, and morality, and energy are compacted together, and animated by the new force of an indwelling supernatural principle. There is still (to use the former comparison) a marvellous harmony; just as when in some great symphony the dominant theme makes itself felt through all the many undercurrents of the lower music, drawing to itself many strange and varied harmonies, and even blending in a subtle harmony what else might seem discords, yet itself still sounding out above them all as the clear note of an angel's voice.

Here, indeed, we may take for the last time the step so often taken before. If we rise to the largest sense of the word 'Natural'—perhaps the only true and complete sense—in which it applies to the whole scheme of creation, describing what Hooker calls 'the first law eternal,' 'which God has set Himself' for His whole dispensation to man, we shall assert that the manifestation of the Lord Jesus Christ is not only 'natural,' but is the only key to the meaning of the dispensation itself. If on such high things it be allowed to speculate, we may even follow out some hints in Holy Scripture, by conceiving the possibility of its assuming other forms, no less mysterious and

The key to the whole dispensation of God.

glorious, under dispensations of God to other orders of his creatures, and being the supreme principle which binds the whole universe together in one divine unity.[5]

VI. It is difficult to exaggerate the importance of a firm grasp of this conception of the true position of Christianity. *Importance of viewing Christianity*

That it is not preternatural—that in the highest sense it is the crown and perfection of the natural—is the truth which lies at the basis of the great argument of the 'Analogy.' In the ages which have elapsed since Butler's days, since with every advance of science the belief in a certain unity of continuous development in all the creations of the Supreme Power has established itself more and more strongly in the minds of men, the importance of that argument has probably increased. Yet its proper force, as Butler himself urged again and again, is to remove objections of an *à priori* character, which profess to preclude all examination of the positive evidences of Christianity, rather than to establish its claims to any absolute allegiance. It is very far from being the whole truth; it is not even that side of the truth by which Christianity has conquered the world. If it be put forward exclusively or predominantly, it must be scrutinised with some jealousy. The celebrated dictum, that 'Christianity is as old as the creation,' has a double edge; it may be, according as it is understood, the motto of the devotion of the Christian, or the half-supercilious patronage of the unbeliever. Nor does this ambiguity attach less seriously to those investigations into 'the science of religion,' which place the Gospel at the head of all the religions of the world. If the difference confessed between it and them be a difference of kind—if they are thought to indicate the longings of which it is the satisfaction, and to afford glimpses of the truth, which it reveals as a 'mystery,' long hidden and now made manifest—then and only then is the principle of such investigations accordant with the claims *as both natural and supernatural,*

---

[5] This extension of idea seems certainly implied in the passages which describe our Lord as the Head not only of the Church and of humanity, but of all created being, 'by whom all things consist.' (See Col. i. 15-17.)

which Christianity puts forth for itself, and by faith in which it has actually grown to be what it is.

<small>With a view to its absolute and universal claims.</small> For it is certain that only by establishing such faith in its unique and supernatural character can Christianity possibly sustain its claim to be an absolute and universal religion. It is, indeed, for want of all pretension to any such character, that, as I have already urged, no other religion can even pretend to fill this place. Judaism, if judged by its own Scriptures, bears upon the face of it the confession of a transitory and imperfect character. When in modern times it claims to be the religion of the future, it has to exchange its distinct prophecies for the dim vision of a very shadowy future, and its strong definite vitality as a religion for the vagueness of a philosophic Monotheism, having probably no Messiah except an idealised humanity. What the Judaism of the Old Testament so freely acknowledges, all religions which rest on the authority of merely human lawgivers or prophets must confess under pressure. A Moses, a Zoroaster, a Gautama, a Confucius, a Mohammed—nay, even the Jesus of Nazareth of all theories which make Him simply the greatest of the sons of men—are but creatures who have 'had their day and ceased to be.' How can it be reasonably held that their authority is to be final? How can it be possibly claimed that their wisdom shall rule and their law direct all nations to the end of time? Most striking and instructive—in some sense most pathetic—it is to observe how, almost by a spiritual necessity, such prophets are apt to be deified in spite of themselves; how (to take the most startling instance) the Buddha, supposed on his own theory to have passed into the Nirwâna of annihilation or absorption, is still invoked by popular devotion in every temple in Ceylon or Burmah as a living power all but supreme on earth. But these things, however natural and significant, are still patent inconsistencies. On every other religion is written the confession of its imperfection. Christianity, on the contrary, stands forth face to face with all theories denying the supernatural, and claiming our worship for the natural, either as diffused in the *universum* or sublimated in humanity. It claims, as a religion, finality, universality,

permanence. But clearly it can do this with any show of reason, only because it avows its Author to be indeed a Son of Man, but yet more than a Son of Man. The Christ who is to be worshipped with full allegiance of faith must be One who was 'in the beginning,' 'was with God,' and 'was God.'

This truth, therefore, must be grasped firmly, and it must be grasped as a whole. At different times and under different circumstances it may be necessary to emphasise now one part, and now the other, of the whole truth. The division, even the antagonism, between those who lay chief stress on each of these parts, is probably as old as Christianity itself. But it ought not to exist; for it cannot but interfere with the full strength and true proportion of faith.

Sometimes it has been especially necessary to show that Christianity is not preternatural. So men used to argue, in the language of our older Apologists, that it was what they called a 'rational religion,' contradicting neither the discoveries of the speculative reason nor—what is more important still—the witness of the practical reason or conscience. So men now have a pride in showing that it can harmonise with itself all the discoveries of science, all the nobler morality of days past or present, all the glories of art, all the free impulses of individual affection, the sympathy of brotherhood, the devotion of loyalty, and, above all, the 'enthusiasm for humanity itself.' So, again, Christians have delighted to survey the religions of the world, in a spirit not of antagonism, but of sympathy, to trace out impartially, and even reverently, the real story of their foundation, to discern what is good and true in them, to understand that in virtue of it, and it only, do they live and rule. All this is well. It is the carrying out of a line of thought which has had noble representatives in Christian theology, since the days of Justin Martyr and Clement of Alexandria; and the wider and more generous perception of its main principles is one of the lessons taught by God to this generation.

The need to assert it as natural.

Sometimes, on the other hand, it is the one thing needful to bring out its supernatural and absolute claims. So it was in the great religious revivals which followed the victorious close of the Deistic controversy of the last century. Against a rationalising infidelity it was well to show how Christianity was rational; but it needed something above reason and morality to overcome the dead weight of practical godlessness and sin, and to rekindle the sacred flame of religious enthusiasm. Such, indeed, has been the experience of all ages of the Church. Christianity has a work to do and a claim to sustain, which imperiously demand a firm faith and a bold proclamation of its unique and ultimate authority. It is not more resolute against the open blasphemy of the more vulgar infidelity, than against that half patronising, half admiring appreciation, which accepts it as one imperfect form of thought, the best perhaps of many, which are all destined to be fused in a higher expression of truth— as 'the last and noblest of the mythologies' doomed soon to vanish away in the cold dry light of science. It must be less than this, or more. If it be only this, then, in order to clear its preachers from the charge of presumption and superstition, its whole history must be rewritten, and its whole language changed. For otherwise that result must be realised which St. Paul holds out as a kind of *reductio ad absurdum*. The faith which regenerates the hearers can only be a beautiful dream; the victorious word of the preacher a falsehood, a glorious falsehood in appearance, but in reality the worst of all lies—a lie in the name of God.

At all times, however, both elements of the truth are necessary; at this present time especially necessary, when the scornful denial on the one side of all supernatural agency, going so far as to obliterate even the line between the material and the spiritual, is met on the other by a kind of reckless delight in all that wears the appearance of the supernatural even in the physical sphere, in a tendency to denounce or decry the advance of natural science, in a rebound towards the superstition, which fancies or multiplies miracles, and turns means of grace into charms.

The necessity of the full truth is urgent. Happily, by all thoughtful Christians that necessity is amply recognised. It will be, as I have said, the object of these lectures to contribute, so far as may be, one to the many voices enunciating this fulness of Christian truth in many tones.

VII. Glancing at Holy Scripture as a whole, I shall seek first to trace out the actual method of its dealing, both in the Old Testament and in the New, with the revelation of God and the spirituality of man, in that close connexion with each other in which all Natural Theology forces us to view them. Here it will be my endeavour to show how it meets the natural searchings of man after God with the calm certainty of a Divine message. In the spirit of St. Paul at Athens, it recognises in them a real, a not unsuccessful search after a God, known to be, though in attributes 'unknown' or dimly seen; and while it accepts for Him 'the ignorant worship,' declares Him as revealed in Jesus Christ for their more perfect knowledge. *The line of thought to be followed.*

Side by side with this evolution of the Scriptural revelation of God, and of man as in unity with God, I shall seek to draw out its teaching on the mystery of evil, in respect of its source, its nature, its present power, and its future overthrow—with a view in this case to show how Christianity meets those needs of humanity which Natural Theology can indicate, but cannot satisfy, by the proclamation of what St. Paul calls a 'mystery, hid from all generations, but now made manifest,' even to the simple and ignorant, those hard workers and patient sufferers who make up the rank and file of humanity.

Possibly this consideration may fairly claim a distinct and not unimportant place in the actual 'evidences of Christianity.' On the belief, tested by experience, that the Gospel can guide men through the perplexities and contradictions of life, and nerve them both to dare and to endure all things, the practical Christianity of the mass of believers rests. On this I will venture to say that it ought always to rest, until it is challenged and often, perhaps, when it has been challenged by speculation and criticism. Many a man may rightly say, with the homely bluntness of the blind man at Siloam, 'Whether it can be proved to be of God' by a proof which shall satisfy every mind, and dispel every difficulty, 'I know not.' 'But one thing I do know,' that without it 'I am *(a) Its force as an intrinsic evidence.*

blind;' with it 'I can see'—see my way through the bewildering mists of temptation, through the gloomy cloud of suffering, even through the thick darkness of death. Till you can offer me some better light, I will walk in this.

But even if this may not be our case, and if accordingly we must go on still to scrutinise the positive evidences on which Christianity bases its claim to the allegiance of faith, still it is clear that the temper in which we shall scrutinise them, and the force of evidence which we shall rightly require for conviction, will greatly depend on our understanding that, claiming to be supernatural, and justifying its claim by revelation of what the natural man cannot conceive, it yet contradicts nothing which he has known about God, nothing which he has felt to be true of himself.

(b) Its function as preparatory to positive evidence.

Hence I believe that this line of thought ought to have a real value, both to the believer and to the doubter. To the believer it should both deepen and widen his conception of the Christian revelation in its twofold aspect, and thus teach him to accept all natural light gladly, though he trusts ultimately in the supernatural. To the doubter, if it cannot bring positive conviction, it may, at least, help to remove some of those difficulties which, prior to all consideration of the evidences of Christianity, incline him to pronounce such examination needless and hopeless.

As this line of thought looks on to the future examination of the actual Christian evidences, so it looks back also to that argument from the many voices of Natural Theology, which has been already pursued elsewhere.

(c) Its relation to the previous argument.

It is as though, by various convergent paths, we had been brought to the threshold of the mystery of God. As we have moved along each towards that central mystery, there has been a light before us and a voice of solemn import in our ears. Now the everlasting doors of the shrine fly open, and One stands before us, claiming to be the manifestation of God. As we gaze on Him, we see that in His crown of light there shine, blended together in perfect harmony, all the various rays of light which have hitherto been our guides. As we listen to the music of His voice, we recognise the tones which have so long been sounding dimly in our ears. But yet in His face there is a glory beyond what we have ever conceived, and the story which His voice tells unlocks to us mysteries beyond our highest thought. What can we do but fall down before Him, and acknowledge that 'God, who in sundry times and divers manners spake to men from the beginning by His servants, has at last spoken to us once for all in His Son'?

CHAPTER II.

THE SIGNIFICANCE OF COVENANT WITH GOD.

'And I, behold, I establish My covenant with you.'—Gen. ix. 9.

THE thesis of these lectures has now been generally stated. Looking upon Christianity as the one accepted representation of 'supernatural religion,' they are to be devoted to show that in Christianity we see the highest exemplification of the great law 'supernatural not preternatural;' which we observe to rule in respect of all the narrower senses of the word 'natural,' and to be, in fact, the principle at once of unbroken unity and continual development, in that which in the largest and ultimate sense is 'the natural'—the whole actual system of the world and man.

The general argument re-stated.

I. In order to exhibit this great characteristic of Christianity clearly at the very outset, it was enough to concentrate our attention for the moment on that remarkable creed of the doctrine of Christ in the Epistle to the Philippians, which set forth His manifestation as the ultimate truth, at once complementary and supplementary to the inductions of Natural Theology. But, if the argument is to be worked out, it is necessary to contemplate Christianity not merely in its central idea, but in its actual historic growth and existence. There are two ways in which this task may be attempted. For Christianity, as to the individual it is at once a faith and a life, so exhibits itself to the world as embodied in a Bible and a Church. It proclaims, that is, on the one hand, a great body of truth, of which that Bible is the authoritative source, and which has been for eighteen centuries drawn out and systematised in the creeds and the theology of Christendom. It professes, on the other hand, to embody in the Church a supernatural power of spiritual life or grace, which

Christianity in the Bible and in the Church.

may be at once the regeneration of each individual soul, and the secret of a spiritual unity or 'communion of saints,' binding all souls together in Jesus Christ.

In both of these aspects it is a matter of deep interest and infinite consequence to consider whether Christianity, as a whole, fulfils the great law already enunciated; for, indeed, on its fulfilment of that law in both depends its power of claiming the allegiance of mankind. For some minds—perhaps of the thoughtful and enquiring few—there is a greater power to convince in the exhibition of truth, confirming, and yet infinitely enlarging, the conclusions of the Natural Theology of ages; for others — perhaps for the more practical many—in the exhibition of a moral and spiritual life, able to take up into itself all the natural forces of our higher humanity, but able, both for the individual and for human society, to work effects far beyond their power. Some (if we may so put it) are led through the Bible to the Church, and some through the Church to the Bible. *The law of its nature in both.*

If, indeed, we consider Christianity as an actual power, it is obvious that both these elements must be combined in our thought, as they were actually combined in its historic development. The Bible grew up, under God's providence, in and with the Church. On the one hand, the Scripture embodies the substance of that word of Christ, prepared for by lawgiver, psalmist, and prophet before He came, carried out by apostle and evangelist after He was taken away, from which the Church itself actually took birth. On the other hand, it is clear that, as the existence of the Jewish nation and race, under conditions certainly unique in history, throws light on the true nature and power of the Old Testament, so the Church, not only by its teaching, but by its very existence, is 'a witness of Holy Writ,' showing that, even as judged by results, it is a book which stands out unlike all other books. Nor is it possible to doubt that it is by the combined force of abstract truth and concrete life that Christianity has gained its mastery of the world, and that it still rules, wherever it does rule, our individual souls. No preacher of Christianity, whether he be an evangelist to extend its sway over new fields, or a pastor *The combination of both in actual power,* to deepen its influence where it is already acknowledged, can ever separate the two elements. For it is not merely the word spoken, but 'the word engrafted' by grace, which he believes to be 'able to save the soul.'

Even in the work of giving 'a reason for the hope' already in us—though, as has been said, this obliges us to *and in evidential argument.* analyse into its various parts what faith grasps as a whole—it is impossible to pursue either line of thought without a constant remembrance of the other, as it is perhaps difficult to determine which of the two is the more substantial and fruitful of result. Wherever we see a great moral and spiritual power ruling human life, we at once search for its basis in some special form of truth; wherever we see, or think we see, a unique discovery of truth, we naturally test its reality by looking for some practical result of corresponding significance in individual and social life.

II. But still, according to the nature of the argument pursued, it is well to choose either one or the other as the *The study now of Scripture* chief line of thought; and the object which is contemplated in these lectures necessarily determines the choice to the former of these two methods. If it is to be shown that Christianity is 'supernatural and not preternatural,' on the ground that it at once confirms the conclusions of Natural Theology, and yet goes beyond them, especially in dealing with that dark mystery of evil which crosses them on every line, then it is as a Gospel that we must consider it. It is on the Bible, as it has been interpreted by the thought and practice of Christendom, that our whole examination must turn.

Now, in such examination, two things are clear. The Bible must be considered as a whole; and it must be con-*as a whole, and in historic order.* sidered in its historic order. In spite of all the differences of time, place, and authorship, brought out even to exaggeration by a discerning and disintegrating criticism, there is really no more a question now than in days past that the book is in substance one book. There is an essential unity—however we may account for it—underlying all these differences; we cannot properly estimate the meaning of any part, even the highest and the most advanced part, if we isolate it from what goes before and from what follows; we may not destroy, but we shall impair and mutilate, the organic life of the whole, if we lop off this or that limb, even if it be one of the members which seem least necessary. But it is also clear that all study of the Bible must be conducted with constant reference to its actual historic development, and in strict accordance with its expressed historic order. Unlike other sacred books, the Bible is, before all other things, a history of man; it has its various elements, but the historical element is the backbone of the whole. By this characteristic it has been noticed[1] that it challenges continual and manifold tests of its truth; by this characteristic we may observe that it gains a solidity of basis, a depth, a permanence, and a variety of influence, which could belong to no abstract teaching, however noble and divine. It necessarily follows from it that, like all history, the Scripture must be looked at not only as a whole, but in the right order of all its parts. Whatever its various elements may be, whether of law, of teaching, or of devotion, still they must be at every point considered in relation to their historic position. The law of all history is the law of continuous development. Hence each part must be examined not merely in itself, but as conducing to the development running through the whole; and the order of a revelation, claiming to be historic, must be considered to be a part of the revelation itself.

I have already alluded to that celebrated work of the old English Deism, 'Christianity as old as the Creation,' written with a view to show that whatever was true in the Gospel was not new, and whatever was new was not true. The Christian must, of course, refuse this interpretation of the title. But the title itself we may well accept, as an unconscious testimony to a great truth which is often forgotten.[2] Christianity does profess itself to be as

Christianity coextensive with human history.

---

[1] See Butler's *Analogy*, Part II. chap. vii.

[2] Modern theology has, indeed, made a great and most wholesome advance in the right direction on this matter. But still there are many reasons why the Bible, more than any book, is studied piecemeal; so that a single book, a single chapter, even a single paragraph or verse, is apt to be dwelt upon as if it stood alone; and all, without considering from what part of the Revelation each comes, are taken to declare to us equally the whole 'mind of God.'

old as the Creation. Its own Scriptures speak of it in idea as ordained in God's counsels before the foundation of the world. In the history of its actual development they start from 'the beginning in which God created the heaven and earth;' and end only with the vision of the 'new heaven and the new earth,' to which these shall give way. It is, therefore, a part of its essential principle to claim to be coextensive with the whole being of man. The essence of Christianity lies in the great facts of our Lord's incarnation, life, death, resurrection, and ascension—considered as the completion of a revelation of God to man, and as the perfect manifestation of God in man—considered as historic facts in the past, living for ever in their effect on the present and the future. The Bible, therefore, consists substantially of two great elements. It is first a record of those great historical facts, of the historical preparation for them, and of the historical sequel to them up to a certain point; and then a series of teachings based upon the facts of this historic record, drawing out their meaning and applying it to the present and future of human thought and life. Accordingly the true method of examination of such a book must be the historical method. One part of it may be more important and precious than another, but no part can be neglected. The great law of 'the supernatural not preternatural' must be sought for in the various historical divisions into which the Bible naturally falls.

III. Before, however, this task is attempted in detail, it is well to consider whether there is any leading idea which runs through all; and, if so, how far that leading idea brings out the great law which we seek to trace.

The leading idea of covenant with God.

We cannot doubt that there will be some leading idea. All history which deserves the name is something more than a mere record of successive facts, or even a picture gallery of collected portraits. Historical study, like the observation of physical science, must be carried on under the guidance of some general conception, which enables us to understand the meaning and connexion of various phenomena and various beings. Now the leading idea, under which the Bible regards the history of man, is very plainly shown by the word used in the text at the very beginning of the regular narrative, and recurring again and again as that narrative proceeds. It is a history of man as 'in covenant with God.' The phrase, with all its simplicity, carries with it a profound significance. It is, indeed, easy to see that (even putting aside its anthropomorphic description of superhuman relations) in its literal sense it cannot be rightly applied. 'Covenants' are properly made between those who are independent of each other. Yet how can man be independent of the God in whom he lives and moves and has his being? How (we may even ask) can God be independent of man, whom He has made, and towards whom it is morally impossible for Him not to exercise His righteousness and love? It has been pointed out, again and again, that the Scriptural description of covenants with God involves certain distinctive characteristics, in which the whole idea stands out above the ordinary notion of covenants between man and man. They invariably originate from Him; they are primarily of unconditional grace and blessing; they need faith and faith only, in the recipient, by which he may accept such blessing and act on the acceptance. But the use of the word 'covenant,' by the very fact of its technical impropriety, has a striking impressiveness.

In the first place it recognises a true living and personal God, whose eye and hand are actually over His creatures. The phrase is worse than meaningless, if it be applied to a mere *Anima mundi*, to an impersonal law, to a stream of tendency which makes for righteousness, or even to a god, like the deities of Epicurus (reappearing in some modern philosophies), who creates the world and then leaves it to itself, bound in an iron network of 'law,' which can in no case be broken. Whether as the Guardian of a chosen family, as the Lawgiver and King of a chosen nation, or as the Father of all mankind, actually or potentially belonging to the Church of Christ, everywhere the conception of a God in covenant with man must present itself to the understanding and to the conscience, to the imagination and to the affections, as a conception unvaryingly and intensely personal.

Its bearing on (a) the personality of God;

But the conception of a covenant with God is not merely,

or perhaps mainly, a grand confession of true Monotheism. It brings out on the other side, even more forcibly, the mysterious reality in man of an individual being— a freedom, however directed or limited, to accept or reject—an unspeakable preciousness in the sight of God. The very fact (as our Lord taught us) that God enters into covenant with man as the 'God of Abraham, Isaac, and Jacob,' carries with it the belief in a spiritual and immortal nature of man. 'God is not the God of the dead, but of the living.' The simplest idea of covenant implies some recognition of the divine in man. It is true that for the full explicit recognition of this truth we have to look to the New Testament. There it grows out into the central mystery of Christianity, the Incarnation of Godhead; there it pervades the whole theory of the spiritual life, regarded as flowing from that Incarnation. It may be true that in the Old Testament it is implied rather than explicit, overshadowed by the grandeur of the recognised presence of God. But, in different degrees of force and clearness, it belongs to all the stages of the Scriptural history. Under the name of 'Hebraism' the Old Testament has been described by a popular writer as involving simply the conception of God over man, almost oppressive in the bare and awful grandeur of its monotheism. To 'Hellenism' alone he ascribes the recognition of the divine in man, in which lies the secret of human freedom and progress. But the fundamental conception of the covenant, which certainly lies at the root of 'Hebraism,' appears to me incontestably to include both of these elements. In fact, it is in its inclusion of the latter that we find the essential characteristic, which in the Old Testament preserves the individuality of man from that absorption into the Deity and that fantastic nonentity, which meet us so constantly in all such Oriental religions as are not drawn from this source. Nor is it less clear than in it we have the great thread of connexion between the Old Testament and the New—a connexion underlying and defying all the superficial 'antitheses' between the two, in the contemplation of which some forms of ancient Gnosticism and some forms of modern criticism have been altogether absorbed.

Yet one thing more must be added. The conception of

a covenant between God and man not only brings out vividly the true personality of God and the true spirituality of man, but it represents the Divine and human natures as having the power of a real communion with each other. Such communion is in some sense intellectual—God revealing Himself to man, and man able to rise to the knowledge of God. It is even more emphatically moral and spiritual; for God is seen as entering by His own free promise on obligations to man, in which 'it is impossible for God to lie,' and man, independently of his own choice, is called to a service of God, which has special blessings and special responsibilities. The whole conception is directly opposed both to the notion of a God 'unknown and unknowable,' and to that belief that He is too infinitely above His creatures to care for their good and evil, which is apt to cry out 'Tush! how should God perceive it? Is there knowledge' of our infinite littleness 'in the Most High?' It is the conception on which alone any true and vital religion can be built. Certainly it is the conception which naturally grows to ultimate perfection in the great central mystery of the unity of God and man in the Incarnation.

These all-important ideas are manifestly implied in the conception of the covenant. It is characteristic of the whole tone of Scripture, that they are conveyed in a concrete not an abstract form; that so they are brought home to the minds of the great mass of men in the very earliest and simplest stages of human development; that their embodiment advances with the progress of man's spiritual education, from the crude simplicity of the beginning of the Old Testament to the lofty perfection of the New. For, after all, it is only by implication and by concrete embodiment that great ideas can ever pervade humanity. The mind, which would recoil in vague perplexity from the contemplation, in philosophical abstraction, of the personality of God, the spirituality of man, the communion between the finite and the infinite, will hail gladly and grasp firmly the reality of such covenants as the covenants with Abraham, with Moses, with David, in which it feels, at least half consciously, that they are representatives of humanity itself.

(c) the communion between God and man.

IV. Accordingly this very conception of 'covenant' between man and God, running through all the Scripture history, seems to me very distinctly to correspond to the two great principles which Natural Theology brings home to us in many ways.

Relation of the idea to Natural Theology:

For, as we have already seen, the evidences of Natural Theology must be considered as falling into two main groups, corresponding to the intellectual and moral faculties of the soul. There is the group of speculative theology—the theology of the intellect and the imagination—leading us to the necessary conception of a First Cause, tracing in the universe the marks of design, discerning in all its parts a revelation of beauty. It is clear that these lay stress mainly on the former of these two great principles. They lead the mind away from all consciousness of self, to contemplate a personal Creator and Sustainer of the universe, in which that individual self is but a speck. The God whom they bid us contemplate is One

on the speculative side;

who sits above,
To us invisible, or dimly seen
In these His lowest works.

To the mind which is guided by them alone the conception of God is the grand and solemn, but vague and almost oppressive, consciousness of a 'high and holy One who inhabiteth eternity;' it is constantly crying out 'Lord, what is man?' inclined in practice to a religious fatalism, in devotion to lay the hand on the mouth, and pay a perplexed and awestruck worship 'mostly of the silent sort.' Yet even from this point of view such a mental attitude is at least questionable. These lines of thought, although they bow the soul before the infinite greatness of the Creative Mind, yet imply that, truly if imperfectly, it is capable of being discovered by the human mind and of speaking to that mind. In proportion as advancing science unveils to us more of the infinite greatness of the universe, it ought to be remembered that every step brings out more and more the spiritual greatness of the humanity which is capable of such marvellous discovery, and which, indeed, shows us the vastness of the unknown mainly by enlarging the bright circle of knowledge. Hence even this group of the evidences of Natural Theology is able secondarily to throw light on the other side of the truth, and to imply—what it does not draw out explicitly—the true spiritual nature of man.

But in the group which appeals to the practical reason—the theology of conscience and the theology of love—the two elements of the truth are seen far more clearly in their inseparable connexion. For all moral conceptions are essentially relative. The witness of moral theology starts from the realisation in ourselves of the moral nature, which a great modern philosopher has declared to be as great a marvel as the starry universe. It recognises God, indeed, as the eternal source of righteousness and love, but in the very recognition it implies that He has relations to us, that we are in some sense like Him, and capable of knowing and serving Him. So vivid is this sense of His relation to us, that it may lead to narrow and inadequate conceptions of God, unless it be corrected by the complementary truth of His infinity, supplied by the other group of evidences. At every moment it brings out, directly and not by inference, the moral and spiritual nature of man, as correspondent with the moral being and attributes of God Himself. on the moral side;

Whether, therefore, we deal with speculative or moral theology, these two great truths—the truth of God and the truth of man—constantly meet us as the ultimate results of our induction. Step by step the conviction of them grows upon us, as we advance along each line of thought, gathering at the same time from the others the confirmation, the correction, the extension, which each such separate line of thought must necessarily require.

But the Bible, be it observed, does not profess simply to swell this manifold strain of gradual conviction, adding, so to speak, one more voice to the chorus of Natural Theology, a voice perhaps somewhat nobler and clearer than the rest. I have said, not that it coincides, but that it corresponds, with these conclusions. It is complementary to them, just as a man's declaration of himself is complementary to the results of the observation and intuition of others brought to bear upon him. For it is evident at the first glance that, while it deals with these same truths, nevertheless it treats them in a wholly different way. as a revelation, not an induction.

It does not regard them as the ultimate results of a long and complex induction. It is not content with a gradual accumulation of evidence upon them, finally rising to moral certainty. On the contrary, it lays down these truths, enunciated in the perfect calmness of absolute certainty, as its fundamental basis. It bids us take them with us as our guiding principles, while it unrolls to us the outward and inward history of man. In its narrative, in its law, in its philosophy, its devotion, its prophecy, every vista of thought is filled up with the solemn declaration, 'I am the Lord thy God.' 'I am the Lord, the eternal Jehovah'—in these words we have the revelation of the Divine personality. 'I am thy God'—from these we infer an assertion of man's spirituality in the very declaration of his communion with God.

The reason of the difference is clear. The Bible, under all varieties of human authorship, claims to be the record of a self-revelation of God to man. The hope of all Natural Theology is to find God; the principle of revelation is that both they who deliver it and they who hear it are alike found by God. In relation to those who speak, there are two constantly recurring phrases in the Old Testament prophecy. First, 'the word of the Lord came to me.' In that phrase is the description of the presentation to man—not of the materials of knowledge, to be worked out by himself into a theory—not of the sense of a Divine Presence with him, breathing thoughts grand and vague ' as the sound of many waters'—but of the revelation of formed and definite idea. ' God spake these words and said, I am the Lord your God.' Next, 'the Spirit of the Lord was upon me.' In that phrase we have the description of a power first lifting the soul above its own thoughts, opening its eyes to see what others cannot see, and then inspiring the tongue to clothe these thoughts in words living and glowing with a fire which is not of earth. Those two phrases taken together describe the office of each messenger of God, leading up to and preparing for the perfect revelation in Him, who is described as 'the Word of God' Himself. Nor is it doubtful that what is thus clearly set forth in regard to those who speak, is recognised, partially in the Old Testament, completely in the New, as extending

[margin: The word of the Lord and the Spirit of the Lord.]

equally to those who hear. The word which comes to them is held to be a word of God, living and powerful in itself, and able to engraft itself on the heart. The Spirit of the Lord is with them to bear witness in their hearts, and so to bring home to them whatever is spoken in the name of God. Hence the whole idea of a Divine philosophy is absolutely distinct from the idea of a Divine revelation. In both, perhaps, God and man work together: but in the one the initiative is from man, rising by slow induction to the ultimate principles; in the other from God, declaring in majestic certainty truth which is at once the Alpha and the Omega, the first and the last. Hence (we may remark in passing) the one is the peculiar privilege of the few, the other is the universal treasure of the world.

Thus it is that the Bible deals with the two great conclusions of Natural Theology, confirming them in the name of a Divine authority, and clenching the 'I think' or 'I hope' of speculation by the calm declaration, 'Behold! I show you the mystery.'

V. But we must now consider how far its message is supplementary to our Natural Theology—how this conception of a covenant with God bears on the great mystery of evil, so difficult even to the speculative side of Natural Theology, so infinitely more difficult to the moral. *Its relation to the mystery of evil.*

Now, in the Scriptural views of this great and terrible mystery, two things are so clear that he who runs may read them. On the one hand, it recognises the existence of evil plainly, sadly, unflinchingly; and it regards it, moreover, as preserving, under all its forms, a fundamental unity, because having its root in the moral evil of man, and bearing, as the fruits of sin, the suffering and death under which 'all creation groans.' Hence it permits no illusion; it strips off all disguises under which moral evil is apt to veil itself, as a mere defect of nature, a result of unhappy circumstances, or a lower form of good. The rebuke of sin, and the warning of retribution here and hereafter, ring like a passing bell from one end of Scripture to the other. Human life and human nature are certainly seen there, not as we desire them to be, but as they are; and they are seen, moreover, to their very depths under the searching light of God's presence. On the other hand, the Bible utterly refuses to hold that this evil in the world is either God's will or man's true nature. Its possibility is, indeed, a consequence of that freedom in man which makes him the noblest work of God, and gives him the capacity of goodness. But in itself it is an unnatural rebellion, both against the true law of God and against the nature of man, which was not in the beginning and shall not be in the end. There is a Paradise of undeveloped goodness and happiness from which man's history starts; there is a matured perfection of heaven in which it closes. The Scripture is too true to reality to acquiesce in a shallow optimism, explaining evil away; it is still less in harmony with the theories of the Pessimist or the Manichæan, which make evil a triumphant or a co-ordinate power.

Now, in strict accordance with this general teaching as to evil, we find that its existence is not conceived as destroying the possibility of a covenant between man and God; because it cannot take away from God the obligation of righteousness and love towards His creatures, and it cannot destroy, though it may mar, the freedom and the moral capacity of man. In any individual soul, a wilful adherence to evil may cut off from God for ever, and by the severance turn spiritual life into spiritual death. But to man as man it is not so; to no individual soul need it be so. 'It is not the will of our Father in heaven that one of the least of us should perish.' But yet the very nature of the covenant allows for the existence of evil; its very object is the conquest of evil in man. The ideas of forgiveness and of salvation from sin lie at the very root of the whole, gradually worked out into clearer definiteness, as 'self-knowledge' in man brings with it at once 'self-reverence' and 'self-distrust.' The completion of the covenant is in the manifestation of One who not only reveals God to man, but is to 'crush the serpent's head,' taking away the sin which is the barrier between them, giving to every soul the immediate blessing of forgiveness and the sure and certain hope of final victory.

Its promise of victory over evil

In this aspect, again, it is clear how entirely the law 'supernatural, yet not preternatural,' applies. Where Scripture recognises the existence of evil in the world and the natural unity between sin and suffering, it simply sets its seal on the discoveries of all thoughtful human experience. Where it declares it to be unnatural, and therefore denies its permanence, it turns into certainty the conclusions which all the noblest thought and aspiration of man have cherished in hope and believed in as probable. Even where it declares that by the existence of evil God's covenant with man is not destroyed, but, on the contrary, has for its purpose and effect the destruction of evil, it does but strike in with authority in the strife of the two voices within us— the one telling the gloomy story of weakness, sin, decay, and death; the other proclaiming the bright hope of strength and purity and life. But where it tells at last how those hopes are realised, how the guilt of sin is taken away, how the new life of righteousness is rekindled in the soul, there it declares us a mystery, inconceivable by man beforehand, even now but imperfectly understood—a mystery which we know, though 'it passeth knowledge,' only by the power of faith in the word and grace of the Lord Jesus Christ. *supernatural not preter- natural.*

What other conception of the mystery of evil—from the theories denying it or explaining it away on the one side, to the Manichæan acceptance of it as an integral law of life, and therefore a law of our God, or our gods, on the other—can have any pretence to stand against it? It is at least a faith consistent with all that we can see of life, even in its strange contradictions, while yet it passes beyond these contradictions to a truth supernatural, on which the mind and the soul alike can rest. *Comparison with other theories of evil.*

VI. Such, as it seems to me, is the bearing of the general idea of a 'covenant with God,' as upon the great conclusions of Natural Theology, so upon the one disturbing influence which casts its shadow on the bright converging rays of their combined teaching. In the various epochs of a progressive revelation the conceptions of that covenant vary infinitely in loftiness, in comprehensiveness, in spirituality, till they come to their perfection in the person of the Lord Jesus Christ. But still at every point they preserve the same great leading thoughts. The personal being of God, the spirituality and freedom of man, the existence of *General conclusion.*

moral relations between man and God, the certainty that those relations cannot be destroyed, though they may be marred, by the terrible reality of sin in us, the sure and certain hope that by them sin (if only we will) can be conquered and cast out—these truths are involved in the very idea of covenant, even in its simplest form. Yet they are all that are needed for the sustenance of the religious life. It is not strange that in the catechetical instruction even of the young, the Church has made the idea of covenant with God in Christ the very pivot of all religious teaching. From the very beginning the right keynote is here struck. As the music of the great symphony of truth grows vaster, that note may swell infinitely in volume, and may be refined into a more exquisite purity; it may gather to it various harmonies, some obvious, some wrought out of seeming discords. But it will still be the one dominant note. Nothing can ever excel, as nothing can supersede, the preciousness of the Divine declaration, alike to the general life of the race and the inner life of the individual soul: 'I, behold I, make my covenant with you.'

CHAPTER III.

GOD AND MAN IN PRIMEVAL HISTORY.

'In the beginning God created the heaven and the earth.... God created man in His own image.'—Gen. i. 1, 27.

FROM the general consideration of the idea of covenant with God, running in various forms through Holy Scripture, and exemplifying the great law of 'supernatural not preternatural'—by at once confirming in the tone of divine authority the two great inductions of Natural Theology, and piercing through that dark mystery of evil which all the light of nature fails to dispel—we have now to pass to the more detailed study, from the same point of view, of the various phases of the Scriptural revelation.

I. The course of our thought leads us at once to those opening chapters of the Book of Genesis, which I venture to call the Scriptural introduction to the history of man. These chapters have a singularly marked and unique character of their own, standing out in obvious contrast with all that follows them. No one who reads the Bible attentively will fail to trace that distinction of character visibly represented by a striking difference of style and treatment. The history, properly so called, after preserving with full and prosaic accuracy the isolated record of the Flood, begins its continuous narrative with the life of Abraham. From that point onward, it may be true history or legendary fiction; but apologue, allegory, poetry, it cannot be. Whatever is recorded, whether it be what we call miraculous, or what we recognise as the ordinary course of God's providence, is recorded simply and unhesitatingly as fact. Nor can I see how the attribution to the Bible of a distinctly unhistoric character can be compatible with acceptance of it as a book of divine authority. No doubt we

The introduction to the Scripture history.

might have conceived a spiritual revelation, which should have nothing to do with historic record. But the Bible is not such a revelation; it claims to be history, and as history it must be judged.

But the portion of the Bible which is anterior to the record of the Flood is obviously of a very different character. <small>Its symbolic character.</small> It is a narrative, brief and vague, in which much of prosaic detail is mingled with more of simple but exquisite poetic beauty. Its purpose is clearly symbolical—to convey, that is, in concrete form, profound spiritual truths. But it should be noted that to call a narrative symbolical does not pronounce on the question whether its symbolical teaching is conveyed in allegory or parable, which is the more obvious and superficial method of such teaching, or in the record of literal fact, which would seem to be the deeper and the truer way. It is proverbial that 'fact is stranger than fiction.' It is equally true that fact is infinitely more instructive than fiction to those who have eyes to read its meaning. As every action, even the slightest, is characteristic, so in God's sight, and in any vision which in degree enters into the mind of God, I cannot doubt that every fact is symbolical, mirroring, that is, in itself the great principles of the system, in which it is but a speck. If it be not so to us, the fault lies in the imperfection of our sight, dazzled and bewildered by the vast and intricate complexity of human history. It is the mark of the philosophic or poetic insight even of human genius to rise in various degrees above the cloud which thus dims man's ordinary vision; for the divine gift of imagination manifests itself, not so much in inventing fantastic worlds of our own, as in discovering and revealing the hidden meaning of the world in which we live. Certainly it is just this insight which St. Paul claims in relation to the Old Testament history. When he would find moral types of the temptations and sins which beset humanity, he finds them in the historical trials of Israel in the wilderness; when he cries out, 'These things are an allegory,' he is dealing with the simple historical narrative of the contest of Sarah and Hagar in the tents of Abraham.[1] That the record of the

---

[1] See 1 Cor. x. 1-11; Gal. iv. 21-31.

creation and the primeval world is symbolical in its purpose is obvious. But the question still remains whether it be record of fact, or poetic parable.

On that question interpreters, all alike profound believers in the divine authority of Scripture, have differed, and will probably differ to the end of time. I must avow my own conviction, that, setting aside what is beyond all human experience, such as the record of creation, and perhaps what appears elsewhere in Scripture as plainly allegorical,[2] the narrative itself breathes the plain simplicity of fact, and even accords with all that reason might conjecture as probable in the earliest condition of man. Nor do I believe that men would have felt so much difficulty in accepting this ancient belief, if they were in the habit of reading what the Bible itself contains, without mixing it up with all those fancies of theologians and schoolmen, whether Jewish or Christian, which Milton has made familiar to us, and which all his genius cannot save from being always fantastic and unreal, occasionally almost grotesque.

Whether in history or in parable.

But, turning aside from this question, and contemplating these introductory chapters, whether historical or allegorical, as having a peculiar character and significance of their own, I would examine in them the relation in which Scripture stands to the speculations of the Natural Theology of man.

II. I turn first to the narrative of creation and the primeval world as it bears upon the conception of God Himself, as it stands, therefore, related to all the forms of thought in which man is ever 'feeling after God,' and trusting to 'find Him.'

The record of creation.

What has it to say on the great question of the 'First

---

[2] The 'tree of life' is thus presented to us in the Apocalypse (Rev. xxi. 2) in an allegorical and spiritual light. But it does not, of course, follow from this that the tree of life in Genesis (which is obviously described simply as an appointed means of sustaining physical life) had no literal existence, as a physical type of which this is a spiritual antitype. In our utter ignorance of the causes which determine the growth, the sustentation, and the decay of that life in man, it would be mere assumption to pronounce such a literal interpretation incredible. The 'tree of the knowledge of good and evil' (which does not thus reappear in the Apocalypse) stands in a different position. The result of the eating its fruit ensues not from any property in the fruit itself, but from the moral character of the act of eating.

Cause' of all the existing world—of which we actually know from science that it did come to be what it is out of something 'without form and void,' but as to which our thought still busies itself with the inquiries, What was the source of being? What was the creative power?

(a) Its bearing on Ætiology.

I have sought elsewhere to show how the thought of man, going back in abstract reasoning to that great First Cause, gradually sweeping away the tentative and imperfect theories of Polytheism and Dualism, comes at last to hesitate in theory between the faith in a living God as the Creator of all, and the Pantheistic conception of an *Anima mundi*—an eternal mind diffused through, and inseparable from, an eternal matter.[3] Unquestionably the history of human thought, as expressed in the languages, philosophies, and religions of men, shows that, wherever it emerges from the region of abstraction to become a power ruling the great currents of human belief and action, it has always embraced the former alternative. Still in theory there is hesitation. Again and again, in the esoteric doctrine of the few, presenting itself now in poetry, now in philosophy, now in scientific theory, the Pantheistic conception of a Nature which is not a God, supersedes or underlies the faith in a personal Creator. Accordingly, with an unhesitating and sublime simplicity, the very first words of Scripture intervene with authority in the conflict of these two great alternatives. 'In the beginning God created the heaven and the earth.' Yet under that simplicity there is a recognition of the profound distinctions which human speculation on this point has delighted to draw. God is spoken of not only as 'making' or 'forming' organised beings out of a primeval matter, but as actually 'creating'[4] even the

---

[3] See the *Boyle Lectures* for 1876, 'What is Natural Theology?' chap. iv.

[4] It is well known that the words referred to are distinct in the original. The word 'to create' is used only of original creation (Gen. i. 1), of the creation of animal life (v. 21), and of the creation of man. In all other cases the word 'made' or 'formed' is used. The distinction is obvious and significant; and though the word 'to create,' being, like all other human words, formed on human analogies, cannot fully express the idea of absolute origination out of nothing—of which we conceive that it must be, but cannot conceive what it is—yet there is no doubt that it is intended to approach as near as possible to that idea.

chaos 'without form and void,' out of which the *Kosmos* of order and beauty was hereafter to spring. He Himself is in the beginning, and He alone. The words, we observe, express clearly, authoritatively, unmistakably, that conception of an eternal Creator which has been a final induction, not unhesitating, of reason. But they express it in simple enunciation as of a known truth, not ' It might be so,' but ' It was so.'

What next has Scripture to declare on the great question of design, and therefore of mind, in the great existing *Kosmos*? Here, again, the history of human thought plainly shows how the mind, coming down from the height of abstract speculation on the dim mysterious past to the intelligent observation of the actual world —surveying it, sometimes with large comprehension of the unity of its various kingdoms one with another, sometimes with minute investigation of the structure and organism of each separate thing, and of the special kingdom to which it belongs—is naturally led, and has actually been led in all ages, to two great inductions. It believes itself to recognise a twofold design—the design of usefulness, in which various elements work to an appointed end; the design of beauty, in which there is, independently of all usefulness, a revelation of the creative mind. Various forms has that recognition taken, both in the analysis of science and in the synthesis of poetry. In its essence it remains fairly ineradicable (I believe) from human thought; yet it has to struggle against the difficulties arising from imperfect knowledge, knowing in some points at once too much and too little of the works of nature; and in the wider generalisations of our own days, it is so overlaid with secondary discoveries of law, and so removed from the actual world by theories of evolution, that it has lost much of the intenser vividness of earlier times. Here, again, the Scriptural record is not silent. We mark how in the detailed history of the successive ' days '[5] of creation—speaking in the letter to

(b) its bearing on Teleology.

---

[5] The teaching of Scripture on this all-important point is obviously independent of all interpretations of the meaning of the 'days' of creation, whether as literal days, as geological periods, or as the steps of that order of development of creation, of which our own science shows us the traces.

the simple and ignorant, speaking in the spirit to the profoundest thought—the Bible takes up that conviction of creative design, enunciating it calmly as a matter of course, describing how, in beautiful order and gradation, the divine purpose fulfilled itself successively in the kingdoms first of inorganic force and matter, next of organic life, lastly of spiritual being, and at every point, 'beholding that which was made,' pronounced it, alike in its usefulness and its beauty, to be 'very good.' Nothing can be more unlike the conception of a Creator starting the world (so to speak) on its course, and then leaving it to the dominion of some power of pervading force and law, or some plastic 'Nature,' itself a kind of secondary deity, not without mind and some shadow at least of personality. At every fresh development of creation, the creative mind is described as present with deliberate purpose of wisdom and goodness; and since we learn hereafter to see that, although the Creator 'rests' from that development of new laws and orders of being which prepared the earth for the dispensation to man, yet He cannot fail to work[6] in the continual production under those laws of individual creatures, we rise naturally to the conception of a sustaining as well as a creating Power, in whom 'we live and move and have our being.'

So the Scripture deals with the two great lines of speculative theology, taking them up (so to speak) from the very first with firm grasp of authority, and turning their inductions into certainties resting on a word of God. Through its simple enunciation of these ultimate truths, thousands and tens of thousands, to whom the speculations of the higher philosophy would be but as an idle tale, have entered half unconsciously into the possession of the great ideas which that philosophy seeks after, and have quietly rested and lived in them.

But what of moral theology? Again we see how the thought of man, uniting the witness of conscience and love within to the observation of the actual course of human nature and history without, has at all times been led to the belief in a God who actually governs the world of human souls—partly by what we call

(c) Its bearing on moral theology.

[6] See John v. 17, 'My Father worketh hitherto, and I work.'

His Providence, ruling all the outward circumstances of human life in its intimate connexion with the physical sphere —partly by what we call the action of the Divine Spirit, moving the wills of men, either by the higher principles of conviction of duty and enthusiasm of love, or by the lower motives of hope and fear in the expectation of retribution. That conception again maintains itself, not only against the negative doubts of an acknowledged ignorance, but against the positive denial and antagonism of evil. But it stands at times with difficulty and pain. Men look up and cry, 'O Lord, how long?' They fall in the struggle against wrong with the dreary cry that 'virtue is but a dream.' They look on the existing confusions, oppressions, cruelties of the world, till they despair of all human progress, sink into a blank and gloomy pessimism, or simply hold that the world is evil and miserable—whether as being the battlefield of rival deities, or as the scene of an imperfect creative power—and that we must be content if we can make it a little less evil and miserable, without speculating as to how it came to be what it is, or whether it has a nobler and happier future. Here, therefore, once more, the Bible strikes in with authority in this moral perplexity. It assumes from the very beginning a moral government of God, and even its embodiment in a law—not ignoring for a moment the possibility of a resistance to it by evil, but asserting it against and through all such resistance. Nor does it leave that government a vague and barren conception. It holds it to be a living reality, working itself out in the life of every day. It marks, on the one hand, the blessing, the intercourse, the guidance to man's innocence; it marks, on the other, the stern retribution, wrung from God (so to speak) by sin, though (in the pathos of a beautiful simplicity) it adds 'It repented the Lord God, and grieved Him at the heart.'

At every point it seems clear in the very beginning that the Scripture thus takes up the various lines of human thought, and, in that simplicity and certainty which alone can rule the mass of men, concentrates them on the one God. As we study its revelation, marking how much profound truth underlies its extreme simplicity, noting the contrast of its plain declaration with the modest hesitations of true induction, and the strange fantastic dreams presented to us in ancient cosmogonies and the imaginations of modern speculation, it is impossible not to feel that here we have a book like no other book, a word which, though it be spoken in the language of man, is in some special sense a Word of God.

But let us turn from the conception of God to the conception of the spirituality of man, and examine in relation to it the first opening of the Biblical record. We find that its attitude towards human thought is still the same. More clearly still, if possible, it takes up and clenches with authoritative certainty the declarations of the higher consciousness of man, expressed in the literature of every age, yet certainly troubled by the knowledge of the terrible power of material laws over us, by the conscious self-degradation of sin, and by the chilling certainty of death.

(*d*) Its bearing on the spirituality of man.

We note the record of the creation of man. It is simple enough, and in its simplicity full of poetic beauty. But there is in it a grave and unmistakable declaration of profound truth. With a decision which modern theories of evolution could hardly surpass, it connects the nature of man with the material world, even with 'the dust of the earth,' making humanity merely the crown of its gradual development. But yet, as clearly, in the most absolute accordance with the actual facts of the unique position of historic humanity, it marks the creation of man as ' a fresh point of departure,' as the introduction of a wholly new power into the world—whether by development or first creation it matters not, if only the continual presence of creative power and design be recognised. United closely to the inorganic and organic world, man is yet a creature 'made in the image of God,' and therefore a master, not merely a member, of the material and animal creation. It would be difficult to conceive any account of the origin of man more completely in harmony, at once with the discoveries of physical and physiological science, and the records of actual human history.

III. But what is here briefly implied is most strikingly developed in its history of primeval man—wonderfully different, as I have already hinted, from that strange fantastic travestie of human imaginations, which Milton has made so familiar to us that we constantly take it for Holy Writ. The very scene of that history is not the ideal Paradise of Dante or of Milton, in its character, perhaps even in its location, far removed from earth; but a region in the high ground of Central Asia, from which again and again have issued the great migrations of the human race, and a region of terrestrial beauty and fruitfulness, needing to be tended by the simple culture of primeval man.[7] The man who is placed in it is truly man, exhibiting, though only in the first germs, all the great elements of historic humanity.

The history of primeval man.

Thus, consecrating from the very beginning the dignity of human work, the Scriptural account represents man as consciously and intelligently a fellow-worker with God in the 'dressing and keeping' of the garden of the Lord, which yielded to him without laborious tillage the fruits of its beauty and fertility, much as in some favoured regions it yields them still. In that record we have the germ of the vast and ever-growing material civilisation of production and of manufacture, which so emphatically distinguishes the progressive reason of man from the stationary brute instinct.

(a) The sacredness of work.

Next, it describes to us the intellectual side of man's nature, when, in language very simple, but singularly profound in meaning, it tells of the origin of the gift of language, as called out under the providence of God through the sight of material objects, but as proceeding from an innate capacity in man. 'The Lord brought every beast of the field to Adam, to see what he would call them.' In that simple declaration, very different from the utterly insufficient theories of ejaculation and imitation with which we have been made familiar, we trace the germ of language, at once the sign and the means of the yet greater mental civilisation of man, day by day advancing its frontiers, because rising to the region of the invisible, while the brute instinct, however

(b) The power of thought.

---

[7] This is made clear by the description of the rivers of Paradise, two of which are undoubtedly the Euphrates and the Tigris.

subtle and marvellous in its narrow intensity of power, lies below, fast bound within the visible sphere.

So far it describes man in himself, as having the power to work and to think. But, passing beyond the individual, it next describes the natural bonds of human society, beginning in the sacredness of marriage, and perfecting themselves in fatherhood and brotherhood—those great natural relations of superiority and equality from which all others spring. In declaring these to be of the essence of man's nature, united indissolubly with the means of his physical propagation, it lays deep in that nature the foundations of duty and love. Men are to be free in themselves, and yet 'helps meet for one another;' their nature is to be at once individual and social. In the harmony of the two principles lies the foundation of the great fabric of human morality, starting, indeed, from instincts individual and social, but guided by reason, and thus elaborated in constant growth to meet all the complex relations of life, and rising in an absolute superiority above the sexual brute instincts, with which some would confuse it.

(c) Man a social being.

But, while it thus recognises these three universal principles of human nature—the energy of work, the insight of reason, the power of social duty and love—it leaves not out that other principle, which, if history can be trusted, is equally universal and ineradicable—the principle of worship. It paints man as having knowledge of God—a knowledge clearly sustained by some spiritual intercourse 'among the trees of the garden'—a knowledge clenched by direct simple law, given (we know not how) by the voice of God. In this declaration we have the recognition of that universal conception of a God, which, however it be accounted for, is a great fact in human nature, destined on the one hand to grow with man's growth in true development, on the other to survive a thousand perversions, superstitions, and perplexities. We have moreover, though in the most rudimentary forms, the two elements of spiritual communion and of positive law, which have formed at all times the religious discipline of man.

(d) Man a religious being.

There is in all this a wonderful completeness of idea,

showing us man as he is and has always been, a being whose nature it is to work, to think, to love, and to pray. Yet these powers undeveloped. But yet at the same time it should not be forgotten that the Bible—again differing utterly from the theories of theologians and the fancies of poets—paints to us the primeval state of man, not as one of full-grown perfection, but of childlike simplicity and immaturity, 'naked and not ashamed'—having in it all the germs of the future, but germs as yet undeveloped, as different from the perfection which we call Heaven, as the full-grown strength and thought of manhood from the lovely weakness of infancy. The picture reminds us not a little of that which is drawn of the dwellers in the West Indian islands, when first the foot of the Spanish discoverers trod their shores, or in some remote island of the Pacific in our own day, fair as the garden of the Lord, which the knowledge and the temptations of civilisation have not yet reached. It is the picture of a true childhood of humanity, not that grotesque mixture of advanced civilisation in thought and knowledge with childishness of occupation and circumstance, which modern poetry has given us in its place. The Scriptural record of human history, therefore, does not stand in antagonism to the philosophic conception of it; it is not, as has been thought, the story of a retrogression instead of a progress, presenting to the thought an ideal original of perfection, to which all subsequent ages are to strive vainly to return. On the contrary, it recognises a development, insisting, however, that this development shall be not from a mere brute condition, but from an immature childhood, containing in itself, just as the childhood of the individual contains, the capacities of all true human attributes. Nothing surely is clearer than this, if we will but study it for ourselves, and put away from us all those strange dreams of imagination which have been allowed to distort it into a fantastic unreality.

Once more, when we compare this record, so simple and yet so profound, with other theories of man's origin, whether offered, as of old, in the name of traditional cosmogonies, or (as now) in the name of scientific theory—when we ask which accords better both with the witness of man's inner consciousness and the plain indications of outward history—

we are inclined to cry out with St. Paul that the 'foolishness' of God's Word 'is wiser' than the maturest 'wisdom of men.' I claim once more that it is 'natural' in its deep accordance with our highest thought; yet supernatural in the clear simplicity of its revelation, as it comes down to us from the distant ages of the past.

IV. Such is the light thrown by this introduction to Scriptural history on the great inductions of Natural Theology, the being of God, and the being of Man. But what has it to tell on the great mystery of evil? On this we must put away from our thoughts not only all speculations of man, but even what the Bible itself in its later portions has told us on this awful subject. When we have done this, what is it which here meets us in the first pages of Scripture?

The record of the Fall.

First, it is boldly laid down that evil is no part of God's creation, and no part of man's true nature. The creation in all its points was 'very good;' man's original condition one of simple happiness and childlike instinctive innocence. His true development would be an unbroken growth, under God's guidance, from the lower to the higher happiness, from the innocence of instinct to the higher purity of thought, of conscience, and of love. All dreams of Dualism, all Gnostic conceptions of an ineradicable gravitation to evil in matter, all fancies that what we call evil is 'a lower form of good,' all despairing theories of an inherent and unconquerable law of sin, are swept away as if unworthy of notice. All was good in the beginning; all shall be good in the end. Whatever God may permit, in carrying out His law of freedom and responsibility in His creatures, His will is for their perfect righteousness and happiness. It is strange, to my mind, that the doctrine of original evil should be supposed to be peculiarly characteristic of Scripture as such. When we look at man as he is, surely it needs no revelation to tell of inborn sinfulness in the individual man, or ingrained evil in society. But what we do need is a Gospel of original righteousness; and certainly we have it in its germ in the first pages of our Bible. We thank God for it; for faith in it is the very principle of all nobleness of life.

Evil not original.

Next, the Scripture describes evil as originating in the

race precisely as it originates in the individual, partly by the misdirection of natural impulses of body and spirit, partly by the presentation of motives to evil from without. Again it should be observed that the temptation, appealing both to the physical and spiritual nature— to the one through appetite, to the other through the desire of independence and of wisdom, by which 'to be as gods'— is simple, childishly simple, as suited the undeveloped childhood of man. Yet it is profoundly significant. The 'knowledge of good and evil,' as separate and co-ordinate rules of life, between which to choose by trial, instead of the knowledge of good alone in itself, and of evil as the mere negation of good, represents clearly the false theory of a merely wilful life, as opposed to the natural discipline of a child of God under the true laws of his nature. The inability of mere retribution to check disobedience, so soon as God's will is looked upon as arbitrary and selfish, and the ease with which, in that mental condition, the reality of retribution itself is disbelieved, are as absolutely true to human nature as is the sad irony of the sentence which follows: 'Their eyes were opened, and they knew that they were naked.' All, absolutely simple, is yet full of a philosophic meaning, and in the whole process the temptation, thus appealing to the instincts of man's nature within, is yet described as presented from without. Man is not the first and only sinner. What is afterwards called a 'law of evil,' a distinct and concrete exhibition of sin as rebellion against God, is represented as being brought to bear upon him, and by his own submission triumphing over him, by precisely that process of 'temptation' with which the experience of the sins of every day makes us too terribly familiar. Few perhaps actually sin without a tempter now; the chain of evil is carried in a horrible continuity from soul to soul, from race to race, from age to age. The Scriptural revelation carries it finally back out of humanity itself to a power of evil which is not itself human.

<small>Evil brought in by temptation.</small>

But—again putting aside the little which subsequent revelation teaches us on this awful subject, and the much which human fancies have dared to invent, and to represent as revealed—we observe that the character, even the personal being, of that power of evil, are here in no sense described to us. The medium of temptation is 'the Serpent,' 'more subtil than any beast of the field,' the chosen emblem in all mythologies and apologues of the lower type of wisdom, earthly and sensual—rather, in fact, a cunning, which adapts means to ends, than a wisdom which knows the true end of life. It is, indeed, true that the very nature of the temptation implies a personal source, a mind speaking to the mind of man. But that source is absolutely veiled from us, as in the temptation so also in the sentence on the tempter—in form describing still the undying enmity between man and the serpent race, while he must be dull indeed who sees no symbolic meaning underlying it. Strange would it be, were it otherwise. Man has proved himself in all ages only too ready to exaggerate and to worship the power of evil. It was well for him to know that evil originates not in himself, that there is an evil power the enemy of man and God, that against this power there is a ceaseless war and a promise of victory. Beyond this we know but little now; beyond this it was certainly not well that the knowledge of the early world should stretch towards the realm of mystery.

<small>The nature of the tempter veiled.</small>

But further, recognising the existence of evil in its three great phases of sin, suffering, and death, the Scripture describes it as having a terrible unity, because proceeding from the one source of sin. It is again necessary to remind ourselves that the book of Genesis itself tells us very little of the nature of the blight on creation, under which we learn hereafter that 'the whole creation groans;' it determines absolutely nothing on the question whether, in the animal creation, decay and death did or did not happen from the beginning in the dread 'struggle for existence.' Nor does it even hint at the more awful penalties of sin on man—the bondage of evil, under which the soul cries out in agony, and the spiritual death, which is the obliteration of the image of God. But it connects with sin, as at once a breach of God's law and a degradation of human nature—first, the heavy labour of weariness and disappointment, laid especially on man; next, the suffering of pain and subjection, of which woman is, with unquestionable truth to fact, made to bear

<small>The penalties of sin.</small>

the chief share; lastly, the decay and death of the body, traced to the withdrawal of the appointed sustenance in 'the tree of life,' but in themselves the culminating result of the unrelieved burden of weariness and pain. Now of the reality of the connexion of these burdens of life with sin in the individual and in society, daily observation tells us much, declaring that, if but two or three gross forms of sin were rooted out, nine-tenths of suffering and decay would vanish like a cloud. Modern science, working out the principle of the mutual action of body and soul, of the individual and the race, of the whole inner and outer life, and constantly ascending towards an idea of unity in all being, may be not unreasonably thought to suggest something more. But once more the Scripture vindicates its position, as supernatural not preternatural, by according with experience and reason, but going beyond either, and by declaring as simple fact what they pronounce upon by long and often doubtful inference.

But, finally, the Scriptural narrative declares unhesitatingly that evil shall not triumph. 'The seed of the woman shall bruise the serpent's head.' The words themselves (as has been already said) describe merely the continual warfare carried on, not without pain and danger, between men and the poisonous race of serpents. *The promise of victory over evil.* But it would be a dull literalism indeed which would refuse to recognise the obvious symbolic meaning of promise, that in some way the seed of woman should conquer the evil to which man now gave way, and that 'the bruising the heel' implied in this conquest the need and certainty of suffering. It would be absurd to read into these words a full Christian meaning. What depths of God's mysterious love lie below them—with what singular appropriateness of meaning future events should endow them—we and we only know. We must divest ourselves as much as possible of all subsequent knowledge, and deal not with the full Gospel, but with the *Protevangelium* of the first pages of Scripture. Can we fail to see how remarkably, in its acknowledgment of the reality of evil, always subordinated to the certainty of the prior existence and final triumph of good, and then in its description of the first origin of evil and its most obvious fruits, it is again 'natural' and 'supernatural,' according with man's deepest thought, yet passing out of the clouds that overshadow that thought into the first clear dawn of a full noonday to come?

V. Without hesitation, in these early chapters of our Bible, which some would banish to the realm of legend, and <small>The Prot-evangelium.</small> which others pass by with uneasiness and perplexity, I trace—what the old Fathers deemed that they had found—a *Protevangelium*. I find the first and simplest exemplification of the general character of the teaching of Holy Scripture, as at once brightening the light, and scattering the darkness, of the deeper thoughts of man. To go back to them from the full and varied life of the present is to trace back the stream of history to its source, not in some mountain of fabled grandeur, like the streams of Eastern legend, nor yet in some dismal morass of purely material or animal life, but (as with the stately river which flows through our great city) to a pure spring, bubbling out in the homely simplicity of a scene, which we can recognise as real, and love for its quiet beauty. True that it is yet but a little stream, showing but slight anticipation of the time when it shall flow on, swollen by tributaries from every side, and bearing on its bosom the emblems of infinite wealth and activity. Yet on its first outburst and its first direction depends the future; we believe that there is an eye which saw that future in the beginning, and guides it to its accomplishment. Therefore in the task of so tracing it back there is not only a vividness, but a certain sacredness, of interest. When we stand at the source of our human history, we feel that our feet tread on solid human ground, and our eyes look up to a presence of God in heaven, not different in essence, though it may be different in phase, from the presence which is about our path in the homely light of every day.

CHAPTER IV.

THE GENERAL AND SPECIAL COVENANTS OF GOD.

'And God said, I am the God of Abraham, and the God of Isaac, and the God of Jacob. . . . I am that I am.'— Exod. iii. 6, 14.

IN this chapter we have to advance some steps further in the evolution of the Scriptural declaration of 'covenant with God.' As yet we have simply considered how in the fundamental ideas involved in such covenant, and in their first illustration through the brief symbolic introduction to the regular history, written in the first chapters of Genesis, the revelation of God is undoubtedly complementary to Natural Theology, as bringing out the personality of a living God, and the true spirituality of man; and how at the same time, though as yet only under the simpler and less difficult aspects, it faces unflinchingly the dark mystery of evil, before which Natural Theology stands at bay—not silenced, indeed, but perplexed. In these considerations we stood at the first source of human history; now we have to trace the stream as it flows down, gradually widening and deepening, till it becomes the great flood, on which we ourselves are borne along.

I. I may remark that here we enter at once on what claims to be a record of a true historic character. Of the world before the Flood we have but the vaguest glimpses, just sufficient to show us that it was a world in essence like our own, although different in some phases and conditions of its being.[1] Still the narrative is symbolic, but symbolic under the simplicity of obvious

The glimpses of the antediluvian world.

---

[1] Such difference is, for example, implied in the longevity ascribed to the patriarchs. This is clearly described as historical. In our ignorance of the determining cause of that victory of the forces of decay over those of reproduction, which we call old age or decrepitude, who can pronounce it incredible ?

fact. We trace the full growth of sin in the murder of brother by brother—its root in sudden jealousy, striking deep into the soil of an ingrained selfishness—its penalty in that outcast loneliness from Nature, from man, and from God, which is the appropriate punishment of selfishness. We trace a gradual separation between the two classes of those who 'call on the name of the Lord,' and those who will not have Him to reign over them—Enoch or Noah the perfect type of the one, Cain or Lamech of the other. We note the profound wisdom, departing from the ordinary type of mythology, which distinguishes between material civilisation, whether of mechanical or fine art, and the moral progress of a religious life—the one belonging to the family of Cain, the other to the race of Seth. We read the record of the primeval existence of sacrifice, presenting itself (so to speak) as a matter of course, under its simplest form as a tribute of homage to the God who gives all—so remarkably corresponding with the universal extension of that strange rite in all its various forms, of which philosophic history has taken note. We find at last—perhaps from some supernatural admixture of evil [2]—the story of an overspreading corruption, in which the probation of that old world came to a tragic end; and we hail the simple beauty of the declaration (for which philosophical abstractions would give but a poor exchange) that throughout that probation God's 'Spirit strove with man,' and that its fatal close 'repented the Lord God, and grieved Him at the heart.' In all this we certainly learn that in that ancient world God and man were still the same. But we learn no more. Thousands of years are noted but in a few scores of words. The Flood, so often paralleled in Scripture with the judgment day, rolls between us and them, and of the further shore we have but dim and shadowy outlines, of which we hardly know the full meaning. From these mere fancy would rejoice to weave a

---

[2] I allude, of course, to Gen. vi. 1-6—the admixture of 'the sons of God' with 'the daughters of men.' Whatever be the difficulties of conception of such admixture, however much we may shrink from the grotesque fables which have been drawn from this source by ancient interpreters, both language and context seem to imply the introduction of some supernatural element into the world, connected in its consequences with the final Judgment.

fabric of many-coloured legend. But with a reserve of fixed purpose the Scripture record passes them by. It is enough to see here in type the great principles of God's moral government. Our business is with the dispensation in which we live. History, properly so called, begins for us only when the great catastrophe of the Flood opens the new world.

II. Accordingly it must be obvious to every thoughtful reader that with the story of the Flood the whole character of the Scriptural narrative changes. The story is told, indeed, with a simple and pathetic beauty, painting, as from the ark itself, the picture of a great convulsion under unknown forces of destruction—'the windows of heaven opened, and the fountains of the great deep broken up.' But it is told with plain, almost prosaic, reality even of detail. It is the beginning of human history, curiously supported (as we know) by the traditions of almost every race, but admitting none of the fantastic additions which we find in these, in itself obviously no mere apologue or legend, but history, and as history claiming to be judged —in relation, if we will, both to the traditional histories of the peoples of the world, and the geological or physiological history written on the fabric of the world itself.[3] There is clearly a fresh start taken when the Flood subsides, and the remnant come forth from the ark. A 'covenant' is given; a new blessing uttered; the old birthright of man in 'the image of God' renewed; the first roll of the peoples of the ancient world recited to us. From that time onward the historic thread is never broken, till it binds the whole world to the feet of the exalted majesty of the Lord Jesus Christ. Laying hold of it as a clue of light in the darkness of antiquity, we may consider the first stages of the evolution of the great fundamental idea of the covenant of man with God.

Now from the very beginning we must be struck with

margin: The commencement of regular history with the Flood.

---

[3] The traditional history in all the great families of mankind—hardly wanting, indeed, in any great ancient tradition except the Egyptian, and in the Chaldean standing out with most striking points of similarity to the Old Testament record — bears strong evidence to the reality of the Flood; the geological and physiological history to its partiality. The Scriptural narrative simply implies its universality in relation to the human race in its primeval habitation.

a twofold aspect of that covenant, corresponding very remarkably to the twofold nature of man. It is at once special and universal; it belongs to the individual, yet in possessing it he is partly the representative, and partly the trustee, of the whole human race. Could it (we may ask) be otherwise? Each man is truly individual, always in his highest consciousness alone with the God on whom his life hangs; yet he is also a member of the great family of mankind, and an element in the greater system of the universe itself. Accordingly it is necessary to any conception of a living relation to God, which shall at once stir the heart and satisfy the intellect, that it shall first be realised by man in the little world of his own soul, and in the relations immediately connecting it with the outer life; and then that it shall be seen in its bearing on the great world without, widening out, like circles on a river, until it washes the shores of humanity on every side. To be a religion, it must satisfy the one condition; to be a philosophy, it must fulfil the other. Thus we see that in Natural Theology the moral witness of conscience and of the affections concentrates our thought on a God who is our God, in whom we ourselves 'live and move and have our being;' the witness of the intellect and the imagination diffuses it (so to speak) over the universe, and bids us identify with this our God the Supreme Power, on which the whole depends. Accordingly any revelation, which is to correspond to the whole needs and various thoughts of man, should certainly bring out the relation to God in this twofold aspect, contemplating it at once in the gathered rays of the revelation to the individual, and the diffused light of a universal revelation to all mankind.

Now this, be it noted, is precisely what the Bible does in respect of its great idea of covenant with God. First, in slight outline, in pale yet not indistinct colouring, it sketches it out as concerning all mankind, and filling the whole canvas of history. Next, it paints over this first outline, stroke by stroke, till the picture lives and breathes before us, the closer personal relation to God of a chosen man, a chosen family, a chosen nation; while at every point the universal conception is seen (so to speak) to form a half-luminous background, on which the brighter painting stands out in softened beauty. The first glance is content to rest on the detailed figures of the foreground; the closer and more thoughtful observation sees that they are but salient parts of a mighty whole. So in a well-known picture the first glance shows us but one figure of an exalted majesty surrounded with glory; the next tells us that this glory is made up of a constellation of angel faces, surrounding the central figure with a living presence of the 'ten thousand times ten thousand,' who stand before the throne of God.

III. We glance first at the original outline of a covenant universal to man; standing at the point, where the waters of the Flood have ebbed away, to leave bare for us the firm ground of the first plain record of human history. Then for the first time the word 'covenant' is used, with all the peculiar characteristics of God's covenants very strongly marked upon it—its origination from His will, as declaring the eternal purpose, which is from the beginning; its perfect freedom and absoluteness, unconditioned by any action of man; yet its value to each man depending on the acceptance, by an intelligent and active faith, of what might otherwise be a mere regularity of law, hiding rather than manifesting the hand of the living God. With these characteristics thus plainly marked, it is set forth in application to all flesh, in all the various families by which the whole earth was to be overspread. That covenant in the very simplest language enunciates, as by the voice of God, three great laws, on which the whole fabric of human life rests.

The general covenant with Noah.

It proclaims first the law of physical regularity and permanence. 'The flood shall no more destroy the earth;' 'while the earth remaineth, seed-time and harvest, and cold and heat, and summer and winter, and day and night shall not fail.' It proclaims this physical regularity, as all religion must proclaim it, to be the expression of a creative will; but it proclaims it as a covenant, that is, as a declaration of that will for the benefit of man, since only by the foresight and reliance on physical regularity can he be 'a fellow-worker with God.' They who have studied

(a) The law of physical regularity.

the 'reign of law,' and searched into its secrets, will know what profound meanings lie below this calm simplicity.

It proclaims next the law of the sacredness of the individual man. Separating his life from the merely animal life, which may be freely sacrificed for our use, it pronounces that sentence, which has sounded through all the centuries its awful irreversible law, 'Whoso sheddeth man's blood, by man shall his blood be shed;' and bases it on the priceless declaration, repeating even to sinful man the first blessing of creation—'In the image of God made He man.' By these words it raises man above the iron regularity of the march of physical law, and out of the bewildering variety of animal being; it gives him right, freedom, individuality, even before the face of God.

(b) The sacredness of human life.

Lastly, by the solemn conclusion to the simple history of the Patriarch's weakness and his son's mockery, the Scripture proclaims, under God's sanction, the sacredness of human relationship, and of the authority which is the lineal descendant of fatherhood. As it has already sanctioned the individual right and freedom, so now it declares that only by reverence can they be preserved, and that he who despises the sacred authority shall be trodden down under the iron heel of brute force, 'a servant of servants' for ever.

(c) The sacredness of authority and society.

It is clear that we have here, first, the grand unity of the physical universe, serving God and man; and next, the two laws of humanity, by the balance of which society is sustained—the freedom of the individual, and the authority which binds all together. We see, therefore, these laws extended to all, and hallowed for all, by the universal covenant of God with man. Here again the Scripture takes up the conclusions of the Natural Theology at once of the intellect and the conscience. Recognising the great laws lying at the basis at once of physical and of moral science, it establishes them—where alone experience has shown that they can firmly stand—on the relation of the eternal God to nature, to the individual man, to human society as a whole. They are all parts of 'one law eternal,' not inferred by reasoning, but declared with authority. So only can they reach and rule the minds of mankind at large. This calm and simple enunciation as of known certainties stands at once in harmony and in contrast with the laborious inductions of our human science.

There is, perhaps, the more need to dwell on this first opening of Scriptural history, because the great universal promise and law to all mankind, marking out for all a fatherhood of God and a moral government of the world, are apt to be obscured to our minds by the far more detailed and vivid painting of the special covenant of the Old Testament. But it is, indeed, the beginning of a general undercurrent of thought, which is to the thoughtful reader perceptible throughout, coming from time to time to the surface in striking examples, gradually asserting itself more and more, especially in the prophetic books, till at last in the New Testament it absorbs all that is special, individual, and national, and spreads in one great spiritual equality from pole to pole. There is even from the beginning a gospel and a law to all humanity. There is a doctrine of God and of man applicable to every variety of human life. It is simple, indeed, and bare enough in comparison with the fuller teaching of the hereafter. But in relation both to nature and to man it asserts what is of the essence of a godly life. *This general covenant traceable throughout.*

IV. From it we pass on to the clear and graphic picture of a special covenant with God, foreshadowed in the promise to Shem, but wrought out in the history of the race of Abraham, under the first rudimentary forms of human society, and the early growth of a material and spiritual civilisation. *The special covenant with Abraham.*

At the first outset we notice that in the union of a speciality of call, knowledge, and privilege given to one man or one tribe, with the purpose of subserving, through him and them, the blessing of all human kind, we trace what observation and history declare to be a fundamental law of human life in all ages and under all aspects. The great steps in material improvement, in intellectual progress, in moral civilisation, are certainly made precisely in this way. Inequality, as truly as equality, is the natural law. Diversities of gifts, duties, and effects under the *Its accordance with the laws of human life.*

unity of one great universal work, form the experience of every day. We have only to look at the actual organisation of any single human society, or the present condition and past history of the nations of the world. Everywhere we see what we call favoured men, favoured classes, favoured races, favoured generations—all rightly recognising their own special privileges—all liable to the natural yet fatal error of supposing that such special privilege is exclusive, and dealing with others as out of the pale of all rights and all sympathies—yet all subserving one great purpose, which they can no more resist, or restrict to themselves, than we can stay the impulse by which light, sound, motion, once imparted, must spread through all the regions of the universe. The whole Scriptural conception of the Abrahamic covenant does but extend to the higher religious history of the world what all observation discloses in the lower realms of that history. The great leaders of mankind, whether individuals or races, are called in various ways to leave their old condition, and go forth they know not whither. To them may be given the lower reward of fame and power and wealth, though so uncertainly that the world's ignorance of its true benefactors has passed into a proverb. But their highest glory, of which no man can rob them, is that, in various degrees, 'in them all families of the earth shall be blessed.'

Very simple is (so to speak) the setting of this great principle in the external history. Few theories, to an unprejudiced eye, break down more utterly on examination than the notion that we have here an ideal history setting forth, under individual names and under the parabolic vesture of narrative, abstract ideas, impersonated races, moral lessons. Symbolic the history may be, and, told from the point of view of God's revelation, symbolic it must be. But plain, prosaic, often homely reality surely breathes in every line; features come out again and again, which no heroic or didactic legend would tolerate. The very migration of Abraham from Ur of the Chaldees has been thought to have been but a single example of a great westward migration. Certainly the whole outward history is but the simple everyday history of a tribe, growing, not without vicissitudes of fortune, not without disruptions and

The simplicity of the external history.

divisions, from insignificance to greatness, until it seems to be merged in that gigantic empire of Egypt, to which it had been attracted again and again.

But it is on the secret spiritual history, underlying all this, that the whole interest turns. The characters of Abraham and Isaac, of Jacob and Esau, of Joseph and his brethren, are of singular variety of type, yet all simple, all strongly marked with human imperfection. *The spiritual history underlying it.* But the leading characteristic of all is the consciousness of a covenant with God, hallowed by solemn sacrifice, marked by the rite of circumcision, accepted in the 'faith,' which 'sees Him who is invisible' as a 'God with them,' or rejected in a 'profaneness' which, however tinged with generosity and nobleness, is a falling back upon the lower earthly life. This spirit of faith shows itself, according to character, in different forms. In Abraham it is strongly marked by energy, freedom, self-sacrifice; in Isaac it passes into a gentleness of submission which is almost weakness; in Jacob it becomes an eager, crafty tenacity of spiritual glory and privilege, darkened by a far stronger admixture of fear; in Joseph it assumes a larger and calmer tone, not unsuitable to the civilisation of Egypt.

But throughout we note, as singularly accordant with the simple condition and the imperfect spiritual education of these early servants of God, that the relation to God is presented in the very simplest form, appealing (as suits all children and childlike natures) mainly *The God of Abraham, Isaac, and Jacob.* to the vivid but narrow insight of affection, and represented to the soul through the experience of human relationship. The patriarchal idea of authority and protection is the leading idea of the race. Accordingly God is known as 'the God of Abraham, of Isaac, and of Jacob'—revealed as a Father of the chosen family, in whom they trust with a simple trust, a free though not irreverent familiarity, very different from the deep and awestruck reverence of the Mosaic period—felt as their protector and their guide to a great future which He has ordained for them, and asking from them, except in one or two great crises, not the co-operation of anxious thought and struggle, but the co-operation of an obedient faith. All the darker, grander, more mysterious aspects of the relation to God, lie far off in the future. What an earthly father is to his children, before they know the darker sins or sorrows of life, God is to the simple natures who live in this early covenant with Him.

Yet (as I have said) in the half light of the background, subdued, yet unmistakable, we see, coexisting with this personal knowledge of God as their own God, the larger conception of Him as the God of the whole world.

The name by which He speaks of Himself again and again is the 'God Almighty.' In that very name are contained *The God* two distinct ideas, bearing upon the divine relation *Almighty.* to the physical universe and the realm of humanity.⁴ In the former relation it describes Him as the Creator and the Sustainer of all those powers, physical and external to man, the contemplation of which belongs to the first awakening of thought, whether it considers in the silent night 'the heavens the work of His fingers' (Ps. viii.), or, in all the freshness and bright colouring of the day, beholds 'the earth and the sea' as 'full of His riches' (Ps. civ.). In the latter it describes Him as the Ruler of all spiritual beings, by a different kind of power, subtler yet not less real than the Divine power over nature; and this latter thought is emphasised in the moral aspect which is its distinctive feature, as when Abraham on the eve of Sodom's ruin looks up to 'the Judge of all the earth,' and knows that He must 'do right.'

In both these conceptions we pass from the narrow intensity of a personal affection to the larger conceptions of the *The union* reason and the conscience. The God of Abraham *of the two* is no mere tutelary God. Outside the bright circle *ideas* of the special covenant, there spreads over the whole universe the gracious light of His countenance. Now and then there emerges (so to speak) from the half shadow, like salient peaks from some great mountain-range, the vision of a Melchizedek, a Pharaoh, an Abimelech, as true servants of God, known to Him and knowing Him, the one in sacredness of office, the others in moral superiority, towering for a time over the patriarch himself. In the foul sensual wickedness of

---

⁴ The distinction is marked by the use of the two words Παντοδύναμος and Παντοκράτωρ in the ordinary Greek version of the Apostles' Creed.

Sodom, as truly as in the purer life of Abraham's tent, man's probation is worked out before God, and ten righteous may save a city. But, independently of these special exemplifications of God's dealing with the outside world, in the very name of 'the Almighty' lies undeveloped a revelation which touches the whole race of man. It is but a germ; the leaves are yet folded within the sheath; but they are there, and are ready to blossom out in fulness of beauty, when the appointed time shall come.

For in constantly increasing clearness a connecting link between these two aspects of the covenant is wrought out in the great promise of a universal blessing through the seed of Abraham to all families of the earth. Perhaps more prominent at the first is the temporal and special promise; it and it alone is gradually unfolded in the successive stages of the patriarch's life. The greater promise, 'In thy seed shall all families of the earth be blessed,' begins and ends the history of Abraham, and is preserved without progress in the history of his successors — still remaining undeveloped, like the tree which flowers only when a hundred years are gone—unchanged (that is) in itself, but necessarily understood better as the spiritual education proceeds. Our Lord profoundly teaches us that in the very thought of a true spiritual covenant with God were involved ideas, incapable of being satisfied in the brief threescore years and ten of earthly life, or by the coarse and comparatively unsubstantial gift of earthly glory. 'God is not the God of the dead, but of the living;' not the God of the earth and the earthly, but of the spirit and the spiritual life. In the very thought lay the germ, as of a hope of personal immortality, so also of the conception of a spiritual covenant widening out to embrace the whole world. As yet, no doubt, it was but a germ. It would be simple anachronism to ascribe to the imperfect knowledge of Abraham the bright foresight of an Isaiah, or the larger insight which is given to the simplest Christian. Yet the human mind, after all, is one and the same, in respect of ideas which change little more than the everlasting hills. Our Lord again teaches us that 'Abraham saw his day and was glad.' Surely that authority more than covers the belief that there was even then some knowledge of the future reconciliation of the special and universal covenant in Him who was to come.

It is hard to conceive any revelation truer to human nature and life, more exquisitely correspondent to the highest aspirations of the theology of man. Yet hardly less appropriate is its silence than its speech. How little as yet is the mystery of evil touched! The existence of evil in its concrete form is plain enough; even the inheritance and horrible development of ancestral sin is not unknown, as (for example) in the development of the conventional falsehood of Abraham or Isaac into the utter baseness of the deceit of Jacob, or again of the selfishness of Jacob into the 'jealousy' which sold Joseph into Egypt, and brought the grey hairs of his old father so near to the grave. Outside the chosen race, the evils of bloodshed, luxury, sensuality, falsehood, run up into poisonous rankness. Nor is there any dimness or hesitation as to the knowledge of God's retribution, whether it simply exile a deceiver from his home to a hard and troubled life, or wave the fiery sword over the lost city of unredeemed wickedness. But of the deep painful consciousness of the bondage and the mystery of evil (unless in the typical significance of sacrifice, itself not yet fully elaborated) we have no trace here. For as in the education of children, first the knowledge of God and of the spiritual being of man, as knowing and loving Him, is to be wrought into the very texture of the consciousness. Then, when they can be borne, and not till then, the darker and sadder mysteries of life can rightly dawn upon it.

Slight reference to the mystery of evil.

In this respect especially this first epoch of revelation stands in contrast with the next epoch of revelation in the law, by which is 'the knowledge of sin.' There is a real truth (though it may be liable to exaggeration or perversion) in the conception of a childhood of the human race, analogous in its needs and capacities to the childhood of the individual. The Abrahamic revelation speaks emphatically to such a childhood, in its realisation of a living personal relation to God, with but a vague secondary conception of His universal sovereignty and fatherhood; in its correspondence with the organisation of the family, the simplest, though the most sacred, of all forms of human

Contrast in this respect with 'the law.'

society; in the comparative abeyance of the sense of the mystery of evil, while the concrete reality of evil is recognised as an exceptional resistance of the dominant law of good; in the simplicity and freedom of its moral life, needing no stern elaborate law, no profound doctrinal teaching. Yet the sadder and more thoughtful manhood of our later days, as usual, finds in these 'first thoughts' of childhood a greater delight, a deeper instruction, a profounder accordance with ultimate truth, than in the revelations, in themselves perhaps fuller and grander, which follow them. In Genesis, far more than in the sternness of the law of Exodus, or the stormy records of the Judges or the Kings, we seem to breathe by anticipation the atmosphere of the Gospel.

V. But we pass on to the next epoch of revelation, in the renewal and enlargement of the covenant to Moses. *The Mosaic revelation.*

This revelation claims to have a distinct continuity with the other. 'I am the Lord God of your fathers, the God of Abraham, of Isaac, and of Jacob.' But far different the circumstances of the receivers. In the place of the bold simple patriarch there rises up the form of a sad, earnest, thoughtful man, trained in all the wisdom of the Egyptians, learning alike by what it could, and by what it could not teach, the deeper things of man and of God. Instead of the free desert-tribe, a great people, dominated by the greater power of Egypt, and from it deriving all the good and evil of material civilisation, increased knowledge, a larger and more complicated form of society. Necessarily, in such a case, with fundamental unity of substance there must be much characteristic and important difference of tone and of scope.

But once more from the beginning we find marked out the universal and the special relations of God to man.

Here, however, the universal relation is marked, not merely by the renewal of the old promise, but directly and emphatically by the introduction of a new name of God, superseding (at least in principal and distinctive use) all other names.[5] *The universal idea in the name Jehovah.*

---

[5] As to this virtual novelty of revelation, Exodus vi. 2, 3 is decisive, whatever explanation (proleptic or other) may be given of the previous use of the name Jehovah in the Scriptural narrative. Henceforth

For the name 'Jehovah,' which was made the sacred stamp of the new covenant with Israel in Moses, is the ultimate, the absolute, the universal name of God—'Ἐγώ εἰμι ὁ "Ων, 'I am He that is.' In that name God is recognised, neither in special relations to a chosen man or race, as 'the God of Abraham, Isaac, and Jacob,' nor yet in His universal dealings with His creatures, in the creation of all things and rule over all persons; but as He is in Himself, the one only Being, self-existent and eternal, in whom, by a mere derivative life, all creatures 'live and move and have their being.' In that name is declared the truth to which all lines of human thought can but approach. They can only tell us distinctly of an infinity relative to us, that is, of power, wisdom, goodness, passing our knowledge. Here is the declaration of absolute infinity in God, existing from all eternity, and existing in sole inherent life.

It is profoundly significant that a name like this, necessarily unchanged and unchangeable in its meaning to all races and to all times, should have been from the very first the peculiar name of the God of Israel. It marked out the race of Israel as in possession of the truth and privilege which are the birthright of man as man, and therefore as representatives and trustees of the whole human race. It brought the Israelite face to face with the absolute majesty of God. Naturally, in the grandeur and the awfulness of that position, the free and simple familiarity of older times passed away. When the name Jehovah is proclaimed, the great lawgiver himself 'hides his face as afraid to look upon God;' when it is first repeated to the people, 'they bow the head and worship;' when at Sinai He manifests Himself in the cloud and in the trumpet voice, they turn away, and will 'not see lest they die;' when it is the accepted name of God, it is held too sacred to be pronounced by human lips. It is impossible for the profoundest Theism, anywhere or at any time, to go beyond the sublime creed of Deuteronomy : 'Hear, O Israel, Jehovah thy God is one Jehovah; and thou shalt love Him with all thine heart, and with all thy soul, and with all thy might' (Deut. vi. 4, 5).

it is the one supreme and ultimate name of God—'above every name,' and regarded with an awful and almost superstitious reverence.

But, existing under the shadow of this universal revelation of God, and intended, indeed, gradually to bring out its meaning, there is, again, a special relation of Israel to God, expressed in the well-known word 'Theocracy,' to be to the people at once a living religion in the present, a half-conscious education for the future. *The special relation of the Theocracy.*

'A religion of the present.' They had passed into a new condition of society, as a nation, not as a family. In that condition God was to reveal Himself to them, at every point of their life, individual and national, not as a Father, but as a King.

'An education for the future.' For by degrees the conception of His kingship over man widened out far beyond the limits of the chosen nation or of the present life. So widening, it prepared for the future manifestation of a kingdom over the whole world, and yet 'not of this world.'

This twofold office of the Theocracy we may trace plainly in the two great developments which mark its earlier periods, both belonging to the sphere of external experience—the conception of 'God in history' and 'God in law.'

'God in history.' It cannot be by mere accident that this is the first epoch of the record of what we call miracle in Scripture. There is described to us an outburst of miraculous power at the time of the Exodus from Egypt and the entrance into Canaan, never to be repeated again in the same grandeur—never, indeed, to be even approached, till the time of the great Baal-apostasy in the days of Elijah and Elisha. Moses, as he has a new mission and revelation, so also is clothed with a power of miracle hitherto unknown. But it is especially notable that the miracles so wrought are in no sense represented as merely exceptional works of wonder. They are spoken of in the same breath and the same tone as what we should call ordinary events; they form an integral part of the history; they only exemplify with special emphasis a great reality which underlies that history throughout. At times they are 'signs' to show that reality to men; at other times they are 'mighty works,' actually efficient and (humanly speaking) necessary instruments of the events to be wrought out. The story of the Exodus, if the records of the miracles were torn out, would be not only mutilated, but *(a) God in history.*

simply unintelligible; by them, and by them alone, the sceptre of Egyptian tyranny is broken, and the people are set free. But throughout they are viewed as parts of a great whole, and manifestations of a universal truth. There is something very striking and profound in this view of miracle. It is essential that all who would understand the Scriptural miracles should consider what in the Scripture itself they claim to be.[6]

What then is that reality, which is thus declared alike in the bright flashes of miracle, and the paler and steadier light of the ordinary course of nature?

It is the declaration of a Divine will in history, working in righteousness and wisdom, working alike through things and through men to an appointed end. It is, indeed, the will of One who makes Israel His own peculiar people, watches over them, guides them, breaks down all that stands against them, punishes in them all that sins against His purpose. But it is the will of no mere tutelary deity, dealing by capricious favour. It is the will of a righteous and merciful God. If Egypt suffer, it is after much warning for insolence and oppression. If the Amorites be destroyed, the blow is withheld for generations, and falls only because 'their iniquity is full.' If blessing be showered in infinite graciousness on Israel, it is only so far as Israel is faithful, righteous, holy. In proportion to the brightness of their peculiar blessing is the deep, dark shadow of the curse—a curse wrung, as it were, unwillingly from the righteousness of God.

<small>A Divine and righteous will.</small>

Nor is all this done for Israel's own sake. Plainly and sternly they are warned of this again and again. They are but instruments in the hands of God, forged by the blows of chastisement, tempered in the stream of an awful knowledge and burdensome responsibility, to work out his promise to the fathers, which is 'the blessing of the whole earth.' Those who measure greatness by bigness have asked at times whether it could be worthy of the Almighty to stoop to special guardianship of so insignificant a people. Yet surely the history even of Greece and England might have taught them how on one little speck in the map of humanity

<small>The mission of Israel.</small>

[6] On this subject of miracle, see Part II. chap. v.

the world may depend. The frail bark of that people of Israel—certainly not the greatest, nor the most enlightened, nor the kingliest of nations—bore the fortunes of the true religion of all times and all races.

It was in the vivid consciousness of this moral government of God over them that the people found the secret of their own national strength and life—a secret which has been in measure read as an ever-recurring lesson in many a Christian nation. But the ideas connected with it—the righteousness of God fulfilling itself, and the destiny of mankind shaped by His far-seeing will—spread far too widely, and struck root far too deeply, to be confined within the limits of that national life, even at its greatest and noblest. The very conception of these was the earnest of the belief in the universal kingdom of God, to be manifested hereafter in the seed of Abraham for the blessing of all families of the earth.

Nor is it otherwise in respect of the other element of the Theocracy—'God in Law.' *(b) God in law.*

The Mosaic epoch is especially the epoch of Law. Still retaining and reverencing the free covenant of God with man, it yet declares that, man being what he is, the existence of law is absolutely necessary for each individual in his relation to nature, to man, and to God. *The unction of law.* For all law is the expression of some sovereign will, proclaiming itself to subject wills, claiming obedience on the ground of authority, and enforcing such obedience by reward and punishment.[7] Now of all law two things are clear. First, that it is necessary because of the weakness, the ignorance, the dependence, the sin of those under it. It claims, indeed, to be but the formal expression of that principle of righteousness which ought to be willingly accepted, and so appeals to the higher nature, in which man is free. But, so far as it is strictly law, so far as it is enforced not by conviction, but by authority, so far as it holds out the blessing and the curse, it appeals to man's lower nature, and sup-

---

[7] This is the only true sense of the word 'law,' in which, for example, St. Paul uses it in contrast with 'the Spirit;' although, by a most unhappy ambiguity, it is made in physical science to mean a simple formula, expressing the fact of regularity, but saying nothing as to its cause; and, by an impropriety less delusive, it is often used for a self-imposed rule, freely recognised and accepted.

plies but inferior motives of obedience; if made the chief principle of action, it degrades the higher humanity. Next, that all law must ultimately trace its authority to the Supreme Power which rules the world. As the 'laws of nature,' so the laws of humanity, if they are to hold and to have power over the individual, must be expressions of the great 'law eternal.' The *vox regis* or the *vox populi* must be the *vox Dei*.

Both these characteristics are plainly stamped upon the law of Moses. It was given just at the time when Israel emerged from the long captivity of Egypt, with all the characteristics of slavery branded into their nature, craving explicit guidance, needing stern restraint, accustomed to lean on the lower motives of hope and fear, incapable as yet of deserving and using freedom. It 'came in as a secondary thing' (παρεισῆλθεν), simply to guard the spiritual covenant, and to educate the people for a higher spiritual state. Those who were under the law had much which was not by the law. To exalt the law, as all in all, became a delusion and an idolatry. But still more striking is the direct, unhesitating reference to the Divine will at every step. The law of Moses was in itself a complex thing. Like all constitutions destined to endure, it grew up gradually with the growth of Israel from slavery to freedom and conquest, and was obviously welded together out of older materials, from the traditions of the fathers and the laws of Egypt itself. But it is stamped with the one great principle of the immediate reference of all things to God. At the root of all tenure of property, all forms of jurisdiction, all freedom in the man, all authority in the ruler, lies the fundamental truth, so often and so solemnly enunciated, 'I am the Lord your God.' In respect of this great principle it makes little difference, except in degree, whether the law be civil, criminal, ceremonial; for these divisions in fact run into each other. Everywhere the place held by the State in Roman law, or by the king in the ancient feudal codes, is occupied by the majesty of Jehovah Himself. He is all in all; judge, lawgiver, priest, and king are but His vicegerents.

Hence it is that the law of Israel, practically unlimited

by the limitations which bound all mere earthly authority, moulded the whole life both of the individual and the nation, and stamped on the tenacious character of Israel an impress, which marked it out as a nation among the nations of the world, and which now, after eighteen hundred years of dispersion, has never lost its distinctive power. Stern, oppressive, searching, it might seem a 'burden too great to bear.' But it certainly laid firm hold of that people, debased and sensualised at once by slavery and by idolatry, with a force which a more spiritual covenant might have lacked. Through it, looking up to heaven, they saw God's will moving over the firmament of humanity, to fulfil or to avenge itself, rejoicing to shower down the genial rain of blessing where it passed freely onward, but ready to shoot forth the lightnings of wrath, wherever anything rose up to resist its march. *Its effect on Israel.*

All this was for Israel alone. But the very essence of that law—in fact, the one direct revelation of God in it—was the moral law, proclaimed at Sinai in the incisive clearness of the Ten Commandments, spiritualised in that 'first and great commandment' of Deuteronomy, which our Lord has sanctioned for ever. In that law are defined and hallowed the three great moral relations of man--to himself, to his fellow-men, to God. These relations, universal and imperishable, look far beyond the time and people of Israel. In them is the law of a covenant which must embrace the whole race of man, and, though in the guise of sternness, 'bless all the families of the earth.' In the history of the world, the power of religion and the power of morality can never die. But the danger is lest they be separated from each other. It was the priceless blessing of the revelation of Sinai to unite them for ever in the solemn utterance of the voice of God. So, once more, what was the strong bond of their national life bore witness to a higher spiritual unity in the future, binding the whole world to the one God of all. *Its universal bearing.*

VI. Thus the characteristic revelations of this Mosaic epoch—'God in history,' and 'God in law'—neither of them the highest kind of revelation, both designed simply as an enforcement of the original idea of the covenant with Abraham, and as an education for a higher and subtler revelation of the Spirit—nevertheless *The relation of both to Natural Theology.*

bring out in singularly clear outline the two great conclusions of our Natural Theology. In the one, the creative purpose and government of God are irresistibly forced on the understanding; in the other, the righteousness of God, impressing and enforcing itself on His creatures, is brought home solemnly to the conscience. In both the truths of the earlier revelations are (so to speak) repainted in stronger and coarser colouring, such as suits the denser atmosphere of the struggle of life. 'He who runs may read them.'

The knowledge of sin by the law. But it is also most natural that in these harder realities of practical life, the terrible power of evil, so faintly indicated in the earlier stages of the revelation, should grow out in dark and threatening reality.

'By the law is the knowledge of sin.' It is the very object of law in all its various forms to unmask the evil lurking in the soul—to bring it under the piercing light of righteousness—to scourge it, thus discovered in all its nakedness, out of the heart and the life of man. In pursuance of that object there rings through all this part of Scripture a peculiar sternness of warning, unwelcome to those who love the easier and brighter aspects of life, perplexing to those who have learnt to understand deeply that God is love. But one thing at least it makes plain—that evil in man, terribly real and powerful as it is, is yet an unnatural thing, which deserves to be scourged, which can and must be conquered, even though it may be through suffering and death. Its stern tone cuts clear and sharp through hazy sentimentalities about an undistinguishing benevolence of God. It scatters, like the sudden cockcrow, the ghostly shadows of speculation as to an inherent power of evil in the world, whether material or spiritual, having a claim to be allowed for in the system of the universe, and to wage a not unequal fight against the power of good. 'The soul that sinneth it shall die'—terrible as the sentence is—is surely better and truer than a denial of sinfulness, which is virtually a denial of goodness, and a promise of escape from the penalty of death, on condition of losing all reality of spiritual life.

This is but to discover evil and to check its development. So far, there is no light thrown on the mystery of evil. But it cannot be a mere coincidence that with this terrible revelation of evil comes the first faint prevision of atonement. Sacrifice has been described as existing from the beginning. In this description Scripture confirms the historical researches which trace its existence in every race. *The institution of sacrifice.* But as yet the idea of sacrifice set forth has been only the simple eucharistic conception of homage and thankfulness, or the higher yet not obscurer notion (enshrined especially in the burnt offering) of a self-dedication to God, even unto death. These are, we observe, taken for granted, merely directed and regulated in the Levitical law. But now, for the first time, we approach the confines of mystery in the formal ordinance of the trespass offering and sin offering, in which is contained the first germ of the idea of atonement.[a] There we have the recognition, not only of the reality of evil, but of what we rightly call the mystery of evil. For there is implied the knowledge that not by the simple act of God's free goodness, not even by the efficacy of man's repentance, can it be taken away; but that some atonement there must be. It is characteristic of the Mosaic law, in this point distinguished from the crude ideas of heathen sacrifice, that this atonement is ordained by God and accepted by God. But still it is offered by man. The very inauguration of the Mosaic covenant is in the great Passover sacrifice, itself uniting all the various ideas and various rituals of the different kinds of sacrifice, and destined, as we know, to be the chosen type of the great sacrifice of the hereafter.

The idea involved in sacrifice must, no doubt, have presented itself in those days in a crude and perplexing form. It could need little spiritual insight to read the lesson that 'the blood of bulls and goats could not take away sin.' Any man who gazed (for example) on the strange and awful ceremonial of the great Day of Atonement[9] would have engraven on his soul at once the need and hope of sacrifice for sin, and the sense that such a sacrifice must be found, not in this ceremonial itself, but in *Its merely typical teaching.*

---

[a] Contrast here Lev. i. 2, ii. 1, iii. 1, where burnt offering, meat-offering, and peace-offering are taken for granted, with iv. 2, 3, vi. 6, where sin-offering and trespass-offering are formally ordained.
[9] See Lev. xvi.

something—God only knew what—which was symbolised in it. Such mingled hope and perplexity was as a spiritual hunger of the soul, forbidding it to be satisfied with unsubstantial 'husks well meant for grain,' and bidding it look on to a true satisfaction hereafter. Here the revelation of God deals with that universal instinct of sacrifice, which the philosophy of man, in its reasoning after God, gave up hopelessly as a strange, ineradicable superstition. For under it there lay a mysterious truth, giving it this inexplicable vitality, not dreamt of in man's philosophy, yet destined, in the fuller light of the future, to solve problems from which philosophy turned hopelessly away.

General conclusion. Such is the brief outline of the revelation which Christianity, embodying the old dispensation as a part of itself, presents in its first great epochs.

It is emphatically a revelation, for it speaks not in speculation, but in certainty. It is emphatically a religion, for it comes home in living power to the individual soul, and deals with the simplest relations of its daily life. But yet it takes up every line of the profoundest human speculation; under its simplicity and personal vividness there lie, in solemn grandeur and in perfect harmony, principles which fill the whole area of humanity.

In this there is that analogy, so often pointed out, to the visible works of God. Under the loveliness of nature, in which each thing freely developes itself in its own unstudied grace, and all together flood the soul with a bewildering richness of variety, there lie great principles of order and beauty, which truly, though imperfectly, reveal themselves to the artist or to the philosopher. In the living human being, under the freshness and freedom of the individual nature, there lie great universal principles of form, both of the body and the soul, which human science can discover, whether by theory or by history. Just in proportion as we enter into the mind of God, we are able to see the universal in the individual, and yet not lose the individual in the universal. Such certainly is the whole principle of the Scriptural record. Its whole idea of God is of One who 'numbers the hairs' of each head, and 'healeth every one who is broken in heart,' while at the same time He 'telleth the number of the stars, and calleth them all by their names.' It can cry out, 'Lord, what is man?' with all the emphasis of the wondering science of nature; but it adds, in the joy of faith, the thankful acknowledgment, 'Thou visitest him,' and 'regardest him.'

CHAPTER V.

THE VOICE OF GOD IN THE SOUL: THE ANSWER OF THE SOUL TO GOD.

'The Lord thy God will raise up unto thee a prophet.... Unto him ye shall hearken.'—Deut. xviii. 15.

ANOTHER step has now to be taken in the attempt to trace out, under the fundamental idea of covenant with God, the unique power of the Scripture revelation, at once to strengthen the conclusions, and illumine the perplexities, of Natural Theology.

Already no inconsiderable advance has been made. We start with the grand idea of God's universal covenant with man, establishing first the great law of known regularity in nature, and next the balance of individuality and unity, freedom and authority, which sustains human life. Under the shadow of this universal conception we come then, as in actual life so also in Scripture, to a special covenant between Him and a chosen man and a chosen family—given, indeed, to them, yet given for the future 'blessing of all the families of the earth,' and extending its light, even in the present, beyond the clear knowledge of the God of Abraham, Isaac, and Jacob, to the dimmer and larger conception of the Almighty, the First Cause of all physical powers, and the moral Governor of all beings in the universe.

Recapitulation.

From this great beginning we go on next to see how in the revelation to Moses the earlier revelation grows into a mightier and sterner majesty, suiting the larger thought and the intenser trials of a growing civilisation; how in the great name Jehovah the absolute and universal conception of God is marked on the very forefront of the whole system of Israel; how under the narrower idea of covenant with the chosen nation, which we call the 'Theocracy,' the knowledge of 'God in history' and 'God in law' is at once the secret of the national life of the present, and the education for a nobler spiritual future.

In both stages we watch with deep interest the recognition of the great mystery of evil. Under the first it shows itself to us faint and simple, as it presents itself to the experience of childhood. Under the second we listen to a stern and awful exposure of the fact of evil, and the certainty of retribution by the law; we hail the dim yet significant representation by sacrifice, at once of the mystery of the existence of evil, and of the promise of an atonement by which it shall be taken away.

I. We advance now to a new stage of revelation of God through prophecy. For it is the peculiar office of prophecy as such to set forth mainly, not 'God in history' or 'God in law,' but 'God revealed to and in the soul.' *The revelation of prophecy.*

It must, of course, be understood that, in thus distinguishing these various stages of the Scriptural revelation, we refer to the dominance, not to the sole existence, of this or that characteristic. It is obvious that in the earlier stages of revelation to Abraham, to Jacob, or to Moses, God is revealed to and in the soul; He speaks face to face with the inner man as alone before Him, and removed by that spiritual communion from the outer world of event and action. It is equally clear that the ideas of 'God in history' and 'God in law' run on through all the later stages of prophetic revelation, increasing rather than diminishing in their emphatic clearness. For man is one; it is impossible to separate the life of outer experience and the life of formal conduct from the spiritual life of thought, aspiration, and devotion. But certainly at different stages different elements of the composite revelation to man's composite being come out with predominant emphasis. Nor can it be doubted that, as might have been expected from the nature of the case, the successive stages of the realisation of the covenant of God enter more and more into the inner shrine of the spirit. The law is represented at Sinai by the whirlwind, the earthquake, and the fire. Prophecy, in the person of Elijah, hears God, not in them, but in 'the still small voice' speaking to the soul. It veils the face from the outer world, that so it may see God within.

In this characteristic we mark a distinct spiritual progress. For the earlier revelations of 'God in history' and 'God in law,' corresponding to the earlier stages of human thought, in what, by no fanciful analogy, we designate as the childhood and youth of humanity, belonged to that outer sphere of human experience, which is so much more intelligible and familiar to the uneducated mind. In the history God manifested His will by actual retribution, often brought out visibly in miracle, alike in the life of the chosen family and nation, and in their relations to the world around; and the very title of 'God Almighty' inferred, by no obscure inference, that the same will ruled the unseen fortunes of the great world in itself. By the law He manifested that same will in the explicit declaration of command and retribution, fulfilling or avenging itself. Both, therefore, turned the thoughts to the outer world of event and conduct; in which, by reason of the medium through which it has to pass, the revelation of God must be comparatively rough and imperfect; and in which, moreover, His will is necessarily represented as dealing with men, not as individuals, but rather as members of a community, and accordingly estimating actions not by their purely moral character, but in large degree also by their consequences to mankind. For in history it necessarily follows, from the unity of human nature, that mankind is dealt with as a whole, 'the good and evil of fathers are visited upon their children.' Law, though it speaks to each individual, yet is in its commands universal and indiscriminate, without special adaptation to the peculiar character of each who falls under its sway; and in its retribution it must be imperfect, as dealing with the coarser material of action, not with the finer fabric of thought. It is true that in what we call the law of Moses there are elements of a higher nature than mere law, in virtue of which our Lord declares that 'the law prophesied.' But, so far as it was law—and the legal element immensely predominates—it has from its very nature an inherent limitation and imperfection, even though it comes from the hand of God.

Those revelations less perfect.

II. The consideration of these imperfections in the earlier revelations of God, and therefore in the corresponding spiritual education of man, throws much light on what has been painfully felt as a perplexity and offence in this portion of Bible history. It cannot be by mere accident that at this stage, and at this stage only, of their spiritual education—under the leadership, moreover, not of the great lawgiver and prophet, but of the simpler and ruder soldier of God—was Israel called to slaughter the Canaanites, as a people not simply idolatrous, but stained with gross moral evil, in respect of which their 'iniquity was now full,' and so to be instruments of that unsparing retribution, which treats a sinful people as a whole, and visits the common sin upon all, even the helpless and the innocent. For it is not, after all, the extermination of a whole people which so much startles us. We cannot but see that, in all which respects the outer life, peoples and nations have a true solidarity, in virtue of which, as they act, so also they suffer, as wholes. We cannot but trace this indiscriminate suffering, even to the extreme of extermination, in the everyday experience of the earthquake, the pestilence, and the famine. Through these undiscriminating physical agencies we can sometimes see— and, if we believe in a God, must believe when we do not see —that a righteous purpose is worked out for the good of the world at large. Behind the evolution of that general purpose we can understand that a common suffering may be distinguished in its actual effect on each life and character by the individualising judgment of God ; and the death which cuts off a hardened sinner in his sin, may be to another a merciful 'release out of the miseries of this sinful world.' *(a)* The slaughter of the Canaanites.

But what really startles us is the extermination by human hands, demoralising (as it seems to us) and degrading these living and conscious instruments. It is natural and morally right, that we should be thus startled, if we transfer to those earlier days our own knowledge and principles. But in that transference lies the error. Not to dwell on the undoubted fact that, in ancient ideas and ancient law, the unit was always the family and the nation, not the individual, nor on the fierce The real moral difficulty involved.

thoroughness of ancient war, unconscious of the noble inconsistencies which limit and alleviate the horrors of war in modern days, we may well consider the actual condition of Israel itself in respect of spiritual education. They were emphatically 'under the law'—the law of the outer life, the law of formal and undiscriminating ordinance. On them had not yet shone that higher revelation, which shows each individual soul as standing alone in sacredness of freedom and responsibility before God, and accordingly to be dealt with separately, as in His judgment, so also, as far as is possible, by those of His servants who have to carry it out. They felt themselves simply to be executioners on a guilty race of an extermination, sad, awful, yet inevitable for the good of human kind, stamping out a contagion which else might have infected their race and the world. That feeling, although we can understand it as one element of our moral consciousness, yet, as an unmixed and predominant feeling, would be impossible to us. Perhaps it might have been impossible in a later age, for subsequent law and prophecy [1] declined to accept absolutely the visitation of the sins of fathers upon children; although, indeed, something of it may still be traced in the whole conception of those 'imprecatory Psalms' which hate not only the sin but the sinner, and look upon the enemies of God's servants as necessarily the enemies of God Himself. But certainly on us—who, by the teaching of our Master, have learned to love the sinner while we hate the sin, to understand the moral efficacy of a mercy, tempering or rising above stern righteousness, and to meet spiritual evils mainly with spiritual arms, limiting as far as possible the scope even of the avenging sword of justice—we hold it inconceivable that such a burden should be laid; and we resent with just indignation certain false applications of this ancient precedent to wars undertaken in Christian days by those who believed themselves instruments of the judgment of God. Even of Israel we note that only in this earlier and ruder stage of their history was such terrible duty demanded from them. In the moral condition which ren-

The condition under the law.

---

[1] See Deut. xxiv. 16; 2 Kings xiv. 6; Ezek. xviii. 4, 20.

dered that duty possible, we trace one evidence of the truth that 'the law,' as law, 'made nothing perfect.'

But, indeed, this confession of imperfection is written on the law itself. Plain and awful as were these revelations of God in history and law, fitted as they were (per- *The imperhaps better than the higher revelation) to educate fection of that condithe people of Israel out of the degradation of bond- tion.* age to the new life of freedom, yet it is notable how the higher prophetic element asserts itself more and more in the last utterances of Moses himself. They are prophecy, not law. The lawgiver is himself the greatest of the prophets of Israel. In his farewell he points onward to the prophets, especially to the Prophet of prophets to come, like unto himself, yet greater still. In his prayer he rises to a yet grander conception: 'O that all the Lord's people were prophets, and that the Lord would put His Spirit upon them!'

But the history shows us that this higher phase of the spiritual life was not yet to come. On the contrary, the period following the epoch of Moses and Joshua is *(b) The retrogression* perhaps the most dreary and painful in all the *of the next* Israelitish history. The people themselves 'fell *period.* away like their forefathers' below their high destiny. In timidity, indolence, unfaithfulness—faintly reproducing the great treason and cowardice of Kadesh Barnea—they failed to do thoroughly the terrible work laid upon them; they did not enter upon anything like their full inheritance; they fell contentedly into a dangerous alliance with the lower, baser life of the idolaters around them. The great epoch of Moses, in which seems compressed the spiritual growth of centuries, was followed (as we see only too often in national history or the individual life) by a time of retrogression— socially towards anarchy, division, mutual strife—morally into a lower and more barbaric condition of base sensual vice, of fierce cruelty and the shedding of kindred blood— spiritually not merely into idolatry, like the idolatry of the golden calf, degrading the worship of the true God, against the solemn warning of the Second Commandment, but even into the acceptance of false gods, violating the yet higher sacredness of the First. The law of Moses, if ever it had been thoroughly accepted, seemed now to fall into abeyance. To such a people only the sterner and ruder manifestations of God's moral government could be brought home, in the alternations of bitter suffering in the time of sin, and temporary relief on occasion of repentance. Proving themselves unworthy of freedom, they fell into bondage; losing the spiritual and moral strength of a people of God, they were overborne, now by desolating invasion, now by the uprising of the ancient races, now by subjugation under neighbouring nations. Over such an age we pass with pain and disappointment. But certainly the whole tenor of this period of the history shows that we are dealing with no ideal or heroic legend; the very imperfections and obscurities of the record carry with them the clear impress of an historic reality.

Even the characters of the 'Judges,' who rose up from time to time in God's name to deliver Israel, bear upon them some marks of the lower spirit of the age, and fall generally far beneath the standard of better days. In their office we have still the two ideas of the earlier revelation. They are the instruments of God's will in the outer region of fact, sustained at times by direct manifestations of His miraculous power. They are also, as 'judges,' the expounders and executors of a law drawing its inspiration from Him. But, in most cases, the former function seems to predominate. They are warlike deliverers rather than peaceful rulers, successors of Joshua rather than of Moses; the enemies against whom they fight are temporal oppressors rather than spiritual principles of evil. Both they, and the people they rule, occupy an altogether lower spiritual position. The great mission of Moses might have seemed a failure in respect of anything like complete immediate success. In that age of Israel, as so often in the times of reaction after a great 'era of expansion,' the seed of higher life, sown in the greatness of the age gone by, seemed, but only seemed, to be dead. It slept, under the long winter of apostasy, in the fallow-ground of ignorance and neglect. When the breath of the Lord came, its grave opened, and the full harvest sprang up.

The characters and office of the judges.

III. That breath of revival came in the Spirit of God, speaking through the prophets. Its first faint whisper sounded in the call of a little child as he lay asleep in the temple of the Lord. It swelled fuller and stronger through the ages, till more and more it foreshadowed the mighty rushing wind of Pentecost, under which (to use the grand simile of Ezekiel) the dry bones of dead humanity stood up, as a mighty army instinct with the new life of God. *The prophetic revival.*

For the essence of the prophetic revelation, whether to the prophet himself or to others through him, was that it was a revelation to the soul itself, alone face to face with God, calling out, not by constraint, but by a free and natural response, the answer of faith, obedience, and love. *The revelation to the soul.*

This is seen in the two phrases already referred to as characteristic of prophecy. 'The word of the Lord came to them.' Here is represented a purely spiritual power—the power of the true teacher, speaking as he himself is taught of God, acting on the soul by the simple presentation of truth, right, love, holiness, as expressed in the will of God and known to be His attributes, disdaining the coercion of material force, and even the lesser coercion of hope and fear. Such teaching the spirit of man, so far as it retains its higher nature, even when it is wearied and burdened by sin, always leaps up to receive. It can love truth, right, love, holiness, simply because they are what they are, simply because they are of God. The 'still small' voice speaks to the soul, and it is enough. Man veils his face in the mantle of reverence, and goes forth to stand before the Lord, and to follow His call, let it lead whithersoever He will. *The word of the Lord.*

Next, 'The Spirit of the Lord was upon them.' There we recognise the inspiration of the human spirit by the Divine —a force utterly different from the absolute constraint of physical necessity, and from the half-constraint which the law brings to bear—a force which, because it is mysterious, we can but describe by paradox, as when we speak of 'a constraint accepted willingly,' a 'service which is perfect freedom;' but which we know well by experience to be the true meeting-point between the sovereignty of God and the free will of man. It is a force lifting the soul above *The Spirit of the Lord.*

itself, sometimes having to overcome the shrinking reluctance of our lower nature;[2] but yet, whether with or without a struggle, it is accepted by the higher nature within, and the whole soul is so yielded to it freely, as to be at once the instrument and the fellow-worker of the grace of God.

Both these gifts belong primarily to the prophet himself. But in both he is the representative of his brethren, receiving in special and miraculous fulness gifts which in their ordinary type belong to humanity as God made it, and receiving these gifts, moreover, not for his own sake, but in order that he might transmit them to the people of God. He is by his very title the mouthpiece of God;[3] of the word which he speaks God is the true speaker; and, when he has spoken it, he still feels, with increasing vividness in proportion to the greatness of his message, that it is spoken in vain, unless the same grace, which gave him the power to understand and to speak, give his hearers the power rightly to hear. Of all gifts the prophetic gift is by its nature the least exclusive. It is given wherever it pleases God to give it, without limit of race or rank, even to those who, like Amos, were 'neither prophets nor the sons of prophets.' It presupposes for its exercise the diffusion in the hearts of the hearers of something like itself. As the natural prayer of the true prophet is the prayer of Moses, 'O that all the Lord's people were prophets,' so the culmination of all the visions of prophecy is the fulfilment of that prayer, when the laws of God shall be 'written on all hearts,' and the prophetic function of teaching shall cease, because 'all shall know Him from the least even to the greatest.' (Jer. xxxi. 33, 34.)

By these powers God is revealed to the soul in the light of His truth—revealed in the soul by the inspiration which opens the eye to see. Clearly it is a far higher revelation. In it we leave the coarser air of the outer world of events

---

[2] See a remarkable picture of this spiritual conflict, and of the victory of the higher principle, won at the price of anguish, in Jer. xx.

[3] Perhaps the best illustration of the true idea of the prophetic office is derived from the simple juxtaposition of two passages (Exod. vii. 1, iv. 16): 'I have made thee a god unto Pharaoh, and Aaron thy brother shall be thy prophet.' 'He shall be to thee instead of a mouth, and thou shalt be to him instead of God.'

and actions for the subtler atmosphere of thought; and as we rise to this more ethereal medium, we see the light of God more and more free from all dimness or distortion, till we even approach to the seeing Him as He is. Clearly it gives a more individual knowledge of God and of ourselves. For we leave the life shared with men, in which the soul is but a single unit, lost in the sum total of humanity. Standing alone face to face with God, we at once realise His unspeakable Majesty, and yet know that He is our own God for ever and ever.

It is by this prophetic power, first appearing in Samuel, carried on in unbroken succession for six hundred years, that Israel rose out of the barbaric and retrogressive period of the Judges, to begin the true greatness of its national life. It is to be observed that, at first united with the temporal power and the priestly office in Samuel, it was rapidly dissociated from both, standing out purely as a spiritual power, kindling in the individual and the nation the fire of the higher spiritual life. *The spiritual power of prophecy.*

We observe how it took up and perfected the earlier forms of revelation of 'God in history' and 'God in law.'

Towards the history it stood forth as an inspired interpreter. By no mere technicality were all the books of the Bible history reckoned among 'the prophets.' It was the prophet's privilege to see, and his office to declare, how God was working out in history His laws of righteousness and love; and, as speaking to the conscience, to draw the practical corollary from this truth, by commanding all men, whether kings or subjects, to recognise themselves as His servants, and to hold it their one privilege to be fellow-workers with Him. It is to be noted, moreover, that, while this teaching applies especially to the history of Israel, yet, in constantly increasing degree, it extends itself to the history of all mankind. The heathen nations are regarded in two different lights—sometimes as aliens and enemies outside the pale of God's covenant, sometimes as being in some sense His people, having something at least of call, probation, blessing, punishment from Him. But as the prophecy advances, this larger and loftier idea swallows up the exclusiveness of the other. The faith in 'God in *(a)* Its relation to God in history.*

history' diffuses its light in various degrees of brightness over all the earth.

It is in this function of prophecy that we must include the office of prediction, so commonly and so unhappily assumed to be the whole of the prophetic office.[4] In the working of the will of God time is nothing. To those who in any degree enter into the secret of that working, the future must in measure be unrolled, as it lies perfectly unrolled before the eye of God. To this divine insight the effect is seen in the cause, the exemplifications of a great moral law in the knowledge of the law itself. It might, moreover, be needful, perhaps as a sign of his authority, perhaps as an integral part of his message, that the prophet should declare to his brethren what he alone, lifted above the earth, could foresee. Prediction is natural, though not essential, to all prophecy. But in the prophets of Israel it was especially natural. For their golden age was in the future. The history of the world was to them not a mere succession of events, ebbing and flowing incessantly, with no stream of progress. All was sweeping on to an appointed end of promise and blessing to all the families of the earth. Yet it cannot be too often urged that prediction was, after all, but a secondary part of their function. Whether in the past, the present, or the future, their true office was simply to reveal God, working out His gracious will, as by the unceasing and unresting stream of physical law, so also by the great tide, stirred by an attraction from above, which moves on its appointed way through all the heavings and surgings of the restless wills of men.

Prediction.

Again, towards the law, and the revelation of God in law, the prophetic office was exactly that which the great Prophet of prophets discharged in His Sermon on the mount. It had first to lead the soul from the obedience of the letter to the obedience of the spirit, from the formal rules to the living principles underlying them, and from the visible fruits of word and deed to the secret root of

(b) Its relation to God in law.

---

[4] The error is probably in part etymological, though a false derivation of the word 'prophet;' partly, no doubt, it arises from an inordinate love and craving for the supernatural, treating lightly the moral and spiritual purposes which the supernatural power was meant only to subserve.

both in thought and will. It had, next, to raise the spirit of obedience from the 'spirit of fear,' obeying because it dares not disobey, to the spirit of love, obeying because it is joy to obey, trusting in the righteousness of God and inspired by His love. Under both aspects it tends (to use the frequent metaphor of Scripture) towards the promised change from the law, written on the hard granite tables of stone, and enforced by the thunders of Sinai, to the law 'written on the heart' within, growing with every spiritual growth of knowledge and power, and proving its own authority in the free response of the spirit within.

But towards that element of the law, which dealt with the consciousness of sin and hope of atonement, and which was visibly represented in the sacrifice and the priesthood, prophecy had a peculiar function. Not, as perhaps might have been expected, to unfold the mystery of atonement, but rather to guard against the fatal tendency to turn the future hope into present superstition, by making the offering of sacrifice a substitute for repentance, for obedience, for faith. The words in which Samuel rebuked the false pretence of Saul, 'To obey is better than sacrifice, and to hearken than the fat of rams,' ring in different tones through all the utterances of prophecy. Taking up mainly the idea of self-dedication, embodied especially in the whole burnt-offering, prophecy taught men to carry it out not merely in symbol but in reality; whether in the glad resolution of the true servant of God to do His will, or in the humble conviction of the sinner that the broken and contrite heart of penitence is the true sacrifice (Ps. xl., li.) Not, be it observed, that the sacrifice, with the idea of propitiation constantly shadowed forth in it, was to cease. On the contrary, the very psalm which declares that 'the sacrifice of God is a broken spirit,' ends in rejoicing that 'when sinners are converted to Him,' then 'shall He be pleased with burnt-offerings and oblations; then shall they offer young bullocks upon His altar.' No! sacrifice was to remain in all its mysterious significance, as a silent witness, reverently treasuring up its secret till the time of revelation was come. But meanwhile the prophecy kept that religious mystery from being turned into a superstitious charm, and

(c) Its relation to sacrifice and priesthood.

bade men see in sacrifice not a substitute, but a means, for true reconciliation of the soul to God.

Thus it was that prophecy (I repeat) carried on those earlier revelations, teaching men not only to feel but to see God's hand in history, and in law to know not only God's will, but God Himself. But its peculiar revelation was the revelation of God, neither in outward history nor outward law, but to and in the individual soul itself.

(d) Its message to the soul itself.

This office of the prophet towards his own generation is perhaps most distinctly seen in the prophets of 'unwritten prophecy'—in Samuel, in Ahijah, in Elijah, in Elisha, and in their less famous brethren of the same early periods. The establishment and succession of the prophets corresponds to the establishment and succession of the kings, in something more than mere coincidence of time. The true theocracy was to be maintained against the danger of the conversion of the kingdom into a mere Eastern despotism of the ordinary type, worshipping material strength and splendour, perhaps idolising the king himself. Whether by friendly guidance or by stern rebuke, by the promise of God's protection or by the threat of His vengeance, it was the task of the prophets to fix the position of the king as simply the vicegerent of God in the department of legal and temporal power, and thus at once to give sacredness to the authority of the 'Lord's anointed,' and to mark out its limitation and responsibility. It has been said with truth that the prophetic power was thus the guardian of liberty, and the representative of the element of progress, in the commonwealth of Israel. But this beneficent work was indirect rather than direct. It was by the assertion in the national life of the true sovereignty of God alone over the spirit as well as the body, that the rights and liberties of His covenanted people were guarded; it was by the declaration of God's direct revelation of Himself to the individual soul, that the spirituality of man, in which lies the secret of progress, was brought out.

IV. It is to be observed, as illustrative of this peculiar character of the prophetic revelation, that in Scripture, immediately following the first entrance of prophecy and actually preceding its full development, occur those books which express the answer of the human

The answer to the prophecy.

soul to the new revelation of God, and shine upon us by the light of inspiration, transfiguring the spiritual life within.

Of that answer of the soul there are two phases—the moral and spiritual answer in the Psalms, the intellectual answer in the books of Wisdom. In both we trace not the word of God to man, but the answer of inspired man to God.

We listen first to this answer, as embodied in the Psalms of Scripture, not confined to the Psalter, but running in a distinct thread through the history and the prophecy itself. Those psalms are the productions of many writers known and unknown, and of many ages, from the days of the Exodus down to the return from the Captivity. But, by consent of all, the highest strength and beauty of the psalmic element of Scripture is enshrined in the Psalms of David, the pupil of the first prophet, and the child of the first prophetic age. They may therefore be best considered as belonging to this stage of the Scriptural revelation.

(a) The 'Psalms of David.'

The psalm is the lyric poetry of Israel, and it occupies very much the place which ordinarily belongs to the lyric element in the development of a national literature. But the question may occur to the mind why the lyric poetry, generally the most varied by virtue of its individuality, should present in this case so remarkable a unity, and why it is that, while other lyric poetry appears to be naturally more evanescent in charm and vitality than other elements of literature, the Psalter is just the one element of the Old Testament which is most permanent, and which through eighteen centuries has been taken up as the utterance of Christian thought and feeling. The answer is simple. It is because it embodies that which in its essence is most unchangeable in various persons and various times— the consciousness of a revelation of God in the secrets of the soul. In this lies the true essential inspiration of the Psalmist's spiritual song.

The communion of the soul with God.

It is true that the Psalmists constantly realise the presence of God in the outer world of event and conduct. Then there are psalms which delight to trace that presence in the outer sphere of nature. Such is the 8th Psalm, the hymn of the earliest astronomer,

Other aspects of the Psalms.

watching the starlit heavens; or the 104th Psalm, that great psalm of creation, surveying it in all its kingdoms of earth, and sea, and sky, tracing all the beautiful gradations of being, in vegetation, in animal life, and in humanity. There are psalms, which are little more than an adoring comment on the history of God's chosen people, and a recognition of His hand working through it all. Such is the great 78th Psalm of Asaph, passing under rapid survey the story of Israel from the Exodus to the kingdom of David, or those later Psalms (Ps. cv., cvi.) which dwell in fuller detail on the early patriarchal days, on the trials and blessings of the Exodus, and the misery of the subsequent apostasies, and end in a call to all Israel: 'Blessed be the Lord God of Israel for everlasting, and let all the people say Amen.' There are psalms, like the 107th Psalm, which are the psalms of life, tracing God's hand in all the changes and chances of this world—the wandering in a wilderness, the darkness of captivity, the wasting away of sickness, the tossing on the great deep—and at every point crying out, not to Israel, but to all mankind, 'O that men would praise the Lord for His goodness, and declare the wonders that He doeth for the children of men!' There are psalms again like the great 119th Psalm, which, through scores and scores of verses, repeats constantly the expression of reverence and thankfulness for 'the law,' 'the statutes,' 'the commandments,' 'the testimonies' of the Lord; rejoicing to plant the foot firmly on the rock of God's declared will.

But the true essential idea of the Psalms, which runs like a golden thread of light through them all, is the sense of a direct and individual communion with God in the soul itself. The very motto of the whole is contained in the famous passage—'Have I not remembered Thee on my bed,' in the solemn thoughtfulness of the night? 'Have I not thought upon Thee when I was waking,' in the first fresh rush of thought and feeling in the morning light? That sense of communion with God may express itself in the tearful cry of penitence, such as the Psalm (Ps. li.) poured out to God and to God alone, when the Psalmist lay prostrate with veiled face before the sanctuary of the Lord. It may, on the other hand, speak in an outburst of thankful-

This the essential character.

ness (Psalm ciii.) 'Praise the Lord, O my soul,' or in exulting confidence (Psalm xci.) in the defence 'under the wings of the Most High' and 'the shadow of the Almighty.' It may assume (as in Psalm cxxxix.) the form of a solemn awe-stricken sense of the unceasing presence of God in the very secrets of the heart, 'trying, examining, judging, cleansing' the soul. But, under whatever phase, the essential thought is the same. The Psalmist closes the eyes to all outward things, that he may see God within. To him the inward witness supersedes the necessity of anxious search into the works of God. To him the voice of the Lord in the soul speaks more clearly than the thunders of the outward law. To him the shrine of God in the soul is a more sacred temple than even the tabernacle, which all the psalmists loved, and at which so many served. We enter with him into a revelation of God to man as man, which we feel to be essentially our own. The history changes age by age; the law in its outward form has passed away; the sacrifices have told their tale; and the altar is deserted and cold. But the word of the Lord, written on the heart, abides to all eternity. The Spirit of the Lord in His action on the soul is the same, yesterday, to-day, and for ever.

But there is another answer of the soul to God, not, as in the psalm, through the moral elements of conscience and love, sublimed into the enthusiasm of adoration, but, as in those books which may be called the philosophical books of Scripture, an answer of the understanding. (b) The Sapiential books. They naturally succeed the other; for there is a reaction of deep thoughtfulness which settles down on the soul, whenever some burst of enthusiasm has passed over it. Their one great characteristic, expressed in many forms, is the desire of 'wisdom.' That desire, searching for wisdom as for hid treasures, with which no earthly gold or jewel may compare, is perhaps not less earnest, but certainly calmer, more self-conscious, and more self-controlled, than the Psalmist's intense spiritual 'thirst for God, yea! even for the living God.' The search for wisdom.

But what is the Scriptural idea of 'wisdom,' as distinguished from 'the understanding,' the faculty by which it is attained, and from the 'knowledge,' which is but the preparation for attaining it?

There is a wisdom of man; and this is the conception of the true design and object of life, for which all faculties and all opportunities are given him, and on which depends what some call his happiness, and others the perfection of his nature.

The wisdom of man.

There is a wisdom of God; and this is the principle of His great dispensation to man—the design which ruled in creation—the scheme or plan which determines all the events of the world, and should rule all the actions of man.

The wisdom of God.

But these two are in some sense one. The wisdom of man cannot be attained unless he enters, so far as a finite creature may, into the wisdom of God—in part seeing it by his understanding, and in part resting upon it in faith. The idea is the grandest of all possible ideas; the loftiest conceptions of the spiritual nature and capacities of man are implied in this consciousness of a power to enter into the very wisdom of God.

The union of both.

This fundamental idea is expressed in many forms.

In the Book of Job it wears the form of an intense desire to know the secrets of God's moral government of the world, and an honest, though impatient, perplexity at the apparent imperfections of His retribution. It ends to Job himself, not in understanding, but in a deeper faith in God's inscrutable wisdom and infinite love. 'The fear of the Lord, that is wisdom; and to depart from evil'—let what will betide—'that is understanding.' It ends to the reader of that magnificent book, in the conception of life as a discipline, in which there is a power of evil making it hard, but a power overrruled in God's wisdom to good.

The Book of Job.

In the Book of Ecclesiastes—that terrible soul's tragedy —we have the teaching of failure after failure in the search after wisdom. The purpose of life is sought by the wise king of Israel,[5] first in self-indulgence, self-consciousness, self-culture; then in the communion with

The Book of Ecclesiastes.

---

[5] It will be, of course, understood that the lesson of the book, with which alone we are here concerned, is independent of all critical questions as to its date and authorship.

men, in the laborious service, or the still more laborious rule of the world. At every step the sense of hollowness, change, suffering, evil, grows upon the searcher, till the sad burden is repeated again and again—' Vanity of vanities; all things are vanity'—' Better were it not to have been than to be— better is it now to die than to live.' Only at last, like some storm-beaten ship, making not what harbour it will, but what it can, he disowns all study and enquiry as a mere 'weariness of the flesh,' and comes back to what he might have learnt at his mother's knee: ' To fear God and to keep His commandments, this is the whole duty,' and therefore the whole wisdom, 'of man.'

Far different from the grand poetry of the Book of Job, and the pathetic speculation of Ecclesiastes, is the calm and oracular sententiousness of the Book of Proverbs. For it represents as already found that wisdom, for which the others profess to search. The proverb, according to a well-known definition, is the presentation of the 'wisdom of many'—the long-tried and accepted discoveries of 'common sense'—under a form stamped with the impress of the 'wit of one.' It has nothing to do with what is vague, imperfect, or mysterious. Accordingly the 'Book of Proverbs,' after a grand poetical opening—not unlike some of the reflective passages of the Psalms, and closely resembling many passages in the Book of Job—settles down into a long series of those clear-cut antithetical maxims which we call 'proverbs.' There are in it proverbs which sometimes startle us by their enunciation of what is called ' worldly wisdom,' regarding the object of life as simply a man's own happiness and peace and safety. There are proverbs of a higher wisdom of humanity, which find that object in the service and the love of men. But the characteristic proverbs, which stamp on the Scriptural book its peculiar distinction from all other books of 'proverbial philosophy,' are those which find the wisdom of man in the knowledge of the wisdom of God, understanding that under it the lower types of wisdom will find their place, since by it alone we learn to work out our own perfection, and fill our place rightly in the world of our fellowmen. This highest conception is especially prominent, as a dominant idea, in the grand introduction to the book, rising

The Book of Proverbs.

again and again to a lofty philosophic enthusiasm. In that sense it is that in the first chapter Wisdom is introduced as 'crying without and uttering her voice in the streets,' in solemn and authoritative tones of entreaty and warning, blessing and condemnation, which are simply echoes of the voice of God Himself. To these succeeds in the next chapters the exquisite description of wisdom in all its intrinsic beauty and its capacity of blessing, as not merely 'the fear,' but 'the knowledge of the Lord.' But above all in the glorious eighth chapter (in which lies the first germ of the doctrine of 'the Word which was with God, and was God') the Divine Wisdom is personified, as 'possessed by the Lord in the beginning,' 'with Him,' when He created the world, and ordained the fortunes of the sons of men. What nobler answer could be given by the understanding to the revelation of God within the soul? Not (be it observed) an answer free from all doubt and perplexity, ignoring those deep shadows which shoot athwart the brightness of the knowledge of God. Otherwise it could not be true to human nature, and to the conditions of this imperfect human life. But an answer nevertheless deep and true, because it recognises and answers a real voice of God within.

V. By these answers to the prophetic message we see how great an advance is made through prophecy in the revelation of God, although as yet prophecy has been regarded only in its first simplicity, not in its full richness of development—only in its message to the present, and not yet in its greater work of preparation for the future. Nor can we well fail to see also how infinitely more vivid, because more spiritual and more personal, it makes the conception of God's covenant with man. But it is important to notice how in it those two ideas of the universal and the special covenant, as yet distinct, though harmonised, under the patriarchal and Mosaic revelation, now almost melt into each other. The sense of the relation to God, just because it is so intensely individual, is absolutely universal; for it is felt to depend on that which in us is essentially human, as distinct from all special phases of life and character, and accordingly it belongs to man as man. The Psalmists are true Israelites;

The advance in spiritual knowledge.

Union of the universal and special relation to God.

they rejoice over the old glory and privileges of their race; they mourn over Israel in her sorrow and ruin; they yearn for the holy city and the temple, when they are far away. But yet the Psalms are just those parts of the Old Testament in which any believer in God may delight; they are just those parts which the whole Catholic Church of Christ has made for ages the food of the spiritual life. The writers of the Books of Wisdom, perhaps even more directly, deal with the truths and the perplexities concerning simply man as man. It has been noted that they represent exactly the time, when the thought of Israel felt most inclined to recognise brotherhood with all the wisdom of the East. The special and the universal covenant thus blend with each other. Nowhere do we find a better earnest of the time, when in the seed of Abraham the old promise should so grow as to encircle the whole earth.

But we note also how nobly both the elements involved in the idea of covenant—the conception of a personal God, and the consciousness of freedom and true personality in man —are here brought out.

The sense of the revelation of God in the soul by the Divine Spirit is simply the assertion of His sovereignty, not only in the outer sphere of physical force and human action, but in the inner realm of thought, which all forms of Stoicism refuse to Him, in the spirit of self-reliance. He is brought near to us; we see Him, not far above or far away, but face to face. We know that the face is the face of a living God. *(a)* The sovereignty of God over the soul.

But even more truly (as I have already hinted) this revelation of God in the soul brings out the other truth of the spirituality of man. If we contemplate only God in nature or God in history, man may be lost in the multitude of God's creatures ruled by necessity or instinct, a mere instrument working out, whether he will or not, the design of the Creator. If we regard only 'God in law,' man may be but as a slave, driven by the scourge of fear, or lured by the promises of hope, while he lives his short span of life, before he vanishes away. But if he can recognise God speaking to the soul within by His word, and guiding it by His Spirit—if he can, with the Psalmist, feel *(b)* The divine image in the soul.

H

that he has the freedom to answer and to obey—if he can, with the writer of the Book of Proverbs, claim to enter in measure into the wisdom of God—then man can be no machine, no brute, no mere slave. He must have the divine image in him; he must be the true son of God. The truth, for want of which so many Eastern religions dream of an absorption of the soul into the deity, or a *Nirvana* in the virtual loss of all individuality, is here brought out clear and strong, and is worked step by step into the very texture of our consciousness.

(c) The existence of evil.
But what shall we say of the terrible consciousness of evil? We must distinguish, as usual, between the sense of its existence and the inquiry into its mystery.

The existence of evil in man, whether it be conceived as sin or as blindness, is brought out with special vividness in both these elements of Scripture. Naturally by the Psalmists it is especially felt as sin, polluting and enfeebling the soul, and calling down the wrath of a righteous God; by the writers of the Books of Wisdom as folly, blinding the mind, and by the very blindness cutting it off from entering into the wisdom of God. But in both phases it is natural that the blackness of evil should be brought out by the consciousness of the light of God's presence. It is a right instinct which says, 'My eye seeth Thee, therefore I abhor myself and repent in dust and ashes.' Where shall we find, even under Christianity, so intense and absolute a confession of sin as in the fifty-first Psalm? Where can we trace, even in the saddest modern philosophy, a more oppressive sense of the blindness, folly, littleness of man, than in the passionate complaints of Job, or the gloomy despondency of the writer of Ecclesiastes?

Yet the certainty that sin is not man's true nature, and that it can be and must be conquered, is necessarily deepened
The hope of deliverance from evil.
by every thought which shows us man as made in the Divine likeness, and living in conscious communion with the Eternal. Accordingly the presence of evil, though it may be felt deeply, is not felt as a hopeless burden on the despairing soul. It is, indeed, significant that there is a far closer approach to such hopelessness in the meditation of the intellectual searcher after truth, than in the spiritual experiences of the Psalmist. But through both

CHAPTER VI.

THE MESSIANIC IDEA IN THE OLD TESTAMENT.

'The Christ is the end of the Law.'—Rom. x. 4.

I. IF in this well-known passage we give to 'the Law' its widest sense, the passage becomes a terse and pointed declaration of two facts, patent to all who study the Old Testament—first, that it has an end, for which it confesses itself to be simply a preparation; and next, that this end is the manifestation of the Christ or the Messiah.

The Messianic idea in the Old Testament.

As yet, in surveying the successive revelations of God in the Old Testament—the revelations of 'God in history,' 'God in law,' 'God in the soul'—we have considered primarily what these were in their present significance, as confirming and supplementing the Natural Theology of man, to those who received them. It is true that secondarily the expectation of a great future must always be taken into account in the study of the Old Testament; for unquestionably such an expectation is stamped on the whole dispensation. The realisation of the first promise to Abraham, in the extension of the special covenant with Israel to become a universal covenant of blessing to all the nations of the earth, is always present in idea, underlying all more immediate revelations. To that end it was obvious that all the history was considered to be moving on. Nor was it difficult to infer that the law which guarded the covenant by stern ordinance, the prophecy which brought it home freely to the spirit, and the answers to the prophetic inspiration in the spiritual devotion of the Psalms and the intellectual insight of the books of wisdom, were all so connected with this historical future, that it must be, in different senses, 'the end' of all. But as yet these expectations of the future have lain for us far away in the background. Now, in proceeding to study the fuller development of prophecy, we must bring this future prominently before our thoughts. It is, as we have seen, a serious error to identify prophecy with prediction. But certainly, in the Old Testament, prevision and prediction are essential elements of prophecy. Not only is it true that of 'the law' in the largest sense—that is, of the Old Testament in all its various elements—the Christ is emphatically the end; but it is clear that, as we proceed to the later prophetic developments of the older revelation, this characteristic grows into brighter vividness, and assumes a more predominant importance.

I venture to say that this characteristic must be patent to all who study the Old Testament, in whatever light they regard it. The unbeliever may consider this faith in a coming Messiah to be only the sublimest of those noble delusions, by which the life of many a nation has been from time to time sustained. The Jew will argue that the prophecies are still unfulfilled, and that the true seed of Abraham is yet to come. The Christian will, of course, hold that the Lord Jesus Christ is the true Messiah, and claim accordingly to illustrate the New Testament by the Old, and the Old Testament by the New. But all alike must, if they study the Old Testament, confess that what has been called the 'Messianic idea'—that is, the faith in a Christ to come—is most certainly there; and, moreover, that it determines the very tone and character of the Jewish Scripture, as it certainly has stamped a peculiar impress on the thought and life of the Jewish people. At times it flashes out into one of those great sayings, which every child knows, and which supply us with an Old Testament lesson for our chief Christian festivals. But far more important and significant is the consciousness that it underlies the whole, and that these bright salient passages are merely indications of the far-spreading veins of gold which lie below the surface.

Its reality and prominence.

The clearness and prominence of that expectation evidently vary greatly at different epochs. Although it is true that the special covenant with Abraham, and those temporal promises connected with it, which were wrought out step by step, were avowedly preparations for a great future 'blessing of all the families of the earth' in 'the seed of Abraham,' yet that promise may have seemed at first vague enough; 'the seed' might be the whole people, or it might be some one future person to arise out of that people. But by degrees it unquestionably cleared into a definite faith in a personal Messiah, in which, like their father Abraham, the people 'rejoiced to see His day, and they saw it and were glad.' Men began to see that 'He saith not, And to seeds, as of many, but as of one, And to thy seed, which is the Christ.' (Gal. iii. 16.)

It is easy to trace the power of the Messianic idea in each of the great elements of the Old Testament record.

Thus it is obviously the end of the history. For it supplies the only reason why the history of an insignificant Eastern people should be preserved and treasured up for the whole world and for all generations. It is the ruling idea which determines why from time to time the history of the great empires of old times should be just touched upon, and then passed by. What St. John says of the actual earthly life of the Christ is true of all the earlier history. 'Many things' of infinite greatness and interest 'were done' 'which are not written in this book;' that only is written, which bears upon the manifestation of the Son of God. The whole history of Israel itself, and of the other nations so far as they were related to Israel, claims to have a certain unique character, alike in the events which we should distinguish as miraculous, and in those which fall under the ordinary laws of nature and humanity; and this unique character belongs to it simply as a preparation for the coming of the Messiah.

(*a*) Its relation to the history.

Nor is it difficult to trace this same idea as underlying, though less obviously, all the elements of the law, properly so called. If we look to what is ordinarily called the 'civil law,' its characteristic is obviously the theocratic principle—that is, the conception of a kingdom of God over Israel, distinct from His universal sovereignty over the whole world of humanity, and yet destined ultimately so to expand as to draw under it all the nations of the earth. This theocracy was indeed to be in some measure realised in every generation. Lawgiver, and judge, and king

(*b*) Its relation to the Theocracy.

were simply vicegerents of the Lord Jehovah. But all these realisations were confessedly imperfect both in power and in scope. The kingdom of God upon earth was yet to come in its perfection. The hope of its coming gathered, as by a natural gravitation, round the expected seed of Abraham, who was 'to bless all the families of the earth;' and we note that the time when the temporal kingdom came to its greatness in David was exactly the time chosen for the new prophecy of the King, at once 'Son of David' and 'Lord of David,' who was to reign for ever and ever.

Less clear and obvious, but far more profound in significance, was the preparation for the Messiah implied in the other elements of the law. The high moral element of the law had, indeed, the power to hold up, and to force on the attention of men, the conception of what was 'holy, and just, and good.' But (as St. Paul, brought up to idolise it, argues emphatically and repeatedly) it could give no spiritual power to obey. It simply brought with it the knowledge of sin. So far as it was mere law, it could restrain the outward exhibitions of sin, and scourge the evil within the soul into a silence, under which lurked an intenser spirit of rebellion. So far as it 'prophesied,' by revelation of the will and attributes of God to the spirit, it might direct into the right way, stirring the inner man to a hope of righteousness, and a longing to be free from the bondage of evil. But it could do no more. By its imperfection it confessed itself (to use St. Paul's metaphor) a mere 'schoolmaster'—a servant trusty and authoritative, but a servant still—whose whole office it was to bring men to the true teacher, able to write the law on the heart.

(c) Its relation to the moral law.

But the law had a ceremonial side. Its conception here was of a holy people consecrated to God in sacrifice. Here, again, its idea was but imperfectly realised. The people were not yet holy in heart and soul. The sacrifice, which represented the taking away of sin, was but a shedding of the blood of bulls and goats, which could not really take it away. In proportion as the knowledge of sin was brought home by the moral law, the sense of the need of some atonement must have forced itself upon every thoughtful mind; and with that sense of need would come to

(d) Its relation to the sacrifice.

those who believed in the covenant with God the cheering encouragement of hope. The visible sacrifices and priesthood would be seen to have little or no meaning, unless there were some true Priest and some true Sacrifice to come.

It would, indeed, seem that the prevision, through this deeper witness of the law, of a spiritual salvation in the Messiah was, at any rate in the earlier ages, far less clear than the expectation of His glorious kingdom, far less clear perhaps than we should have expected. In the perfection in which we can grasp the idea, it was made manifest only by the event. It would be a sheer anachronism to ascribe to the most thoughtful Israelite, or even to the greatest of the prophets of Israel, the profound conceptions either of the Epistle to the Romans or the Epistle to the Hebrews. But one thing at least is clear, that the future kingdom of the Messiah was looked upon as one in which there should be neither sin nor sorrow, and in which the law of God was to be written on the heart. In such a kingdom the mystery of sacrifice must have found its solution, and the sternness of the law, as written on the tables of stone, would pass away, because the spiritual regeneration had come.

Next we may turn from the Law to the Psalms and the philosophical books. It is obvious that in these books, proceeding as they do from the side of man, the expectation of the Messiah must generally be of a peculiar kind.[1] He will be looked upon emphatically as the Son of man, of whom all sons of men, so far as they preserve their true humanity, are imperfect types, and who can be known by them through sympathy, in proportion as they rise to the likeness of His perfect humanity and ceaseless communion with God. The Psalm had, as we have said, for its essential principle, the sense of a true inner communion with God through the moral and spiritual faculties of man. It sprang at once to full maturity and beauty, just at the time when the great promise to David foreshadowed the Messiah more distinctly than ever. It was but natural that the

(*e*) Its relation to the Psalms.

---

[1] There are, indeed, some Psalms directly prophetic (like Psalm cx.), looking outwards in the prevision of fact, rather than inwards in the foreshadowings of spiritual consciousness. But these are exceptions to the general rule referred to above.

Psalmists, in proportion to the spiritual depth of their inspired utterance, should have felt themselves, and have been recognised by others, as prefiguring the Messiah—sometimes in distinct prophecy, more often simply through this conception of a communion with God and an exaltation of humanity, which could only be perfect in Him.

Less direct and plain, but again singularly profound, was the expectation of the philosophic books. It was, indeed, in some respects like that of the Psalm; for it taught that the wisdom, the knowledge of which is promised to man, is the power to enter into the wisdom of God, and, since it is obvious that no mere man can perfectly 'know the mind of the Lord,' it thus made the knowledge of every wise man who learned this lesson an imperfect earnest of some perfect knowledge to be revealed hereafter. But, over and above this, it had a peculiar phase, which moulded hereafter the more philosophic thought of the Jew, especially in Alexandria. For it contemplated an impersonation of the Divine Wisdom 'with God' and 'possessed by God' 'in the beginning,'[2] in which there was undoubtedly the foreshadowing of that doctrine of the *Logos* or 'Word of God,' which St. John consecrated to the fullest and deepest revelation of the Christ.

(f) Its relation to the Sapiential books.

But it is, above all, in the richer development of prophecy which belongs to the later ages of the kingdom, that the conception of the Messiah to come starts out into a clearness, a beauty, a frequency, before unknown.

(g) Its relation to prophecy.

In some prophets the vision of the future kingdom of God is more distinctly 'Messianic,' bringing out the reign of the personal 'Messiah the prince.' In others it is more what we call 'Evangelical'—that is, it dwells rather on the manifestation of the spiritual kingdom, than on the personal glory of its Head. In the greatest of the prophets, the two elements, the Messianic and the Evangelical, are united in the most perfect harmony. But, in various methods and various degrees of clearness and beauty, the outline of the promise to David is so filled up as to present a bright and living picture. Nor is this merely one prophetic theme among many; it is really the one chief subject of prophecy,

[2] See especially Prov. viii. 22-31.

as such; and the foresight of the Christ runs through all, like a golden thread, on which the jewels of divine teaching are so strung as to form a perfect whole.

In all these various ways the study of the Old Testament itself justifies the sweeping declaration, that 'the Christ' is, in every sense, 'the end of the Law.' In this or that detached instance it may be doubted whether a Messianic application is real or fanciful. Possibly to modern study the broad general lines of the Messianic idea may be more certain and more impressive, than the detailed fulfilments of prophecy, on which earlier ages delighted to dwell. But making all allowance for fantastic imagination, putting out of consideration all which is ambiguous, it is still absolutely clear that the Messianic idea remains, pervading in different degrees the whole of the Old Testament, and essential to the true understanding of its meaning.

But here also the study of the Old Testament itself receives striking illustration from the history of the people, who received it and drew from it the food of their religious life. Nothing is more certain historically than that the expectation of the Messiah became the settled faith and the inspiring principle of Jewish life. In the later ages of the Jewish history, from the Captivity downwards, when the temporal glories of Israel slept in abeyance, and the voice of prophecy had ceased to sound, this expectation had been worked into the very hearts and minds of the people—especially the mass of the people, as distinguished from the philosophic schools—till the very Gentiles saw it in their actual life, as clearly as if it had been stamped upon their foreheads. Even by heathen testimony it is certain that the birth of our Lord found the age of His appearance strung up to almost an agony of expectation of the great Anointed of the Lord, the King of all humankind. (*h*) Its effect on the history of the people.

II. Now it is this Messianic conception which makes the Old Testament something more than the sublimest revelation of Monotheism. It is the elimination of this conception which has condemned the bastard Judaism of Islam to spiritual barrenness. It is the full development of it from the germ of the Old Testament belief, which marks out Christianity as unique among the religions of the Its bearing on the covenant with God.

world. Hence, even in the earlier stages of development, the study of this idea must be of paramount importance. Without it the religion of Monotheism would not be in a true sense the religion of humanity ; and the Scriptural revelation could not hold that relation to Natural Theology for which I contend, confirming in it whatever is strong, and supplying whatever is wanting.

For it is obviously the perfection of the pervading idea of God in covenant in man, and in it all that is of the nature of promise in that covenant finds its fulfilment. This will be best seen by examining its bearing on the three chief principles contained in that idea—the personality of God, the spirituality and dignity of man, and the removal of the evil which is as a barrier between earth and heaven.

Of these three principles it seems to bring out first and most emphatically the second—the revelation in the Messiah of the highest exaltation of man. He is emphatically the Son of Man ; his human character is marked from the beginning, while on that human character are gradually accumulated attributes rising to the divine. This will be clearly seen by considering the chief epochs of Messianic prediction.

(a) As an exaltation of humanity.

The Messiah is first described as the 'seed of Abraham,' the inheritor of the covenant, who is to unite under its blessing all the families of the earth. The simple patriarchal authority over the tribe, founded not so much on material power as on moral reverence, is for Him extended over the whole of mankind.

The seed of Abraham.

Next, He is the heir of the royalty of Judah, the 'Shiloh' or Peace of Israel,[3] to whom 'the gathering of the peoples shall be.' The idea is here the same, but carried out more fully than before. The conception of mankind is enlarged from the many families to the many nations ; and accordingly the simple earlier picture is drawn afresh in deeper

---

[3] Gen. xlix. 10. I take the grand old rendering, supported by all the ancient versions, by all Jewish traditions, and by high linguistic authorities, 'till Shiloh come,' and not the tamer rendering proposed by some ancient and many modern critics, 'till he (Judah) come to Shiloh.' Whether 'Shiloh' is to be rendered 'the Peace,' or 'He whose right it is' ($\tilde{\phi}$ ἀπόκειται) is a matter of some critical difficulty, but affects little the use I have made of the passage.

lines of royalty. The Messiah is the giver of peace to His struggling people, and the homage of all nations is to be paid to Him.

Once more, from the lips of the great lawgiver and prophet, able to recognise in the spiritual influence of prophecy over the soul something higher than the royalty of power and law over the visible world, He is declared to be the Prophet of prophets, whose lightest word must be hearkened to by every soul which would not be cut off from spiritual life. *The Prophet of prophets.*

Then again, when in the person of David the glory of kingship and the inspiration of the prophet met together, the Messiah is at last known as the 'Son of David,' crowned with the triple glory of the king, the prophet, and the priest. His royalty is to spread not only over all nations, but over all ages, because He is exalted to the right hand of Jehovah; His prophetic power is to rule the minds and the souls as well as the bodies of men. He has a priesthood like that of the priest-king Melchizedek of old, 'having neither beginning of days nor end of life.' *The Son of David.*

Here the full outline is drawn. Each succeeding prophet has but to fill it up, till it seems to breathe and glow on the canvas of prophecy. Sometimes, as in Daniel, it is simply the royalty which is emphasised. The 'Son of Man' is seen 'in the clouds of heaven' 'at the right hand of the Ancient of Days;' and 'there is given to Him dominion and glory, and a kingdom' exalted over the great empires, which are shown in vision to have their day and cease to be. 'All peoples, nations, and languages are to serve Him, and his dominion is an everlasting dominion, which shall not pass away.' Sometimes, as in Jeremiah or Joel, the stress is laid rather on the spiritual sway of the Prophet, realising the noble prayer of Moses, when the Lord shall 'put His laws in men's minds and write them on their hearts,' 'pouring out His spirit on all flesh' in the great day of the Messiah. Sometimes, but perhaps less clearly, the idea of His Priesthood is brought out. Described emphatically as Himself the Righteous One and the Servant of Jehovah, He is to 'make His soul a sacrifice for sin, and bear the iniquity of the many;' or, again, He is the 'Messenger *The fulness of Messianic prophecy.*

of the covenant,' coming into the temple 'to purify the sons of Levi themselves, that they may offer unto the Lord an offering in righteousness' which shall be 'acceptable unto Him.' But for this union of the three great dignities no mere man is fit. Accordingly, as the picture is more and more fully drawn, there gather round His head rays of glory far too bright for any human brow, until He is hailed (to take only one specimen, the greatest of all) in words which no conception of poetic license or Eastern hyperbole can explain away,—the 'Wonderful in counsel, the mighty God, the Father of eternity, the Prince of Peace.'[4]

But still throughout He is the Son of Man, the true representative of humanity, as made in the Divine image and joined in the covenant of communion with God, at once the Heir and the Dispenser of all blessings, spiritual and temporal, for men. Most distinctly, therefore, the religion of the Old Testament, as seen in this light, contains the essence of what has been called the 'religion of humanity'—recognising in man freedom, wisdom, righteousness, a spiritual nature and an eternal life, which make his nature the true image of the Divine—utterly refusing (like other religions of the East before and since) to believe man to be but as one creature out of many, the mere instrument of destiny, cut off by an immeasurable distance from the majesty of God, destined to live (if indeed he can be said really to live) for a time, and then, as his greatest blessing, to pass away, absorbed into the Deity or into nothingness. All that in man rebels against this dreary and crushing theory of human nature and destiny, and seeks to justify that rebellion by what we call progress, in dominion over nature, in the light of knowledge, in the glory of righteousness and love—all this is freely accepted and solemnly consecrated in the conception of the Messiah. But there is this characteristic and immeasurable difference between the religion of Scripture and the modern 'cultus of humanity,' that the glory of humanity is not worshipped, as diffused through the race; it is not, by a strange confusion of thought, acknowledged to be imperfect and sin-stained in all men

The worship of the Messiah a 'religion of humanity.'

[4] See Dan. vii. 13, 14 ; Jer. xxxi. 33 ; Joel ii. 28 ; Isa. liii. 10, 11 ; Mal. iii. 1-3 ; Is. ix. 6.

considered individually, and yet by mere extension supposed to be exalted and purified in society, regarded as a whole. It is conceived as concentrated in One, perfect in righteousness, in wisdom, in goodness, whom every soul may know face to face, and, so knowing, may worship with a direct and personal worship. It has been already urged that this spirituality and immortality of man are implied throughout in the very idea of covenant with God. But what was elsewhere only implied, or at best imperfectly realised, is here brought out explicitly and perfectly. Down whatever vista of thought we look, the Christ is at every point the object on which the eye of hope rests. Every Israelite felt the peculiar dignity of kinship to the Messiah; he cherished accordingly the hope, not only of the wisdom of the Greek and the righteousness of the Roman, but of that purity, consecrated by nearness to God, of which neither Greek nor Roman seemed to have any adequate idea. Yet he should have understood that in this Israel was but the representative of mankind, and that in the Messiah's kingdom all peoples, nations, and languages should find their place, as a people holy unto the Lord.

But yet this exaltation of the Messiah is not the greatest example of that apotheosis of mere man, so familiar to us in polytheism; nor is it the perfection of that 'hero-worship,' which has been put before us in modern days as a kind of religion, protesting vehemently and not unsuccessfully against the idolatry of the race. Had it been so, it would have been utterly irreconcilable with the sublime Monotheism of the Old Testament. The Lord Jehovah could not then have been 'One Lord.' There is another side to the Messianic doctrine; in which it is made clear that in the Messiah, although He is so emphatically the Son of Man, there is a visible manifestation of God. *(b) As a manifestation of God.*

In this respect also the appearance on earth of the Messiah is the key to much which in itself might seem perplexing, and even self-contradictory, in the representations of God in the Old Testament. *The key to the antithesis pervading the Old Testament.*

There, on the one hand, He is represented, in the light suggested by the great name 'Jehovah,' as the Infinite, the One Source of all being, the One Eternal Self-existence, Creator of all things and all men. As such He is invisible, unapproachable, inconceivable. The idolatry, which seeks to represent Him visibly, is sternly forbidden and punished, as a blasphemy against His majesty, and as the degradation of all true religion. Everything which approaches that idolatry in practice by formalism or superstition, or which approaches it in thought by claiming to grasp the whole conception of God, is discouraged with equal determination. 'As the heaven is higher than the earth, so are My ways higher than your ways, and My thoughts than your thoughts.' The servants of God even cry out in disappointment, 'Verily Thou art a God that hidest Thyself.' 'I go forward, and He is not there; backward, yet I cannot perceive Him.' Yet they know that it must be so. For man to see God face to face were to die; even the angels veil their faces before His glory. Nothing can be more solemn and sublime than this recognition, essential to a true Monotheism, of the invisible, the infinite, the inconceivable majesty of God.

God infinite and unapproachable.

Yet, as has been already noted, side by side with this adoration of the invisible and infinite God, we find certain special, local, peculiar manifestations of Him in close relation to man, as the God of Abraham and the God of Israel. His hand is visibly unveiled, in miracle or in ordinary providence, in the history of the chosen people; His voice heard in the giving of the Law on Sinai: 'I am the Lord who brought you out of Egypt.' There is a tabernacle or a temple where He is pleased to put His name, where man may come before His immediate presence, and where the cloud of His glory rests. He is always the eternal Jehovah, and yet 'He dwells between the cherubim.' There by inquiry before the oracle, or at the lips of the prophet, men find a special word of the Lord. There the rites of sacrifice offer a special means of approaching Him, in certainty of forgiveness and purification.

God manifested to Israel.

The contrast is striking, yet it is not (as some would have us think) a mere confusion of thought, or a remnant of barbaric superstition, gradually giving way before a larger and freer light. It is certainly an intentional contrast; and it is preserved through the whole revelation. It served, indeed, an immediate purpose. In that local and special manifestation of God there was, according as man used or abused it, an education for the true spiritual religion, or a subtler idolatry of form and ordinance, which in the later days of Israel superseded the older and grosser idolatry, driven away for ever by the Captivity. But, in itself, it must have stood out as a strange and perplexing contrast—this local Temple, and the temple 'made without hands,' for Him to whom 'heaven was the throne and earth the footstool'— this special law, dealing so much with the body and the outer life, and the universal kingdom claiming for itself the inner life of the soul—this God, invisible and infinite, and these special and local manifestations of His peculiar presence.

Where lay the key? The answer undoubtedly is in the conception of the Messiah as one who (to use the words of Isaiah) was an 'Emmanuel,' God with us. In the 'Theophanies,'[5] foreshadowings (as they have been called) 'of the Incarnation,' there come out, from time to time, glimpses of a manifestation of a divine presence, thought worthy of the worship due to God alone, yet in human form. But these have little significance in themselves, although they may borrow a deep interest from that of which they are as types. It is in the appearance of the Messiah, not in vision, but in the reality of a true humanity, that the only key to this apparent contradiction is found. All these visible and special manifestations of God are seen to be preparations for a perfect and universal manifestation in Him of God upon earth. The kingdom of the Messiah is the kingdom of the Lord Jehovah Himself, directly and visibly manifested to all mankind. The Messiah is 'Jehovah our righteousness;' in His appearance 'the Lord will suddenly come to His temple;' the voice which cries before Him bids that 'the way of Jehovah be prepared,' 'a highway for our God.'[6] If we start from the side of the humanity of the Messiah, we have seen how His office gradually rose and swelled in its greatness, till it was seen to need (as all absolute royalty over the souls of men must need) divine

The Messiah as Emmanuel.

---

[5] On these mysterious appearances, and the various interpretations of their meaning, see an admirable sketch in Liddon's *Bampton Lectures* (Lect. ii.).

[6] See Jer. xxiii. 6; Mal. iii. 1; Is. xl. 3.

attributes. There is on this side an apotheosis of man, such as that of which the religions of the West held out hope and promise. But on the other hand, starting from the side of God, we see the Lord Jehovah Himself stooping to earth, manifesting Himself in the Messiah, not in the transient incarnations of which Eastern religions are full, nor imperfectly and in condescension to human weakness, but absolutely and for ever; so that He might be known face to face, as truly, although, of course, not as perfectly, as we know man. This conception is complementary to the other. On this side the Messiah is not the Son of Man, concentrating in Himself all the dignity and glory of humanity, but there is in Him an indwelling of the infinite and invisible God.

Hence to this conception we look for the enforcement of the other great truth of all religion—the true personality of a living God capable of being known to man. The Deity is no Law, no 'stream of tendency,' no diffused *Anima mundi*, no power unknown and unknowable, but a living Person, the Father of all men. It was this truth, which by all the various manifestations of the special covenant with Israel, in history or law, in ritual or prophecy—in spite of the obvious danger, too often actually realised, of lowering the conception of the Godhead, and so localising His peculiar presence as to forget His universal omnipresent majesty—had been worked into the whole thought and faith of Israel. Here again the Christ was the 'end of the Law.' In His manifestation this spiritual education was complete, and the truth which it had taught was fixed for ever.

But if it be asked, how such a manifestation of God can be possible without a degradation and limitation, by a virtual idolatry, of the infinite greatness of Deity, the answer is suggested by observing that by the presence of God in the Messiah it is the moral nature of the Godhead which is brought out. Let a kingdom on earth be ever so wide and so glorious; it can but imperfectly manifest the glory of the Creator of the universe. Let wisdom and light be ever so brightly embodied in any revelation to man; there can be here also but an imperfect and limited outpouring of the wisdom on which all being hangs, and of the light which transcends all know-

The revelation of God a moral revelation.

ledge. But righteousness, love, purity, these are the attributes which depend (so to speak) not on their scope, but upon their intensity. They could be perfectly manifested in a pure human nature, and exhibited in a kingdom over men. It was, therefore, in the revelation of these that the true glory of the Messianic revelation was contained. 'This is the name whereby He shall be called, Jehovah our Righteousness.' In this it does but carry out the principle of the whole of Scripture. The revelations of 'God in history,' of 'God in law,' of 'God in prophecy,' had always been moral revelations—a moral government, a moral standard, a moral inspiration. This conception of the principle of God's manifestation places the Old Testament in marvellous and instructive contrast with all legends of manifestations of God in mere power, as (for example) in the Creator, the Preserver, the Destroyer, of Indian mythologies. In the Messiah, this line of thought also reaches its perfection. For this is, indeed, the only Divine revelation which is possible. On the knowledge of God, as manifested in righteousness and love, hangs all religion that is really worth the name.

Perhaps this side of the Messianic idea is, from the nature of the case, less clearly marked out than the other. Certainly in actual fact it far less completely possessed the mind of the Jewish people. In the preparation for the Christ as the 'Word,' or Revealer of God, the New Testament accordingly called to its aid, as we shall see hereafter, the conception of an incarnation of the Divine Wisdom, shadowed forth in the Sapiential books, and afterwards worked out by the philosophy of the Schools, especially in the mystic atmosphere of Alexandria. But yet in the Messianic revelations it is clearly implied, although, being the deeper part of the idea, it was worked out more slowly and less perfectly by the mass of men. The divine 'Wisdom.'

But these great principles, so perfectly exhibited in the conception of the Christ—the exaltation of the human nature, and the manifestation of God to man in man—are both crossed by the terrible consciousness of evil. It is sin in man, which forbids his entering on the full heritage of all his glorious capacities. It is sin in man, which invests any revelation of God's perfect righteousness with (c) The bearing on the mystery of evil.

terror as well as majesty. Naturally, therefore, the very first characteristic of the kingdom of God in the Messiah, which is set forth again and again in the prophetic books, is that it should be purged from all taint of sin, and therefore of all sorrow and suffering. But how should this be? The whole tenor of 'the law,' in all its various phases, had been to bring out with startling and pitiless emphasis the reality both of the guilt and power of sin. How could these be shaken off by that humanity, to which they had become a second nature?

The answer was not yet clearly given. It is true that the kingdom of the Messiah is described as exhibiting to the full all the influences which can guide and foster the higher spiritual life. In it was to be a perfect knowledge of the laws of God in their spirit and not in their letter; there was to be a perfect exhibition of righteousness of the Messiah to draw all men to follow Him; there was to be a purifying and enlightening power of the Spirit poured out on all flesh. But all these, as the prophets knew well, had been in measure brought to bear on sinful humanity, and yet so far in vain, that the bondage of the soul under sin was but partially broken, and the sense of the guilt of sin, as seen by the pure eyes of God, remained absolutely untouched. The kingdom of the Messiah must have some power to wipe away this guilt, and break this spiritual bondage, over and above this perfection of the spiritual forces, which had been, in their imperfect developments, tried in vain. What must that power be? Where should men look for some type or anticipation of it?

<small>What was revealed and understood.</small>

The Scriptural revelation, as completed in the New Testament, answers this question very plainly by unfolding the ideas which were implied in the priesthood and the sacrifice. But by the mind of Israel this side of the Messianic doctrine was far less firmly grasped; the great question was not resolutely asked, or, if asked, was not seen to have received an answer, even by anticipation. That the Messiah was to be a King with a universal sway over nature and humanity, over body and soul—that He was to be a Prophet, having in fulness, and giving to others in measure, both the word and the Spirit of the Lord—these

<small>What was as yet mysterious.</small>

things they understood well. When, on our Lord's last visit to Jerusalem, they accepted Him as the Messiah in the loud welcome of the Hosanna, it was in this twofold character that they hailed Him, as the 'Prophet of Nazareth' and the 'King of Israel.' But the conception of His Priesthood and the hope of salvation in Him as their Sacrifice, entered little, if at all, into the popular conception of the Messiah.

Yet our Lord Himself, looking only to the Old Testament Scriptures, declared that in this they were 'fools and slow of heart.' The sacrifice stood out in the law in all its significance and in all its mystery, pointing to some antitype in the future; and they knew that the whole of the future of Israel centred round the Messiah. The very name of the Anointed of God included under it the office of the priesthood, to which, indeed, the anointing first belonged; and the inference from this was clenched by the attribution to the Messiah of the name of 'Priest for ever,' and that too in a priesthood—'the order of Melchizedek'—older and greater than the priesthood of Aaron.

The sacrifice and the priesthood.

The two ideas taken together might, as it seems to us in the light of subsequent events and teaching, have suggested some anticipation of a new and perfect sacrifice, corresponding to the new and perfect covenant in the Messiah. But this was not all. The appeal on this point is not only to 'Moses,' but to 'all the prophets.' Side by side with the predominant declarations of the glory and majesty of the Messiah—brought out, it is true, in an undertone, and almost exclusively in the later books of prophecy—there are many teachings on the suffering of the Messiah as connected with the sins of men. Such an utterance as the fifty-third chapter of Isaiah from without, or as the twenty-second Psalm from within—both accepted by Israel as referring to the Messiah—ought to have had an unmistakable significance. It might, indeed, be seen that they shadow out the great law of Mediation of man for man, which seems to be a fundamental law of human nature, and through which every good man, who has zeal for God's glory and love for his fellow-men, bears in his measure and degree the suffering of the sins of others. Hence in this or that prophet or psalmist—a David or a Jeremiah—they might have

The suffering Messiah of prophecy.

some imperfect fulfilment. Still, even before the event, the more thoughtful Israelites knew that in the fulness of their meaning they could belong to no ordinary man, and in accordance with the pervading expectation of the Messiah to unfold all mysteries, they did refer them to Him; although it seemed so difficult to reconcile them with the prevailing visions of glory, that they actually dreamt the strange dream of two Messiahs, the one to suffer, the other to reign. For there the words stood—whatever they might mean—connecting this mediation of the Messiah with sacrifice. 'My righteous servant'—a 'servant' in humiliation, yet 'righteous' in His unique sinlessness—'shall justify many;' for 'He shall make His soul a sacrifice for sin,' and 'shall bear their iniquities.' A Messiah for sinful men must not only bear suffering, but in that suffering must justify through sacrifice.

Then, besides this explicit witness of prophecy, there was an implicit witness always borne by the very existence of the priesthood. Every priest is, by the nature of the case, a mediator, or intercessor, between man and God. Now all experience confirms—what certainly the Old Testament declares repeatedly—that in the humiliating consciousness of weakness and sin man naturally, and almost invariably, seeks for one to stand between him and God. This Israel had desired at Horeb; and Moses was then their mediator, partly as the mouthpiece of God, partly as an intercessor for the people. So in the perplexity of the great enquiry, how God, who made man as he is, can yet judge him for the weakness or sin which seems his second nature, the Book of Job had expressed the longing of man for a 'daysman'—that is, an arbiter between God and man, not clothed in the terror of God's majesty, who should be at the same time also a witness to plead for man with God, as man pleadeth with man. Was this desire to be satisfied? The institution of the priesthood replied in the affirmative. Day after day the priest in the Temple did thus stand out as a mediator, representing God to man, and man to God—as representative of man offering for the people a sacrifice which they could not offer, and passing for them with the incense into a shrine of God's presence, which they

The mediation of the priesthood.

could not enter—as representative of God, consecrated by His ordinance, and commanded to bless the people, as accepted through sacrifice in His name.

Thus there existed (so to speak) in suspension all the various elements of belief in this most mysterious aspect of the office of the Messiah. But they were not yet fused together and precipitated in visible solidity. In this point, far more than in the others, the teaching of the event was necessary; in this, above all, the actual Christ of the New Testament is infinitely greater than the ideal Christ of the Old.

III. Still, however, it is true that from every point of view, although in different degrees of clearness and fulness, the great Messianic idea gives life and unity to the Old Testament witness, both on the two great truths of Natural Theology—the revelation of God and the knowledge of man's spiritual nature—and also on the great perplexity of that theology, the existence of evil. Yet, being of the nature of an expectation as yet unrealised, and necessarily corresponding but imperfectly with the future fulfilment, it at the same time marks that witness as being incomplete in itself, and therefore as needing for its right appreciation the consideration of the New Testament also. Under the light, therefore, of this Messianic idea, it seems natural at this point to endeavour to sum up the Old Testament witness, in its strength and its weakness, its truth and its imperfection.

The completion of the Old Testament revelation.

In regard to the great truth of Monotheism as a living religion, recognising not an ultimate abstraction, but a personal God, it is on the almost perfect strength of that witness that the mind is inclined to dwell. For in the vivid realisation by faith of the one true and eternal God—as a Divine Person speaking to the personality of man—as a Creator and Sustainer of the whole fabric of nature—as a Ruler, a Teacher, an Inspirer of every human soul —even the Gospel can hardly go beyond the revelation of the older Testament, except in sanctioning the familiarity of true sonship, and the gradual conquest of fear by love. The Old Testament stands out for Judaism, for Christianity, for Mohammedanism, perhaps for philosophic Deism, as the fountain-head of a true Monotheism. What can go beyond

(a) Its perfection as a revelation of God.

the magnificent passage, 'Hear, O Israel, the Lord our God is one Lord, and thou shalt love Him with all thine heart, and with all thy soul, and with all thy might,' which our Lord Himself has consecrated as His 'first and great commandment'?

But it is in respect of the other two great truths that the Old Testament is seen as preparatory and insufficient without the New.

The belief in nothing else than the eternal greatness and majesty of God, so long as it is absolutely dominant, may easily produce such painful consciousness of man's weakness and littleness, as to paralyse all human energy and progress, leading the mind either to question man's individual being altogether, or, at any rate, to doubt his freedom, to lay him at the feet of an absolute sovereignty, and bid him utter the 'Kismet' of hopeless fatalism. When the soul recovers from that terror, and begins to feel that it has in itself real power, freedom, light, then, if the old religion can offer it nothing beyond the simple utterance, 'God is great,' it ceases to be undisputed in its sway. It vainly seeks to check the stream of human progress; and that stream, as it grows stronger and deeper, sweeps men's souls away from their anchorage on the old truth, leaving it in desolate grandeur, like a seaport from which the waters have retired. How completely this has taken place in the religion of Islam all history tells us. If Judaism has not suffered this utter barrenness, it is because it has still some form of Messianic hope, although it has refused to accept that which claims to be its fulfilment, and which certainly has shown through that claim an all-conquering energy.

(b) Its imperfection as a religion of humanity.

Now in respect of this religion of humanity, complementary to the simple faith of Monotheism, and harmonising perfectly with it, it is confessed by all, that the Old Testament is still imperfect, and that the Christ of the Gospels is infinitely greater, fuller of light and inspiration, than the Christ as painted even in the noblest prophetic utterances of the Old Testament. But, while this imperfection is obvious and full of significance (especially in its bearing on mythic theories of the origin of Christianity), yet it cannot prevent the acknowledgment, that in this respect the witness of the Old

Testament, culminating in the Messianic idea, is living and powerful. In it the truth of the greatness and dignity, the spiritual and immortal being, of human nature, is worked out with constantly increasing force. Even in the first conception of covenant with God, I have contended that 'Hebraism' really includes this conception. But, if we consider the perfection of that idea in the Messiah, it stands out with such vividness and power as to resist all the Pantheistic, Materialistic, Nihilistic theories which would destroy it.

But it is in respect of the mystery of evil and the hope of its removal that the Old Testament witness is most certainly imperfect. To the Jew, as such, resting simply on his older Scripture, the Cross has always been a stumbling-block, although he has nothing to put in its place as a theory of atonement. To the man *(c) Its imperfection in relation to the mystery of evil.* who believes in God and believes in the spirituality of man, and who yet, in the consciousness of sin, alternately doubts these truths and trembles before all that they imply, the Old Testament will give something, perhaps much, of hope, but certainly no full rest or satisfaction. Like the Ethiopian eunuch (Acts viii. 30, 31) he may read there the promise of deliverance from sin through suffering, and perhaps believe that in some way it will be realised, but yet will need another voice to lead him through promise to fulfilment.

It is clear, then, that in the contemplation of the Messiah as foretold, the mind advances boldly towards the full knowledge of God and man, yet is still far from its full attainment. Without that contemplation it may (to *General conclusion.* carry out a former comparison) be held to have passed, through the outer region of nature and the inner court of human life, to the shrine of God's spiritual presence to the soul. But, when we stand before the shrine, can we venture to enter in? Prophecy paints to us the figure of a mediator who will make for us a way. That figure is the form of a perfect Son of Man, in whom we feel that our own humanity is exalted and renewed to the Divine likeness. On His brow we see shining, with a radiance not fitful or veiled like the light on the face of Moses, the unfading glory of an indwelling presence of God. If He will lead us on, we may advance where without Him we should not dare to tread. But yet there is one veil still before which we pause; it is the veil woven by the consciousness of a sin, which blinds our eyes and estranges us from God. The Holy of Holies is not yet laid open to us. As we learn to know the promised Mediator, the veil may seem to tremble, and the light from within flash out in glimpses of an exceeding brightness. But it is not yet rent in twain. For that consummation of all hopes we must wait till the Messiah of prophecy becomes to us the Christ of the Gospel, and till, instead of simply hoping for an atonement, we stand beneath the Cross.

CHAPTER VII.

THE SPIRITUALITY OF MAN AND THE RESURRECTION OF CHRIST.

'Jesus Christ our Lord . . . made of the seed of David according to the flesh; and declared to be the Son of God with power . . . by the resurrection from the dead.'—Rom. i. 3, 4.

I. THE doctrine of the Messiah appears in the Old Testament as a fruit-bearing germ of the religion of humanity, engrafted on the stem of a sublime Monotheism, and by contact therewith drawing to itself the power of a supernatural life. The doctrine of the Christ in the New Testament traces the development of that germ in a marvellous actual growth, spreading beyond the narrow limits of its native soil, so as to fill the whole world with its fruitfulness and beauty. *The Christ in New Testament.*

In the consideration of this doctrine of the New Testament it will be well to adopt the method which has been our guide in tracing the earlier stages of Revelation, by following the historical order of its enunciation, rather than by attempting any artificial analysis of its full-grown development. The preaching of the Gospel, like all proclamations of truth which are to pervade and transform humanity, was still to some extent a gradual process. In seeking to estimate its true character, we shall start best with that first phase of Christian teaching, which had the points of closest contact with the ancient doctrine of the Messiah. *Relation of the idea of the Messiah.*

Now if, in relation to that doctrine, pervading the whole of the Old Testament in different degrees, we seek to estimate the light which it throws on each of the great ideas involved in the belief of a covenant with God, the result has been already considered. It brings out with extraordinary vividness the exalted spiritual nature of humanity; it next emphasises, though with less completely striking emphasis, the conception of the manifestation of God to man; least clearly of all does it deal with the mystery of evil, and with that knowledge of salvation from evil which is needful for the full realisation of the other two leading ideas. Hence to those who looked eagerly for the Messiah of the Old Testament, filled with the simple ideas of His glory, visible and spiritual, it was perhaps natural, though not justifiable, that the Cross should be a stumbling-block.

Now it has been remarked that, considering Christianity, as distinct from simple Monotheism, to depend (as the Apostles' Creed shows) on a declaration of the great stages of our Lord's manifestation to man—the Incarnation, the Atonement, the Resurrection and Ascension—the order of Christian preaching reversed the historical order of events. It proclaimed, first, Christ risen and ascended; next, Christ crucified; and lastly, Christ incarnate and pre-existent before the Incarnation. Speaking roughly, we may find these phases of doctrine represented in the preaching of St. Peter, St. Paul, and St. John, respectively. It would be, of course, absurd to contend that at any time, or from the lips of any apostle, these great declarations could be separated from one another; for each necessarily implies the others, if brought out in its full meaning. But, in regard of prominence, the general statement appears sufficiently correct; and it will suggest the true order, in which to examine the actual doctrines of Christianity, in their relation both to the light and to the darkness of the Natural Theology of man. This reversal of the historical order of events is no arbitrary thing. When we examine the basis of any deep-rooted faith, just as when we dig down to the foundations of the earth, we uncover first the strata which were last deposited, and so gradually come to that primeval rock which is, so far as we can discern, the first substantial beginning of all things.

The stages of Christian preaching.

The first preaching of the Christ, addressed by Jewish preachers to Jewish hearers, naturally represented Him mainly as the promised Messiah, and so appealed to the expectations founded on the ancient doctrine. How did it do this? How could it do this, after the apparent failure of His ministry, as closing in re-

a) The Resurrection the seal of His Messiahship.

jection and death? To the most careless reader it will be evident that the witness of the Resurrection, described in the outset as the very purpose of the apostolic ministry, was carried out as the main subject of the apostolic preaching—whether by St. Peter at Pentecost, at the Beautiful Gate of the Temple, or in the house of Cornelius, or by St. Paul to the Jews in Antioch, to the heathen philosophers at Athens, before the Sanhedrim at Jerusalem, at the Roman tribunal at Cæsarea. The reason of this method of preaching it would be easy to infer. But we are not left to inference. It is declared in the text to be simply this--that 'Jesus Christ,' already by the hearers themselves known to be 'of the seed of David according to the flesh,' was now 'declared to be the Son of God in power by the resurrection from the dead.' The Resurrection was proclaimed generally as the seal of His Messiahship; it was set forth in detailed argument as the fulfilment of the aspirations of Jewish psalms, and of the brightest promises of the great epochs of Jewish prophecy. By it (said St. Peter, challenging the allegiance of the very Sanhedrim which had shed the blood of the Lord Himself) 'let all the house of Israel know assuredly, that God hath made this same Jesus, whom ye crucified, both Lord and Christ.'

It is singularly interesting to observe how this method of preaching corresponds in idea to the whole representation of the life of our Lord on earth, as it is painted to us in the first three Gospels, and as it was declared to the first Christians by the apostolic witness out of which these Gospels sprang. *(b)* The climax of the Gospel narrative. At once, or after a brief notice of His birth and infancy, that Gospel record—for in substance it is but one—suddenly places us by His side at the baptism which sealed Him to His ministry, and then bids us (as if with little previous knowledge of His nature) follow Him through that ministry, watching thoughtfully His acts, listening to His words, gradually receiving the impression of His personal presence, till finally, by an inductive process of reasoning, we arrive at some conception of who and what He is. The climax of that induction is placed invariably in the Resurrection and the Ascension, which are but two parts of one great act. It is in the light of the knowledge of the resurrection, that the conclusions, gradually dawning and growing upon us, flash out at last into the clearness of moral certainty.

Thus, for example, the history records from time to time exhibitions of miraculous power, partly as signs of His au- *Of the signs of miracle.* thority, partly as integral parts of His redeeming work, and means of manifesting it to the world; and these powers of miracle are claimed expressly by Himself as fulfilments of the predicted tokens of Messiahship. Step by step, if that record be accepted as a true history, the conviction grows upon us, that these mighty works must argue the existence of a divine power working with Him, or rather in Him; for He works by an inherent authority, to which no mere man could lay claim. But the climax of all, the one miracle of miracles (in comparison with which all else are as nothing), is the resurrection from the grave and the ascension into heaven. Of it St. Paul says, what assuredly he would have said of no other miracle, that if it be not true, the Christian 'faith is vain,' and the Christian 'preaching is false witness for God.'

Thus, again, the evangelists and the first apostolic preachers delight to trace in the Lord the fulfilment of the *Of the fulfilment of prophecy.* ancient prophecies, sometimes in their great leading principles, sometimes even in slight and striking details. Gradually, by the accumulation of such fulfilments, incapable of being accounted for on any theory of mere coincidence or assumption by Himself of the signs of Messianic character, the conviction will grow on any reader, who accepts the substantial truth of the record, that (to use the words of the first disciples) 'we have found Him of whom Moses in the law and the prophets did write.' But the whole line of these fulfilments of prophecy culminates in the resurrection and ascension. On it alone St. Peter dwells under this aspect in the first Christian sermon at Pentecost; St. Paul describes it as the 'hope of Israel,' to which, 'serving God night and day,' they had through centuries 'hoped to come.'

Then, once more, we watch through the history the actual humanity of the Lord Himself, unfolding gradually, in the midst of His lowly lot and spirit, a unique power and dignity, a perfect sinlessness, a superiority to all material influences, to which no other child of man has ever shown even an approach. The belief will grow upon us, that in this picture—which all acknowledge to have been entirely beyond the power of the early Christians to draw as an ideal picture—we see the true Son of Man, and therefore the true Son of God, made perfectly in His image, showing what that image should have been, had not sin come into the world, and death by sin. In the triumphant suffering on the cross the powers of evil themselves might seem to be conquered. But 'the last enemy to be destroyed is Death.' Till the resurrection-day tramples Death under His feet, and the ascension opens heaven, that humanity is not seen as really made perfect. The whole description of this superhuman humanity needs still its climax, and finds it in the broken tomb and the ascension from the slopes of Bethany.

Of the exaltation of our Lord's humanity.

In fact—take what line of thought we will—the whole Gospel record works up to the Resurrection and Ascension, the new coronation-day of the self-discrowned King of the kingdom of heaven. The one conclusion to which all various inductions converge is expressed in that great declaration of our Lord Himself, spoken in the new life of the Resurrection, and on the very eve of the Ascension, 'All power is given me in heaven and earth;' 'make all nations my disciples;' 'teach them to observe all things whatsoever I have commanded you.' 'Lo! I am with you alway, even to the end of the world.' In that declaration there is undoubtedly the claim to be 'the Son of God with power.' But that claim could be held reasonable only when the resurrection had declared His Divine sonship. The Apostles themselves then—and (as the earlier history shows) not till then—entered into its full meaning.

II. Whether, therefore, we examine the accounts of the earliest Christian preaching, or study the actual history on which that preaching was based, we must come to the conclusion that it was the message of 'Christ risen and ascended,' as the true Messiah, which first proclaimed to the world that a new and all-important epoch had dawned in the revelation of God to man. Under this light, therefore, first we must consider the relation of

The order of the teaching of Christ risen.

Christianity to those great points of Natural Theology, to which we have so often recurred, because, in fact, the soul of man must dwell on them in all its hours of deeper thought. What has the Resurrection to declare on the nature of God, on the spirituality of man, and on the great mystery of evil?

Here, again, the enquiry should observe the historic order, and consider the actual method under which, in the early days of Christianity, the Resurrection was actually declared, first to the inhabitants of Jerusalem, and then to the world at large. It will be found that, in the first proclamation of the Resurrection (as might, indeed, have been expected) the one great object is to bear witness to the fact. In the very place where He died, to the very persons who had stood by the cross, perhaps who had helped to condemn Him to the accursed death, the fact was testified again and again, by those who had seen Him die, who had seen the sealed stone upon His tomb, and who had also seen, heard, even handled Him, when he came back from the grave. On that witness they utterly refused to keep silence; to bear it they professed to live, and they were certainly ready to die. For they did not declare it as simply an historic fact, greater and more wonderful than other facts. As they pressed upon their hearers its infinite spiritual importance to their salvation, so they showed in their own persons that the conviction of its reality had been to themselves a new source of light and energy. A new source of light; for they who had before been as 'fools and slow of heart to understand' now spoke with a firm and definite faith, and with a wisdom which their enemies could not gainsay or resist. A new spring of energy; for they who had 'forsaken Him and fled' now stood forth, counting it all joy to suffer and to die for Him. As it was with the Twelve, so also it was with the great Apostle of the Gentiles. To enemies and to disciples alike the one account which he gave of the great spiritual change of his conversion, and the one foundation of his claim of apostleship, was that he had seen the risen and ascended Lord, and that the truth of the Resurrection had been revealed to him, as to 'one born out of due time.'

(a) The declaration of the fact.

It is obvious that the first Christian preaching, as reof material laws; that, as sin had no strength to defile, so death had no power to destroy Him; that earth was but His temporary dwelling-place, and heaven His true home; that, being true Son of Man, He was yet something more than Man, even the Son of God. In him, therefore, as risen and ascended, all that the various lines of Messianic teaching had foreshown was more than fulfilled. Therefore all, and more than all, the reverence, the loyalty, the adoration, due to the Messiah, was claimed for Him. Prophecy was at last fulfilled. The triple crown of the prophethood, the priesthood, and the kingship rested on His brows, and each of its bright circlets was now tinged with the light of heaven, before unconceived and inconceivable. Hence, under each aspect, the claim for unlimited faith in Him was boldly put forth. As the Prophet of prophets, His word was to be accepted as the complete and ultimate truth, known by the perfect knowledge of one who 'is in heaven,' and set forth to be the light of the whole world. As the King of kings, His royalty was to be recognised, as universal over the souls as well as the bodies of all men, claiming an unreserved obedience and an unbounded faith, both by the grace of the present and by the promises of the future. As Priest (though as yet this aspect of His salvation came not out in the forefront of preaching), it was to be understood that in Him and by Him alone sin and death were overcome.

His Messiahship.

Thus on every side He was preached, and actually accepted, as 'the Son of God with power,' as soon as His life and death on earth were read in the light of the resurrection. It was not so till then. While He was seen and heard on earth, only a handful of men were gathered round Him by the work of years; when He was known as risen and ascended, three thousand souls were made His in one single day. So it was in actual fact, and it was clearly reasonable that it should be so. It would have been impossible to preach Christ as the apostles preached Him, if it was believed that He, like other prophets and kings of men, had simply lived His day and then died the death of all men. The human race, by a true instinct, has always taken the chief steps of progress by faith in those natural leaders to whom we rightly ascribe a 'mission,' as its teachers and examples, as its rulers and inspirers. But still it retains,

CHAP. VII.   THE GOSPEL OF THE RESURRECTION.   129

corded to us, turned invariably, not upon abstract argument, nor even on prophetic exhortation, but on this witness to the Resurrection. Therefore it was that it conquered the world. For, to the mass of men at any rate, it is an infinite relief, on these mysterious subjects, to exchange the vagueness of speculation and the feverish eagerness of hope for some solid witness to fact, and thus to feel firm ground under the foot, which has sought in vain for a resting-place in the troubled waters of a fathomless sea. It was, therefore, the highest wisdom of the first preachers to begin thus with the tale of their own eye-witness. So St. Peter began, when to him was given the charge of first opening the Gospel both to Jews and to Gentiles. So did St. Paul, when long after, preparing to enter on the deep spiritual meanings of the resurrection before the enquiry or scepticism of Corinth, he laid the foundation of all in a recital of the various witnesses to the fact itself, in language which has all the precision and almost the formality of a creed (1 Cor. xv. 1-8).

But, as soon as the fact thus emphatically testified, had in spite of incredulity, in spite of dissuasion, in spite of threat, sunk deep into the conviction of the hearers, then it was inevitable that the preachigns hould leave it, as a foundation surely laid, and go on to draw out the spiritual significance which from the beginning it had been declared to imply. Of that exposition, as is, indeed, natural, we can trace two successive phases—first, the enforcement of the significance of the Resurrection, so far as it concerned the Lord Himself; and, next, of its significance, as it extended to all humanity. *Its significance,*

What it was declared to be in relation to the Lord Himself is clearly described in the text. It marked Him as 'the Son of God with power.' It was, indeed, the great sign of His authority. On it He had staked His truth again and again; had He not risen, His life would have been but the noblest of human lives, His death but the grandest and the most awful of all human martyrdoms. But, like all His miracles, it was not only a crowning sign, but an all-important part of the revelation of Himself. It showed with the most startling clearness that His nature, even in the body, was not under the dominion

(b) In relation to our Lord Himself.

K

or should retain, its freedom of judgment, and its expectation of still greater progress in the future. For mankind is, after all, greater than the greatest of mere men. In none can it place an absolute and unreserved faith. It must be a sign of short-sighted presumption, if one, who acknowledges himself to be a mere man, although a prophet of God, claims to declare the truth to all times and to give laws for all generations. It strikes us as a virtual idolatry, if ever such claims are advanced for him by his followers, when he has passed away. Certainly it startles us as a strange inconsistency, when, in the case of our Lord Himself, those who hold Him to be, or rather to have been, only the wisest and the noblest of mere men, speak of taking Him still, after eighteen centuries of human thought and experience, as being, either in knowledge or in morality, an absolute guide. Only as manifesting Himself something more than a mere man—only as fulfilling in the Resurrection and Ascension His own simple and majestic declaration : ' I came forth from the Father, and am come into the world; again I leave the world and go to the Father,' can He possibly claim that which Christianity has always claimed for Him. It was a right intuition which first represented in the glory of the Resurrection the light which was to shine from one end of the heaven to the other. St. Paul's words are as true as ever. 'If Christ be not risen,' and be not in heaven now, He may have been (though even this can hardly be reconciled with His own self-assertion) the wisest, purest, noblest of men; but a 'Son of God,' with enduring and universal power, He can never be.

Such, accordingly, was the first explanation of the significance of His resurrection. It was, for the time, all-sufficient. Under the spell of its influence men crowded into His kingdom. Without any deeper enquiry, Jews, Samaritans, Gentiles, all found there the truth they longed for, the authority they needed, and the new spiritual life by which they might conquer sin and defy death. There is a singular simplicity and beauty in the first recorded Christian confession :[1] ' I believe that Jesus Christ is the Son of God '—

[1] Acts viii. 37. The passage, indeed, is of doubtful authenticity. But, if it be not genuine, it is an early gloss, embodying the simplest

'the Son of God with power by the resurrection from the dead.'

But, as time went on, as Christian teaching developed itself in all its fulness, and especially as the Gospel drew to itself the highly civilised races of the West—the great masters of that philosophic thought which studied, above all other things, man's nature and destiny—the significance of the Resurrection had to be unfolded in its wider reference to the whole race of man. This extension of significance was not derived simply from the inference, however cogent, that, since Jesus Christ was emphatically the 'Son of Man,' in all things taking the human nature upon Him, He must show in His own person what were the true capacities and destiny of humanity, pure from sin and in perfect communion with God. For He Himself had expressly declared that for all He was 'the Resurrection and the Life,' and that He went to heaven ' to prepare a place' for us. Hence this extension of the significance of the Resurrection was declared as a matter of course. The same apostle who lays such careful stress on the fact of the Resurrection, and attributes to it such infinite importance, declares that to suppose it not to touch all mankind is virtually to deny that it is in itself true: 'If there be no resurrection of the dead, then is not Christ risen.'

(c) Its significance in relation to all mankind.

What, then, is that wider significance? It appears to be the direct development of just those two great truths which were involved in the idea of the Messiah; while, at the same time, it less directly implies the other great truth, which in that idea is but faintly represented. It declares in Christ the glory of God and of human nature, in virtue of the manifestation of the Divine image in it; but it simply prepares for the doctrine of the Cross. Thus it exemplifies the great principle for which I have contended as characteristic of all revelation; it takes up what had been declared in old times as 'the hope of Israel,' to confirm what in it was known, and to open the revelation of what was unknown.

form of Christian faith, and so bearing witness to the one thing needful for discipleship.

III. We observe that it is taught under two forms, as having both its present and future consequences to every man. But in itself it is one. It is, beyond all else, the demonstration of the truth of the spirituality of man. This truth must imply, first, as to the nature of man in itself, that man is not bound in the iron chain of physical causation, as a mere instrument of some irresistible force, but that he has a will free to originate action, a reason which sees invisible truth, and a conscience which recognises a moral majesty of right, ruling the soul in perfect independence, perhaps in victorious opposition to all compulsion from without. Next, in relation to man as he actually is, it implies that in that spiritual life there is a power to overcome all hindrance and temptation from without, and to struggle against the capacity, or even the full-grown habit, of sin within. There follows, thirdly, the belief that there is an undying personality in man, incapable of being destroyed by all the changes of outward life and circumstance, and especially in the last terrible change which we call death. Yet, since man cannot be a god, living by an independent and inherent life, and therefore partaking of the nature of the uncreated, these convictions can be based only upon the faith that man has the power of a spiritual communion with the Eternal Creator and Supreme Ruler of the world—a power which necessarily implies some spiritual likeness to Him.

The spirituality of man.

These four points, inseparably connected with each other, are involved in any firm belief in the spirituality of man. They are often combined in very different proportions. Sometimes one or other sinks into insignificance, leaving only faint traces of itself, like rudimentary organs in a changed species. Sometimes the consciousness of the spiritual power to discern truth as it is, and as it is to all eternity, gains an all but exclusive predominance. Sometimes the certainty of a moral conquest of evil, begun here and to be continued hereafter, appears to be all in all. Most of all we notice a kind of conflict between the strong sense of the spiritual in man himself and the idea of communion with God, in which either the former throws the latter into the background, where it is acknowledged rather than realised, or the latter tends to the belief of an absorption of human personality in the infinite God. But yet all the four points are integral parts of the true idea, and it invariably suffers grievously in vividness and power, if any one of them is left in abeyance.

Now it is impossible to glance, however cursorily, at the history of human thought, as expressed in the various literatures, or embodied in the various religions and philosophies of the world, without being convinced that this idea of the spirituality of man's nature is fairly indestructible. It may, indeed, become dim and vague; it may express itself in visionary and even grotesque forms; it may have to live only in a state of constant spiritual warfare. For it has against it the whole force of appearances. The vastness of the universe and the greatness of physical force as against the littleness of men—the actual power of evil in the world, degrading the soul and binding it through the body to this transitory life—the awful phenomena, bodily and spiritual, of death, and the horror of impenetrable darkness which lies beyond—the sense of the infinite and inconceivable greatness of God, too high for human knowledge or communion—all these things (I say) are at continual war with the various elements of that lofty belief. Constantly it is found unable to dispel the various doubts, which overcloud the hopes of man for himself, and still more unable to show how these hopes can be worked into harmony with the great scheme of the universe and the conception of God. But still it does maintain itself, 'perplexed but not in despair,' man's convictions, here as elsewhere, are far stronger than the reasons he can give for them.[2] It is more than doubtful whether, in respect at any rate of the practical and moral side of his nature, the most purely materialistic philosopher can live from day to day, without using words and doing acts virtually implying the belief which he speculatively disowns. The stronghold of

(a) The difficulties of belief therein.

---

[2] This is most strikingly seen in the immortal *Phædo* of Plato. The idea of communion with the Divine being, at most, very faintly realised, the arguments for an inherent immortality in man naturally pass into an abstract and transcendental phase, contrasting most strikingly with the firm faith of the dying Socrates himself. We feel that his death argues more forcibly than his philosophy.

the higher faith is still bravely maintained against all the forces which press from without, although its banner may from time to time seem to waver, and the battle-cry of its defenders to wax faint, or to be overborne by the clamour of the enemy.

But besides all the doubts which rise up against the belief in the spirituality of man, there is a further perplexity in the question 'What is man?' 'What is the relation' (it is asked) 'of the soul, with its transcendent powers and capacities, to that body through which we are linked to the material world? Is the body a part of our true self, or merely an imperfect instrument, a temporary vesture, of the soul?' The natural tendency in all who believed in the spirituality and immortality of man was to embrace the latter alternative. Many religious and some of the noblest philosophies held that even in life the body was but an encumbrance or a prison-house, and accordingly, in any conception of the hereafter, rejoiced to think that it had mouldered into nothingness, and left the soul naked and free. But the fuller investigation in modern days of the complex being of man—of the power of physical influence over him, of the need of physical machinery, not only for act and word but even for thought, of the undoubted action and reaction of body and soul on each other—soon dispelled this first conviction. Even if it did not induce the belief that the soul was a mere function of the bodily organisation, destined to perish with it, it at any rate showed that the body is a part of man's true self. But the body is dissolved in death. How can man still exist in his true nature and personality? The difficulty of answering this question, and of conceiving a true personality in a disembodied soul— the mere 'shade' (as ancient poetry has it) of its former self—threw a gloom of vagueness and darkness over the future world, which prevented its being realised with any vividness of power; and indeed, after an almost grotesque device for putting off the perplexity by a notion of transmigration of souls, often ended in the conception of an absorption of the soul into the *Anima mundi*, perhaps to pass away altogether in respect of individuality, perhaps to be sent forth again into another cycle of earthly existence. The

(*b*) The question as to the body in speculation.

very conception of a resurrection of the body would have seemed, as indeed it did seem when St. Paul preached it at Athens, a thing to mock at: yet for want of it even the cherished belief in the immortality of the soul trembled in the balance.

The belief of the Jews was far stronger. For, as our Lord Himself taught the Sadducees, the very conception of covenant with God carried with it a profound belief in the true personality and spiritual nature of man, which forbade the fear of annihilation or absorption after death. But the idea was implied rather than explicit, and the whole tone of the Old Testament shows that it had not yet gained a complete victory. At times, as the Psalms and Prophecies and even the Books of Wisdom tell us, the light pierced through the mists of doubt, and disclosed the future for the moment in all its brightness; but then the darkness closed in again. Gradually, however, the belief won its way, and by the time of our Lord's appearance it had settled down, even in the popular faith, into a clearer perception of the truth than the subtlest philosophy could teach elsewhere. But the belief was still an inference, not clearly declared even in the later Scriptures, and unsupported by the supreme Mosaic revelation, and therefore often denied by those who rested simply upon the written Word, and defended, on the other side, by appeal to a supposed oral law handed down by tradition. It wanted the vividness and certainty necessary to give it spiritual force. Humanity waited still for some clear unwavering light, which might at once scatter the darkness of doubt, and light up the dulness of a merely formal belief.

The belief of the Jews therein.

IV. That longed-for light was certainly given by the declaration of the Resurrection in all its full meaning. As a matter of fact, it spread from one end of the world to the other, and everywhere the souls of men rose up to welcome it, as that which they needed and expected, and yet could not have discovered for themselves.

The bearing of the resurrection:

For, first, if believed, it brought the present spirituality of man out of the region of mere speculation. Crowning, as it did, the perfect life of the Son of Man upon earth, it showed visibly what humanity

(a) on the spirituality of man in the present;

ought to be, what in Christ it had been, what for His sake and in His kingdom it was to be for all His faithful people. The Apostles did not hesitate to say, 'Ye are risen with Christ;' 'Your life is hid with Him in God;' and to draw out, as inferences from this truth, all those ideas which have been already described as involved in the spirituality of man—freedom from the bondage of the flesh, detachment from the mere visible world, ability to mortify the power of sin, capacity of seeing and knowing God. They declared thus a present resurrection of the Spirit, and based it on words of the Lord Himself: 'He that heareth my word and believeth hath the eternal life' already, and 'is passed from death unto life.'

Then, as inseparable from this, came the certainty of a future resurrection, brought, again, out of speculation and hope to the plain light of day. The minds of ordinary men could hardly enter into the subtle reasonings of philosophy, nor yet be wholly content with mere promise. They found it hard to dispel, either by mere probability or mere hope, the darkness which hung over the grave, and into which men went down and made no sign. But they could very well understand such declarations as this—'Christ has risen for you; as He rose, you who are His shall rise: for such resurrection is the privilege of your redeemed humanity. Christ is ascended into heaven; He is gone to prepare a place for you, that where He is ye may be for ever. In the hour of martyrdom ye shall see Him rise up to receive you at the right hand of God.' They could understand it, and they showed that they did understand it. What had been at best the speculation of the wise or the dream of the saintly became the treasure of all, fixed as one of the great convictions of humanity. How, by the knowledge of it, men have actually conquered the flesh, defied death, lived in the glorious future of heaven, all history tells us. (b) the immortality of man in the future;

But it is to be observed further how, in respect both to the present and to the future, the resurrection of Christ dealt with that great perplexity as to the body. It showed distinctly that the body was a part of our true self; that in the future perfection of man it (c) the true nature and destiny of the body.

should have its appointed place. For it is the temple of God, and, so consecrated, it cannot wholly die. In that belief very much is implied. First, surely the sanction of that which all modern science teaches so distinctly—that the body is now a true and powerful factor in our actual nature and character, acting upon the soul and acted upon by the soul, and forming the link between our individuality and the great universe to which we belong. Next, the condemnation of the merely ascetic theory, which, holding the body to be an enemy and not a faithful subject of the spirit, would seek perfection by crushing it, and so cutting off the individual from the visible world of things and persons, that he might dwell in an unnatural isolation, fancied to be nearer God. But, besides these ideas touching the present, how wonderfully this conception of a resurrection of the body brought out the true personality, the vivid reality, of the future life! In the person of the risen Lord it was seen that the body of the future was the same and yet not the same—with a true identity, subtilised and glorified, and capable of passing to the unknown region of bliss in the presence of God, which we call heaven. True that in our promised resurrection faith has to contemplate a yet greater marvel. For it was declared that His 'flesh saw no corruption;' ours, we know, moulders away, and the actual particles of which it is composed pass into other bodies. So, even from the first, those who professed belief in the risen Christ yet asked the two natural questions, 'How are the dead raised up?' By what power (that is) shall the dry bones live? 'With what body do they come,' now that their old body is absolutely passed away? But these questions the first preachers of the resurrection put aside, as neither admitting nor requiring any complete answer. The one all-important point was that which the resurrection of our Lord, if believed, made abundantly clear—that the body laid dead in the grave could be raised up again, and transfigured to a new and more glorious condition, from 'a body of humiliation' into 'a body of glory,' and that the state of future perfection involved the continued existence of that twofold nature of body and soul which belongs to man here. If this were true, the difficulties raised by further questions, whether they could be solved or not, appeared to them not to touch the root of the matter. The identity of the body, even in this life, depends not on the mere material particles, which are being dissolved and renewed at every moment, but on the impress of individuality, which these changes do not impair, and which gives to the body a distinctive character in each one of the countless millions of human kind. It cannot be incredible that this process of decay and reconstruction—slow and gradual in our earthly life, though strangely sudden and complete in lower organisms—should culminate in the decay of death and the newness of resurrection. St. Paul's argument is irresistible, when he dwells on the mysterious power which from the seed or the first simple cell assimilates, under some hidden law of the internal structure, the simple physical elements, so as to develope out of a common material the distinctions of species and race, even of family and individual, till the perfect human being stands out, 'fearfully and wonderfully made,' and urges that the same power is surely adequate to work out the change— be it what it may—which shall clothe us in the body of the future, the same, yet not the same, as the body which has mouldered to dust. Most emphatically, therefore, the proclamation of the resurrection brought out that doctrine of the spirituality of man in his whole complex nature, which is perhaps the most prominent in the old Messianic idea. Under this aspect, as in the more direct reference to the nature of our Lord Himself, it stood in the closest relation to the Messianic promise, and by no figure of speech could be described as realising the 'hope of Israel.'

V. But still, like the old Messianic idea, it was a revelation also of God. In this respect it forms part of a true religion, as distinct from philosophy, or from what calls itself a religion of humanity; and therefore can approve itself in the minds of those who believe above all else in the absolute and sole eternity of God. *The resurrection as a revelation of God.*

For this spirituality and consequent immortality of man, if they be conceived of as belonging to him by some inherent power of his own nature, make him as a god in himself; they become confused with the self-existence which is divine, and must, therefore, be extended back into a pre-existence which had no beginning, as onward to a future which has no end. In that conclusion, avowed in some philosophic schools, and implied in the reasoning of others, there is a kind of *reductio ad absurdum* which must either make men disbelieve the immortality of the individual man, merging it (as the modern 'religion of humanity' teaches) in a (so-called) immortality of the race, and tending ultimately even to question any true personality of the individual being, or (with many mystic schools of the past and present) making the soul to be only an emanation, to be absorbed hereafter into the Eternal Spirit from whom it came.

But the resurrection of man, as preached by the Apostles, clearly places the future life in a wholly different light. Christ as man is raised, we men are raised in Him, by 'the glory of the Father.' 'God giveth the future body as it pleases Him.' The immortality of man is set forth as sustained by the continued will of God. As by His word we now 'live and move and have our being,' bodily and spiritual, so shall it be through all the ages of eternity. Even in those aspects of the resurrection, which belong to Christ and to Christ alone, as one in whom dwelt the fulness of the Godhead, the same truth holds. When, in words which no mere man could use, He asserts that He had life in Himself, and therefore says of His human life, 'I have power to lay it down, I have power to take it again,' He still adds, 'This commandment have I received of my Father.' But in us it is made clear, again and again, that our eternal life consists in communion with God through Him. On that, and on that only, depends the certainty of our resurrection. In this is carried out the truth which has been already contemplated as implied in the belief in the Messiah. The glory, the spiritual life, the immortality of man, are looked upon simply as a manifestation in man of the glory of God—originating in His will, sustained now by that same will, resting its promise of an endless future on the imperishable continuance of that 'gift of God which is without repentance.' By that view, not only is the reference of all things to God preserved, without which the essential monotheism of all true religion is impossible; but the belief in the immortality of man is cleared from all those impossible consequences, by which its reality must be fatally discredited to every thoughtful mind. We shall see, as we proceed in the consideration of the actual order of Christian teaching, how this conception of 'God in Christ,' with all its consequences, works itself out more and more vividly and distinctly. As yet it is only implied, but implied most clearly at every point. The exaltation of humanity is never for a moment contemplated, except in virtue of the communion with God, and the indwelling of God in man.

Such is the significance of the doctrine of the resurrection as set forth in the earliest teaching of the Gospel, especially as we gather it from the Apostle who has been called 'the Apostle of the Circumcision,' as appealing primarily to Jewish thought and faith; and who has been called 'the Apostle of Hope,' because he dwells so emphatically on the dignity, the freedom, the promise of Christian life. In it Christianity seems to occupy mainly the former of the two positions which I have throughout assigned to it, and stands out as strikingly confirmatory of the great truths of Natural Theology. Like the doctrine of the Messiah, which it crowns, and the whole doctrine of covenant with God culminating in the Messianic idea, it takes up the great induction of the spirituality and immortality of man in his whole nature, to which the human mind, along the various lines of intellect, conscience, imagination, and affection, has against all difficulties struggled on and won its way. It takes this up, but not as merely an induction. It meets it by the witness of a transcendent fact, manifesting the true nature of the Christ, and disclosing through Him the actual capacities and destinies of humanity. In the proclamation of that fact it solves the great problem of the destiny of the body, which so often perplexes the defenders of man's spirituality.

The actual 'power of the resurrection.'

Nor does it fail to take up the other great induction of Natural Theology—the belief in a God who is the Eternal Being, and yet has moral relations to His creatures, and can be known and served by them. For the manifestation in Christ of the spirituality of man, in accordance with the whole tenor of Bible teaching, is made to be the crown and completion of the covenant and communion of man with God.

Not in himself, but as made in Christ the son of God by adoption, has man his spiritual being. God is still all in all. Man still rests absolutely on the fatherhood, to the embrace of which he is restored in Christ.

The experience of ages has shown its power to bring life and immortality to light. It has not yet shown the slightest indication of any adequate substitute for it. What speculation, or theory, or hope, can take the place of the words, 'I am the Resurrection and the Life,' as spoken on the brink of the grave, or of the promise, 'I go to prepare a place for you,' as addressed to those who look on (as man by his very nature is formed to look on) to some ultimate future? The Gospel in declaring the resurrection has, indeed, its own positive evidences to present, and fears not the most jealous scrutiny of them. But surely it is no bad preparation for those who need to study them, it is no uninstructive task for those whose faith is already established, to see how, here as elsewhere, Christianity meets the highest hopes, and supplies the most urgent needs, of the spiritual life.

VI. In regard of the other great function which the Scripture revelation professes to discharge, as supplementary to our Natural Theology, especially as dealing with the great mystery of evil, this aspect of Gospel preaching is like the Messianic idea which it crowns; it deals with the solution of it rather by implication than explicitly, although the implication is infinitely more obvious and emphatic. In proclaiming the victorious spirituality of man, and promising him a future in the perfect communion with God, it obviously implies that the guilt of evil, separating man from God, is done away, and the bondage of evil over the soul effectually broken. Every preacher of Christ risen ends his pleading with a promise that to those who will repent and believe sin is blotted out, and the new life of grace kindled in the soul by the fire of the Holy Spirit. St. Paul, when he takes up the message, declares emphatically that in Him sinners are 'justified' before God, as afterwards that Jesus Christ was 'raised again for our justification;' and that, 'as He was raised up,' so we are risen 'to walk in newness of life.' But for the full and explicit treatment of this great subject—for the consideration of the doctrine of Atonement and the means of justification—we have to look to a further stage of Gospel preaching. Here, as in other cases, the fact of forgiveness and deliverance is proclaimed, and men are invited to test it by experience, before searching into the principle on which it is based. The glory and dignity of the Messiah are first brought home to Jewish hearts, that they may be able to receive hereafter the preaching of the Cross, which was to them a stumbling-block. For only in the light of the resurrection can the Cross itself be understood.

It is, indeed, with the human race, as the Gospel record declares it to have been with the chosen disciples of the Lord, when He came to them from the grave. At first they believe not for joy and wonder; and step by step, time after time, the great fact is borne in upon them, till even the most sceptical can doubt no more. *Preparation for fuller teaching.* Then with the fact itself is joined the promise and gift of the spiritual life, more than renewing to the redeemed the old birthright of humanity. It is enough; the 'disciples are glad' with the joy of unclouded faith; they cry out in adoration, 'My Lord and my God.' After this it is that His first recorded teaching tells how 'the Christ was to suffer,' and so 'to enter into glory;' and His last charge is to preach in His name 'repentance and remission of sins.' That teaching had been—so the Evangelists with one voice declare—spoken from the same lips before, yet spoken in vain to those who could not or would not understand. Now it comes home because spoken after the resurrection. It is only through the knowledge of 'Christ risen' that man can enter into the preaching of 'Christ crucified.'

His victorious presence with His servants was and is all-sufficient. At all times—to borrow a figure from a grand scene of the old Scripture history—there is a fiery trial, testing mind and heart and spirit, to be *Conclusion.* gone through by those who will not bow down to the golden image of material power in the worship of nature or humanity; they have to enter it, bound in the bonds of their own earthly garments, in the chains of their physical nature, and of the power of sin, which clings to them from their birth; they enter, not knowing whether the power of death is or is not to shrivel them up into nothingness; yet they can enter it in hope, as believing in a God who is their God, although a God unseen and infinite. But in the midst of the fire there is One, who comes as a true Son of Man to pass with them through its hottest fury. At His coming the bonds fall from their hands; the fiery death passes by and leaves them unscathed. Of Him even the world sees that His 'form is like the Son of God.' They who follow Him know that not in form, but in reality, He is 'declared to be the Son of God with power by the resurrection from the dead.'[3]

[3] On the whole of this subject see Professor Westcott's *Gospel of the Resurrection*.

CHAPTER VIII.

THE LAW OF MEDIATION AND THE MEDIATION OF CHRIST.

'There is one God and one mediator between God and men, the man Christ Jesus, who gave Himself a ransom for all.'—1 Tim. ii. 5, 6.

I. In these words, in which, almost at the close of his career, St. Paul sums up the main subject of his apostolic preaching, we may trace the second chief phase of the doctrine of the Christ, as it was actually set forth in the first preaching of Christianity. It followed necessarily on the teaching involved in the declaration of the Resurrection; it could not have preceded it, nor perhaps at first have been co-ordinated with it. The earliest preaching (as especially represented in St. Peter), addressed to Jews, naturally took up, in the proclamation of the Resurrection, the fulfilment of Messianic glory and Messianic hopes, rather than the Cross, which, viewed alone and in itself, was a stumbling-block. That proclamation was brought home to men in all its meaning by a teaching which, after emphasising with all possible energy the actual fact of the resurrection, passed on immediately to its significance in relation to the Lord Himself, 'declared' by it 'to be the Son of God with power,' and on still further to its significance to humanity at large, as a demonstration of man's spiritual and immortal life, and a consecration of his bodily nature as a part of his true self. The wisdom of this appointed method of preaching proved itself by results. So proclaiming the resurrection, 'the sound' of the Gospel 'went out' literally 'into all lands, and its words to the ends of the world.' For it came home as a Gospel of good tidings to those who sat trembling under the oppressive burden of physical law, under the blight and cloud of sin, and on the edge of the shadow of death.

The doctrine of mediation.

But soon the thoughts of men began to search into the reason of this inseparable connexion between the resurrection of the Lord Himself and the spiritual life, here and hereafter, of all humanity. That there was such a connexion He Himself had expressly declared, and the first preaching of Christianity had unhesitatingly taken up His word. But on what did it depend? Why was His resurrection so utterly different in its spiritual significance from the resurrection of Lazarus or the translation of Elijah? Each of these, if accepted as true, might be held to show, by an exceptional and miraculous manifestation, what was the true birthright of humanity. For, from the rising of him who had been dead four days, it was clear that the corruption of the body in the grave did not hinder its reunion with the soul; and the translation of Elijah showed how humanity was capable of rising to perfection without passing through the shadow of death. In each there was type and promise. But why was the resurrection of Christ something more than a greater type and a brighter promise? Why was there in it not merely (as was obvious) a greater evidence of glory and power in Him, but an entire difference of meaning; so that He should be declared to be in it, not our example only and our leader, but the 'second Adam,' whose heavenly image all would bear; so that all men should be said to be risen, not with Him, or like Him, but 'in Him'? The question might at first be answered by simple faith in the word of the Master Himself. But as Christianity won its way to the notice of the civilised and sceptical world, it was necessary for the disciples to give to enquirers 'a reason' or 'defence' 'for the hope that was in them.' That reason was contained in the declaration of the fundamental principle of Mediation, embodied in the text in one of those clear-cut maxims in which the Pastoral Epistles delight. 'There is one God;' there speaks the sublime Monotheism of the Old Testament. 'There is one Mediator between God and men, the Man Christ Jesus.' In this declaration, emphasising His humanity, yet distinguishing Him from 'man' generally, we have a doctrine of which we can trace the germ in the Old Testament, but which bears its full fruit in every line of the doctrinal and practical teaching of the New.

It is to be noted that this great principle of mediation actually presented itself in the preaching of the Gospel (as the language of the text suggests) in especial rela- *The doctrine* tion to the mystery of evil, and to the death of our *of the Cross especially* Lord upon the cross as being a deliverance from *preached,* that evil—whether as 'a ransom' or redemption, as it is called in the text, which is an echo of certain recorded words of Christ Himself, or as a 'sacrifice' or 'propitiation,' which name He more solemnly stamped upon it at the institution of the Holy Communion. St. Paul, indeed, at one time summed up his whole preaching of the one Mediator in the celebrated words: 'I determined not to know anything among you save Jesus Christ, and Him crucified.' Under this aspect it showed itself supplementary to the Messianic preaching in the resurrection; for it dealt with that great perplexity of Natural Theology, which in that earlier teaching was touched only by implication. Under this aspect, therefore, it was felt to be especially necessary to the completeness of Gospel revelation.

But it ought never to be forgotten that the idea of mediation extends far beyond the preaching of the Cross. In it the Incarnation, the Atonement, the Resurrection, *but only a* the Ascension, the Intercession, the Judgment to *part of the doctrine of* come, are all included, as the salient points of the *Mediation.* great office of the one Mediator for the salvation of souls. We may even say that the idea of suffering and death is not necessarily involved in the idea of mediation as such, but only belongs to mediation so far as, being exercised in a world like this, it comes into collision with the power of evil. Could we venture to conceive of the first great act of our Lord's humility without the second, and picture to ourselves a manifestation of Himself without either death or resurrection, in which the ascension should present itself simply as the climax of a perfect and glorious life on earth, just as it is represented in His own words: 'I came forth from the Father and am come into the world, again I leave the world and go to the Father'—still His mediation would remain. Still, though without the special adaptation of that mediation to humanity, as oppressed by the power of evil we should have to confess that there is 'one Mediator between God and men, the Man Christ Jesus.'

Now in respect both of the general principle of mediation, and of its special application in an atonement for sin, Christianity, more distinctly than ever, assumes for itself the position of a truth, 'supernatural, not preternatural.' The law of mediation is a law of human nature. The Mediation of the Lord Jesus Christ is preached, first as the highest type of that law, and next as being itself unique and transcendent, passing into regions and exercising powers which our reason can neither discover nor perfectly comprehend.[1] Moreover, the assertion of this unique Mediation is especially directed to grapple practically with that mystery of evil, which unsolved is a terror and a despair to human nature, and yet from the solution of which most religions and philosophies are apt to shrink, and pass by on the other side.

The mediation of Christ supernatural and preternatural.

II. If we consider what mediation really is, all study of human life will show us that some mediation between man and God is a fundamental law of human nature. For mediation (as the very word implies) is the power of one human soul to be the means of spiritual communion between others and God, either by bringing them into new relations with Him, or by renewing to living energy and fruitfulness relations already existing, but as yet dormant or forgotten. Now, since the establishment of the true relation of the soul to the Supreme Power must be, on any hypothesis, a leading element in its right development, it follows that mediation thus conceived is a part—the highest and the most striking exhibition—of the power which is exercised on the growth of the individual soul to its natural perfection by other souls, whether in their individual action or in the collective influence of human society. Of the reality of that power no one could ever

The law of mediation in human life.

---

[1] It is, of course, needless to acknowledge the debt which all study of this subject must owe to Butler's celebrated chapter on Mediation (*Anal.* part ii. c. v.). It might have been sufficient to refer to it, had not the course of Christian theology since Butler's day brought out a larger and higher conception of the Mediatorial work of Christ, and so marked more decisively the points in which it exemplifies, and in which it transcends, the general law of mediation.

reasonably entertain any doubt, and modern thought has brought it out with an extraordinary vividness.

It is exercised in many ways, which, however, fall generally under two categories, according as they affect the outer or the inner life of the individual. In both they take for granted free and responsible action in him, sometimes preceding, sometimes accompanying, sometimes following it. Thus in the outer life *The spiritual power of soul on soul in various phases.* this influence from without may precede all action, by affecting a man's circumstances or opportunities, giving or withholding the things which afford him scope for action, bringing him into new relations with persons, from which follow important results for evil or for good. It may accompany action, to assist or to hinder it, either indirectly by supplying or refusing means, or directly by support or opposition of actual power. It may follow action, stepping in between a man and its visible consequences, saving him from himself when his action is foolish or evil, or robbing him of the proper fruits of action wise and good. So, again, on the inner life this human mediation may act in the same relations to the individual action, by bringing to bear on the mind various influences—by presentation to it of principles of intellectual or moral truth, by the application of motives of hope and fear, by the exercise of personal ascendency or the dominating force of public opinion. But in none of these ways is it, strictly speaking, a compulsion. That it is in some way harmonised with individual freedom and responsibility, in spite of the paradoxical exaggerations of semi-fatalism, we feel sure, although the method and the proportions of that harmony it is often very hard to trace. There are lives in which this external power seems so strong, for good or for evil, as to overbear the individual freedom, and (as we fancy) to weaken or destroy responsibility. There are lives, on the other hand, in which the internal force, moral or intellectual, seems either to grow unaided from without, or to overcome all external influences, almost without effort, by a sturdy self-assertion. But still the coexistence of the two powers remains a fact, acknowledged in universal language and practice. The growth of the soul we call its 'education,' that is, the drawing out by external influence of capacities which lie within; and though of that education some part depends on simple contact with the world of things, yet far the largest part is due to action upon the soul, conscious or unconscious, of the world of persons. We are being educated from the cradle to the grave—by fathers, teachers, guardians in our youth, in manhood by the great leaders of thought and by the spirit of the age. Yet all the while our freedom remains, and with it our responsibility to that perfect judgment, which judges a man within the limits of his opportunities, 'according to that which he hath, not according to that which he hath not.'

This action of others upon the soul, affecting it as a whole, must tell in different degrees on all its three great relations to self, to man, and to God, although it is most patent and effective in the second sphere. Now, mediation, as commonly understood, is that form of it which deals with the highest relation—the relation to God—telling, both directly and indirectly, not only on the moral and intellectual, but also on the spiritual life. It is strange, it might seem all but incredible, that it should be able to exercise any power in this sphere, where man stands face to face with his Creator. But this abstract improbability vanishes before actual experience. There can be no doubt that, by all these means of influence both on the outer and on the inner life, men can so act on the intellectual and moral and spiritual nature of others, as to aid in bringing them to the knowledge, faith, and love of God, in which a religious life consists; and if they believe in God as the ultimate Worker of all things, they will hold that they do this simply by bringing others within the reach of some light and grace of God, which otherwise they could not enjoy. This work upon the souls of others they can perform, they can neglect, or they can oppose. As they can be workers with God, so they can stand aloof, or be workers against Him. But, whether used, neglected, or misused, the reality of their power cannot be questioned. Every man may be in his degree what (for example) the great lawgiver and deliverer of Israel is called by St. Paul, a 'mediator' between God and the souls which He has made for Himself. It is, indeed, true, that in this highest relation the influence over the inner

Mediation the highest form of this power.

one by a network of spiritual ties, strengthened by mutual needs, and quickened by mutual affections. These ties may be what we call 'natural,' such as the ties of family, nation, race. They may be ties, like those of friendship or marriage, which are self-chosen on the ground of harmony of character, but which, although self-chosen, yet carry with them duties, such that it is not necessarily within our power to relinquish them. But in any case it is in virtue of the unity which these ties produce that this action of man on man, of which mediation is the highest spiritual phase, is possible. This action, moreover, for anything like perfection, seems to require actual sympathy, which is a conscious recognition of this unity, implying a certain harmony of nature, distinct from mere identity, through which one soul is able to enter into the thoughts and feelings of another, while still keeping a certain reserve of what is peculiarly its own. Generally we may say that our power to mediate for others varies with our degree of unity with them, both in the actual relationships of life and in the recognition of those relationships by sympathy. Hence it belongs especially to the more advanced conditions of human society; it is almost rudimentary in the loose cohesion of barbarism; it increases every day in formidable power as civilisation grows in its complex unity.

(b) Mediation dependent on unity between man and man.

Now this power of action upon other souls, of which we trace the most striking exemplification in mediation, belongs to human nature as such. From the beginning man was not alone; even as regards his fellow-men no man 'lived or died to himself.' In itself, therefore, like the exercise of all natural powers, it is a privilege and a delight. It is, indeed, one of the highest privileges and the most exquisite delights of which human nature is capable; for it is that energy of the soul which bears the nearest likeness to the spiritual creation and sustentation of the soul by God. Nothing can be farther from the truth than the notion that mediation, as such, is made necessary only by the existence of evil in the world, or that it necessarily implies suffering in the mediator himself. In a condition free from all evil—a paradise or a heaven—humanity would still be one even in its relation to God; the

(c) Mediation does not in itself imply suffering.

life is more circumscribed than in any other, by the individual freedom on the one hand, by God's direct action upon the soul on the other. At times it seems to be scattered like a cloud by the sudden meeting of these two powers. But it is real. From it more than from any other influence men may shrink, in fear of too great a responsibility; yet to exercise it and to feel it are necessities of spiritual life.

Now of this power of mediation, in whatever sphere it be exercised, two things are clear.

First, if we believe in God at all as the Creator and Ruler of the world, it follows necessarily that this spiritual influence is His ordinance; that in exercising it we have a mission from Him, so that we are His representatives; that the power which seems to be ours is His gift, simply ministered by us; that, just in proportion to our knowledge of Him, our likeness to Him, our communion with Him, we are able to wield it for the spiritual benefit and salvation of others; and that, even then, it depends ultimately for success upon His action upon their souls, inasmuch as it serves mainly to bring them within the scope of that divine influence, and then stands aside that He may work all in all. This must be true of all forms of influence upon the spiritual growth of others; but obviously it is most distinctly true of the highest phase of that influence, in which it bears directly upon the relation to God. There we are most vividly conscious of the free individual soul on the one hand, of God Himself as the one great Worker on the other; and of our own action as merely secondary and intermediate, able at most to break down barriers between the soul and Him, or to rouse it to the knowledge and acceptance of His working. Hence the word mediator is strictly applicable. The mediator is simply one who makes himself a medium between God and man, through which the current of spiritual communion may pass. Viewed from the side of man, he is the representative of God; and this he cannot be, unless he himself has spiritual unity with God, in fuller degree of perfection than those whom he would perfect and save.

(a) Mediation an ordinance of God.

But, on the other hand, it is to be observed that the whole power of affecting the spiritual development of others depends on the fact that mankind is bound together in higher natures would still find their true mission and their highest bliss in aiding the lower and weaker in their approach to Him.

But it is true that, wherever mediation is exercised within the sphere of our actual experience, in a world (that is) which groans under the burden of evil, it does bring with it, in different degrees, labour, struggle, suffering. For wherever it implies conflict with sin, either in the individual souls, over which it has special power of influence, or over society as a whole, those who exercise it must be ready to undergo suffering, in proportion to the greatness of their influence and the purity of their own character. This suffering is due to various causes. It is undergone, partly because each soul, in the attempt to save others, will have to bear some of the external consequences of sin, which otherwise would fall on them—which to them (be it noted) would be punishment, which to the soul of him who saves them are suffering, but in no true sense punishment; partly because, through sympathy with the sinner, it enters into his spiritual state, and feels—what he cannot feel with anything like the same perfection—the horror of sin, its deadliness to man, and its outrage of the righteousness and love of God; partly because its action kindles a positive hatred and antagonism of the powers of evil, perhaps in the soul which it would save, perhaps in others who would prevent its salvation. Every day the experience of fathers, teachers, brothers, children, shows us these penalties so plainly, that men have come to recognise them as in the actual order of the world a thing of course, and wrongly to infer that they belong to mediation as such, and are the measure of its reality and value. But it is not so. The power of mediation in any case is a part of the dignity and glory of human nature; it is only because the world is sinful, and just so far as it is sinful, that the crown of this dignity is a crown of thorns.

Therefore it is an error, though a natural and even a noble error, to suppose that the suffering of mediation is always an exact measure and test of the reality of its efficacy for others; and accordingly to seek suffering in itself, and to fancy that one who suffers for others must necessarily, just in proportion to his suffering, win the power of saving and helping them. So far is this from the truth, that the sorrow of mediation never destroys its natural joy; mostly it is entirely subordinate to it. Of all who strive against sin at the inevitable cost of suffering it may still be said that, in their measure, 'for the joy set before them they endure the cross, and despise the shame.'

But while the existence of sin chequers the joy of mediation with the dark shadow of suffering, yet it also makes media-
<small>(e) and is made more necessary by sin.</small> tion itself infinitely more necessary. Perhaps, in actual fact, it is generally either sin, or its consequence in sorrow, sickness, and death, which calls out the daily mediation of man for man. Certainly it is in meeting these evils that we find the chief function of human charity in the lower spheres of being; nor is it otherwise in the mediation which concerns the higher relation to God. If every soul was sinless, and therefore strong and happy, as it would need but little aid from charity in its earthly life, so it would be possible to conceive (though even then the inference would be more than doubtful) that each could live its spiritual life alone before God, working out unaided its appointed work for Him, needing no companionship in the spiritual communion with Him. But, when sin has come between the soul and God, then in the gloomy consciousness of guilt and in the misery of spiritual bondage, it most needs the hand of a brother to raise, to cheer, to guide it back to the house of the Father; and that brother's hand is powerful in its beneficent work, just in proportion to his own sinlessness and the perfection of his own communion with God.

Such is the power and such are the conditions of human mediation. It can be exercised by all, but in very different
<small>(f) Mediation especially belongs to the leaders of men.</small> degrees. There is the ordinary mediation of every day—the power by which individuals, living or dead, the spirit of the age, and the inherited traditions of the past, tell upon our spiritual state. There is the exceptional mediation which belongs to the great leaders of humanity. How extraordinary and almost terrible is the power exercised by these few choice spirits, not only on the intellectual, but on the moral and spiritual

life of thousands whom they never see or know, of generations yet unborn! By the teaching, the acts, the life, of a mere handful of men, the whole world seems spiritually to live or die. They may do infinite service in bringing it to the knowledge of God, and to a spiritual communion with Him, or they may, as apostles of godlessness, stand between God and His creatures, and cast a long shadow over the faith of ages. To these leading spirits—'inspired men,' as we rightly term them—belong accordingly at once the highest joy of mediation and the heaviest burden of sorrow. In both they are alone, knowing what we ordinary men cannot know. Not only a power of mediation in general, but an exceptional power of mediation in special men, must be held to be a law of Nature—that is, a part of the dispensation of God, carried on by mingled equality and inequality of gifts and powers, all capable of showing forth His glory, because all capable of subserving the spiritual good of mankind.

All this is matter of actual experience. It seems to prove incontestably that mediation between God and man is a law of human nature. The theory of a bare individualism will not stand in any sphere of human life. The notion that (to use a common phrase) each man's religion is 'a thing between himself and God,' in which he cannot affect others or be affected by them, must, if it be taken literally, be scouted as a vulgar error. It is indeed true that mediation (as Butler long ago reminded us) belongs to an intermediate phase of the spiritual life, perhaps not to its beginning, certainly not to its close. In the end, every man must stand before the judgment-seat of God, to give account for himself. But in its own sphere it is a power real and great, on which largely depend the growth of each individual soul and the spiritual progress of humanity. A religion which includes no principle of mediation in its creed is clearly out of harmony with human nature, and especially unsuited to the world as it is.

III. But it is next to be considered how far the mediation set forth in Christianity, while it exemplifies this general law, is itself unique and supernatural.

Here, indeed, lies the crucial point of separation between the thoughtful Christian and the thoughtful unbeliever. No man can question that, in actual fact, the life and death of Jesus of Nazareth have been a high—perhaps the highest—example of mediation in the spiritual sphere. They have already affected the religious life of millions, and they still maintain their power so to affect the growing life of humanity. We read how Napoleon, dwelling on the actual kingdom of Christ over the souls of men, declared it to be a thing unique and inconceivable, infinitely transcending the highest examples of the power of earthly empire over men's bodies and minds, of which he of all men best knew the capacities and the limits. Most men, moreover, will allow that this kingdom is in some sense exercised of moral right ; for they accept His truth and His inspiration as the highest, truest, noblest, which the world has seen. There are, indeed, those who, struck with the fact of His own self-assertion, and rightly seeing that no wise and good man, as merely man, would have ventured upon it, have half-unwillingly questioned His goodness and truth. There are those who, in hatred of what Christianity actually is, have broken out against its Founder in virulence of coarse or refined blasphemy. But these are few; the world at large acknowledges that, in a very high degree, He has proved Himself a mediator between God and man. Nor is the Cross always a stumbling-block. Men will allow even that the suffering of Calvary was, in some sense, and a very peculiar sense, a blow to the power of sin, by the knowledge of which thousands of souls have risen superior to the sins which beset them. But the Gospel calls Him not a mediator, not the greatest of mediators, but the 'one Mediator.' It asserts for Him a power at once natural, as accordant with human nature, and supernatural, as infinitely transcending it.

<small>Mediation of Christ supernatural and absolute.</small>

<small>Limitation of all human mediation :</small> For it is easy to see the limitation of all merely human mediation, even the highest.

<small>(a) in scope;</small> I do not refer only to the obvious limitation of this power in any one man, or in any age or race, in respect of space and time. It is seen at once that men and races have their day and cease to be, and, in great degree, though seldom completely, their thoughts and deeds perish with them. Even while their power lives, it extends

CHAP. VIII.   THE GOSPEL OF MEDIATION.   157

over a certain area, great or small, beyond which mankind seems quite untouched by it. But it might be held that the race endures, and that the limited influence of individuals is thrown into the stock of the universal and undying power of mankind. Hence it is of more consequence to observe that all human mediation, whether of the individual or of the race, is definitely limited in the very nature of its power.

It is exercised both over the outward circumstances and over the inner life of man. But there is a marked difference in its character in these two different spheres of influence. *(b) in nature.*

In relation to the first, it can touch what may be called, in the widest sense, the circumstances of a man's life without the consent of his will. It can affect, for example, almost indefinitely his physical well-being, and even, as in the transmission of hereditary characteristics, his constitution of body and mind. It can give or withhold opportunities and aids of spiritual growth. Both by individuals and society this is done every day. As the world grows older, it seems that this power of influence grows with it; till we are even puzzled at times to judge how far individual responsibility remains, in apparent absence of all opportunity for good, and presence of irresistible temptation to evil. *In relation to circumstances.*

But if it is to act upon the spirit itself, it must be by consent of the will. For this action on the spirit is carried on partly by the free influence of principle, in the presentation to the soul of truth, of right, of beauty, of holiness—in other words, in the revelation to it of the attributes of God—partly by the half-compulsory influence of what we call motives, by hope of reward, or by fear of punishment—partly by that subtle ascendency, mostly personal, though in some degree belonging to the spirit of the age, which works like a magic spell, sometimes through sympathy and enthusiasm, sometimes through awe and fear, so as to exercise a marvellous dominion over the soul. But in all cases the will must consent. Men may shut their eyes to the inculcation of principles, either deliberately or idly. They may steel themselves against hope and fear; and as they grow older, they do so more and *In relation to the soul itself.*

more. They may resist the power of personal ascendency, and defy the spirit of their age. Just so far as they do so, this mediation, obviously far the deepest and truest, absolutely fails.

These limitations of human mediation are often a cause of infinite sorrow to every true servant of God. But it is clear that they are the safeguards of individual freedom; and any system which in theory or practice overbears them is unnatural in itself, and deadly in its fruits.

But we may see that these limitations are imposed by the limitation of the unity of the mediator with God and with man. Because he is not perfectly one with God, he cannot bring the Divine power to bear in all its perfection on the soul; the fulness of the stream is limited by the finiteness of the channel through which it flows. Because he is not perfectly one with man, there are recesses of human nature into which his influence cannot penetrate; and even where it does reach, the contact is not absolutely perfect. If both these limitations could be removed—if in any Son of man the unity with God could be perfect, so that the Divine power both over the outer and the inner life could be exercised by him without measure—if, again, the unity with man were perfect, so that he could draw men's souls wholly to himself, to enlighten them by his knowledge, inspire them with his own spirit, and conform them to his own likeness—and if at the same time it were universal, unfettered by space, number, or time—then these limitations of mediation would vanish utterly, and his mediation, both before and after the consent of will, might be absolutely perfect. But obviously such a power as this can belong to no created being. Such a mediator as this must be not merely the Son of man. He who is the one Mediator between God and man can be none other than the Son of God.

Dependent on limited unity with God and man.

Now this is exactly the kind of mediation which the Gospel claims for the Lord Jesus Christ; and this inference as to His nature is precisely the inference which it draws. It represents Him as, on the one hand, having perfect unity with God, and exercising the Divine power without measure or limit; and, on the other, as

The mediation of Christ unlimited,

(in His own words) 'drawing all men unto Him,' and having a universal and perfect unity in spirit with them. Sometimes, as, for example, in St. Paul's four great Epistles to the Corinthians, Galatians, and Romans, this power is described as applied to the individual. Every man, considered by himself, is said 'to be in Christ,' ' to be buried and risen with Him,' ' to put on Christ,' as the beginning, the progress, and the end of his spiritual life. Sometimes, as in the Epistles of St. Paul's first Captivity, He is said to 'gather humanity,' as a whole, to Himself, to be the Head, of which the Church, coextensive with all humanity in capacity and promise, is the one body. But, whether we regard the individual or the corporate life, it is in virtue of this perfect unity with God and man that He is the one Mediator. It is through this universal and perfect Mediation, possible to no created being, that His Divine nature is contemplated and gradually understood.

IV. Now this Mediation, strictly speaking, describes the whole office of the Christ, as (to use the common definition, drawn from the ancient covenant) Prophet, King, and Priest. It applies to His prophetic revelation of God. Because He is one with us, we see God (so to speak) through the eyes of Jesus Christ; because He is one with God, we see God manifested perfectly in Him. It applies to His power over the soul as King, by grace here, in the glory of heaven hereafter; for this can belong only to One who is the perfect representative of God, and only because He is in us are we said to be already risen from sin and death to the new life, and even ascended into heaven. *as Prophet, King, and Priest.*

But it was especially in the light of His office as Priest, offering Himself to God as a sacrifice for sin, that the mediation of Christ was at first regarded, and has always since been regarded, in the preaching of the Gospel. For indeed this followed by a spiritual necessity. When, through the preaching of the Resurrection in all its meaning, the spirituality of man was recognised in its present and its future reality, there followed naturally a strong conviction of sin as sin. From the knowledge of what man's nature ought to be in perfect communion with God, came the sense of the evil actually *but especially as Priest.*

marring the spirituality of that nature, and felt to be a wilful breach of that Divine communion. From the same knowledge there followed also the conviction that this evil was not an integral part of human nature, nor even an inevitable disease, to be palliated and forgotten as much as possible, but a power which ought to be, could be, must be, overcome. Hence the very light of the Gospel, thrown upon human nature, first cast the dark shadow of the consciousness of sin, and then lighted up that shadow with the promise of the conquest of sin. It is by no accident that the solemn and even awful teaching of the Epistle to the Romans on this terrible subject stands in close connexion with the glad proclamation of the Gospel of the Resurrection. The special aspect of the mediation of Christ, which shone out in the light of the proclamation of Christ risen, was that which represented it as taking away sin.

Now in the conviction of sin there are two forms of consciousness.

There is the sense of the corruption and bondage of sin, as destroying the spiritual capacities of man's nature—felt in evil habit, especially in relation to sensual sin, as an unnatural power enslaving the will. No one who has to study evil in its concentrated intensity in the world, or who reads his own soul under the pitiless light of remorse, will hold that the terrible picture of that bondage in the seventh chapter of the Epistle to the Romans is unreal or overcharged. It is a bondage created by man for himself, intensified by the accumulation of inherited evil. It cannot be broken, independently of himself, without destruction of responsibility; yet by himself it seems incapable of being broken.

(a) The bondage of sin.

It is in relation to this consciousness that the mediation of Christ is, in the words of the text, regarded as a Redemption or ransom. Under this aspect the work of salvation is viewed as starting from the side of God. The Son of God is represented as coming down from Heaven, in order, by the unique power of an unlimited mediation, to enter into the souls of men, and thus to give to each that power, which in itself it could not have, of breaking the bondage of sin, and escaping the

Christ's mediation as redemption.

spiritual death in which it ends. It is declared that, in order to gain the power to deliver, the love of God sent His Son to live and to die as man. His earthly life and His death alike constitute this price of ransom. The soul, which had cried out in hopeless bondage, ' O wretched man that I am! Who shall deliver me from the body of this death?' is bidden to answer, in the knowledge of Christ's redemption, ' I thank God through Jesus Christ our Lord.'

But besides the consciousness of the bondage of sin, turning the eyes of the soul upon itself, there is the sense of the guilt or sinfulness of sin, turning the eyes upward to the outraged majesty of God. Can sin—which is resistance to the all-righteous Will, keeping all creation in harmony and safety—can it be forgiven? The contemplation of that will, as expressed in physical law, seems to cry emphatically, ' No! The soul that sinneth, it shall die;' here no simple repentance can annul the doom; seldom can after-exertion avert it. The contemplation of the same will, as expressed in the laws of humanity, seems to give an uncertain sound. On the one hand, stern law declares that, for the sake of all, there must be penalty; those who are burdened with the charge of the welfare of society must punish, even though they weep for the necessity. On the other hand, the love of a father forgives not seven times, but seventy times seven; and even the king has the privilege of saying, ' I will chastise him and let him go.' The two voices seem then to contradict each other. There is room for hope, hardly for certainty. The question still stands, Can we dare to say with confidence, ' The Lord hath put away thy sin. Thou shalt not die'? Moreover, in this uncertainty whether sin can be forgiven simply on the repentance of the sinner, the law of ordinary mediation seems absolutely to fail us. For the one thing which no man can bear for another is individual responsibility, individual guilt. The visible consequences of evil-doing may be warded off or borne for us; but as to the guilt of sin, declared and visited by God's judgment, the Psalmist's declaration simply expresses the irreversible verdict of man's conscience: ' No man may deliver his brother, nor make agreement with God for him.' Alone before God, man has

M

to face the great question, 'Can sin be forgiven?' If he feels unable to save himself, he can turn to no human mediation to save him.

Now to that great question the rite of sacrifice—so strangely universal among men, and in the Old Testament sanctioned, guarded, and purified—suggested an answer. For when we look at the essential idea of sacrifice, in which it differs from all other acts of worship, we find it in the idea of an atonement for sin, both ordained and accepted by God, but offered by man. It could suggest an answer; it could not do more. For it needed little spiritual discernment to understand that 'the blood of bulls and of goats could not take away sin.' The substitution of the victim for the sacrificer implied in all sin-offerings, unless it represents something as yet mysterious, is purely arbitrary, and may easily lead to gross superstition. The sacrifice, therefore, might suggest the need and promise of a true atonement. But it left the great problem still unsolved.

<small>The rite of sacrifice.</small>

Moreover, contradicting, as it seemed, the impossibility of all human mediation, the sacrifice involved the action of a mediator. For the sacrifice could not be offered except by a priest; and every priest, claiming to be ordained and consecrated by God, and yet to be the representative of man in the access to God, is necessarily a mediator. Yet no priest can be really and spiritually one with the countless offerers of sacrifice; still less can he be one with God, so as to open to them the communion with God. Clearly the priest, like the sacrifice, could only be the type of some greater reality; and if, forgetting this, he claimed to be a true mediator in relation to the inalienable guilt of sin, the claim was simply usurpation and superstition. But if there could be a great High Priest, who could unite all humanity to Himself, and, being sinless, yet assume their sins as His own—if at the same time He could be one with God, so as to open to them through Himself a living way to the Divine presence—if He could be at once Priest and Victim, not offering an arbitrary substitute for men, but offering in Himself the humanity which He had taken upon Him—then the answer, which could before be

<small>The mediation of priesthood.</small>

only suggested, might be given. There might be a propitiation for the sins of the world.

It is, therefore, in this second light that the mediation of our Lord is also represented. Here it is (so to speak) viewed from the side of man. As the true Son of Man, representing all the human souls with which He is one, bearing death as the penalty of their sins, bearing their sins in His ineffable sympathy, bearing the concentrated enmity of the Prince of Evil and his servants, He is declared to offer the sacrifice which His Father's love both ordains and accepts. Emphatically He is the Mediator between God and man, because He is 'the Man Christ Jesus.' *Christ's mediation as propitiation.*

Such is a brief sketch of the second great phase of Christian doctrine, declaring the mediation of Christ in relation especially to the great mystery of evil. In itself it is declared to be a mystery, beyond our thought either to have conceived, or even now fully to comprehend. Why salvation should be wrought in this way, how it was wrought out, we cannot know. If we believe it, it is only from the word of Jesus Christ Himself; and why we should believe that word must be hereafter considered.

V. But we are at present concerned with the relation of this phase of Christian teaching to Natural Theology. Again it fulfils the condition of being supernatural, and yet accordant to the natural. While it goes beyond all human reason, it yet accords with all men's deeper thoughts on this great subject. *The bearing of this doctrine on Natural Theology.*

For it recognises evil as really sin, not only against our own nature, but against the will of God. It holds that it brings with it a spiritual bondage, which for ourselves we cannot break. It holds that it must bring down judgment —the death of separation from Him on whom our spiritual life hangs. It teaches that, man being what he is, free and responsible, sin cannot be taken away, unless humanity works together with God, and in some way bears the just penalty of sin. Then, finally, it takes up the great law of mediation, itself unquestionably a law of human nature, and raises it to that perfection in Christ, which alone can make it availing for the atonement for the sins of the world.

This relation of the Gospel to the Natural Theology of men is singularly striking as a preparation for the consideration of the direct evidences on the ground of which it claims our faith. It is no slight matter that, if it be rejected, no other solution of the mystery of evil can adequately take its place, either to meet the deeper speculations of the enquiring mind, or to give practical strength to conquer sin, and to defy death in sure and certain hope.

Not yet, indeed, has the doctrine of Christ reached its full development. But naturally, in a Gospel to a world like this, the truth of mediation assumes a paramount importance, and stamps Christianity with the sign of the cross. For under the cross, if we believe all that the Gospel declares it to imply, we learn to face, without subterfuge and without despair, the darkest mysteries of life. Although the sun of God's love be shining still, there is a darkness over the earth of ignorance, of sin, of death. Through that darkness the cry of humanity goes up, ' My God, why hast Thou forsaken me ? ' It is a cry half of despair, half of faith—of despair in the sense of separation from Him—of faith in the sense that He is our God still. It is under the cross that we especially feel that darkness, and hear that bitter cry. But it is only there that we hear the word of victory, ' It is finished,' and know that, sin notwithstanding, death is but the receiving of the spirit into the hands of the Father. This is what we need to know in this life. It is enough to rest upon; we are content, even if, for what lies beyond it and beneath it, we have to wait till ' we know even as we are known.'

<small>The message of the Cross to humanity.</small>

CHAPTER IX.

THE REVELATION OF GOD IN MAN—CHRIST AS THE WORD.

'In the beginning was the Word, and the Word was with God, and the Word was God.... And the Word was made flesh, and dwelt [tabernacled] among us.'—John i. 1, 14.

I. In these words of St. John, which, both historically and ideally, form the completion of the whole cycle of the New Testament teaching, we find the fullest expression of the doctrine which is the ultimate foundation of the Gospel. On it rest the great secondary strata of Christian teaching, and to it, having passed through these, we must necessarily come at last. *The final doctrine of Christ as the Word.*

There was a gradual progress by which, in the wisdom of God, the whole truth of Christianity emerged to the eyes of men, growing upon them continually as they were able to bear it. The great facts of the Resurrection and Ascension were made the proclamation in Christ as risen, first of the perfection of Messianic promise, and then, as implied in this, of the true spirituality of man in Him and through Him, beginning here, and passing through death to the glory at the right hand of God. Then, when, accepting these truths, the mind of man sought for the key to the mystery they involved, the Gospel set forth the Mediation of Christ, at once according with, and infinitely transcending, the general law of mediation in human nature. In this was set forth explicitly what in the spirituality of man is implied—the recognition of unity between God and humanity, especially manifested in the removal, by one great atonement, of the bondage and the guilt of sin. Now, in these two phases of preaching it is clear that the figure of the Lord rises before us, first as the true Son of Man, crowned with the triple diadem of Messiahship, in whom we see what humanity can be in perfect unity with God; next, as at once true Son of Man, and yet something infinitely *The previous stages of teaching.*

above man—'the One Mediator between men and God' in a regeneration and redemption of the whole world which no mere man could dare to undertake.

Then comes at last the inevitable question: What does all this imply as to His nature? If He is the 'Son of Man,' if He is more than man, what is He in Himself?

The answer is in some degree already given by implication in these previous declarations. There is claimed for Him, as the true Messiah, a kingship over all mankind in every age and in every land till the end of time— extending beyond that outward life, which earthly royalty is content to rule, to the inner life of the soul, and claiming there the allegiance of unlimited faith and love— destined not only to continue through this life, but to manifest itself anew at the resurrection to judgment, and to determine the eternity which follows it. What must this imply? Every instinct of freedom and responsibility revolts against attribution of such power to any created being. To claim it for a mere man, even if he be in the highest possible degree inspired by God, and by that inspiration the noblest, wisest, purest of men, is an obvious and gross idolatry. If we conceive of a superhuman being, standing highest in the created hierarchy of heaven, and offer such homage to him, still the answer must come: 'I am thy fellow-servant; worship God.' Even in the Old Testament, as the conception of the Messiah grew out and defined itself before the eyes of Israel, there were constantly heaped upon His unquestioned humanity epithets which could belong only to God. When the full truth of the Resurrection and all that it implied burst upon the doubting apostle, we do not wonder that the earlier confessions, 'Thou art the King of Israel,' 'Thou art the Christ, the Son of the living God,' finally merged themselves in the transcendent confession, 'My Lord and my God.' Trace this line of doctrine alone, till it culminates in the declaration, 'All power is committed unto Me in heaven and earth;' 'Make all nations My disciples;' 'Teach them to observe all things whatsoever I have commanded you.' 'Lo! I am with you always'—not in memory, but in living power—'till the end of the world.' What must the conclusion be? Either with the Jews to cast stones at

(*a*) The significance of universal kingship.

the blasphemer, or to fall down and worship in Christ the indwelling presence of God.

But still more decisive is the significance of the deeper conception of the 'one Mediator between God and man.' Grant to the full the reality and value of human mediation, yet between the individual soul and its ultimate relations to God who can intervene? The burden of responsibility, and the guilt and penalty of sin, no created being can take from us. A power over man, even for salvation, absolute and unlimited, is inconceivable in man. There are times, again and again, when, in the strong yearning of compassion and love, we would perhaps die to win such power over one who is dear to us as our own soul. But it cannot be; we must 'let that alone for ever.' We need, therefore, only think what it means to declare that for all the millions of human souls, in their perfect individuality and infinite variety, there is One who is the absolute Representative of God and the only Being who can lead them to the Father—who has borne their sins and taken them away—who can breathe into every redeemed soul the grace of a new life—and all this for ever, in this world and in the next. We ask in wonder, 'Who can this be?' Can He be a man—an angel—a Being above angels and archangels, highest in the order of Creation? No! He must be One who can say, 'I and the Father are one;' 'Thou, Father, art in Me, and I in Thee;' and therefore all men can ' be one in us.' *(b) The significance of universal mediation.*

Ultimately, therefore, both these conceptions of the Christ lead up inevitably to the declaration of Godhead in Him. Perhaps only through them could this declaration be understood. The idea of 'God in man' is so tremendous an idea, if it be seriously pursued along any line of thought which brings the infinite into contrast with the finite, that only gradually, through practical induction rather than abstract speculation, it dawned upon the soul. Men learned to trust in the Christ, and then through infinite trust they came to worship. They learned to pray to Christ, and in that prayer they felt and knew His Godhead. But at last a time came at the close of the apostolic age, when the eyes of human thought were bent *(c) The ultimate declarations.*

in the deepest earnestness on the Christ, and the very air was full of speculations of all kinds as to His relation to God, seeking to bridge over by Gnostic theory the gulf between the finite and the infinite. Then at last came forth such full declaration as we read in the text: 'He was in the beginning,' 'He was God.' 'In Him the Godhead tabernacled in human flesh.'

This passage is quoted from St. John; but the idea must not be supposed to be peculiar to him. The theory of a Petrine, a Pauline, a Johannine Gospel, as distinct, and even in part divergent, from one another, will not stand against any careful study of the New Testament, unless, indeed, we arbitrarily reject as spurious whatever will not square with our theory. The various phases of teaching melt into each other. Just as St. Peter's first proclamation of the risen Lord leads on to the thought of the mediation in the Atonement, so St. Paul's characteristic preaching of the one Mediator changes in the later Epistles, and bears a strong likeness to this full doctrine of St. John. Thus, for example, in the Epistle to the Colossians, written clearly in view of early Gnostic speculations of many emanations from God, of which Jesus was but one—speculations strangely mingled with the last mystical forms of Judaism—we cannot but observe the emphasis with which St. Paul passes on from the thought of the mediation of the Christ, 'in whom we have redemption through His blood, the remission of our sins,' to speak of Him, in the same breath, as 'the Image of the invisible God,' 'first-born before all creation' ($\pi\rho\omega\tau\acute{o}\tau o\kappa o\varsigma$ $\pi\acute{a}\sigma\eta\varsigma$ $\kappa\tau\acute{\iota}\sigma\epsilon\omega\varsigma$), 'Creator of all things in heaven and earth;' 'in whom all things consist.' Similarly in the Epistle to the Hebrews, belonging probably to about the same period, and written, as all criticism shows, not by St. Paul's hand, but under his inspiration, we observe that, while its main object is to work out in detail the doctrine of the mediation of the true High Priest and the true Victim, yet it goes down to the ultimate truth in words uniting to the glow of adoration the clear precision of a creed. It speaks of the Son as (to use the strict translation of the original) the 'emanation of the Divine glory, the visible expression of the essence of God,' 'through whom the

The late Epistles of St. Paul.

worlds were made,' and who 'upholds all by the word of His power.'[1] In both these remarkable passages it is clear that all which has been implied in universal kingship and in universal mediation is visibly assuming a clear explicitness, as the time and the circumstances advance, and as the great Apostle of the Gentiles draws towards the close of his ministry.

But history tells us that there was one apostle who survived, like an old giant of the forest amidst the trees of a younger generation, for at least thirty years after the day when St. Peter died upon the cross, and St. Paul's head fell on the road to Ostia. St. John in his old age occupied an exalted place in a Church, now covering the whole Roman empire, rather as a teacher of established truth than a preacher winning his way against ignorance and error. He (it has been said), and he only, had a 'school' of disciples. To him we naturally look for the full expression of the ultimate truth of the Gospel. Nor do we look in vain. As we open his writings, the very style, both of tone and of idea, indicates a 'going on to perfection;' it belongs, in its calmness and precision, to the full development of what had long been gradually unfolding itself. His Gospel, obviously in intention and substance supplemental to the rest, records the self-revelation of our Lord, not, as in Galilee and to the multitude, by indirect witness of miracle and authority, but to the leaders of Jewish learning and Jewish thought at Jerusalem, or to the inner circle of His disciples, by the distinct testimony of His word. Yet he leaves not even this without comment. In the opening of his Epistle, and in the preface to the Gospel, gravely, thoughtfully, unmistakably, with all the simplicity of an undoubting certitude, he uncovers to us the ultimate foundation of Christianity in the Deity of the one King and the one Mediator, the Lord Jesus Christ.

II. This final development is marked by the phrase,

The teaching of St. John.

---

[1] See Col. i. 14–17; Heb. i. 2, 3. In the former passage the translation given of πρωτότοκος πάσης κτίσεως might be doubtful if we considered merely the words themselves, but is put beyond all doubt by consideration of the context. In the latter, if the ἀπαύγασμα τῆς δόξης might be construed as mere Gnostic emanation, the χαρακτὴρ τῆς ὑποστάσεως can be nothing less than the visible manifestation of the Godhead itself.

unused elsewhere in the New Testament, in which he expresses the nature of the Christ. He is the 'Word of God.'

The title is not drawn from the series of Messianic revelations in the Old Testament. For they started from the side of man, gradually ascending to a dignity and a glory far above the level of the earth, but still emphasising the humanity of the Messiah. They might be accepted and woven into some Gnostic theory of emanations. St. John's phrase starts from the side of God. Historically it has a double parentage, from the peculiar and exclusive faith of the Jew, and from the Greek philosophy, pervading and moulding the thought of the civilised world.

The origin of the name 'the Word of God.'

On the one hand it is in idea the descendant of the impersonation of the Divine 'wisdom' in the philosophic books. Who can refuse to trace the first dawn of the noonday of St. John's teaching in the words of the Book of Proverbs (viii. 22-30) in which Wisdom declares:

(a) The 'Wisdom' of the Old Testament.

' The Lord possessed me in the beginning of His way,
' Before the works of old.
' I was set up from everlasting,
' From the beginning, or ever the earth was.'
' When He prepared the heaven, I was there;
' When He set a circle on the face of the deep.'
' I was by Him, as one brought up with Him:
' I was daily His delight, rejoicing always before Him.'

It is, indeed, but a faint dawn, which might pass away as a mere poetic imagination, or which might brighten into a steady light of truth. But, whatever it was, it belonged to heaven, not to earth. The 'wisdom of God' in the abstract is His creative design and dispensation to man. Hence this wisdom personified shadows out a manifestation of God in some Being, through whom the worlds were made, and by whose power they are sustained.[2] As yet there is no hint that this manifestation of God should be in man, such as is the leading idea of all the Messianic predictions. Vaguer, accordingly, and more shadowy than they, the revelation is

[2] In the Palestinian Targums this idea is carried out in the use of the actual phrase 'the Word of God,' as a gloss for the name 'God,' in describing His manifested Presence on earth. This 'Word' is the embodiment of the Divine 'Wisdom.'

more incontestably divine. This 'wisdom' might or might not be a distinctly personal manifestation, but it was certainly a manifestation of God Himself.

On the other side, the title of the 'Word of God' (as it is best known to us through Philo) bears the impress of the Greek thought of the Platonic school. That thought, deeply realising in man a spiritual insight into the invisible, recognised great principles (ἰδέαι) of truth, of right, of beauty, which the soul did not create for itself, but on which it gazed, as the eye gazes on the light, till the very sight kindled the love of them in the soul, and transformed the soul itself to their likeness. Those who, like Socrates and Plato, united this conception with a certain faith in a living God, ventured perhaps to recognise those principles as His attributes, certainly to speak of them as living and energetic powers in the creation and the guidance of the world. So far they advanced towards the conception of a manifestation of the Divine, which might bridge over the gulf between the Infinite and Ultimate Being and the phenomenal world of finite existences. So far, but no further; and even so far their advance was hesitating and their conceptions vague and impalpable. But at Alexandria this fundamental principle of Greek thought was taken up by those Jewish teachers who had learned in the Old Testament to know God with a clearness of which Plato never dreamt. Whatever ambiguity might attach in common use to the name *Logos*, their Jewish learning bade them see in it not only a Divine 'Reason,' but a 'Word of the Lord,' a manifested presence of God. In it they accordingly saw, more distinctly than their Platonic teachers, an impersonation of all the attributes of God, perfectly manifesting His being to man. It is certain that they spoke with some hesitation and inconsistency, now making it a mere personification, now investing it with a true personality.³ Their philosophy might have remained barren of all religious results—a mere cloudlike speculation of the schools, melting away in the open air of ordinary life. It was probably in itself only the treasured idea of the learned, un-

(*b*) The 'Word' of Alexandrine Platonism.

---

³ Perhaps this was caused by the ambiguity of the word Λόγος noticed above. See Westcott's 'Introduction' to the Fourth Gospel in the *Speaker's Commentary*.

known to the Jewish people who looked for a visible and human Messiah, unintelligible to the carnal polytheism of the Gentile world. Still it existed, and—what is of infinite consequence—it belonged to both Jew and Gentile; it was a link between the knowledge of God, so jealously guarded by the one, and the free range of thought in which the other delighted.

There is a deep interest in this history of the growth of human thought, gradually ascending towards the conception of a perfect revelation of God Himself. Its relation to the Gospel of St. John illustrates once more the position which is claimed by believers for Scripture—the position of a supernatural revelation, taking up, confirming, correcting, completing, the natural inductions of human reason. For in St. John's application of the phrase it obviously passes at once out of this vagueness into clear and certain assertion of a true personality in the Word, and moreover connects itself inseparably with the belief of an incarnate Messiah, hitherto rather coexistent than united with it. Thus, in the preface to the Gospel, he declares that in the beginning ' the Word was,' ' was with God,' ' was God,' distinct yet inseparable from ' the Father.' To the Word he ascribes the twofold power of the Godhead—the power of creation of the visible world, and the power of a life-giving illumination to the souls of men. Every word implies a true personality; and in the whole description there is not one touch of imaginative metaphor. As truly in this philosophic declaration as in the great vision of the Apocalypse, the ' Word of God ' is a personal Conqueror of evil, ' King of kings and Lord of lords.' But, lest there should be any shadow of doubt, he goes on at once to connect this manifestation of the Godhead with the incarnate Messiah of the Old Testament prophecy. Then passing without a pause to the witness of the Baptist, he shows us through it the actual Jesus of Nazareth, as the ' Word made flesh, and having His tabernacle among us; ' so that under the veil of flesh they ' beheld His glory, the glory as of the only begotten of the Father.' Similarly, in his Epistle, with striking emphasis he dwells on that ' which we have heard, which we have seen with our eyes, and our hands

St. John's use of the phrase.

have handled, of the Word of life.' In the very phrase, 'the only begotten,' he adopted the well-known title of the Messiahship, through which the Lord Jesus had been first proclaimed. In the declaration of 'grace and truth coming by Him,' so that 'of His fulness we all receive,' he brings out in a remarkable form the truth of the Mediation which had grown out of the truth of the Messiahship. But he passes on beyond these great titles to answer explicitly the questions which they suggest: 'Who is this King of all mankind? who is this one Mediator between man and God?' None other than He who is the manifestation in a true personality of all the attributes and nature of God—the Word, who 'was in the beginning,' who 'was with God, even the Father,' 'who was God' Himself.

III. This ultimate revelation is, indeed, infinitely beyond those thoughts of men, vague and tentative, feeling the truth rather than grasping it, formerly embodied in that phrase ' the Word of God,' which it now took up and made its own. So great the truth which it contains, that (as has been said) even in the apostolic preaching, and even in the Holy Scripture which contains it, it was, perhaps it could be, only worked out gradually. So great that in the Church hereafter, when Christianity emerged from its long struggle, to be acknowledged as the dominant religion of the civilised world, and when men accordingly attempted to comprehend this mystery in logical systems, it cost the distracting controversies of a century and a half before its place was fixed in the faith of Christendom. But of this, as of the preparatory declarations of the Gospel, I contend that it accords marvellously with the highest thoughts of men, while it goes far beyond them in scope, and rises above them in the calm certainty of its knowledge of the ' deep things of God.' *The relation of this revelation to human thought.*

For the chief steps in human thought, starting from a belief in God, and feeling after Him, are clearly marked.

It is clear that to His creatures God must be manifest in His works. But in what works shall we hope to seek and find Him? At first, indeed, as the early Nature-worship shows, that manifestation was sought for in the visible grandeur and tremendous *(a) God manifest in His works.*

forces of nature; just as, in the first revelation even to Israel, the Lord gave, as visible tokens of His presence at Sinai, the whirlwind, the earthquake, and the fire. Nor was this conception of the manifestation of God either erroneous or unfruitful. In nature 'God left not Himself without a witness,' and the acceptance of that witness is obvious in all the literatures and religions of the world. But, with the strictest philosophic truth, St. Paul notes (Rom. i. 20) that through it the chief direct revelation was of ' eternal power and Godhead,' with only the inferences of wisdom and goodness, and even these inferences not wholly unshaken by the contemplation of suffering and apparent failure in Creation, of sin and its deadly fruits in Humanity.

But as man became more conscious of himself and of a spiritual nature, both moral and intellectual, higher and greater than this lifeless grandeur, he began also to believe (as again the history of the religions of the world plainly shows) that God must be manifested best in man, His greatest earthly work. The various mythologies accordingly dreamt of temporary Avatars of the Godhead, or of beings, called by the name of Gods, dividing and diluting the essence of Deity in natures which were but forms of humanity, exalted, indeed, but often exalted in power or wisdom rather than goodness. The philosophy, which gradually rose upon the ruins of such mythological beliefs, still preserved in a nobler and more rational force the same leading idea. It passed, as the Greek philosophy shows us, in its search for the foundation of being, from the material bases of the Ionic school, through the 'number' (that is, the 'law') of the Pythagoreans, to the creative 'mind' of Anaxagoras; and it then went on to realise the nature of the Eternal Mind through the mind of man. The soul, as Plato emphatically taught, has the power of seeing the invisible, and of entering into the great principles, unseen yet underlying the whole world of sense. In that power lies its true humanity. These principles, indeed, it does not create for itself: they have an independent existence; they must necessarily be attributes of the supreme power. Yet man can not only see them, but, by seeing, grow into their likeness, and, both by word and act, can reproduce

(*b*) God manifest in man.

them, however imperfectly, to others. He has, therefore, the power not only to have communion with God, but also to manifest God, as being in His likeness, as being (to use St. Paul's quotation at Athens) 'His offspring.' There is in man something more divine, something more really manifesting God, than in all the glories of nature, before which he seems so weak, so insignificant, the mere creature of a day. Through them, or without them, there is a true voice of God to him—whether the 'trumpet voice exceeding loud' to the multitude, or the 'still small voice' to the individual soul. That voice he can, in measure, transmit to others, and thus be to them the manifestation of God. This consciousness of the Divine existing in man, and capable of being manifested through man—as the *microcosmus* embodying in his own nature the great elements, physical, animal, and spiritual, of the great world itself—marks the first great achievement in the search after God; which it is certainly retrogression, rather than progress, to surrender, in order to go back to the belief in a primeval matter somehow organising itself, or the belief in law, which, after all, is a mode, and not a cause, of being.

Yet the next step is taken through the consciousness, not of the reality, but of the imperfection, of this manifestation of the Divine in and through man. If we look to the individual, how imperfect is the manifestation of God in the very noblest of men, even in virtue of the finiteness of his intellectual nature! He cannot comprehend, still less can he manifest, the fulness of God. (c) The imperfection of such manifestation in each man. In what he knows, he is conscious there are in him 'thoughts beyond his thought;' yet how much there is in which he does not even know his own ignorance! It was this imperfection of knowledge which pressed hard upon the thought of the Greek. But there was a deeper consciousness still, of which he knew but little, but which was brought home forcibly to the Jew— the consciousness of sin. How could a sinful nature, unable to rise even to its own standard, much less able to bear the judgment of the pure eyes of God—how could it be God's offspring? how could it have communion with God, and how manifest God? No wonder that, under the consciousness of the blindness and sin of human nature, the very couception of the divine in man was but a wavering light, burning dim in the thick air of doubt, flickering in the blast of dissolution, always more able to maintain itself than to account for itself, even in the profoundest thought. Clearly the manifestation of God in any man, even the best and the wisest, was, after all a poor thing, on which the soul could not rest, however much it might strive to satisfy itself with hero-worship, or to attribute a prophetic infallibility to its teachers. At times it even fell back from this imperfection on the vague grandeur of nature. At best it could but accept it as the earnest of some better thing to come.

But is there an escape from this disappointment by taking refuge, as some ancient and modern philosophies *(d)* In the suggest, in the manifestation of God in the race, race. and so accepting the *vox populi* as literally the *vox Dei*? It is true, no doubt, that in the contemplation of humanity at large, all the strength and glory of the individual nature is indefinitely multiplied. The greatness of humanity is seen intellectually in the steady progress and accumulation of human knowledge, of power over nature, and of civilisation. It is shown morally in the massive common-sense which rebukes individual vagaries, and in the dominant force of the public opinion which shames individual baseness and selfishness. It shows itself, so to speak, physically, in the concentration and harmony of individual forces, and the (so-called) 'immortality of the race,' in which the effect of the short-lived individual existences endures, when they themselves have passed away. Collective humanity in its various forms is certainly a grand thing. We cannot wonder that men have found it more tolerable to worship their family, their country, their race, the brotherhood of all human kind, than to worship any individual man. But—not to dwell on the fact that no multiplication of the finite will yield the infinite—it is obviously and terribly true that by this multiplication the evil is magnified as well as the good. It is a commonplace to cry out against the injustice, the fickleness, the blindness of the praise or blame of men, which are the judgments of society on each of its members. It is a truth only too familiar to our daily experience, that a community is often more selfish, more ruthless, more shameless, than an individual. The power of evil, as it spreads by contagion and becomes engrained and accumulated by inheritance in a society, is felt every day as an all but Satanic power. Hence, if the worship of humanity is on the whole a nobler thing than self-worship or the worship of individual wisdom and power, yet still it is the worship of that which is still imperfect and sinful, and which has some features of exaggerated imperfection and sin. There is a residuum of the individual freedom and consciousness from which it cannot claim allegiance; and if this be usurped, the end of the slavery to society is still as truly described in the words of the dying Wolsey as the end of the slavery to the individual. The *cultus* of humanity, as a complete manifestation of the divine, is not only vague and transcendental, because we do not know what form of humanity to worship, but it is false in principle, mistaking (so to speak) bigness for greatness. Why should we worship a mere enlargement of human nature, in its imperfections as well as its glories, in its sin as well as its nobleness?

Once more, baffled here, philosophy had recourse to the conception of an ideal humanity—as when Stoicism set forth the claim of the perfectly 'wise man' to be the true king of men, rising above all physical and human force, not only a sage whose sound opinion was to correct all vulgar error and be the standard of truth, but almost a prophet, who was to see the truth in itself and to reflect it to others. To that ideal all ordinary goodness and wisdom approach, and up to it perhaps the race itself shall grow. May we not (it asked) in this find a manifestation of the Divine which we may worship? To that question the ordinary common-sense of the world answered, emphatically and almost contemptuously, in the negative. Speculatively considered, this ideal humanity was a mere fancy of the Schools, having no solid reality. It could hardly be conceived, much less worshipped. Morally it was seen that in their attempt to rise to it men passed into a self-reliant and disdainful isolation, becoming really inhuman in the hope of realising a higher humanity. So rejected both by mind and by heart, the very name became a byword and a jest; and the world turned away to worship objects which, if they

(e) The conception of an ideal humanity.

were imperfect and unworthy, had at least a real personality and a real human sympathy.

IV. But the Gospel recognised in this ideal belief a feeling after the truth, and it stamped it with an authoritative sanction on two all-important conditions. First, that the ideal man, if we are to worship God in him, must be not an unreal abstraction, but a living person—a true Son of Man, perfect in sinless purity, in all-discerning wisdom, in ascendency over the souls of men, but yet making Himself a sharer of the common life and work of the mass of men, and becoming one with them in a love which embraces all humanity, and rekindles in each the power to love. Such an ideal man the Gospel declares in Jesus of Nazareth, whose life, death, resurrection, and ascension are the actual development of the true humanity, in which God is revealed, and so furnish at once the pattern of imitation and the object of an adoring faith. Christianity is therefore a religion of humanity, but of humanity as culminating in the person of the true Son of Man. So, indeed, alone can it have vital power as a religion. A philosophy may be contented with an abstract ideal as its ultimate conception; but a religion must have a true personal being as the object of its worship. Hence the reality of the person of Christ is the fundamental truth, which early Christianity grasped firmly against all mere Gnostic abstractions, and which came out prominently in its preaching of His resurrection and His mediation.

The ideal of the Gospel a true man.

But He must also be infinitely more than man. If we are to see and worship God in Him, there must be in Him a power of communion with all the fulness of the Godhead, which no created being can have. There must be in His manifestation of God no limitation of time and place, such as clings inevitably to all creatures. He cannot otherwise so manifest God as to be 'a light that lighteth every man,' shining through all ages of time, and going not out in eternity. Hence he must not only be a son of God, as other men are, differing from them only in degree. Nor, since He is clearly man, can he be, like the Christ of the higher Arianism, a being intermediate between

A being more than man.

true Godhead and humanity, whom, indeed, an expiring Paganism might call a God and consent to worship, but whom the clear conception of a true Monotheism would sternly degrade to the rank of created beings. He must be an 'only-begotten Son,' 'before all creation,' or (to clench all by one complete declaration) He must be the 'Word of God'—that is, the full expression of the divine nature—One who 'in the beginning was with God, and was God.'

In this declaration the Gospel (as I have said) reached the climax of an inevitable development. Guarding earnestly the truth of His manhood, it now laid emphatic stress on His true Deity. For clearly nothing less than this is sufficient, if it is to claim to be in any sense a religion absolute, universal, final. Nothing less can justify the claim of universal kingship or the claim of universal mediation. Judaism without a Messiah, and the other religions of the world involving no incarnate Godhead as the basis of their faith, cannot rise to the height of such a claim. Nor can those forms of a professed Christianity really maintain themselves which, like Arianism, exalt Him simply on the pedestal of a superhuman created being, or, like Socinianism, reverence Him only as the true Son of Man. These theories say too much or too little. The opposition is between the Christianity of the Catholic Church and simple Deism or Atheism—between the acceptance in Christ of a perfect revelation and the denial of all special revelations as of ultimate authority. *In this the climax of Christian doctrine.*

In this, therefore, we must trace the final exemplification of the harmony of the supernatural with the natural in the Gospel. The two great conceptions of Natural Theology—the belief in a personal God, and the consciousness of a Divine image in man—are here not only confirmed, but manifested in complete union by the Incarnation of the Godhead in man, and in their union it is taken for granted that the mystery of evil, separating God and man, is overcome. Accordingly in it men found, as a living practical religion, what they had been groping for in philosophic conceptions or legendary fancies of a manifestation of God in humanity. They laid hold of it *The final harmony of the natural and supernatural.*

as a divine hand, yet a warm and living hand, in the spiritual darkness or twilight, and were ready to be led by it towards the central light of God.

In this consummation of the doctrine of Christ all else is implied. We find that, following closely on this declaration of the perfect manifestation of God in man, came naturally the declaration of the Divine Spirit, inspiring the soul to understand and accept that manifestation, and conforming it to the divine image in the likeness of Christ. The belief in the power of a Divine Spirit is certainly an element in any true belief of God. Without it the sovereignty of God cannot be asserted in the inner life of the soul, and, as that inner life becomes prominent in the more advanced human thought, so the conception of a divine inspiration rises to a chief place in all human religions, co-ordinate with the other two great convictions of the providence of God and of His revelation of Himself to man, which had stood out pre-eminent in the earlier stages of religious consciousness. How strikingly the doctrine was foreshadowed in the Old Testament we have already seen, by the connexion in the prophetic revelation of 'The Spirit of the Lord was upon me,' with 'The word of the Lord came to me.' But it is in the teaching of Christ Himself, and by the knowledge of Christ as the Word of God to us and in us, that it grows out into completeness, revealing to us in the Holy Spirit not a mere influence or mode of Divine action, but a true Person; till in the central mystery of the Holy Trinity we have the highest of all examples of the true nature of the Gospel, as absolutely supernatural, beyond thought to discover, beyond thought fully to comprehend, yet certainly the ultimate basis of the spiritual truths which we know naturally, in the observation of human life and in the depths of human consciousness. That mystery is (in the words of the Athanasian Creed) brought home to us 'by the Christian verity,' implied (that is) in the full manifestation of God in Christ. In that implicit form is it generally taught in Holy Scripture, and probably in that form grasped by the thought and faith of ordinary Christians. It is sufficient, therefore, for the purpose here contemplated if, without entering into the consideration of that mystery of the Trinity in Unity, and of the various foreshadowings of it which Christian teachers have found or fancied in the religions and philosophies of the world, we fix our thoughts simply on the completed development of the manifestation of Christ, as the Alpha and Omega of our Christianity.

I say 'of Christianity,' not merely of Christian doctrine. For though Christianity is a life as well as a truth, yet the truth and the life are inextricably blended together. Nothing is clearer, both to friends and foes, than that Christian morality has a peculiar stamp, dependent upon Christian doctrine, incapable of being retained if that doctrine be given up. For it is at once a 'godly morality' and a true 'human morality.' It is a godly morality; for it finds its basis, not, with one school of moralists, in the sacredness of intuition, nor, with the rival school, in the inherited experience of utilitarian laws, but in the declared will of God; and it holds goodness to be developed by a conscious obedience to that will, growing by love into the likeness of God Himself. Accordingly it recognises profoundly the horror of that moral evil, which unquestionably exists around us and in us, as not only vice against self or crime against man, but as sin against God; and it proclaims, as the source of man's power to conquer sin, God's forgiveness and God's grace in Jesus Christ. Hence it takes up heartily, as the dominant principle of moral life, the old commandment, which is the very creed of Monotheism, 'Thou shalt love the Lord God with all thy heart, and soul, and strength,' and then only adds, as second to it, and as accordant with it, 'Thou shalt love thy neighbour as thyself.' Yet it is a true human morality; for its essence consists not in law, enforcing obedience to the Divine will, perhaps even sinking the human will in an absolute submission, but in free conviction and love of the soul within, accepting that will gladly, and working with God by the energy of a spiritual nature. In the presence, therefore, of evil, whether in the guilt or bondage of sin, it is serious, but not despairing, because it holds that, as unnatural, it can and must be overcome. It looks up to God as really our Father, and therefore it bids man be reverent, but not abject, in the Divine presence. But it

The effect on Christian morality.

unites these two characteristics—in other systems of morality so often divorced from each other—simply because it rests on the faith of God and man really made one in Christ, and of a power to reproduce the life of Christ in every man. Take away that faith, and the two elements of morality will fly asunder. Neither will prove itself sufficient to maintain that union of firm stability with elasticity of constant progress, on which depends the growth alike of the individual soul and of the human society. Hence for acting, as well as for believing, to learn from Christ and to learn Christ are still the sum and substance of Christianity.

Nor is it otherwise if from moral action we turn to consider the inner principles of the spiritual life itself. Here also we find *Our spiritual life.* the same connexion between the Christian knowledge and Christian life. It is, indeed, notable that to the three successive stages of the preaching of Christ, there may be seen to correspond the three great principles of the inner life. The preaching of 'Christ risen' appeals to the indestructible instinct of Hope, which is the confidence of future perfection, and on which therefore hangs the true human life of freedom, of energy, and of progress. The preaching of the one mediation, on the other hand, calls forth the response of Faith, in which is involved the sense of weakness and sin, but of weakness and sin overcome by dependence on the grace of God, and which is, therefore, the central principle of a godly life. By no mere accident we find, lastly, that the teacher of the final truth of Christ as the Word of God is emphatically the Apostle of Love. For in love is the living sense of unity, first between man and God, and then between man and man; and it is the knowledge of the Divine in man which is the assurance of such unity. There is something very remarkable in this correspondence of the preaching of Christ to the spiritual capacities of man. In it the law, which has been dwelt upon throughout, exemplifies itself again. For that which corresponds to man's nature must be natural, and yet certainly from the mere capacities of that nature could never have been evolved the supernatural conception of the Gospel preaching.

Thus in relation to Christian doctrine, Christian morality, Christian spiritual life, the cycle is completed in the proclamation of the eternal 'Word of God.' The contemplation of this ultimate truth is full of instruction, as throwing light at once on the unity and the finality of the Scriptural revelation. However we may account for it, it is certainly true, that up to this, in fundamental unity and continuous development, all previous teaching had led, from the *Protevangelium* of Genesis, through all the various stages of the ancient knowledge of God, in history and law, in psalm and prophecy, and even through the earlier phases of the revelation of Christ Himself. At no previous stage could we vaguely stop: for nowhere else could we find any adequate completion of the great pervading ideas of covenant with God. But beyond this we cannot go. For it has to do not with earth, but with heaven—not with time, but with eternity.

CHAPTER X.

CONCLUSION.

IT remains now briefly to recapitulate the chief points of the present investigation, and to show its connexion with the enquiry into the direct evidences of Christianity, as such, which will occupy the second part.

I. My object throughout has been to examine the relation in which the main doctrines of Christianity stand to the two chief conclusions and the one great perplexity of Natural Theology. Holding that in a true sense 'Christianity is as old as the creation,' I have thought it best to carry out that examination by studying in the Bible as a whole the actual historical development of the chief doctrines of the Gospel. Since the first glance at the Bible shows that its one great subject is 'God in covenant with man,' and that this subject has its completion in the full manifestation of Jesus Christ, it follows that the conception of this leading principle determines the chief lines of our investigation.

The general line of argument.

For it obviously involves three main ideas: first, the belief in a personal and living God, having communion with man; next, the conviction of man's spirituality, and his freedom to be a fellow-worker with God; lastly, the certainty of the conquest of the power of evil, which raises a barrier between God and man. In the first and second of these principles we trace the substance of the teaching of Natural Theology; in the last we are brought face to face with its one great perplexity. The covenant with God, if realised in faith, must necessarily confirm the one and dispel the other.

II. The investigation proceeding on these lines of thought carries us on through the various sections of the Scripture history.

The stages of investigation.

We have first the outline of the whole in the great introduction to the regular Scripture history, shadowing out in a brief and impressive simplicity, which carries with it profound symbolic meanings, the creation, the primeval condition of man, and the end of the first dispensation in the Flood. It has been called not unjustly a *Protevangelium*, in its anticipation of the three great principles of the whole Scriptural revelation. (a) The introduction to the Old Testament.

Passing next to consider the Old Testament as a history of Israel illustrated by the teaching of prophecy and the response of psalm, it is not difficult to trace in its various periods the gradual working out of these principles in detail. (b) The Old Testament

Looking to the revelation of God Himself in His relation to man, the Scriptural narrative shows us, in distinct accordance with human experience in life and history, the coexistence of His universal 'covenant' to all mankind with lesser covenants of special relation to a chosen family and nation, not for their own sake, but as the channels of a blessing to all the families and nations of the earth. In that twofold aspect there are worked out successively the manifestations of 'God in history,' ruling by a supreme moral government the whole course of human action and life; 'of God in law,' formally declaring and enforcing His will on human action; of 'God in the spirit,' proclaimed and manifested in the prophecy, acknowledged in the Psalms and in the Books of Wisdom, as enlightening the soul by His word and inspiring it by His grace. as revealing a living God.

Then, secondly, in relation to the belief in the spirituality of man, it is obvious that the very idea of a covenant with God carries with it freedom and responsibility, which are the essence of a spiritual nature. Thence traversing the same ground as before, we see how the sterner teaching of history and law, wrought out mainly the sense of a glorious and awful responsibility, and how the spiritual experience of the Prophet and the Psalmist testified to the reality of freedom, yielding itself not by constraint, but willingly, to the light of 'the word of the Lord' and the inspiration of 'the Spirit of the Lord.' as bringing out the spirituality of man;

Lastly, in the same order, seeking for some light on the

great mystery of evil, we find it laid down as a fundamental principle that evil is no part of man's true nature; we find its origin in the world traced to a superhuman temptation to rebellion against God, yielded to by the human will. We see the reality of the power of evil deeply and terribly brought out in the experience of history, in the rebukes of law or prophecy, in the self-revelation which comes from communion with God. But the very existence of a covenant with God implies that evil is not dominant in man's nature over good, and that, by the communion with God, it can be, and must be, overcome. In the great rite of sacrifice, inaugurating the chief epochs of that covenant, ordained and accepted by God, and wrought into the religious life of the people, we find a typical prophecy—to us clear, to those of old time still veiled—of the supernatural method of some future conquest of evil.

<small>as dealing with the mystery of evil.</small>

Thus far this consideration of the subject deals with the Old Testament as if it were complete in itself, and as if its teaching concerned only the religious life of Israel as a people of God. But to confine our thoughts to this view would be to contradict every page of the Old Testament itself. Necessarily we must go on to consider the germ which it contains, and gradually unfolds, of something greater than itself—the Messianic idea unquestionably running through it, by which it is linked to the New Testament. Considering the idea of the Messiah, as it gradually brightens and stands out more prominently, we recognise in it the engrafting of a true religion of humanity on the stock of a sublime monotheism. Looking at it in relation to the same three great principles, it is impossible not to see in it, represented in a startling distinctness, the exaltation of humanity to a glory invested with all the attributes of Deity; to see less fully, but yet very distinctly, brought out the visible manifestation of the invisible and eternal God; least clearly, in fact rather by implication and suggestion, the promise of a conquest of evil by a sacrifice which should take away sin and overcome death. The idea of the Messiah stands out as a grand promise, which supplies the principle of life and growth to the ancient dispensation, but

<small>The Messianic idea.</small>

which was utterly incapable of anticipating the full reality of the future fulfilment.

From this glorious promise in the Old Testament the thoughts next turn to the full revelation of the New—still keeping to the historic order of the preaching of the Christ. First, as 'Christ risen,' fulfilling the Messianic hope, asserting the supreme authority of Jesus as the Prophet, Priest, and King of all humanity, and connecting this by His own sanction with the spirituality of the human nature in the present time and in an eternal future. Next, as 'Christ the one Mediator,' especially as 'Christ crucified,' taking up that element of truth which was least fully worked out in the Messianic hope, and by supernatural exaltation of the natural law of mediation, setting forth the conquest of sin and death. Lastly, in that ultimate truth which both the others implied, as 'Christ the Word of God,' true God as well as true Man, manifesting in humanity all the fulness of the Godhead. *(c) The New Testament. Christ risen. Christ the Mediator. Christ the Word of God.*

III. Everywhere, in different aspects and in different degrees, it has been my endeavour to show that the revelation of Christianity is in its substance at once natural and supernatural. Natural in its accordance with all the lines of the higher thought of man, as he searches out his own nature, the nature of God, and the relation between both. Supernatural, first, in the contrast of the calm simplicity of revelation with the laborious anxiety of the induction which it confirms; next, in the substance of the truths revealed, transcending human discovery, and, although satisfying the spiritual necessities at once of thought and life, incapable of having been evolved from them. *The harmony of the natural and supernatural.*

If this has been in any degree shown, what should be the inference? Not any absolute inference of the truth and authority of Christianity. For this it needs, and it presents, positive evidences, to the variety and convergent force of which, as they present themselves to modern thought, it is the object of the Second Part to direct attention. But at least a removal of some presumptions which are pleaded as sufficient to preclude the *The force of the argument.*

necessity of examining these evidences altogether, and the creation, on the other hand, of a presumption in favour of the truth of these evidences when presented to the enquiring mind. This is the scope of all presentations of analogy between the Gospel and the results, whether of actual experience or of the reasonings of Natural Theology, from the immortal work of Butler downwards. It is a work necessarily incomplete, but never unimportant, least of all to be neglected in our own days.

It was directed in the Jewish law that if a prophet, even with the attestation of signs and wonders, proclaimed a message as from God, it was to be examined as to its accordance with the main points of the revelation already given. If it contradicted these, then, whatever its apparent credentials, it was to be rejected with abhorrence, for God could not contradict Himself. If it agreed with them, then it was to be accepted, as carrying on to new developments the ancient message of God to His people.

This principle is of wide application.

The light of reason and of conscience is the universal revelation of God to the soul of man. No true revelation can contradict either the one or the other. Every appearance, in that which claims to be a revelation, of speculative or moral contradiction, either of itself or of the light of nature, shakes, though it need not overthrow, our faith in its authenticity. Every proof of accordance with the Natural Theology, recognising this universal revelation to the soul as coming from the same God, is, so far as it goes, a preparation or a confirmation of that faith. If, however, there be accordance in method and substance, and nothing more, it follows necessarily that, though the revelation may be true, it need not be special and authoritative, and it cannot claim the absolute and permanent obedience of the world. But if, while there is a perfect accordance, there is also that which goes far beyond all reason, both in certainty of knowledge and in the scope of its substance, then there is presumption, not only of truth, but of authority. In it there is advance beyond reason; if that advance lead to truths in their nature ultimate, there is presumption of finality.

IV. At all times, therefore, there must be value in this line of thought, but perhaps some especial value now. Rightly or wrongly, there is in educated thought an indisposition to lend ear to the strong 'evidences of Christianity' wrought out so carefully in days gone by. This reluctance is due to one of two opposite assumptions. Sometimes it is taken for granted that Christianity is preternatural, contradicting the conclusions of advanced reason, discordant, or very imperfectly accordant, with the highest morality, and that accordingly no amount of positive evidence can prove it true. Sometimes that Christianity is merely natural—one out of many religions, all invented by human thought and evolved out of human needs—one which has done higher service to humanity than any other, but which must in its turn give way to some higher generalisation of knowledge, or to the conviction of necessary ignorance. In this case it is, of course, idle to claim for it perpetuity or absolute authority. These two assumptions, far more than any intelligent doubt as to the fulness of Christian evidence, lie at the root of much scepticism of the day—sometimes maintained by deliberate and careful argument, sometimes loosely thrown out, as if they needed no argument, in popular literature. They must be familiar to all educated men; some accept them with all their inferences; many, without accepting them, feel half-consciously their unsettling effect. I venture to question both. Of those who, fully or partially, have felt their influence, I would ask that they consider how far they can stand with the careful examination of what Christianity actually is, not in any abstract theological systems, but in the historical order of its living development in Scripture. Even to those by whom these assumptions have not been accepted, there may be some use in the study of that order, so full of beauty, consistency, and harmony with truths otherwise discovered, to deepen in the mind the existing conviction of faith.

From these considerations it is natural to pass on to the positive Christian evidences, for which they are properly a preparation. But there are many minds to which these considerations in themselves may serve as a direct and sufficient introduction to Christian faith, without any further study of evidences at all. It is true that their force is simply preparatory; but it should be remembered that even what we call positive Christian evidence differs from them in this respect rather in degree than in kind. All Christian evidence, direct or indirect, professes only to be thus preparatory. It is necessarily the belief of Christians that all which is possible, all which is necessary, for Christian faith, is to bring men in thought to Christ Himself, content if we can put away all the supposed hindrances which keep the soul out of the range of His presence. Let this be once done, and we hold that there are, first, the signs of miracle and prophecy, which weave a halo of glory round His head, and draw men to Him as to one who may be at least presumed to come from God; that there is, next, when men are drawn near to Him, the intrinsic truth, beauty, purity of His life and teaching—accordant (in a sphere in which we are able to test it) with all the highest thoughts and aspirations of men— which bow the soul before Him, as having certainly the words of eternal life. Beyond this there lies—what no study of evidence can supersede—the acceptance, in the faith so established, of His teaching of 'the heavenly things' of His own nature and office, which He alone can know. That faith by the nature of the case must lead us far beyond the conclusions of our own reasoning; it can be tested only by its fruits in the regeneration of the soul to peace, holiness, and love, and in the regeneration of human society to a higher and nobler corporate life. In these last spiritual processes lies the vitality of Christianity as a religion. To these the mass of Christians come at once without any evidential argument at all; to these some may be led at once from the consideration of that relation of Christianity to Natural Theology on which we have already dwelt; while others may require to approach these only through the study of the various positive evidences of the Divine mission of Christ. In any case to the law of Induction must be added the law of Faith.

It may be remarked, in conclusion, that in the assertion of that law the Gospel gives one more illustration of its true character, as at once natural and supernatural. For it must be obvious to every student of humanity, whether in the handwriting of his own personal experience or the great book of history past and present, that the law of faith is a natural law, and, moreover, that it is a supreme law of human life, moving the whole world as no other power can move it. But the faith which Christianity claims is supernatural also, because it is —what no faith in man can be—absolute, permanent, universal, crowning the principle of faith in man by uniting it with faith in God. In it, if it be accepted with the whole heart, is necessarily 'the victory which overcomes the world.' What are the true grounds and what the full scope of such faith, must be considered in the Second Part.

The province of faith.

PART II.

THE POSITIVE EVIDENCES OF CHRISTIANITY.

CHAPTER I.

THE FUNCTION AND METHOD OF CHRISTIAN EVIDENCES.

'Be ready always to give an answer to every man that asketh you a reason of the hope that is in you.'—1 Pet. iii. 15.

FROM the strong indirect evidence of Christianity, which is presented to us in its relation, at once complementary and supplementary, to the inductions of our Natural Theology, we now go on to consider the positive and direct evidences of what I maintain to be a 'manifold witness to Christ.' In these lectures that witness is necessarily considered in obedience to the command to be 'ready to give an answer to every one who asks a reason of the hope which is in us,' whether he asks in the tone of serious inquiry, or in the tone of defiant unbelief.

I. But it will probably help our investigation not a little, if we first satisfy ourselves of the true function of these Christian evidences in the actual growth of Christian faith. What part do they play in the growth of a reasonable Christianity in the world at large? What have they to do in any one of us with the answer to the question 'Why am I a Christian?' To that question, itself a short and simple question, any answer, which is to have much general truth or value, must be a complex answer. In the answers, indeed, to almost all questions which touch the ultimate foundations of any kind of truth, speculative or moral, simplicity of form has

The grounds of actual belief.

mostly to be purchased at the expense of accuracy and fulness. So it would be here. In individual cases it may often be possible to single out some one special reason, drawn either from thought or from experience, on which the Christianity of this or that soul is built; just as it may be quite possible to point to the particular moment or circumstance, which is to any individual a time of conversion or revival, and so a turning-point of spiritual life. But, speaking generally, it seems clear that our actual Christianity is the product of many influences. Something we receive from without by inheritance and by teaching; something we gain for ourselves by experience and thought. A Christian, of course, will trace in both operations the power of the Spirit of God, working through the race and in the individual, to ' testify of Christ.'

Something we receive undoubtedly from inheritance and teaching—influences which come from without. For Christianity, as embodied in the Bible and the Church, is an historic thing; it professes to be a treasure, given to the whole race of men, and enduring for ever. The Bible itself grew up through many centuries, and has lived through many more centuries in its full development. The Church is a society which has an absolute continuity of inner principle, and a continuity, within limits, even of outward form and operation, living on through the lapse of ages, and extending its influence over all varieties of race, place, and character. It would contradict the fundamental idea of Christianity, if the faith of each individual or each age claimed to start *de novo*, either by fresh revelation or by original discovery. As with all the chief treasures of humanity—knowledge, morality, art, civilisation—the very progress of the human race depends on inheritance from the past, and the possibility of individual growth involves some education by direct teaching in the present. To say ' I am a Christian because I was born a Christian,' or ' because I was taught to be a Christian,' is indeed a very imperfect answer, but it is not an absurd or an untrue answer, as far as it goes. If, indeed, it were altogether inadmissible, and if each man's Christian faith claimed to be an entirely new, independent, and original growth, then we should be inclined to doubt whether Christianity could be

(*a*) Inheritance and teaching.

one of the great powers destined to rule humanity, and to grow with its growth towards the appointed end.

Something, on the other hand, is due to what is individual, to practical experience and abstract thought. First, (b) Practical experience. in this process of education, as in all others, comes generally the teaching of practical experience, testing by its fruits the doctrine which has been received. Christianity must submit itself to that test in many ways. It presents itself as at once a philosophy, a morality, and a spiritual life; it professes to guide men to truth, to exalt them to righteousness, to give them a communion with God. These claims can be tested by each man's own experience, by himself and for himself alone. If he finds that they are practically true—if (that is) he finds that the Gospel does really throw a sufficient light on the great problems of the being of nature, of man, and of God, so that he can walk in that light—if he finds that Christian grace supplies a new moral force, adequate to kindle, sustain, and develope the life of truth and righteousness—if in Christianity he finds a power of communion of the soul with God, and therefore a hidden spiritual life, in which it lives and by which it is exalted above the earth—then he has (in Scriptural language) 'tasted for himself that the Lord is gracious,' and verified, by manifold spiritual experience, that which he received originally by inheritance and by teaching.

But out of that experience there naturally grows up in different degrees, according to education or capacity, the (c) Abstract thought. abstract thought, by which each man ponders, tests, corrects, enlarges the truth inherited and taught, which experience has thus proved to be in some sense a reality. It is the work of such thought to examine it in itself —what it says, what it means, what it implies; to examine the grounds on which it rests, and the claims which it makes on our understanding, and obedience, and faith; to examine perhaps its relation to other forms of truth, other claims of authority, other spiritual influences, which move the world. When to inheritance and teaching from without are added the experience which verifies, and the thought which illuminates, from within, then, and then only, does the process of growth in Christianity stand out in full completeness. No exhortation is commoner in Scripture than the exhortation not merely to accept and to hear, but to test and to think. The Christianity of our own days, always appealing to an open Bible, urges that exhortation with special emphasis. There is a function of the Church as a whole towards each individual member, teaching with authority and ministering grace; but it is absolutely necessary for anything like a living faith that each man should not only 'mark and learn,' but should 'inwardly digest,' by the combined power of practical experience and abstract thought.

We appeal thus to the combined power of both; but it cannot be forgotten that, for the great mass of men, in respect of their education in the knowledge of all kinds of truth, scientific, moral, or religious, experience is the leading element, and thought, although not excluded, is distinctly subordinate. Certainly we find that in religious truth, far more than in any other form of truth, great abstract ideas are apprehended by the mass of men, of whose capacity schools of science and morality make but little account. Still even of religious truth the general law holds, that the apprehension of it must be more practical than theoretical in mankind at large; and indeed it is so obviously true, that men are constantly led by the sense of it to what seems to me an unwise depreciation of all theology in the abstract. If a man is asked, 'Why are you Christian?' he will answer, 'Because, having inherited Christianity, and having been taught to be a Christian, I have tried the truth and the grace of Christ for myself, and I have found in them the words of eternal life.'

II. The answer is practically a sufficient answer. Even if we do not rest satisfied with it, and become in some sense theologians—entering on that exercise of scientific thought which is as much decried in relation to this form of knowledge as it is exalted in relation to all others—still, for most men, and for most ages of the Church, the object is more exegetical than apologetic. We rather study Christian doctrine in itself, accepting its basis as true, and drawing out various deductions from it in application both to truth and to life, than set to work to examine what are called the evidences

Examination of Christianity in itself.

of our Christianity—the basis on which its claim to authority rests, and the relation in which it stands to other truths, other laws, and other powers in the world of humanity. Naturally, in most cases we prefer to spend our thought in surveying all the beauty and variety of the domain which God has given us, rather than in scrutinising its title-deeds, or strengthening the points in which other domains may possibly infringe upon it.

Even when we pass from this survey of Christian doctrine in itself and in its applications, to consider how it vindicates its claim to supremacy over human thought, still we seldom in the first instance examine its positive evidences. Supposing that we have already grasped that fundamental belief in a true and living God, which men have called (not untruly in the right sense of the word) the 'Natural Religion' of man, since to it we are led irresistibly by the convergent power of many witnesses along many lines of thought—supposing (I say) that, with the great mass of men in all ages, we do with more or less of certainty rest on this foundation truth—then generally the thoughtful mind inclines to something like the path which in the last series of lectures I endeavoured to tread. Its natural impulse is to examine what the Christian doctrine is, first in relation to the two great truths of a personal God and a spiritual nature in man, to which Natural Theology leads us all but irresistibly; and next in relation to that great mystery of evil in all its forms of suffering and decay, sin and death, before which our Natural Theology stands aghast, dismayed though not confounded. If it finds that the Gospel proves itself to be at once natural and supernatural, confirming the conclusions of Natural Theology and going far beyond it, not only turning its hopes into certainties, but also dispelling the terrible darkness which enshrouds the mystery of evil—then perhaps in most cases the mind searches no further. Christianity (to use a common phrase) carries with it its own evidence; and, when pressed by doubts and questions, men are apt, as has been already said, to take up the words of the man healed at Siloam, 'How these things may be, I know not. But one thing I do know, that, whereas I was blind, seeing very much dimly, and

Examination of its relation to natural religion.

in many things seeing not at all, now I see. Till you kindle for me some better light, I shall walk contentedly in this. Till you find me some greater salvation, I shall own Him for my Saviour who has given this light.'

Accordingly, it is this study of the Gospel which occupies, and rightly occupies, the chief place, not only in ordinary Christian thought and teaching, but even in the great fabric built up through the ages by Christian theology. Happy (as it seems to me) are those minds and those generations, for which it is all in all. Even in our own critical days, if we enquire into the real origin of the Christian faith existing in the world at any moment, we shall find that it arises mainly from the appropriation, by individual experience and such individual thought as I have endeavoured to describe, of the historic Christianity inherited from the past, and taught by the Church in the present from the Book of God. In small degree is it actually due to an examination in cold blood of what are called Christian evidences. It would, indeed, be strange if it were. For I find no corresponding condition of things in respect of great scientific laws, of gravitation, electricity, physiology; in respect of great political and social institutions, such as those which are the glory of England; in respect of great moral principles, on which depend our individual humanity and our common civilisation. The mass of men in each age receive the knowledge of these by inheritance and teaching; and they are content, in ninety-nine cases out of a hundred, to test them by practical experience, or, if they learn them scientifically at all, to learn what they are, and to what they lead, rather than how they can be proved.

III. But Holy Scripture and common sense, while they refuse to trace to mere study of Christian evidences the existence of the living plant of Christian faith, yet lay on all who have that faith, and cherish the hopes which it creates, the duty of giving in right time and manner, 'an answer,' or, (as it is properly,) 'a defence,' of the hope that is in them, 'to every man that asketh it.' The initiative is taken on the other side. If our right to our domain is challenged, we must look to our title-deeds, even though the task of searching for them and

Examination of Christian evidences.

interpreting them be dry and difficult. Now, no one who studies the condition of our age will doubt that this right is challenged, with a degree of boldness, peremptory and almost arrogant, to which most other ages have been strangers.

Sometimes (as the founder of these lectures foresaw) the challenge comes from those who deny or question the belief <small>In answer to the atheist;</small> in God and in the spirituality of man altogether, and who honour Christianity with their especial hostility, simply because it—and possibly in a lower degree the Judaism in which it was cradled, and the Mohammedanism which is a wild offshoot from the same stock—form the vital and aggressive religions of the world. Wise in their generation, 'they fight neither with small nor great, but only with the true King of Israel.'

Sometimes the challenge comes from those who accept a belief in God, and hold to the sacredness of religion, but <small>In answer to the 'deist,'</small> to whom an ultimate and authoritative revelation is incredible, and to whom Christianity is but one out of many forms of religion—all at once true and untrue in their gropings after God, and differing only in their degree of truth and untruth—all probably destined to be superseded by something higher and better in the future. Sometimes we are even bidden to look on Christianity as a retrogression from the simple monotheism of the old creed of Israel, as it is preserved in modern Judaism or in Mohammedanism—a retrogression from which—with perhaps the gain of some lessons learned from the Master, whom we are supposed to have misunderstood—we must, as soon as possible, return.

So it was in days past when these lectures were founded; but certainly never more than now. As we look down from our walls, we see now one, now the other, form of attack emerge. At times we even notice that our enemies are divided against themselves. The Pantheist or Materialist host turns contemptuously on the ranks of mere Deism, and bids them let Christianity alone, if they mean to believe in God at all, and have no more vital religion to put in its place. The believers in God, of whatever type, at times desist from the attack upon our positions, in order to struggle against the growing power which menaces both us and them. At times, on the other hand, both combine against us, and leave their own battle to be fought out hereafter. But, whatever the changing aspect of the conflict, so long as it lasts, and in proportion as it is fierce against Christianity, we must be prepared to defend the hope that is in us.

But it is with the latter form of challenge that we are now especially concerned. To the question, 'Why are you a Christian?' it is (to say the least) a very insufficient answer to reply: 'Because I must have some religion; I cannot live without God; and Christianity is, on the whole, the best I know.' This faith is, indeed, far above mere Agnosticism or unbelief. Nor could we dare to pronounce that it is beyond the range of His acceptance who once declared, 'He that is not against us is on our side,' and said to one who knew simply the love of God and man, 'Thou art not far from the kingdom of God.' But certainly it is not the kind of faith which the Gospel claims. It is as different from the faith of the New Testament as the dim beauty of the twilight from the warm colour and life of the noonday. Such a faith could never have conquered the world, nor will it bear the soul safely and triumphantly through life and death. For Christianity, if it is true at all, must be by its very nature something more than one religion among many. It declares itself as old as the creation; it looks forward to the end of all things as simply its consummation. Starting from the belief of the universal fatherhood of God, it boldly declares of all men, whether they know Christ or not, and of all ages, whether before or after His manifestation of Himself: 'There is none other name under heaven given among men, by which we must be saved, but only the name of the Lord Jesus Christ.' *The actual claims of Christianity.*

Now, if by the question, 'Why are you a Christian?' be meant (as must ultimately be meant), 'What are the grounds on which you accept this claim, so unexampled in its importance and boldness?' and if, in order to answer it, we look to what are called Christian evidences, even then the answer is not a simple, but a complex answer.

In this respect the witness to Christianity stands in the same position as the witness to natural religion. It is a manifold witness. In dealing with the evidence on which rests the belief in a true and living God, we must contend, as I have already urged elsewhere, for three important considerations. It is, first of all, to be remembered that the witness to God, starting from that universal instinct which has expressed itself in all the languages and religions of the world, is worked out by maturer thought, not along one line of thought, but along many. It has its speculative evidences appealing to the understanding and imagination. It has its moral evidences in the voice of conscience and of love. It is to be urged, next, that it is a fatal error to rely on one line of evidence only, as if it stood alone, and were intended to be all-sufficient; and that it is an almost equally flagrant error to treat the result of these various forms of witness as if it were only the sum total of the evidences of each, instead of being (as all laws of evidence, scientific or forensic, allow) infinitely stronger, in virtue of the convergence of independent evidences, than the sum of all put together. It is to be shown, lastly, how, by all considerations, both of reason and of analogy, we are irresistibly drawn to the expectation of some revelation of God Himself to the race as a race, clenching the moral certainty of all these combined evidences of Natural Theology, and adding to the law of induction the law of faith.

The manifold witness for Natural Religion.

For exactly these three principles I would contend in respect of Christian evidence. I hold that it is a complex evidence, having its various appeals to the reason, the conscience, the affections, and the spiritual aspirations of man. I hold that, next, the conviction produced by these various reasons for coming to Christ is infinitely greater than the sum of all put together, rising, as all convergent evidence must rise, with extreme rapidity from bare probability to absolute moral certainty. I hold that, lastly, the work of Christian evidence is done when it has brought men to Christ with the profound conviction that 'none can do what He does, except God be with Him,' and that, having 'the words of eternal life,' He can reveal what no mere man can discover or fully comprehend. Then, for the rest, comes in the law of faith. We have to sit at His feet, and, through faith rather than investigation, 'learn to know what passes knowledge, and so be filled with all the fulness of God.'

The manifold witness for Christianity.

CHAP. I.   THE FUNCTION OF CHRISTIAN EVIDENCE.   201

It is in this last contention of the need of an unreserved faith in the word of our Master, that Christians, as such, part company absolutely with those who believe in God, but, if they accept Jesus of Nazareth at all, accept Him only as one of His prophets. Perhaps in desire to appeal entirely to reason, perhaps in reluctance to break up the ranks of the host of Theism, the absolute necessity of this last contention has often been imperfectly dwelt upon by Christian apologists, and a stress accordingly has been laid on Christian evidences which they can hardly bear.

IV. But it is infinitely important to have a clear view of what the Christian position is or ought to be. To sum up, therefore, what has been now put forward as to the actual and reasonable origin of the Christianity of the nineteenth century, I should trace out its various stages thus. *(d) Summary of results.*

We are Christians, first, because we have inherited our Christianity under God's providence, just as we have inherited our freedom, our knowledge, and our civilisation. We accept the position, and teach our children 'to thank God that He has called us into this state of salvation.' *Inheritance.*

We are Christians, next, because through the Bible and the teaching of the Church, which is its witness and keeper, we have been taught from our earliest days to learn from Christ what He says, and to learn Christ, what He is. Such teaching we hold to be the debt of society to each individual born into it. We accept it for ourselves, we resolve to give it in our turn to others. *Teaching.*

We are Christians, again, because we have tried this Christian teaching and privilege by experience, and found in them a guide through the perplexities of life, a light to the understanding, a strength to the conscience, a new inspiration of our affections, and a satisfaction of our spiritual longings. *Experience.*

So far, and so far only, all must go who are to be true Christians. Thousands stop there, contented, and reasonably contented. In faith so inherited, so learned, so verified by experience, they have Christ dwelling in them, and 'in Him can do all things,' both for life and for death.

But there are stages yet beyond, which to many it may be a duty and even a privilege to tread.

Here men are Christians because they have learned to study Christian truth, not only in its effects but in itself, and to draw out in a true theology the knowledge of God, the knowledge of man, the knowledge of God made one with man in Jesus Christ; and because, as they thus study, the truth grows upon them, and possesses their souls with an ever-deepening conviction of its reality, its sufficiency, and its supremacy.

Study.

So far it is a high privilege to go; but by necessity we may have to go further still, and say: 'We are Christians because, having been challenged to give a defence for the faith in us, we have looked into all the rich variety and complexity of that witness which leads men to Christ; we have convinced ourselves that it stands still, as it stood of old, unshaken by speculative or moral difficulty. Whatever points may still be dark, waiting for fuller light, still what we can see is sufficient, and more than sufficient, to teach us that "He is the Christ, the Son of the living God."'

Evidence.

But, when we have done all, still, for the full understanding of the Christian mystery, we must at last rest by faith on Christ—in His word, His life, and His manifestation of Himself—content to believe that He knows what we do not know, and that what seem to us irreconcilable truths are to Him in a perfect harmony. Our religion is not a philosophy, but a faith; it rests not on abstract principles, but on a Divine Person.

Faith.

Of this course of thought the present series of lectures has only to do with the last two stages. They are directed to two objects—to show, on the one hand, the variety and convergent force of Christian evidence; to assert, on the other, the necessary limitation of its function, as designed to lead on to faith, not to supersede it.

V. Before entering, however, on the examination in detail of Christian evidences, it will be well to consider the true order and method of that examination.

It seems to me right to start in thought, as we start in practice, with the actual power of Christianity in the intellectual, moral, and spiritual spheres of our being, rather than go back at once to its first manifestation in the past. For it is surely true that, while the great principles of Christian truth must always be the same, yet there need not be, and cannot be, the same unalterable character about the evidences by which the mind is led to that truth. The tide of thought advances here and recedes there. The hand of Time adds in one direction, while it takes away in another. Hence it would seem to be a mistake to throw ourselves back, so to speak, by historic imagination, into the earliest ages of Christianity, and to seek to reproduce—what is really incapable of any perfect reproduction—the power by which, in those days, the Gospel of Christ forced itself on a half-reluctant world. The real question rather is, what are the forces—partly the same, partly not the same—by which it is brought home to us as living in this nineteenth century? *The order of Christian evidences for us not the same as in the first age.*

Thus, for example, when the Gospel was first preached to the world, we know the stress laid on two great evidences —the fulfilment of prophecy and the witness of miracle. It was perfectly natural, almost inevitable, that this course should be followed. For the fulfilment of prophecy claimed the past for Christ, and His miracles, bodily and spiritual, showed His power over the present. But it does not follow, as is sometimes assumed,[1] that these must be the chief evidences of Christianity to our day. We have a new past and a new present of our own; we equally claim them for our Master, but our method of advancing that claim may not be the same as that which was so cogent in days gone by.

The argument from prophecy was addressed to a people to whom the prophecies of the Old Testament were the chief spiritual treasure, bound up with the very life and hope of the Jewish dispensation, familiar as household words, habitually viewed in relation to the coming *(a) The argument from prophecy,*

---

[1] On this point I venture to doubt whether even Butler is to be implicitly followed, when he says (in Part II. c. vii. of the *Analogy*), that 'miracles and the completion of prophecy' are the 'two direct and fundamental proofs' of Christianity, compared with which all others are subsidiary.

of the Messiah. To show them fulfilled in Christ—whether in broad general principles or in vivid details—was an argument of marvellous power. It was, as has been said, to claim for Him the whole of the glorious past of Israel, and of the covenant which she held in trust for humanity; by showing that through the centuries, in ways often dark at the time, and made clear only by the event, the hand of God was preparing for His manifestation, as the one fulfilment of all the hopes of Israel, and as the culminating event of human history. From this it was most natural to begin, as St. Peter began on the day of Pentecost. But is it equally natural now? I doubt it; for to do so now is to sin against that very principle of the original teaching which gave it so vivid a power. Then the prophecies were living and familiar realities, connected with the actual spiritual life of the hearers. Now they have receded into the dimness of a far antiquity; they are to us, in some measure, only historic memories of surpassing grandeur; in parts their meaning is obscure to us, and has to be approached through subtle criticism and speculation; even when we can understand them and listen to them as still living words of God, we have to translate them out of ancient forms of thought into modern language and idea. They are certainly not the chief food of our spiritual life. It is not impossible that from this distance we may be able intellectually to estimate them better as a whole, to subordinate to leading principles the details which caught the eye of a nearer contemplation, and to view them in the instructive light of the event. But they cannot come home to us as they came home to St. Peter's hearers, in that vivid force and beauty which tell upon the heart. If the evidence of prophecy is not less substantial, it is certainly less immediate and less persuasive. It is not to it that we should turn at once, in confidence that by it we can forthwith make the minds and hearts of men burn within them. When we approach it, it should be through the medium of something which is more absolutely and familiarly our own.

So far we lose something. But there is a glorious compensation for our loss. History with us takes the place then occupied by prophecy. There is now a new past of eighteen

CHAP. I. THE FUNCTION OF CHRISTIAN EVIDENCE. 205

centuries which visibly belongs to Him; in which His manifestation is contemplated, not by prospect, but by retrospect; in which the power of His light and grace has been seen actually working to subdue to Him the human soul and human society, proving itself a power unique in man's experience, and at least suggesting the belief that it comes from above. Through them surely it is natural to go back to the past. It must be a mistake to fix the mind at once on the dim remoteness of prophecy, without approaching it through that other evidence, cognate in nature and surely not inferior in power, which is afforded us by the actual history of the kingdom so long foretold.

_{supple-}
_{mented by}
_{our argu-}
_{ment from}
_{history.}

Nor is it otherwise in respect of the evidence of a divine mission in Him and His apostles afforded by the working of miracles. It must surely argue a great ignorance of common human nature to doubt that for the mass of men, at the time of the first manifestation of Christ, the power of miracle, wrought before their eyes or told by eye-witnesses, must have been all but irresistible; and indeed must have been, humanly speaking, almost the only means by which a handful of men, comparatively poor and ignorant, could have induced the world to stand still even for a moment, and listen to the claim of universal kingship for One who lived in obscurity and died in shame. Our Lord's simple appeal, on this ground, to the doubting disciples of St. John the Baptist was obvious and irresistible, even before the great miracle of all miracles—the resurrection from the grave. But when that wonder had been wrought, crowning the whole of the wonderful works of His earthly life, the Apostles themselves, converted by it to a wholly new spiritual faith and energy, stood up with just confidence to preach Jesus of Nazareth, as long ago 'approved of God by wonders and signs,' and now 'declared to be the Son of God with power by the resurrection from the dead.' The witness of miracle, of course, was never appealed to as if it stood alone; it was but a means to an end; it led up to the preaching of the Gospel by word, and could be rightly estimated only in that connexion. But in its right place it was a witness of transcendent power. From it, whether in

(b) The argument from miracles

narrative of the life of Christ, or in visible manifestation in the upper room at Pentecost and at the Beautiful Gate of the Temple, the first Christian preaching did surely well to start.

But how stands the case with us now? Certainly we have lost the vivid power of actual eye-witness, or of ear-witness from those who actually saw the miracles worked, who had actually handled the glorified body of the risen Lord, and who now staked their lives on the declaration, and considered it an adequate power to convert others as it had converted them. The witness of miracle may tell the same story still, and, we believe, that its message will emerge from all tests of criticism, substantially unimpaired in its ancient credibility; but its voice sounds faint and far away from us; so that it seems far less difficult, far less absurd, than it would have seemed in early days, to shut our ears to its meaning altogether, or to explain that meaning away.

<small>supplemented by our argument from actual power of Christianity.</small>

But here again, if we lose something, how great is our compensation! The significance of the miracle is its manifestation of a divine power over the present in the person of the Christ, when it pleased Him to veil his glory in human flesh. But we have in present reality that unique and transcendent power which His truth and grace are at this moment exercising over the world. This may fairly be called a moral and spiritual miracle, which, if He be but a mere man, is fairly inexplicable, and which, therefore, like the miracles of old, bows men to His feet in the confidence that only the finger of God could work as He works. It is absurd to refuse to dwell on the historic miracles of our Lord's life and resurrection: they tell their story to us in the pages of the Gospel, and it is in essence the same story which they told to those who saw them. In some points we may even have a larger, though far less intense, apprehension of their significance. But we should not begin with them: it is surely reasonable to approach the contemplation of these historic miracles of the past through the nearer perception of the spiritual miracles of the present.

So it must be every way. God gives to each age its own signs to lead men to Christ. We in this nineteenth century have signs different from those of the apostolic age. They may be greater or less; they are perhaps both greater and less at once. But they are certainly different. We cannot reasonably expect to estimate the full force of the witness to Christ, if, in vain attempt to recall what cannot be recalled, we throw away that which is peculiarly our own. We stand face to face with an actual Christianity, unquestionably the most marvellous spiritual phenomenon in the world's history. Through it we may best hope to understand what was the great reality from which it originally sprang. It cannot be right for us to endeavour to 'learn Christ' by proceeding as if we could obliterate eighteen centuries, and forget that there is such a thing as a living Christianity.

Now, when we do thus contemplate Christianity, we perceive that every way 'Christianity is Christ,' in a sense to which there is not any analogy in the other religions of the world. As an intellectual system, the Gospel is the setting forth Christ as the Light of the world, and the Word (or Revealer) of God. As a moral force, it is simply the reproduction of the life of Christ, not only by His light drawing the soul to Him, but by His grace conforming it to Him. As a spiritual life, it is a communion with God by a mysterious unity with Christ Himself. Thus at every point it discloses to us Christ as wielding a certain extraordinary power over the minds, souls, and spirits of men, such as no mere child of man ever has wielded, or could ever have a right to wield. So, through the consciousness of this present power, it bids us next, in the enquiry who and what He is, go on to study the manifestation of Christ on earth; because this is the central point, visible to us in the eternal life which the Gospel ascribes to Him—a life, which has in itself neither beginning nor end, but which is necessarily invisible to us before He came down to earth, and since He has ascended into heaven.

(*r*) The examination of the life of Christ.

So we go back necessarily to that life of Christ on earth. We seek through it to know Him. How much of it can we expect to see for ourselves? For how much must we be content to be taught by Him?

It is a familiar truth to us that even in the life of a

man like ourselves, but greater, wiser, holier than ourselves, there is, indeed, much which the world may know, and even more which his personal friends may know, partly by observation, partly by sympathy: but there is also much—the deepest part of that life and the best worth knowing—of which he alone can tell us, both what it is and what it means; and we have to accept his self-revelation in faith (a faith, of course, necessarily liable to some reserve), if we are to understand it at all.

The province of knowledge.

Infinitely truer must this be of One who confessedly stands on a level entirely above that of all other humanity. We may know Him in part for ourselves. As we look on the life of Christ, we see signs, which by their convergent power draw us to Him, and enable us to understand that He is the perfect Son of Man, that He is from God, perhaps that in some special sense He is the Son of God. The three forces which dominate human nature are power, wisdom, and goodness. They are in themselves the attributes of God; all manifestations of them on earth argue mission from Him, and likeness to Him. Now in the Lord Jesus Christ we find One who did mighty works, which none other man ever did, alike over the realm of nature and the realm of humanity. We hear from Him words of wisdom, which we could not have discovered, but which we can appreciate and know to be eternally true—words which 'never man spake like this man.' We behold in Him a perfectly stainless and peerless life; He could boldly challenge those who doubted His truth with words which in us would be presumption: 'Which of you convicteth Me of sin?' 'And if I say the truth, why do ye not believe Me?' We see that wonderful life closed by a death of perfect conquest over suffering and infinite self-sacrifice of love, and renewed by a resurrection from the grave, leading on to an ascension into heaven.

Now what does all this tell us? That He is the Messiah, for whom all history had been preparing, and all humanity waiting? That He is the true Son of Man, 'a light to lighten the Gentiles,' as well as 'the glory of His people Israel'? That He is in some special sense the Son of God, that God is not only with Him, but in Him?

CHAP. I.   THE FUNCTION OF CHRISTIAN EVIDENCE.   209

Yes! all this; but not more than this. The rest—the mystery of His nature and the mystery of His office, the reality of the Incarnation, the Atonement, the Mediatorial kingdom, the future Judgment—we cannot discover for ourselves. We must necessarily ask Him, 'Who art Thou? What sayest Thou of Thyself?' With His disciples we may have already learned that 'He has the words of eternal life'—that He cannot be deceived, and cannot lie. But what these words are, no Christian evidences can ever teach us. This ultimate truth, if it is to be learned at all, must be learned by faith. Such faith He unhesitatingly claimed; such faith all Christians have unhesitatingly given. If such faith be impossible, contradictory to reason, inconsistent with responsibility, Christianity is itself impossible. For, except in connexion with such faith claimed and given, Christianity cannot be judged, and, indeed, Christianity cannot live for a day. *The province of faith.*

Such I believe to be, drawn out in brief outline, the true order of the consideration of Christian evidences; and such the limitation of the function which we have a right to assign to them. This outline must, as far as possible, be filled up in the succeeding lectures.

VI. But in the meanwhile it may not be premature to draw two practical inferences, which seem not inappropriate to this present time. *Two practical inferences.*

The first bears on the question of the right attitude of the individual Christian towards the doubts and denials of Christianity, of which the very air is just now full. The Church, as a whole, must, I am convinced, deal with them. The disease of unbelief lies far too deep to be cured by the mere anodyne of pious sentiment or the wholesome distraction of beneficent activity. They who have to be teachers must, in different degrees, have some cognisance and understanding of them. But what of the individual Christian? To my mind all depends on this—whether they actually trouble, in himself or those for whom he is responsible, the power of Christian faith and the growth of spiritual life. If they do not, and if in daily life and thought he knows by experience the divine power of the Word and the grace of Christ, then he *(a) The right attitude towards doubts.*

P

need trouble himself but very little about these threatening but ever-changing spectres, hovering round the precincts of our Christianity. At most they should only drive him to study more deeply the actual truth of the Gospel, with that positive study which is often the best safeguard against the doubts and denials of the age. But if they do cross his path, and impede his spiritual progress, then let him look them seriously, patiently, and boldly in the face, without fear, but with the deep seriousness which is appropriate to momentous issues. Let him still rather contemplate the positive claims which Christianity has upon him, and so deepen and build up a positive faith, than distract his mind by an incessant refutation of this or that objection. Nor let him ever forget that, after all, Christianity is, and must necessarily be, a thing partly of understanding, partly of faith. If he has enough ground for faith, he may be patient even under some difficulty and perplexity, always seeking and praying for greater light, but waiting for it to grow in God's good time.

The other lesson is this—that in this gravest of matters, as in all others, it is our wisdom to accept cheerfully the age in which God has set our lot. We feel, indeed, its peculiar trials; we may think that there are points in which it is less happy than days gone by. But there is great truth in the conviction that 'God has set one thing against another'—that He gives us special grounds of faith to meet special trials, special compensations for special losses. The field of our observation enlarges as the ages roll on. If no larger share of light is given, the light diffused through the wider sphere will perhaps necessarily lose some of the intense brightness of the days when it was gathered into one narrow field. But the light itself is not diminished; and our eyes will grow familiar with the larger and dimmer radiance. There will be a 'reason for the hope that is in us,' not perhaps exactly the same, but yet as real and true, as that which satisfied the ages past. In it we must stand—for in no other can we stand—till, both for us and for them, hope passes into present reality.

(b) The true accordance with the spirit of the age.

CHAPTER II.

CHRISTIANITY AS AN INTELLECTUAL SYSTEM.

'Christ Jesus is made to us wisdom.'—1 Cor. i. 30.

'THE Greeks' (said St. Paul) 'seek after wisdom.' The reference is clearly to the eager speculations, physical and metaphysical, characteristic of that self-reliant and progressive intellect of the West, of which the Greek presented the liveliest type. But the search after wisdom belongs to man as man. After a different fashion, but with not less real earnestness, did the old Arab patriarch, in the stately immobility of Eastern life, cry out, 'O where shall wisdom be found, and what is the place of understanding?' Wisdom is like happiness in this, that all men seek for it, and few men find it. But what is wisdom? It is not 'understanding;' it is not (that is) simply a richness, depth, or subtlety of intellectual gifts. It is not 'knowledge,' although such knowledge were boundless as the sand on the sea-shore. No! it is the true conception of the meaning of life—the solution (to use a modern phrase) of the great problem of being.

The search for wisdom.

St. Paul declares that 'Christ is made unto us wisdom;' and he proceeds to dwell on the immeasurable difference between 'the wisdom of the world'—as exemplified especially in the keen, eager Greek race, the intellectual ruler of its duller and stronger conqueror, which he was then addressing—and 'the wisdom of God,' as revealed in Christ, and written by the Holy Spirit on the heart. In other words, he refers to the Gospel, on its intellectual side, as a Divine philosophy, giving the solution of that great enigma of life, which none else could read; just as the Lamb of God in the Apocalypse is represented as opening

Christianity as a philosophy.

the sealed book of mystery, which to all other beings was absolutely and hopelessly closed.

It is on this side that we may now proceed to consider it, in pursuing the course already marked out. In respect of the function, a true but limited function, of Christian evidence in the development of Christian faith, two principles have been laid down. First, that, like all other means by which great powers and truths are known, it is a complex thing, converging by many lines to one ultimate truth; and next, that for us, living in this advanced period of the world's history, the true order of thought should lead us to the manifestation of Christ in the past through the contemplation of the Christianity which professes to be a manifestation of Christ in the present, and the enquiry what it actually is now, as a system of thought, a moral force, and a spiritual life. For the knowledge of Christ in actual history, and of Christ in the living power of the present, is, I believe, to us in great degree what the fulfilment of prophecy and the manifestation of miracle in Him were to the first age of Christianity. It discloses to us signs of an extraordinary and enduring power through all ages and over all races of the world, which lead us to Christ, and prepare us at least to believe that He may well be the true King of humanity, and the only possessor of the words of eternal life. Of that past and present power of Christianity I take but one element to-day. I would seek to enquire whether St. Paul was really speaking the truth, and speaking it to all times, when he declared that 'Christ Jesus is to us wisdom'—that is (I repeat), that in Him is the true solution of the great problem of being.

Of that great problem there are clearly two parts. Man is conscious of himself in his own individual life. On this side wisdom is the knowledge of the meaning of that life—the Γνῶθι σεαυτόν of the old Greek philosophy—the answer to the three questions which even the simplest and the most unthinking occasionally puts to himself: 'What am I?' 'Whence am I?' 'Whither am I going?' Man, again, is conscious of a great world—not himself, although it is related to him and he to it. On that side wisdom is the knowledge of the scheme and pur-

CHAP. II. CHRISTIANITY AS AN INTELLECTUAL SYSTEM. 213

pose of the universe, what it is, whence it is, and why it was created. If Christ Jesus is wisdom, He must give the key to both kinds of knowledge—of the 'I,' the thinking subject in the little world within the breast, and of the ' Not I,' the object contemplated in the great world without. Man has always been seeking such a key to unlock to him the secrets of both worlds. What can Christianity offer to reward his search? *The solution offered in the Gospel.*

I. Man, as I have said, is conscious of himself. However his nature may have been evolved in some prehistoric past, however closely it may be linked to other orders of being in the present, yet he is conscious of an actual nature perfectly unique in the existing universe. *Individuality:*

First, he can think. Like the lower orders of brute creatures, he has his senses, and on the impressions of these senses he reasons in the visible sphere. So far no marked line can be drawn between human reason and brute instinct. But, unlike them, he can ascend from the visible and concrete to the invisible and abstract; that step involves at once the possibility of language, and unlocks range after range of thought. It is a truth so familiar to us as almost to lose strangeness, that this puny inhabitant of a world, which is but a little speck in the universe, can to a very large extent survey and discover the laws which rule in all its wide expanse, and can actually, millions of miles away, weigh the density and test the substance of every star. Every extension of our conception of the wonders of the universe in its two great infinities of vastness and minuteness, while it humbles us by the disclosure of the physical littleness of man, at the same time, by way of spiritual compensation, deepens our sense of the wonder of the intellect which attains to that conception. Yet even then that intellect is not satisfied. There is another and a subtler world in humanity itself—a world of ideas, thoughts, feelings, imaginations—a world invisible yet well known, distinct from the visible universe, which yet it interpenetrates. In that world the mind not only sees and discovers, but creates, for itself and for others, systems of thought and fabrics of beauty. Nor even then is the range of human intellect exhausted. By all human literature, by the philosophies and religions of the world, it is *(a) in thought;*

made evident that man will scale the starry walls of the universe—the *flammantia mœnia mundi*—in the search for the Supreme Power, by which all these things were made. He is capable, in some degree, of contemplating and understanding that mysterious Power, of seeing the invisible, and knowing the unknown.

But man can not only think: he can will. Unless every mental consciousness is sheer delusion, and all languages and institutions of men mere organised hypocrisies, man can at will originate thought, resolution, and, within limits, action. No physical force can crush will, though it may crush the life out of the body. No human power or authority can turn it from its course, except by conviction. No theory, which ascribes the seeming volition to an irresistible power of antecedent circumstances [1] or immediate motives, will stand against careful observation. The Supreme Power of the universe, whatever it is, though it may influence and rule the will, does not constrain it and does not destroy it. Under whatever 'law' it works, that law does not destroy a freedom which is absolutely unlike the simple instrumentality of physical machinery. It is a fact—account for it as we will—that individual human will, guided by individual thought, is an efficient factor in the working of the universe itself. It cannot create, but it can mould and direct both matter and force; it actually changes, within limits, the face of nature; it determines, within limits, the destinies of humanity itself. It is true that, when it emerges into the physical sphere, it has to work under physical conditions; but it works and knows that it works, and it is actually the one aggressive and advancing power. For while our knowledge of the greatness of nature increases, yet, through the practical use of that knowledge, the vastness of merely physical power is more and more encroached upon by the power of will.

(b) in will;

---

[1] In 'circumstances' I do not include antecedent mental condition, which (as our consciousness of the power of habit tells us) determines in some degree—and we know not in how great a degree—the action of any moment. For I contend, of course, that this mental condition is itself the result, not only of antecedent circumstances, properly so called, but of antecedent volitions. Nor can I think that the familiar and vivid consciousness of sudden resistance by a new impulse from within even to the power of this mental condition can be explained away as a self-delusion.

Lastly, he can love—or rather, he can be 'true in love'—and so realise certain spiritual ties which bind him to other beings. He can be true—that is, he can recognise that there is a right, in his own nature, in relation to his fellow-men, in relation to the Supreme Power; and that, once seen, it must be embraced, by an obligation different in kind from physical necessity. He can be true in love—that is, he can not only recognise duties, but rejoice in them; he can not only acknowledge that his freedom must be limited by the rights of others, but he can identify himself with others, and lose all thought of self in the enthusiasm of unity.

(c) in conscience and love.

So (to extend the old saying) he thinks, he wills, he loves : therefore he is, and knows that he is. That consciousness is simply indestructible. It matters not that extending knowledge tells him his infinite physical littleness. It matters not that both science and experience show him how greatly his life is affected by circumstance, bodily constitution, human influence. It matters not that, to his infinite wonder, he finds this treasure hidden in a mere earthen vessel, always in decay, liable at any instant to be shattered. In some sense it matters not that consciousness shows him his blindness of thought, his weakness or sinfulness of will. In spite of all, the simplest child and the wisest philosopher alike know that there is in them a distinct individuality, armed with these three great powers to think, to will, and to love. Knowing this, man cannot but ask, 'What is this "I" —this thinking, willing, loving soul? Whence came it? Whither goes it? What shall it profit to gain the whole world without, and yet lose this soul? And yet, if I am to save it, must I not know its true being, and source, and purpose?'

The indestructible sense of personality.

Now it is certain that any true wisdom must answer these imperious questions. It is of no avail, in place of an answer, to distract the soul by bidding it forget itself in gazing on the magnificent spectacle of the universe, whether under the guidance of science which discloses the wonder of its laws and forces, or under the guidance of poetry and art which reveal its beauty. It is almost as idle to exhort the soul to lose itself in the greatness and

Wisdom must acknowledge it.

immortality of the race, and to rebuke it sharply for paltriness and selfishness, if it refuses to consent to this moral self-abandonment. It is of less use still to suggest that all individuality is a simple delusion, to be got rid of, if it may be—that the soul is a link in a great physical chain of causation, or a fragment of a pervading Mind, 'becoming' (whatever that may mean) 'in humanity conscious of itself.' For a time it may be possible to distract the attention and perplex the understanding, so long as the soul muses half-passively in vague speculation; but one call to action, one strong impulse of conscience or love, scatters all these vague dreams to the winds. When we stand on the mountain height of contemplation, we may be for a time lifted out of ourselves, absorbed in the magnificent greatness of the view which spreads illimitable on every side, lost perhaps in the play of the great forces of nature, the whirlwind or the earthquake, the avalanche or the thunder-cloud. But let one pang of pain shoot through body or mind; let one cry for help come from a human voice; let the eye even catch for a moment a glimpse of our distant home; let one accent of the still small voice be heard, asking 'What doest thou here?' then all the grandeur around vanishes like a dream; the soul feels itself again, and feels itself alone, whether before man or before God.

Wisdom, then, must recognise the individual personality within, and must tell us whence it comes, what it is, whither it goes. We know how frankly and boldly the Gospel meets the challenge. It has made familiar as household words of practical life what were once the speculations of the philosopher, the aspirations of the poet, the secret mysteries of the initiated. For it puts forth, again and again, the most positive declarations that this individual nature is divine, not indeed a god, or an emanation of God, but yet made in His image; that it has a spiritual life now; that it has an immortality beyond the grave. It strikes in with a tone of unhesitating certainty in the conflict between the material and the spiritual, raging over the mystery of the relation of the individual to the universal. To use its own words, it 'brings life and immortality' out of darkness or twilight 'into light.' But

The recognition of it in the Gospel.

how does it do this? Whence comes this authority to settle questions as old as humanity itself?

The answer is easily given by looking at the wording of its declaration. It is not 'Christ teaches us wisdom,' but 'Christ Himself is made to us wisdom.' In this as manifies its peculiar and triumphant power. The nature and the destinies of humanity are not taught in an abstract philosophy, arguing what must be or what ought to be, trying to discover an ideal humanity under all the varieties and imperfections of actual men. They are set forth to us visibly in the actual person of the true Son of Man, Jesus Christ Himself. There is an infinite force in a teaching which says, not 'I think,' or 'I hope,' but 'Behold! I show you the mystery.' Certainly it was always by this method—the only one which can really conquer a world—that all the great acts of our Lord's manifestation on earth were declared to be revelations of mystery.

as manifested in the life of Christ.

The Incarnation is at once the renewal and the revelation of the image of God in human nature, making it fit to be the tabernacle of Godhead. The earthly life of Christ is the manifestation of the spiritual dignity, strength, and beauty of the individual human life, divested by the Divine Providence of all extraneous aids, whether from the world of nature or the world of humanity—standing out through poverty, obscurity, hatred, loneliness, in its own intrinsic majesty. The death of Christ—what is it even to the eye of man but the manifestation of the glory of perfect self-sacrifice, conquering by spiritual strength all suffering and contempt, the power of wickedness, and the bitterness of death? The Resurrection and the Ascension to heaven—these are the visible proofs of what is man's immortal nature and heavenly destiny. Those who first proclaimed Christianity as the 'wisdom of God,' laid emphasis on the fact that they themselves had seen these things with their own eyes; and they stood out not as reasoners or teachers, but as simple witnesses of what they had seen. In the manifestation of the Son of Man they saw, and through their eyes the world learned to see, what true humanity really is.

For although He is declared as more than man, yet He is also—to use the name which He most often applied to

Himself—the true 'Son of Man.' Up to His humanity the Gospel declares, in every form of direct teaching and illus-

<small>Christ the true Son of Man.</small> trative metaphor, that all men, if they will, may certainly grow. It does not falter in that declaration, even in the presence of the horrible consciousness of sin in us; because, while it recognises it in all its hideous reality, it declares that in Christ Jesus there is, for sinners who will lay hold of salvation, no hopeless bondage of sin, no looking forward to condemnation. It does not falter in the presence of death. For instead of those speculations and hopes—so much stronger in themselves than the arguments on which they are based—which are all that the highest philosophy could utter from the lips of the dying Socrates, and which are apt in most men to shrivel up to nothing at one touch of the cold finger of death, it dwells on the unity of men with Christ, who is 'the Resurrection and the Life,' Himself risen and raising all to be with Him; and in that belief it finds not a high and precarious, but a sure and certain hope.

This is the answer which 'Christ as made unto us wisdom' gives us to the great problem of being, so far as it concerns our individual nature. It is an answer unlike any other in its living power and unhesitating certainty—an answer which at least confirms all man's noblest hopes and speculations, and inspires him to do and to suffer all things in the conviction of a high destiny.

II. But it deals so far with only half the truth. The true difficulty, it will be said, meets us when we try to reconcile

<small>Unity:</small> this view of the individual humanity with the phenomena of the great world in which it is but a speck. What has the wisdom of the Gospel to say on this?

The problem itself is soon stated, for it is familiar to all ages of human thought.

We gaze on the great world of physical nature in all its bewildering variety and beauty. As we look beneath the

<small>(a) in nature;</small> surface we see what we term 'laws,' under which all the various forms of being are seen to fall into classes, to move in regular order, to act and react upon each other: we see how, under these laws, all varieties of force and matter constantly approach to unity, and lead us

to some one ultimate Power, clothing itself in many forms, from which all comes and in which all lives. Irresistibly, whether in the calm accents of philosophy or in the glowing utterances of poetry, we speak of Nature as one. We bestow upon it, considered as one, the admiration and reverence which could not be given to any one of its parts, or to all as a mere aggregate. Before the ever-extending sense of its greatness—whether in the immeasurable vastness of the starry system, or in the inconceivable minuteness of the clouds of microscopic germs—it is hard at times to keep our intellectual independence, and not to cry out, in utter abjectness of humility, 'What is Man? What am I?'

We turn to the world of humanity. Even there, in different degrees, the same impressions grow upon us. Through all individual, all national, all secular variations, (*b*) in humanity. great laws of human nature make themselves visible, write themselves out prosaically in tables of averages, or paint themselves more grandly on the great recurring movements of history. Under these laws, again, we seem to come to simplicity, almost to unity, of the great forces which rule individuals. We look to the spirit of the age, the public opinion, the science of this or that day, as something more than abstractions; and, almost perforce, we personify nations, ages, races, as something more than mere collections of individuals. Increasing knowledge shows how even these cannot be looked upon in isolation—how age acts upon age, nation upon nation—so that humanity itself must be regarded as a whole, having a life and development of its own, extending through all ages and over all lands. Again we come to the idea of a great unity of life and power; and as our science teaches us with ever-growing distinctness how wonderfully the body and the soul, nature and humanity, act and react upon each other, the conviction grows upon us that it is the same power which rules in both.

But what is that power? It cannot be merely a material power; for, in spite of philosophic desire for unity, and scientific imaginations of unknown potentialities of What is its matter, we cannot really believe that such a power ground? can rule will or evolve thought and conscience and love. It cannot be merely humanity; for, after all, humanity is utterly unable to guide or rule physical power, before which it again and again confesses itself conquered. The one great alternative must at last force itself upon us. Is it the universe itself— the vast body with a vast pervading mind? or is it a true, personal, and living God? On that depends the further question—Has it what we understand as a design, a purpose, a government, recognising man's freedom and thought and moral energies, in order at once to give them scope and guide them? Or is it simply a growth, without beginning or end, except in recurring cycles, in which the individual life, or even the life of a race, is no more than the life of one of the millions of coral insects, which die to build up slowly a huge fabric, itself already dead in part, and doomed to die continually as it rises?

It is wisdom in the great outer sphere to find the answer to these great questions. In all ages men have wearied themselves to find it. They have cried out to the unseen Power, 'Verily Thou art a Power that hidest Thyself.' 'Only show Thy glory,' whether it is the bright mist of an impersonal presence, or the face of a living God.

Here, again, Christianity gives a decisive and unhesitating answer by teaching her simplest children to believe in ' one God, the Father Almighty, who made heaven and earth, and all things visible and invisible.' The answer proclaims the ' one God ' as the answer of all true Monotheism. In this sense Christianity is 'as old as the creation.' But that which is especially emphatic in it is the addition of the declaration that the eternal God is ' the Father ; ' in virtue of which, even before any deliberate thought, every Christian child is bidden to pray to ' Our Father which art in heaven.' But how is it that this answer to the great question of all questions is given with this all-important addition, and with a familiarity of certitude which makes it a household word?

The answer of Christianity.

I have already ventured to contend that even the thought of man, if it embraces all the faculties of his nature, will decide the great issue between Theism and Pantheism. The firm belief in the one God is held, and I believe rightly held, to be the fundamental article in the 'natural religion,' underlying all the religions and many of the philosophies

CHAP. II. CHRISTIANITY AS AN INTELLECTUAL SYSTEM. 221

of the world. There is a natural theology of man, in which the concurrent voices of the intellect, the imagination, the conscience, and the affections, all bear witness to the truth, and develope the universal instinct of God into a deliberate and thoughtful belief. Nor must we fail also to contend that, in this searching after God, man is not left to himself—that both abstract probability and historical testimony point to the idea, which runs through the Old Testament, that revelation is also 'natural,' and that God has actually met this searching of man by direct revelation of Himself; till the belief of natural religion rises into the sublime creed, ' Hear, O Israel, the Lord our God is one Lord Jehovah; and thou shalt love Him with all thine heart, and with all thy soul, and with all thy might.' *The light and darkness of natural religion.*

But the sense that this eternal and invisible God is really ' our Father' is comparatively faint in ' natural religion '—not, indeed, absent, but apt to be overborne by the sense of awe, increasing in proportion as we see more and more of the infinite majesty of God. Even in the creed of Israel, in spite of the claim of that love which is the very spirit of sonship, the perception of Him as the Creator, the Ruler, the Lawgiver, the Judge, was far more prominent than the idea of His fatherhood. In the Gospel, on the other hand, while the faith in His eternity and infinite majesty is heartily accepted, it is exactly this doctrine of Fatherhood which is brought into especial prominence and ' revealed even to babes.'

Why and how is this? The answer, as before, is : 'Christ is our wisdom.' In Him the Gospel finds an ' Emmanuel,' ' a God' not only above us, but ' with us.' Hence, first, we actually see the one God in the face of Jesus Christ, as a true and living God. The grand vagueness of Pantheistic theory vanishes like a cloud before the conception of God, which the Gospel brings out in all the spheres of being. Thus in the physical sphere we understand that just as truly as Jesus of Nazareth, by the visible power of God, created and sustained being, ruled the winds and the sea, healed the sick body and raised it from the sleep of death, so the Divine will by *The revelation in the life of Christ: (a) of the one God;*

design and purpose, in righteousness and love, did create all in the beginning, did rule all at every stage of development, did and does guide all to an appointed end. In the spiritual sphere we understand that the graces which we call in men wisdom, righteousness, purity, love, and which accordingly we see developed to absolute perfection in Jesus Christ, are simply manifestations in man, so far as man can manifest them, of the attributes of the Divine nature. In the actual kingdom of Christ, as guided by truth and inspired by love, to work out present salvation and final judgment, we see the kingdom of God, and discern His moral government, which all things physical and all actions of men work together to fulfil. Of all that belongs to the true conception of the one God—His creative power, His perfect moral nature, His actual rule over all the universe—the declarations ascribed to the Lord, startling as they are, are literally true. 'No man hath seen God; the only begotten Son, He hath revealed Him.' 'He that hath seen Me hath seen the Father.' There is for vital religion an infinite difference between a God, towards whose invisible and inconceivable majesty man can but look up through the veils of secondary causes, rather feeling than knowing that He is, and a God whom we know face to face, as manifested to us visibly through the manifestation of Jesus Christ. The old faith of Monotheism, without losing its awful sublimity, glows with a new warmth and life.

But of yet greater moment is the addition of 'the Father.' We know by experience that the bare grandeur of Monotheism in looking up to one God, whose mere creatures we are, to be done with as seemeth to Him good, cannot of itself satisfy man, when he comes to feel that divine image in himself, and so to feel that, little as he is, he has powers, and even rights, before God. Marvellously has the picture of that noble perplexity been wrought out to us in the Book of Job, and pronounced, even while for its presumption it 'abhors itself,' to be truer before God than the grandest ideas of His absolute, inconceivable, unquestionable majesty, of which the minds of the three friends are full. That perplexity took visible form in all the strange fancies of idolatry, bridging over the gulf between earth and heaven, now by deifying men, now by dreaming of

(*h*) of the Father.

various emanations from God. Nor was it less clearly, though it was less grossly, visible in the constant and (as it seems to us in our happier state) inexplicable weakness, in which the Israelites shrank from the awful greatness and purity of their monotheistic creed. We see still the want which it indicates, when we observe that the grand bare simplicity of that creed of Islam, which has been borrowed from Judaism, while it can inspire with a true religious faith the poor and the simple, and while in Africa at this moment it can even conquer savage tribes from gross idolatry, yet cannot coexist with the growth, by education and civilisation, of a vivid conception of the Divine in man.

Christianity meets this want frankly. In Christ the one God is seen in all His absolute perfection and in all His eternal majesty; but He is seen revealed in man and to man. Hence He is known especially not as our Creator or our King, but as really ' our Father,' whose children are like Himself, and whose delight it is that these children should not be slaves, bowed down before Him, incapable of even raising their eyes to heaven, but children indeed, growing into His likeness, knowing and trusting and loving Him. Such a spirit of sonship is the dominant power in the earthly life of the Son of God and man. It is the characteristic of the Gospel—in this respect (as St. Paul so often pleads) infinitely above the law—that it says (what no system of simple Monotheism can clearly say) : ' The Spirit beareth witness with our spirit that we are sons of God.' ' Now are we the sons of God . . . and, when He shall appear, we shall be like Him : for we shall see Him as He is.' The capacity of a spiritual progress, which can fill the whole sphere of this life, and which, having conquered the world, shall yet extend infinitely beyond the grave, is involved in the very essential idea of Christianity.

It will be seen at once that, in giving this answer to the question as to the origin and meaning of the great world without, the Gospel at the same time confirms its teaching already given as to the true spirituality and dignity of the nature within. The two react upon and illustrate each other. Through the consciousness of the Divine in man, as the son of God, we ascend to the living conception of the eternal Father Himself. Through the contemplation of the Father visiting us in His righteousness and love, we deepen in ourselves the consciousness of our true sonship. The two conceptions, elsewhere apt to be isolated or even antagonistic to each other, are here unquestionably made one.

But perhaps even more unique is the power of this 'wisdom' of the Gospel in the boldness with which it faces the great mystery of evil—the one great contradiction to both forms of faith, the faith in humanity and the faith in God—the one great hindrance to the conception of that unity of God and man, which is the special glory of Christianity.

<small>The light thrown on the mystery of evil.</small>

It will not consent to explain it away, in a spirit of mere optimism, by ignoring its existence altogether, by treating it as a mere superficial excrescence, capable of being removed by better laws and social arrangements, by identifying it in man with simple ignorance, or by audaciously insisting, against all reason, to say nothing of conscience, that it is a lower form of good. Yet it equally refuses, with the Pessimist or the Manichæan, to exalt it into an inherent power in man and in the world, capable of an endless strife, whether by positive antagonism, or by a negative inertia of evil, against the power of good. It confirms unhesitatingly the observation which is in itself able to tell us that evil is, and that it is deadly—as sin in the individual soul, blinding, paralysing, polluting the spiritual life—as a burden on the great world, under which 'all creation groans,' both in itself and in its bitter consequences. The characteristic doctrine, which gives to Christianity its visible emblem in the cross, brings out both these forms of evil with a plainness so unsparing and so awful, that the very existence of evil in man's nature is wrongly supposed to be a peculiar doctrine of Christianity. But the peculiarity of the Gospel rather is that, on the other hand, it boldly declares, in the manifestation of Christ Himself, that evil is not the true nature of man, and that it is not the will of God; that for the world it was not in the beginning and shall not be in the end; that for the individual soul there is no need for any to grovel hopelessly in sin or despair under inevitable condemnation.

CHAP. II. CHRISTIANITY AS AN INTELLECTUAL SYSTEM. 225

On this mysterious subject we cannot but note in what marvellous accordance with reason, speculative and moral alike, it holds that straight way to truth, from which these opposite errors diverge on either hand. No wisdom suits the world as it is, which either ignores evil or deifies it. The Gospel does neither. Christ as our 'Wisdom,' like a wise physician lays bare the actual disease, but considers it only in relation to the original health, and to the remedy which is to restore that health for ever.

III. Such is, in brief outline, the aspect which the Gospel presents, in view of the great problem of life, as a Divine philosophy, as a 'wisdom of God,' in the simple manifestation of Christ Himself. It speaks for itself; but yet we may well incline to believe that it stands out in more wonderful and striking force, if it be compared (as St. Paul compares it) with other forms of wisdom, claiming to answer the enigma of self, the enigma of the world, the enigma of evil. *The philosophy of the Gospel.*

It cannot surely be necessary to compare it with the theories of other religions—the extinct Polytheisms of days past, the strange mythologies and rituals into which the sterile beauty of the Vedas has degenerated, the bare Nihilism of the Buddhist theory coloured secretly by creature worship, or the cold morality of Confucianism. In these comparisons no one will question its infinite and obvious superiority. *Comparison with pagan religions.*

Perhaps it is hardly necessary to compare it even with the grand Monotheism of the Jewish or Mohammedan systems. It is hard to believe that the latter has any great future. If there is yet a future for the former— if the Israelites, as they believe and we believe, are yet to play a great part in the world's history—it must be by a true Judaism, which has found and worshipped not humanity, but a personal Messiah. We need not consider its claims, till it has accepted a Messiah in Him whom once it rejected, or has found some one who shall be greater than He. *Comparison with Judaism and Mohammedanism.*

Probably it will be concluded that if a religion is to rule, it must be Christianity, but that the era of philosophy has now dawned. For what philosophy, then, shall we put the

Q

wisdom of the Gospel aside? Shall it be for the mere Humanitarianism of an individual type, which either, in what men call Agnosticism, puts off all question of the Supreme Power, or, in a bare Deism, acknowledges it as existent and passes it by—in either case resting in our own humanity, as the only thing we know, working with this, in contented disregard of any other power, and supposing that somehow all will come right in the end? Shall it be for the simple Materialism, tracing all to physical law or force, so breaking down the barrier which all consciousness and experience raise between spirit and matter, and necessarily denying our distinctive humanity? Shall it be for the Pantheism which, acknowledging spirit and mind in terms, yet ignores utterly the indestructible consciousness of our individual existence, and our moral responsibility? Shall it be for the newer forms of the 'Religion of Humanity,' sinking our individuality either in a mere abstraction, or worshipping in the concrete human society a many-headed idol, which reproduces all individual defects, and is incapable of ruling with any absolute sovereignty?

Comparison with modern philosophies.

It is almost under protest that, even for a moment, we contemplate the Gospel as a mere intellectual system, a philosophy of being. Yet even so, need it fear comparison, in respect at once of a fair recognition of all the facts, and of a magnificent unity of idea including them all, with any of the rival forms of the wisdom of the world? May not the Christian, after eighteen centuries, still acknowledge with St. Paul that the 'very foolishness of God'—the simplest and rudest conception of Gospel truth—'is wiser than' the wisest of 'men'?

(a) Its abstract completeness.

But yet, to increase the wonder, we have to note that this wisdom is not for the few thinkers only, but for the many, the workers and sufferers of this life. So our Lord expressly declared it to be, and thanked the Father that it was so. So His Church has ever rejoiced to acknowledge and to pay the debt of teaching, not only to the Greek, but to the barbarian—not only to the wise, but to the unwise. For this is the result of the fact that the wisdom of the Gospel is set forth, not in abstract speculation or argument—though it fears neither and uses both—but in

(b) Its intelligibility to all.

the manifestation of Jesus Christ. Now the simplest child or the most unlearned peasant can learn to know Jesus Christ. He can understand that in Him there is the true Son of Man, whom by love and imitation he can follow. In Him he can learn to know God's righteousness and love, and to understand that sin is, and yet that it is forgiven and can be conquered. In Him, even under the shadow of death, he can cherish the sure and certain hope of immortality and heaven, though his conception of both may be vague and childish. There is a simplicity of power in the contemplation of wisdom in the concrete and personal form of the life of Christ, through which thousands and tens of thousands, who could never enter into the depth or subtlety of an abstract philosophy, find light, even if it shine 'amidst encircling gloom,' to 'lead them on.' But, at the same time, that life, while it is simpler, is yet deeper in its meaning than all the abstract principles which can be drawn from it; from these the profoundest thinker comes back to it, and, as he studies it again and again, finds in it new revelations of the mysteries which underlie all human nature and life, and which press themselves on those who not only act but think. This wisdom is open to all who seek it in simplicity, whether the unconscious simplicity of practical experience, or the simplicity of conception, which is the fruit of the maturest thought, knowing at once its scope and its limitation.

Whence came that wisdom? So far as human origin is concerned, it sprang out of the narrow exclusive system of Judaism, in which there was, indeed, a steadfast belief in the one God, but in which there seemed (c) Its actual origin. to be no capacity of spiritual growth, no free scope for human thought and energy. Its Author was but a Galilean peasant, unlearned in the lore of the schools, trained in the simplicity of the carpenter's house, despised and persecuted as a fanatic or impostor, by all who sat on the seats of Jewish learning. Its first preachers were a handful of poor men, fishermen, publicans, and the like, with but one man among them of high education and genius, and this one man won by miracle from the foremost ranks of persecution.

Yet out of this there rose—to speak only of its intellectual aspect—a light of wisdom, which has pervaded the whole atmosphere of modern society in the leading races of the world—which has fostered all the forms of human thought, progress, freedom—which has outshone all the systems of the profoundest students and thinkers, and thrown a radiance on all the forms of the great problem of being— which, if it disperses not every cloud, yet at least illuminates the two worlds of human consciousness, with a brightness growing more and more towards the full noonday of the hereafter.

IV. What shall we say to this? The simple answer, which has suggested itself again and again to simple minds, is the cry, 'This is the Lord's doing, and it is marvellous in our eyes.' With St. Paul they will thank God that, when by its own wisdom, searching in vain into the mysteries of life, the world 'knew not God,' and in the fullest sense knew not even man, it pleased Him, by the simple preaching of Christ, to show what 'eye hath not seen, nor ear heard, neither hath it entered into the heart of man to conceive.' They will hold that it is of God, not of man, that 'Christ Jesus is made unto us the true wisdom.'

Conclusion.

But, if this seems to us too hasty an inference, yet at least we may fairly see in this intellectual greatness of Christianity as a philosophy of life, one step at least in the preparation for the acceptance of Him to whom it bears witness. My contention is here, as throughout the whole argument, that the cord which draws the soul to Christ is manifold—that the evidences of His Divine nature appeal to all the various faculties of our humanity, and converge by many lines to one point. This is the first. We need not be afraid to try its strength in itself, while yet we remember that not on it alone, but on it in conjunction with others, the stress of the great argument lies.

Let us try its strength in itself. The air is full of other theories, advanced with confidence as destined to supersede the philosophy of the Gospel, or possibly, like the old Gnosticism, condescending to weave that philosophy into some wider and more perfect system. It needs some calmness to stand firm against bold assertion, and the presentation to us, in the name of science, of a sweeping simplicity of theory, which, in application to such a life and nature as ours, is really a *primâ facie* evidence rather of falsehood than of truth. But let us look thoughtfully at the answer given by the Gospel. Let us see whether, in recognising all the facts, acknowledging both the *Ego* and the *Non ego*, enforcing the sacredness both of the individual and the collective life—in acknowledging the reality of evil, and yet resolutely depressing it to a secondary place and a transitory power—in presenting the wisdom of God as embodied in that personal life, which at once appeals to the simplest and the most universal intelligence, and yet satisfies the deepest and the most ultimate study—there is any that can be put either beside it, or even second to it, in the history of humanity. If not, then we may at least see that, in what we can understand and test, 'never man spake like this Man;' and accordingly we may at least be prepared to listen not unwillingly, when He goes on to claim that right to speak of the 'heavenly things' which can belong only to one who is the Son of God as well as Son of Man.

CHAPTER III.

CHRISTIANITY AS A MORAL FORCE.

'Christ Jesus is made unto us righteousness.'—1 Cor. i. 30.

Christianity as a moral force.

FROM the contemplation of Christianity as a divine philosophy, we pass to consider it as an effective moral power, in the history of the past and in the experience of the present. In so doing we enter on a consideration of even greater importance than the other; for the search after wisdom belongs almost entirely to the few who are the leaders of the many, but the 'hunger and thirst after righteousness,' as a necessity both of individual and of corporate life, comes home to the better moments of every human soul. If only Christianity shows itself to be a supreme and unequalled moral force in the world, men will often be prepared to accept it on that sole evidence, either dispensing with all consideration of its abstract theory, or being inclined to believe that theory to be true simply on the ground of its moral results. So it certainly was in the early Apostolic days; so it has always been, but perhaps never more strikingly than in our own times. The consideration of the morality of the Gospel, not as an abstract system, but as a living and quickening power, is put forward now more than ever—on the one side as a ground of faith, on the other as a reason either for rejecting Christianity altogether, or for extending a condescending toleration to it, as an imperfect system destined, after having done some not inconsiderable service to humanity, now at last to vanish away.

I. In entering on this consideration, it might at first sight seem as if we had to investigate two questions—first, whether Christianity has shown itself to be a moral force of commanding power in the history of the world; and next,

CHRISTIANITY AS A MORAL FORCE.

whether that moral ascendency has been such as to accord with the claims which the Gospel makes for its Master—claims which, whether true or false, are obviously unparalleled and final. But a moment's consideration will show that of these two questions only the latter really calls for discussion. No one who studies history can possibly doubt that Christianity—in which I include both the proclamation of the Gospel and the formation of the Church—did introduce a new and very remarkable moral force into human society. It appeared at a time when old religions, old moralities, old civilisations—Greek, Roman, and Asiatic—were dying out. It was, in the first three centuries of its existence, the one growing and living power, both as abstract in thought and as concrete in life; and that power was in no sense material, and was not mainly intellectual. It was beyond all else a moral and spiritual power, and it proved its vitality by overrunning and pervading the civilised world. Then came the collapse of the old Roman Empire, and the irruption into Europe of those races, roughly and vaguely classed as 'barbarian,' some of which passed away, while others became the progenitors of modern European society. There is no historical doubt that, as a matter of fact, Christianity was the moral force which laid hold of these races and civilised them. Their civilisation borrowed much of its framework and system from the old Roman law, but the spiritual vitality which animated that framework was undoubtedly Christian. In fact, on the degree in which they accepted or rejected Christianity depended mainly the power which they had of assimilating civilisation, and so asserting their place as factors in the European society of the future. So it was in the foundation of modern Europe; and if we trace step by step the gradual building up of the national life in the countries which are the leaders of modern civilisation and the rulers of the modern world, it is impossible not to see—whether we rejoice or mourn over it—that the impress of Christianity is deeply marked upon their actual moral life, sometimes in the rigid lines of law and institution, sometimes in the subtler and more spiritual forces of opinion, tone, and faith.

Its reality and greatness historically certain.

Hence, as it seems to me, the first question answers itself. All searchers into history, whether they be believers or unbelievers, whether they accept Christian morality as eternal, or reject it for their own times or for the future to which they look forward, will with one voice avow that Christianity has been a leading moral force in human history.

The real question is the second of the two proposed. Of what nature is that moral force? Is it only one of many moral influences, possibly the best hitherto known, but destined to be superseded by something better as the ages roll on? Or is it in itself a moral force, so unique, so deep-rooted, so permanent in vitality, as to be worthy of its high pretensions? For these are neither more nor less than a claim for its Founder of a kingdom universal and eternal, extending over body, soul, and spirit, through all peoples, nations, and languages, and through all ages till time shall be no more.

<small>The question is of its absolute supremacy.</small>

II. Now, in considering this question, it is important, just as in examining the 'wisdom' of the Gospel, to gather (as from St. Paul's great saying in the text) what is the nature of the moral force which Christianity has introduced to the world. As we are told 'Christ Himself is our wisdom,' so we are also told that 'Christ is Himself our righteousness.' It would be out of place here to enter into any of the deeper meanings which Christian doctrine attaches to this declaration. It is enough to look at it simply as describing the moral force of Christianity exhibited in the world. That force is not a system of laws, however holy and just and good, or of religious rites, however sacred and full of significance. Christianity has, of course, its laws and its rites: it necessarily uses both in order to mould the outer life. But the moral force of Christianity itself depends on something wholly different and infinitely greater. Nor, again, is it a philosophy, an idea, a moral principle. Christianity has, indeed, its philosophy, and it necessarily deals with ideas and principles, when it has to give an account of its relation to the conception of truth and the moral nature of man. But Christianity, as a moral power, is what the text implies by calling

<small>The peculiar character of this moral force,</small>

Christ Himself our righteousness. It is the reproduction of a life; it is the stamping upon human natures the likeness of the life, death, and resurrection of Jesus of Nazareth. To be a Christian is to 'put on the new man, created after the image of God,' but that new humanity is no ideal or abstraction. It is the image of Christ. 'To put on Christ,' 'to be found in Christ,' as our righteousness, is the sum and substance of Christian morality. 'I live, yet not I, but Christ liveth in me,' is the startling language of one who felt and knew the new moral force of the Gospel.

as a reproduction of the life of Christ,

There is a close connexion between 'Christ our wisdom' and 'Christ our righteousness.' Christ is our wisdom, as manifesting to us at once what is the perfection of the humanity which we find within, and what are the true attributes of the Supreme Power above. Christ is our righteousness, as teaching us to embody this knowledge of man and of God in a 'service which is perfect freedom.' The light of thought and the moral energy of life thus interpenetrate each other. Even in this lower sense there is a profound truth in the text, 'In Him was light, and the light was the life of men.'

Now it should be noted that this conception of a new moral force is absolutely unique in the history of the world. For no king or lawgiver, for no great philosopher or poet, for the founder of no other religion—a Moses, a Zoroaster, a Buddha, a Confucius, or a Mohammed—was this reproduction of his life, as the principle of moral regeneration and growth, ever claimed. All of these had, and they professed that they had, 'their day,' and then 'ceased to be.' What lived after them were their laws, their works, their poems, their philosophies, their religions—not themselves, whom, indeed, the best and noblest desired most utterly to efface. What such a claim implies as to the nature of Him for whom it is made, and whether there is not a strange inconsistency, when the life of Jesus is accepted as an absolute permanent type of righteousness by those who make Him simply a man, I do not now stop to enquire; and, indeed, I might easily leave that enquiry to be answered by any thinking man for himself. But, putting

unique among the religions of the world.

this aside, what we are concerned with is that this was the moral force which Christianity claims to introduce into the world, and which those who have lived as Christians and died as martyrs have declared to be the secret of their power to rise to a new life and to defy death.

It is important to discern the relation of this moral force to the nature of man as it actually is. Christianity is, indeed, a 'religion of humanity' in acknowledging the Divine in man, with that free recognition which is the condition of all progress, and which under a bare monotheism, like that of Islam, is seldom found. Its moral principle is therefore a free development from within of the image of God in close conformity with the life of Christ. But it regards human nature not as we desire it to be, but as it actually is. It acknowledges—what all thoughtful and honest observation must surely acknowledge —a corruption of man's nature as such; and accordingly it holds that the reproduction of the life of Christ implies the 'casting off of this the old man,' as well as the 'putting on the new.' The two are, in fact, the negative and positive sides of the same process, just as a right medicine to the sick body by the same action drives out the poison of disease, and fosters the health and strength. But Christianity always declares—what only a revelation from God can turn out of mere hope into certainty—that this sin or corruption was not a part of man's true original nature; that, in virtue of the life and death of Christ, the soul is purified and restored to its place in the family of God; and that no individual soul need ever sink hopelessly into corruption, or fear that the spiritual life may go out in what we call death. The one ever-recurring declaration is, 'There is no condemnation for those who are in Christ Jesus.' 'They are raised from the death of sin; they can walk in newness of life.'

Its relation to humanity as it is.

But, while Christianity is thus a religion of humanity, yet the moral force which it introduces is also, in the strictest sense, a derivation from God. For the life of Jesus Christ is looked upon as the manifestation of God in human flesh, especially in the beneficence which is essentially divine. Sometimes this

Its relation to the power of God.

divine manifestation is expressed in the metaphor, 'In Him was light'—the mysterious force which is one condition of physical energy, and of the existence both of vegetable and animal life—the one gift absolutely free, absolutely pervading the whole world, capable of being reflected, diffused, refracted, by earthly things, but in no sense of being created or increased. Sometimes, dropping all metaphor, 'in Him was manifested the love of God,' as recognising a true unity of nature with His creatures, and therefore not only protecting, guiding, ruling, but loving with an unwearied love. Hence the strength of the moral force of Christianity, because the secret of the life of which it is the reproduction is placed in the same Supreme Power which created and sustains the physical universe, which made the soul of man, and which rules both his outer and his inner life. Christianity is never weary of repeating, 'God was in Christ, reconciling the world to Himself.' 'Your life'—your moral and spiritual life—' is hid with Christ in God.'

These characteristics of the moral force of Christianity are of infinite moment. It is the reproduction of a real human life by free development of our human nature. It deals with man as having in him corruption, but as already redeemed from that corruption, and able to conquer it. It places the first source of all spiritual energy in the love of God manifested in the life and death of Jesus Christ.

For from these characteristics there is much that follows at once.

First, a certain practical simplicity and vividness of power. It is true that the study of character is the highest and deepest study, and the discovery of an ideal humanity the ultimate aim of the profoundest philosophy. But the moral influence of an example—the example of one not dead but living—to draw men unto Him, is a power which lays hold of all. The youngest child, the simplest peasant, the poorest slave, can understand, love, and reproduce the 'mind of Christ Jesus.' They know what it is to follow Christ, as to the cross on earth, so also to the glory of heaven. They understand well enough that in Him the God, whom, by the universal instinct of humanity, they grope after, and feel rather than know, has manifested

Its practical simplicity.

His truth and holiness, but above all His love. In that knowledge accordingly they actually find a new moral force—'a new man' to put on, 'created after the image of God in righteousness and true holiness.'

Next follows an absolute universality of this moral force. It belongs to man, simply as man. Born in the narrow precincts of Judaism, its growing life burst through all limitations, even though stones, once sacred, were by that growth riven and split asunder. The words were always on the lips of Christian preachers: 'There is neither Jew nor Greek, barbarian, Scythian, bond nor free;' 'Christ is all in all.' Of all the divisions of mankind that moral force has destroyed none, and yet is limited by none. Distinctions there have been, and there will be, of characters, classes, nations, races; but separation there need never be. The meanest slave and the greatest prince, the simplest child and the profoundest thinker, the lowest and the highest of the races of humanity—all are capable of the life of Christ, as all have been redeemed by His death.

Its universality.

But, again, this moral force comes home, not to the purer and loftier spirits only, but to sinners, who know that they are sinners. With a boldness which, as in His own life, perplexed the severe and frightened the timid, Christianity from the first came down from the pure mountain heights into the dense and polluted air of ordinary human life. It cried out to warn those who in vice were sinning against themselves, degrading their nature, ruining their souls. It stood between those who in crime were breaking the laws of truth and love, and preying on each other. It bade men understand that vice and crime were also sin—outrage on the righteousness and love of the God who made both themselves and their fellow-men. But its attitude has never been chiefly one of rebuke. It is an attitude of pity and hope. 'Why will ye die, O house of Israel?' 'It is not the will of your Father that even one of His little ones should perish.' In the words of the Master, its message is, 'Thy sins are forgiven.' 'Go and sin'—for thou needest sin—'no more.' It holds up the highest ideal of holiness and love; but it

Its applicability to sinners.

promises, even to souls utterly weakened, stained by sin, that, if they will, the 'Christ' shall be 'formed in them.'

Lastly, this moral force is absolutely detached from all those frameworks of human life which necessarily pass away. Codes of law, systems of government, institutions, and civilisations, theories of philosophy, forms of language and literature — it can live with and rule all; it is identified with none. As one by one they perish, its life may be for a time disturbed and shaken, especially if it has clung to them too closely. But it is only for a time. Soon it has adapted itself to the new conditions, and shown itself as vigorous and progressive as ever. Thus, as it is universal in space, so it promises to be, and claims to be, universal in time. It deals with man as man, not (as some philosophies had done) with an ideal man detached from all surroundings, but the actual man, as he exists in them all. Hence, so long as humanity lasts, it claims to be able to endure. *Its permanence.*

These are the necessary results of the peculiar characteristics of Christianity as a moral force. It has simplicity of application, universality of scope, appropriateness to the world as sinful, and independence of all the perishable forms of human society. We have next to consider in actual fact, how have these forces actually worked upon the moral nature of man?

That nature is obviously twofold—at once individual and social. The very name 'man' applies both to the individual as individual, and to the race as a whole. Here we are brought again face to face with that great duality of consciousness which meets us intellectually—the consciousness of the *Ego*, the inalienable individuality of the soul, and the consciousness of the *Non ego*, the great world of which the individual soul is but a part. But that great world in the moral aspect is far narrower, for it is only the world of persons, not of things; yet it is far closer to us, for we do not only gaze on it—we are bound to it by spiritual ties, and must realise that unity by action. Now a true morality must meet both phases of this twofold consciousness. *The twofold nature of man.*

On the one hand, each of us has an inner life of thought,

emotion, aspiration, will, which no other human being, nor all society put together, can either understand or rule. No system of thought or life can be morally sound, which, either directly or indirectly, ignores or overbears this individuality, whether by despotic authority, or by levelling tyranny of society, or even by a worship (as men call it) of humanity. On the other hand, all of us are bound together by a marvellous network of unseen spiritual ties, into some of which we are born without our will, while some we make for ourselves, but often cannot unmake; and, moreover, these ties are strengthened and protected by mutual needs, and quickened by mutual affections. No system, therefore, which virtually isolates man, making society not a necessary law, but a simple convention—not a sacred thing, but a matter of pure convenience, in which 'every one is for himself,' 'and God' (if there be a God) 'for us all'—can possibly claim the allegiance of a thoughtful mind. Individuality and unity—how shall they both be preserved? how shall they be reconciled? It is this question which underlies almost all the great controversies—social, political, ecclesiastical—which now or in days past have exercised human society. For by the right harmony of these two principles that society must be sustained, as truly as our planetary system is kept in its marvellous order through balance of the force by which all its various bodies are drawn into one, and that centrifugal velocity which is at every point a tendency in each body to pursue the straight line of its own independent course.

Individuality and unity.

Now, if we consider the moral force which Christianity declares itself to introduce into the world, we see that it guards both these principles, not by a formal balance of them, but by a perfect cultivation of both. This reproduction of the life of Christ is at once individual to each, and yet absolutely common to all. There is, therefore, in it a unity of all mankind; but it is not a unity binding man directly to man, and so liable to fetter his individual freedom. It is a unity binding each in perfect individuality to God in Christ, and so binding all indirectly with one another. The metaphor, so familiar as to have become hackneyed, is the metaphor of

Both harmonised in the moral force of Christianity.

the body. But in a body the members are not directly tied together—the hand to the foot, or the ear to the eye. If they were, how could each be perfect and free for its own peculiar function? They are one because all are united to the one centre of nervous energy, which we call the head, or to that centre of blood-circulation, which we call the heart. Such exactly is the conception of unity reiterated in many forms in the Gospel. Christ—that is, God in man—is 'the Head of each man;' with whom each has a spiritual union, reproducing the life of Christ in his individual nature. That union no power from without can interfere with for a moment; and for its sake He expressly declares that all other ties, even the sweetest and most sacred, to parents, or wives, or children, must, if necessary, be sacrificed. But, on the other hand, Christ being thus the head of all, the whole body is one. 'If one member suffer, all suffer with it' in community of pain. 'If one be honoured, all rejoice with it' in the thrill of a common gladness. There is a wonderful difference between the grand theories—so often repeated since Plato's time in many forms—of a 'Divine Republic,' in which the individual is lost, and the well-centred spiritual kingdom of God, in which each individual lives by perfect union with the Divine King.

III. Accordingly we have to observe, first, how the new moral force of Christianity has guarded the individual thought, life, freedom of each human being, as one for whom Christ died and as one in whom Christ lives. *The guardianship of individuality.*

First it does this with the greatest emphasis and plainness where it is most necessary. I mean in the protection of the weak. It dignifies especially those virtues which are at once the grace of the weak and the self-restraint of the strong—humility and modesty, patience and gentleness, forgiveness and self-sacrifice. It is obviously wisdom so to do, for it is in the weak that individuality needs especially to be guarded. *In the weak.*

This is best seen by considering the various embodiments of weaker humanity—the child, the woman, the poor, the slave.

For the child it is impossible to exaggerate the new

sacredness given to childhood by the declaration of Christ, when He made it the very type of the spirit of His kingdom, and said, 'Whosoever receiveth one little child receiveth Me.' An old heathen moralist spoke nobly of the reverence due to childhood; but it was reserved for Christianity to realise this in practice. Of the many ways in which it has taught this reverence, it will be enough to take one, perhaps the most striking of all. It teaches it, even in relation to the parental authority, rightly, because naturally, held sacred, but often, as in the old Roman law, invested with an unnatural and unreasonable absolutism. Under Christianity the children are not only the children of men. By the fundamental ordinance of the Church they are recognised as children of God, taken out of the arms of their parents to be sealed as His in the sweetness of their infancy. Hence they, as truly as their parents, have their rights. They are not only to be shielded from evil and cruelty—not only to receive in the name of Christ nurture and education—but also to claim an education which shall not be one of hard compulsion and sternness, recognising freedom in the child as well as duty, and appealing to that freedom by the spiritual forces of duty and love. For the softer influences of home, and for the moral force of education, we have had to look mainly to the teaching of the Gospel.

The child.

The woman Christianity, like nature itself, recognises as not lower, but weaker, than man. Accordingly it is certain that under the Gospel the whole position of woman has been raised—first, by the sacredness of marriage, made actually a type of the great central mystery of the Incarnation; next, by the dignity of motherhood, consecrated anew in the high privilege of her who was 'blessed above women;' lastly, by the scope given to the exercise by women of spiritual functions, and especially of that sweet and tender beneficence of ministration in the Church of Christ, in which women so infinitely surpass men.

The woman.

It is true that Christianity plainly recognises—what both nature and experience emphatically assert—that there is a leadership of authority in man, earned by his assumption of the greater share of the burdens and sacrifices of life, and sustained by greater strength, physical, intellectual, and moral. But the Christian conception of man's authority is of a leadership of wisdom and love, not a tyranny of force; and woman's position is one of free subordination rather than mere subjection. That conception has made its way, and raised the position of woman in Christendom far above what it is and has been under other religions, whether of the East or of the West, whether of ancient or of modern days. Perhaps in the fabric of our legal and social system there may still be some elements unjust and oppressive towards women. But their origin is to be traced to the traditions of the old Roman law, or the necessities of the feudal system. Christianity has nothing to do with them. On the contrary, the Gospel testifies emphatically against them by the enunciation of the great principle of the true relation of the sexes, consecrated in the most solemn form by the comparison with the central mystery of the relation of Christ to humanity. The only respect in which the Church was ever false to that principle was in the adoption for a time of the spirit of asceticism, degrading the relation between the sexes in an inordinate admiration for celibacy, and involving not unfrequently something of an ignorant depreciation of woman. But the Christianity of the Gospel itself, even the Christianity of the Church, which at that very time made marriage a sacrament, have always protested against this delusion, and have always tended to the protection and exaltation of woman.

The poor, in strength, wealth, or influence, need protection against the self-assertion of the strong, and the tyranny of society. Christianity in Christ Himself has ac- *The poor.* cordingly dignified poverty, and given a new life to the exertion of active beneficence in aid of its weakness. 'Each man shall bear his own load' ($\phi o \rho \tau i o v$) is the stern yet beneficent dictum of nature, acknowledged also in the Gospel. 'Bear ye one another's burdens' ($\beta \acute{a} \rho \eta$)—the loads (that is) become oppressive—is declared emphatically to be 'the law of Christ.' It is better, no doubt, that the former principle should be as far as possible realised; that every man should have the opportunity, and that every man recognise the duty, of free and self-supporting action. At times, perhaps, Christian morality has sinned in carrying to excess the duty and

R

privilege of beneficence; and so has fallen into serious errors—the error of tolerating too laxly the inequalities of condition, which it can thus redress, and the error of aiding so lavishly what seems weakness, but may be idleness or cowardice, as to sap the sense of independent responsibility. But after all, there will be always large scope for beneficence, and there will be need to maintain it earnestly against selfishness. Under any system, the poor—that is, the weak, the helpless, the suffering—there will always be. For inequality, physical, intellectual, and moral, is, quite as truly as equality, the law of human nature. If an artificial equality of circumstances were enforced to-day, yet, if men were left free, inequality would recommence to-morrow. In fact, this inequality increases with individual freedom. In modern society we give men more and more an equality of social privilege and power, and thus increase for every man the opportunity of independence. But, on the other hand, increase of freedom and cultivation tends to develope natural inequality, bringing out more and more the differences between man and man, class and class; and, this being so, the beneficent guardianship which Christianity exercises over this form of weakness, rather grows in value as the ages roll on.

But what of the slave, whether the actual slave, 'the living chattel,' bought and sold in the market like a brute beast or the virtual slave, under the hard tyranny of selfish wealth and power? Christianity, it is true, did not in its first ages preach or enforce emancipation. It even taught the slave submission, dignifying slavery by making it a service of Christ, and cheering it by the promise of the common reward in heaven. But it enunciated the great principle, 'Not a slave, but a brother in Christ,' and left it to work slowly and surely in the centuries to come. That it has worked, is a matter of simple history. It is Christianity, not mere philanthropy, which has struck off the fetters of the slave. The disintegration and gradual destruction of the ancient European serfship must be traced mainly to the influence of the Church and the Gospel. When England in the last generation by an unexampled sacrifice wiped out the guilt of the slave trade, those who fought and won the battle of humanity were certainly marshalled under the banner of the Cross. When in our own time the great Transatlantic abolition of slavery effected itself, almost against the will of those who ruled the fortunes of the United States, the real centre of the force of this beneficent revolution was in what men deemed the fanatic Christianity of the old Abolitionist party. It may be that some virtual slavery still lingers among us. There may be 'white slaves' under the tyranny of individuals, classes, society itself, though it is absurd to compare the most oppressive phases of such tyranny with the absolute despotism of actual slavery. But if so, this bondage is the law of the world, in spite of constant protest and influence of Christianity. On this point the Gospel cannot falter in its message, 'Masters, give your servants what is just and equal, knowing that ye also have a Master in heaven, and there is no respect of persons with Him.' It must necessarily bear this witness; if its power to enforce it be still too weak, yet it is a power which is very far from being unfruitful.

So the moral force of Christianity has clearly guarded individuality in the weak; and I am inclined to connect with these direct forms of protection the great emphasis which it lays on purity and chastity. For these the New Testament pleaded with an impassioned earnestness, needful to purify an age which was a very sink of civilised corruption. Now of the two great moral virtues which may be called self-contained and self-regarding—manliness and purity—purity is obviously the virtue which belongs to the weak as well as to the strong, and which, indeed, is in some sense the special glory of natures otherwise weak and helpless. As such, it needs emphatically reverence and protection. For, while it is true that impurity is something much more than an oppression of the weak, yet certainly it is, in practice, very constantly a gratification of the vile lust of the strong, the wealthy, the powerful, to the utter ruin, body and soul, of the weak and helpless. What can be more unchristian, more contrary to the infinite pity of Christ for the 'woman, who was a sinner,' than the indulgence of society in this matter to the

The stress laid on purity.

strong, and its cruelty to the weak—its condonation, almost approval, of impurity in the man, and its ruthless and absolute condemnation of it in the woman?

But the bearing of Christianity as a moral force on purity needs a fuller consideration. It is hardly too much to say that in European civilisation it actually created the idea. Of temperance and self-restraint the ancient morality spoke much, but it regarded these simply as means of so checking the bodily appetites as to give full scope to the higher energies of man's nature. Of purity, as in itself a noble and beautiful thing, it knew but little. Nor, indeed, had it the conception on which alone this love of purity must ultimately rest. For if it depend only on self-respect and self-reverence, it is clear that, in proportion as self-knowledge teaches humility, it is weakened, and it is clearer still that as corruption is admitted, the reverence of the corrupted self becomes less possible. But Christianity taught men to believe that there was 'the Christ' in every soul, and that it was that Divine Presence, making the body a temple, which called for reverence. Purity became holiness; and by that change was regenerated to a new glory and strength. As soon as the question was 'Shall I take the members of Christ, and make them the members of a harlot?' 'Shall I defile the Temple of God?' the answer could not fail to be, 'God forbid!' Hence it has come to pass that Christianity, as a moral force, raised this reverence for purity to a new and dominant power. There have even been times when this reverence has passed into extravagance, and exalted not natural purity, but the celibacy which was supposed to be identical with it, as the ideal of the highest humanity. But perhaps in those days it was only by this exaggeration that effectual witness could be borne against ages of savage brutality and sensuality. Certainly at all times, in spite of intellectual cultivation, social refinement, even lofty enthusiasm, the protest of Christianity has been needed, and it has been nobly and effectively borne. Nor can we fail to notice, with more sorrow than surprise, that with the growth of anti-Christian theories of life, the earnest solemnity of this protest has been smiled at or seriously condemned.

CHAPTER III. CHRISTIANITY AS A MORAL FORCE.

IV. Perhaps, however, this function of the moral force of Christianity may be acknowledged, and even admired; but it will be urged that it is inadequate, and even one-sided, in its theory of moral excellence. If it guards the individuality of the weak, what shall we say of its bearing upon the individuality of the strong? *Its sanction of individuality in the strong.*

It has been said that Christianity looks but coldly on this. It is thought even to discourage the masculine type of character, as manifested in that right self-assertion of manliness, which involves a sense of dignity, a claim of freedom, a resolute maintenance of rights, and a bold exertion of individual energy. In that saying, now not unfrequently repeated, there is just this shadow of truth—that the New Testament lays comparatively little stress on this class of virtues, dismissing them, indeed, with but one exhortation, 'Quit you like men, and be strong.' But for this there is a very homely, yet all-sufficient reason, that these virtues can take care of themselves. They command universal admiration; they bring their immediate reward; they are in themselves a continual delight. At the time of the first preaching of the Gospel they had in the morality of the day run to excess, and needed accordingly, not to be stimulated, but to be tempered. *Its care to temper it.* After all, it is simply a question of experience whether Christianity has really checked the development of manliness, in courage and freedom, resolute individuality and victorious energy. The answer must be, that, instead of checking these, it has actually brought them out in some very remarkable and characteristic forms, not so much by direct encouragement, as by kindling in each man the consciousness of having the life of Christ in him, and deriving from this the sense of an individual responsibility to 'stand fast in the faith,' and to be 'a fellow-worker with God.' The spirit in which the apostles confronted the demand of the Sanhedrim for obedience, has never died out: 'We must obey,' but 'obey God rather than men.'

For it is not only true that under the influence of Christianity all the ancient heroic energy of manliness survives untouched and even increased; but there are three developments of it, which have certainly flourished especially in Christian times, and which may be fairly considered to have been especially fostered by Christianity.[1]

Its development of it in characteristic forms.

There is the spirit of resolute martyrdom, at times running even to the exaggeration of defiant or self-trustful martyrdom, but in its true Christian form, a humble, and yet a willing and even a joyful martyrdom. It is true that this spirit is not peculiar to Christianity. Other causes may count their martyrs. Science or philosophy may boast a few; patriotism, loyalty, or philanthropy may count many. But it is also true that here Christian faith stands out in unapproachable pre-eminence. Where other causes count martyrs by scores, she can count them by hundreds and thousands; and, moreover, she shows the extraordinary power of calling out a strange and superhuman courage in souls least prepared for it by nature. The humblest and the most timid, the tender child and the sensitive woman—even these she has taught to assert a noble individuality, to defy the whole power of the world, and often by suffering to conquer it.

Martyrdom.

Next, akin in some sense to the spirit of martyrdom, is the spirit of asceticism. I do not here examine that spirit, to disentangle the noble and the base, the true and the false, the selfish and the self-sacrificing elements, so strangely and mournfully mingled in it. But whatever else may be thought of it, surely it must be confessed that it brings out in singular force the dominant power of the spirit over the flesh; the firm iron will, too often crushing natural feeling and affection; the contempt of all the power and the opinion, the prayers and the sympathy of the world. It is, in some sense, a Christian Stoicism. For again, though asceticism belongs in some degree to all religions, and to many philosophic systems of morality, it is to Christianity that it owes, for good and for evil, its great development in Europe. All strong ascetic movements —from the old vows of chastity and purity to the modern

Asceticism.

[1] On this subject, see Lecky's *History of Morals*.

pledge of total abstinence—have had in them a strong Christian tinge. Hence asceticism may fairly be claimed as an evidence that Christianity looks on the strong individuality of man in a spirit of watchful sympathy, desiring to temper and to mould, but never to destroy it.

But perhaps most characteristic of all is that third phase into which the spirit of martyrdom and asceticism passed—the spirit of chivalry, a spirit unknown to ancient moralities, a spirit developed marvellously under the shadow of the cross, which was its frequent emblem. It is heroism indeed, but heroism tempered by the peculiarly Christian influences of reverence for the weak and suffering, reverence for humility and purity, and solemn devotion under the blessing of God and the sign of the cross. Yet these influences are so far from weakening in it the spirit of manly daring, that in chivalry it actually ran to a noble but fantastic excess, of which ancient civilisation knew nothing; they are so far from chilling the vivid sense of personal dignity and honour, that it also, in the days of chivalry, rose to a magnificent extravagance. That spirit which we call now the 'spirit of a gentleman'—a spirit which, except in its accidents, depends on no conditions of rank, wealth, even culture, and which is the lineal descendant of the older chivalry—is a spirit all but unknown to the greatest ancient civilisations of the West. In its union of elasticity and enterprise with dignity and self-restraint, it has no parallel in the civilisations, ancient or modern, of the East. It represents unquestionably the individuality of courage and nobleness, of 'self-reverence,' as well as 'self-distrust,' as tinged by the influence of the Gospel, and stamped with the image of Christ.

Chivalry.

These three peculiar developments of the individuality of the strong—found not merely in the ranks of those whom the world honours as martyrs, ascetics, or knights, but in many a Christian character which none knows but God—must be sufficient to show that the charge of stunting or neglecting manliness is utterly groundless. The Gospel not only gives it scope, but actually moulds it into a higher dignity and beauty.

V. So it is, then, that Christianity guards the freedom and

the growth of the individual soul, which is the seat of moral energy. We have now to turn to the other side of morality, and to see how far it guards unity of society, and bids the individual give up himself for his fellow-men.

Its guardianship of unity.

It is hardly needful to argue that a religion, whose very sign is the cross, must encourage, and must enforce, as the first of duties and the highest of privileges, the spirit of self-sacrifice—the facing of labour, danger, suffering, death, for the society in which our lot is cast. But this duty of self-sacrifice may be recognised either towards the human society as a whole, as in what we call patriotism to a country, or towards the authority which at once rules and represents that society, as in what we call loyalty to a sovereign. It would certainly appear that Christianity, as a new moral force, has tended to quicken and regenerate more especially the former—perhaps the wider and greater—of these two principles. It is essentially a religion, I will not say of equality—for equality, according as we use the word, is either a sacred truth or a dangerous falsehood—but certainly of fraternity.

Christianity a fraternity.

It is true that it acknowledges and sanctions loyalty; it teaches reverence for 'the powers that be,' holding that the very existence of authority is a necessity to human society, and therefore an ordinance of the God who made it—holding that the worst government is better than mere anarchy, and that rebellion, if it be causeless, is a sin, and, even if it be necessary, is a resistance to the natural law, which must bring down a lighter or heavier judgment. But this is hardly its main or its most characteristic teaching. Even the marked emphasis with which the duty of obedience is occasionally enforced in the New Testament was probably designed to meet some special tendency in the new-born freedom of the Gospel to disregard civil authority and social custom. In the days when in English history loyalty became a passion, almost an idolatry, we notice that in all its allusions to Holy Scripture the very phrase, 'the Lord's anointed,' which was its watchword, shows that it drew its chief inspiration from the Old Testament and not from the New. So, again,

Its sanction of loyalty true, but secondary.

whenever the spirit of absolutism has sought to raise its head in the Church, it has naturally borrowed the analogy of its sacerdotal authority rather from the hierarchy of the Jewish high-priesthood than from the teaching of the Apostles in the Christian Church, or from the more sacred words of Him who said, 'Be not called father; for one is your Father, which is in heaven.' 'Be not ye called master; for one is your Master, even Christ, and all ye are brethren.'

For in these words is expressed the true and characteristic teaching of Christianity. Its absolute loyalty is paid to one King, and one only, the Lord Jesus Christ Himself, as enthroned at the right hand of the Father, and enthroned also in every heart. All other authorities, of family, of State, or of Church, are but brethren—elder brethren, it may be, to whom we owe faith and deference, but brethren still. The spirit of brotherhood, and what has been called 'the enthusiasm of humanity'—this is the attitude of the soul towards human society which the Gospel especially teaches.

Now this spirit does not merely imply a strong sense of duty to society above the coarser requirements of law, shown mainly in perfect truth and righteousness. For, in the sense of duty, individuality still comes first, and unity second. We first recognise ourselves, we see our own individual freedom and power, and then ask, 'What am I bound in equity to do for my fellow-men?' Duty, therefore, is like a golden cincture which binds together many units—all, it is true, pressing on each other, but all perfectly distinct. But the spirit of brotherhood, as taught by the Gospel, goes much beyond this, and beyond even the calmer and more prosaic willingness to sacrifice self, which we call 'public spirit.' Its main principle—the 'old commandment,' old as humanity itself, made new in the Gospel—is love. Now love absolutely sinks, forgets, denies self. It places unity first, and individuality barely second. It is not like a golden cincture binding separate units together, but like the network of some great organism through which one common life glows and thrills. Nor is even this all. The love of the Christian, as of his Master, delights especially to take the form of mercy—that is, of love towards the weak, the blind, the sinful—neither asking

Its brotherhood of duty and of love.

nor expecting any return, except the inner blessedness which comes from 'giving rather than receiving.'

Now the creation or re-creation of this universal conception of brotherhood is a principal part of the new moral force of Christianity in the world; and it must especially be observed that its universality, or catholicity, is an essential part of the idea.

Its essential catholicity.

There are three forms of natural human society into which each man is born—the family, the nation, and the race.

As to the family tie, it is true that Christianity exalted it and made it more sacred, by the very fact that Christ Himself entered into it and reverenced it in the home of Nazareth, and in the person of His Virgin mother, except, indeed, when it stood in the way of a higher tie. No slight thing it is to have driven utterly away the polygamy, which is a danger and an outrage against it. Nor is it a slight thing to have made sacred for ever the marriage which is its bond. It is the profound teaching of one of the grandest epistles of the New Testament, that all the ties which bind the family together—the ties between fathers and children, husbands and wives, even between masters and servants—are sacred, being types of the relations of God to man, in the fatherhood of God, in the mystic union between Christ and His Church, in the kingdom of which 'the service is perfect freedom.'[2] Here Christianity stands absolutely and irreconcilably opposed to those socialistic theories, ancient or modern, which seek to maintain universal fraternity by ignoring the sacred family ties. Yet it did not create this unity of the family— old as the creation itself—which was found in all religious sacredness in the ancient Judaic and Oriental society, and in firm, if somewhat rigid, massiveness of power in the ancient system of Rome. Nor does it teach us to idolise it after the fashion of some modern literature, which, having given up Christianity, seeks with a pathetic earnestness to create a new domestic religion—to substitute the worship of the Penates of each hearth for the worship of the one Father of all.

Its sanction of the family.

[2] See Eph. v. 22—vi. 9.

Still less does Christianity seem to have found it needful to stimulate and enforce the national spirit of loyalty and of patriotism towards those of our own country and our own blood. Never, indeed, does it ignore it. Our Lord loved and served 'the lost sheep of the house of Israel,' and wept over the doomed city of Jerusalem. An Apostle could even dare to wish himself 'accursed' for the sake of his brethren of the chosen race. There is an unmistakable significance in the historical fact that, under the rule of Christianity, national life has grown up so luxuriantly that the nation is now the unit of modern society, and affinities of race are, at this moment, most powerful factors in the history of the world. But it is still evident that Christianity did not create or especially stimulate enthusiasm for this form of unity. The typical examples of patriotism we still draw from the ancient histories of Greece and Rome. The Scriptural home of national loyalty is in the Old Testament—in the history of the chosen people dwelling alone among the nations, or in the prophecy and the psalm, which rejoiced with the joy and wept with the weeping of Israel. For it was not, and it is not, necessary to blow to a whiter heat the fire of national spirit. In early Christian days the foreigner was still the enemy. In modern days we may see national spirit so far from languishing that, in antagonism to common humanity, it may even become a fierce and unrighteous passion. As in respect of the family, so in respect of the nation, the spirit of Christianity contents itself with watching over the quenchless fire, in order to keep it pure, to restrain it within its needful bounds, and, if necessary, to keep it from polluting the free pure air of that sky which stretches alike over all.

Its sanction of the nation.

But the unity which, as a living reality, Christianity did create or re-create, is the unity of all mankind. The Church, born in the narrowness of Judaism, was in its very idea Catholic, embracing all races, all ages, all characters. Even beyond the limits of that Church, until the day when those limits shall be co-extensive with humanity, lies the world, for which Christ died, and towards which, therefore, His followers should feel something of a living tie of brotherhood—seeking always to

Its creation of the brotherhood of humanity.

draw all men within the Church which should be their real home, but yet not counting them altogether aliens, even while they are wandering from it.

It has become almost a commonplace to remark that in the language in which the New Testament was written, there was in heathen usage no word for 'love' which did not savour of individual passion ($\mathit{ἔρως}$) or personal friendship ($\mathit{φιλία}$). The word 'charity' ($\mathit{ἀγαπή}$) in its general sense is itself an invention of Christian thought; and this invention does but visibly embody the fact that the conception which it represents was itself a creation of Christianity. For necessarily in the common grace of Christ, in the common salvation, and in the life of Christ as capable of reproduction in every soul, there was the first bond of a unity which made literally all men one.

It was the first bond of universal fraternity. We must hold still that it is the one which is most real, living, and permanent; though we cannot speak contemptuously of other systems which have perhaps, at least in part, learned this conception of unity from the Gospel, and sometimes even claim its Divine Author as a half-conscious harbinger of what they believe to be a more thorough and effective unity. For we cannot but remember that they could never have arisen, had Christians been truer to their Christianity.

There are three great forces of union which bind men together. There is the tie of mutual need, represented in the action of commerce, and strengthened by the spread of material civilisation. But this, as experience unhappily proves, is too often marred by selfishness, deceit, and inhumanity, and never can go down into the depth of our nature. There is the unity of common light, knowledge, science, intellectual civilisation. But in this there is too much of an aristocracy of intellect, perhaps of individuals, perhaps of races; it has been found only too often compatible with contempt and tyranny and pride. There is the unity of true religious brotherhood under the love of the one Father. Under it there can be no selfishness and no pride. All, however unequal, have in it a fundamental equality; for all, however weak, and ignorant, and dull, and even sinful, there is room and welcome.

Its supreme power of unity.

Where has this universal brotherhood before God been even shadowed forth, except in the Gospel and Church of Christ?

Such, then, has been Christianity as a moral force—preserving at once individuality and unity, and therefore at once exalting each man and the whole race of human kind.

VI. The chief points which are here brought forward are so plainly historical, that they can hardly be questioned. But against the inference which we draw from them there are, in these days, three main objections made, intended to show fatal imperfection in Christian morality. Of these the first is advanced confidently from the social side, charging Christian morality with selfishness; the second speaks in the name of individual liberty, branding it with intolerance and persecution; the third relies on what are called its 'failures' to regenerate the world.

Objections to Christian morality

To the first, however eloquently urged, I find it difficult to attach much weight. It ought rather to be considered a peculiar glory and beauty of the moral force of Christianity, that it has so resolutely preserved the individuality, as well as the unity, which belongs to human nature as such.

on the ground of selfishness;

It is curious to see that, whereas, before Christ, the inclination of human morality was always to the cultivation of the individual or of the narrower unities of life, now the reaction is in the other direction. We are told that Christian morality is 'selfish,' inasmuch as it teaches us to work out our own salvation, and seek a personal immortality. We are bidden to sacrifice the individual utterly on the altar of 'the religion of humanity,' to live entirely in our fellow-men, and to be content with the 'immortality of the race.' A nobler extreme is this than the other, perhaps because it has learned something from the very system which it condemns. But it is equally one-sided and equally unnatural. What men call 'Altruism' has about it a certain simplicity, in its fundamental doctrine that virtue is merely self-sacrifice, and in its practical depreciation of that individuality for which philosophic systems of law can find no room. But it is always easy on all subjects, whether scientific, social, political, moral, or spiritual, to gain simplicity by the sacrifice of unmanageable truth. Life and human nature being what they are, we have generally to choose between a simple formula that will not cover the fact, and a complex formula that will. Christians may well be thankful that Christianity has chosen the wider and more difficult alternative. For man, after all, is individual as well as social. The Gospel, under one supreme allegiance to a personal Saviour and a Head of the whole race, can harmonise the individuality in which each is alone before God with the unity through which he lives in his fellow-men.

But what is to be said on the second point, urged by the advocates of unrestrained individual liberty; branding Christianity with the charge of intolerance, and the guilt of blood shed in persecution?

on the ground of intolerance;

It seems clear that the temptation to persecute must beset any form of belief, which recognises the practical importance of abstract truth, and dwells on the interests and rights of the society rather than the individual. For those who hold these points strongly cannot acquiesce in the shallow idea that all opinions, if sincerely held, are held irresponsibly, and that at any rate the truth or falsehood of each concerns only the individual who holds them, and is nothing to his neighbours. They see clearly that all toleration of opinion which expresses itself in word and action has certain limits, which the existence of society itself lays down. Hence, wherever they see falsehood—knowing that every falsehood is fraught with evil, and especially those falsehoods which touch the ultimate foundations of our being, and knowing, moreover, that, in respect of such effects, no man liveth or dieth to himself—they are tempted, if they have the power, not only to denounce such falsehood vehemently, but to oppress it by force, and at last quench it in blood.

This temptation besets all religions which are earnestly held; yet not religions only, but also all strong beliefs of every kind not purely scientific, especially where they assume anything of a socialistic character. If it has shown itself signally in Christianity, it is simply because Christianity has been the leading spiritual influence of the world. Men the world, it is clear that, like all other moral forces, it must be capable of being resisted by the idleness, the folly, the blindness, and the sin of man. Only slowly, struggling through the clouds, comes, either for the individual or for the race, the dawn of the spiritual day.

We might, indeed, have expected a more speedy and universal triumph. Such has always been the natural expectation of the servants of Christ, under which they have cried out, 'How long, how long? Come quickly, O Lord Jesus!' That earnest impatience may be morally beneficial, if it makes Christians take shame to themselves that they do so little to hasten—so much, perhaps, to hinder—that triumph. On the other hand, it has been in great degree the parent of that spirit of persecution at which we have already glanced, chafing at the slowness of voluntary conversion, and eager to 'compel men to come in.' But I observe that the Lord Himself never encouraged these expectations of speedy and cloudless success. He spoke of the growth of His kingdom as slow, quiet, gradual; not without admixture of evil, not without spiritual waste, not without conflict of opposition; liable to the conditions under which all moral forces work, and declining to overbear them by supernatural compulsion. Looking on towards the end, He even spoke of 'iniquity abounding, and the love of many waxing cold.' He and His apostles foretell the struggle of evil against the truth, as continued obstinately, apparently as waxing fiercer and fiercer when the end draws near. The final triumph itself would seem to be represented as due to some new supernatural manifestation of Christ, for which all that now testifies of Him is only the slow imperfect preparation.

It is clear, therefore, that Christianity predicts what men call its failures, and the slowness of its spiritual progress. In the individual soul its working here professes to be but preparatory to a spiritual progress, perhaps a further spiritual probation (though of this hardly more than a glimpse is given us) on the other side of the grave. In the world at large it claims for its completion a period long in itself, though short indeed compared with those which science claims for great natural changes. That it has given have rightly held that all falsehood is hateful in God's sight, and must draw down His judgment. In their eagerness to be fellow-workers with God, they have wrongly arrogated the power and anticipated the judgment which is His.

Yet we may boldly say, not merely that the spirit of persecution belongs not to Christianity as such, but that Christianity bears witness against it, in the direct teaching of the Lord Jesus Christ Himself, and in its great leading principles of morality, as requiring not only adhesion, but free and glad adhesion, of the will, and substituting for the compulsion of law from without the influence of grace within. Gradually, although too slowly, that teaching and those principles have prevailed, to limit the natural eagerness to fight against falsehood by any weapons, and to be more zealous for the honour of the Lord than the Lord Himself. If Christians have been, and still are, imperfectly true to their own faith in this respect, yet, looking to the forms of belief and power which seek to supersede Christianity, we may trace in them germs of a far fiercer intolerance and persecution, and we may incline to believe that the day will yet come when Christianity shall be (as it has been) the great protest against spiritual despotism, and the guardian of the freedom of individual thought.

Far more perplexing than either of these objections is the sense of what men call 'failures of Christianity.' Why, after eighteen centuries, is the world still what it is—so madly eager for war, so fatally selfish and dishonest in peace? Why has not the moral force of Christianity absolutely and irresistibly conquered? on the ground of failures.

But it is clear that a moral force must work under moral conditions. Under these, it is not submission, but free submission, of the will which is the one thing needful; and the process is as essential an element as the result. To constrain obedience would be to destroy its moral value. It has been said by a celebrated man of our own day, that he would rather be wound up like a clock, with a certainty of going right, than be free, with the risk of going wrong. But, in the moral sense, no mere machine ever goes right. On the capacity of moral right there must wait the possibility of moral wrong. So, when the new moral force of Christianity comes into an earnest of its moral victory, history seems most unequivocally to declare. On the very theory of Christianity, it is only an earnest; by that theory, rather than by the longings of friends or the requirements of foes, it must be judged. The slow progress and the failures of Christianity are, indeed, scandals and perplexities, but they are signally insufficient as objections to its truth and authority.

VII. Such, then, appears to be the actual power of Christianity as a moral force. Again, as in relation to Christianity as a divine philosophy, the question must press on every thoughtful mind, how there could have arisen *Conclusion.* in an obscure corner of Palestine, through the unlearned simplicity of its first preachers, from a Founder whom the world despised, rejected, and persecuted, this extraordinary power—so strikingly unique in its leading idea, so simple in its practical force, so universal in its scope, so marvellously accordant with the two great principles of our human nature, so absolutely dissociated from all which in that nature is capable of change, weakness, or decay. What answer can be given? The answer of Christianity is a simple and a sufficient one. Not by any human power or wisdom, but by the manifestation of God in Him, is 'Christ made to us righteousness,' and His life of righteousness reproduced in thousands and millions of human lives at this day. What other answer can be reasonably put in its place? Secondary and auxiliary causes there may have been, such as those which Gibbon[3] once so carefully elaborated; but the study of these must convince us that none of them singly, nor all put together, can be adequate to give account for so unique and marvellous a result.

Even if the mind, though convinced that these must be put aside as insufficient, is not yet ready to accept the Christian answer, yet, at least, the consideration of the moral force of Christianity will add another witness to that which is derived from the contemplation of its wisdom. Compared with all else in the world's history, it stands out as a kind of moral miracle. Like other miracles, although it cannot in itself tell the whole story of His nature and His office, yet it may

---

[3] *Decline and Fall of the Roman Empire*, chap. xv.

well bring us to His feet, by showing us that He has not only the enlightening word, but the regenerating power, of eternal life. The Gospel here repeats with variation His own challenge, 'Which of you convicteth Me of sin?' Who can find moral defect or weakness in the life of Jesus Christ, thus made, by reproduction in His disciples, a moral force pervading the world of humanity? If not, why not hold that in His deeper revelations 'He speaks the truth'? Why not, even beyond sight, be ready 'to believe Him'?

CHAPTER IV.

CHRISTIANITY AS A SPIRITUAL LIFE.

'Christ Jesus is of God made unto us sanctification.'—1 Cor. i. 30.

IN the brief Scriptural record of the primeval condition of man, he is represented to us, not only as an intellectual being, having the power of thought and language, not only as a moral being, able to work and to love, but as a religious being, recognising a law of God, and 'hearing the voice of the Lord God among the trees of the garden in the cool of the day.' In the early childhood of the race, undeveloped by the teaching and experience of ages, it traces thus the germs of the great principles of humanity, the growth of which is testified by every history, every literature, every religion in the world. There is, as has been already urged, a life of the intellect, seeking wisdom, and learning to solve, at least in part, the great problem of being—sometimes by gazing on all that is without us, sometimes by reflecting back the thought on all that is within. There is a life of moral duty and love, practically recognising at once the sacredness of individual freedom and responsibility, and the unity which binds all men in one. But there is also what men call, by an instructive interchange of expression, now 'the religious,' and now 'the spiritual life.' In it the soul turns away from all lower forms of being, and relaxes the strain of discursive thought, of moral resolution, and of emotional affection. The double consciousness of the *Ego* and the *Non-ego* must, of course, remain; but as to the latter, the soul refuses to rest on the visible, the particular, the finite phenomena, with which in the other spheres of energy it has largely to do. It will go down to the ultimate foundation, and pierce to the inner life of all this *Kosmos* of phenomenal

The spiritual life.

being. It is at such times (as has been well said) conscious of but two existences—itself, and some Supreme Power which is to it as a God. In that consciousness it finds its only spiritual rest in the present; in that consciousness it looks on by inevitable aspiration to some higher future. There is hardly any soul so narrow, so distracted, or so degraded, that it knows nothing of this high spiritual consciousness. For it grows upon us, as upon the Psalmist (Ps. lxiii. 6), in the thoughtful calm of evening or night, or in the first waking freshness of the morning. It flashes upon us at times suddenly and terribly, when some great shock of joy or sorrow, some glimpse of the solemn meaning of life, or some anticipation of the sure-footed approach of death, seems to open a chasm in the smooth floor of our ordinary existence, and show us the infinite depths which lie beneath. It has been the secret of the loftiest poetry, the deepest philosophy, and the holiest aspirations of humanity.

In surveying Christianity as a living power, I have tried to show how to the intellect it solves the great problem of being, and to the conscience offers a new moral force to regenerate the world. What can it do to fill this third and yet more sacred sphere? Christ

The Gospel promise of sanctification.

Jesus (says St. Paul in my text), as He is made to the understanding 'wisdom,' to the conscience 'righteousness,' so to the spiritual aspiration is 'sanctification.' 'In Him' (to use the words of the same Apostle elsewhere) 'we can set our affections on things above the earth:' 'Our life is hid with Him in God.'

For the idea of sanctification embraces both those elements of consciousness of which I have spoken. It is growth in holiness; and holiness, rightly understood, is purity, but a purity consecrated to God. In purity is implied the love of all that is true and noble and lovely, in itself and for itself, without any thought of relative duty and obligation; and therefore the life of purity is that spiritual life which I have sought to describe, considered simply as a hidden life, concentrated on itself. But holiness contemplates purity as emanating from the Supreme Power, sustained by communion with it, and consecrated to that communion. It considers the spiritual life not only as hidden, but as hidden in God. Accordingly it brings into harmony the two forms of consciousness—the consciousness of our own soul, and the consciousness of God. In declaring that Christ is Himself our sanctification, the Gospel, as before, seeks to establish that harmony, not by any abstract process, but by realising in the life of Christ the life of One who is at once God and Man, and in whom the communion of the two natures is perfect and eternal.

Now the harmony of these two principles, while we feel that in some way it ought to exist and must exist, is a thing of infinite difficulty. Consciously or unconsciously, the mind of man has constantly sought to cut the knot of difficulty by virtually ignoring either one or the other. The two forms of spiritual consciousness.

II. Man strives sometimes to realise himself and virtually to forget God. When he turns his thoughts inwards to self-consciousness, he is always led at once to 'self-reverence' and 'self-distrust.' He cannot but reverence himself, in the consciousness of the spiritual life which is actually his. In spite of feebleness and shortness of life, he feels the marvel of his understanding, able to scan the whole world of matter, and to move with originative power through the whole world of thought. He is conscious of the still more marvellous freedom of will—able, without constraint from below, from around, or from above, to follow what he sees as right—able, by a still more extraordinary power, to do what he knows as wrong. In these powers, as we have already seen, he realises a spiritual life in himself, which he must reverence. But yet he learns 'self-distrust' even from this, that he cannot be satisfied with what he is— that he feels an undoubted capacity, and longs with a constant longing, to grow to a higher perfection. Thought is never satisfied with what it has gained, nor has it ever to weep because there are no new realms to conquer. Like the gods of the Indian legend, it dives downward and soars upward for ever, and yet the reality which it surveys stretches infinitely beyond through all eternity. The energy of freedom can never rest; it acts because it lives. The moral aspiration of man, if it be healthy, is always yearning for higher purity, truer The instinct of perfection.

righteousness, and deeper love. Even the imagination, just in proportion as it discerns beauty, is dimly conscious of some more perfect beauty which it has not yet seen, but of which it knows that it is. There is in every soul this instinct of perfection, made up of a sense of infinite capacity, and a consciousness of the incompleteness of our present attainment. Hope remains always: disappointed again and again, yet rising against disappointment; often 'doomed to death' by bitter experience, yet 'fated not to die.'

This self-knowledge in man may combine these two elements, the consciousness of attainment and the instinct of an unattained perfection, in different proportions, according to differences of character and age and circumstance. But it always seems to contain both and we observe that it is not destroyed, indeed in some sense it is intensified, by that consciousness of evil within, of which certainly each man's experience, and all collective human language and literature, are full. The evil may be conceived as simple blindness and error, or as disobedience to some law of our nature, or as a pollution of the inner life. But, in whatever form it is seen, there comes with it to every soul, which is not yet utterly degraded, the sense that it is evil indeed, dark, lawless, and foul, yet that it can be and must be conquered. The victory may be sought negatively by self-chastisement, scourging and torturing the body, cutting off all joy, beauty, and love from the soul, till there actually rises up a strange delight in this cruel self-conquest. It may be sought positively, by new light, new moral culture, new sense of beauty, new energy of freedom; or sought perhaps, as in the ancient Mysteries, by the aid of some mysterious power known only to the few. In any case the sense of evil simply creates disturbance and provokes a struggle of indignant antagonism, in this consciousness of a spirituality striving towards higher perfection. It never destroys it, till the spiritual nature itself has lost all vitality and hope.

The consciousness of defect and evil.

The self-concentration of the spirit.

Now in this spiritual life the soul is certainly alone as regards all the lower forms of being. It breaks suddenly or gradually loose from the appetites and sensuous delights which bind it to the world of things. In various forms it always learns the lesson of 'subduing the flesh to the spirit' by temperance or by abstinence; it soon comes to understand that 'the things of the flesh'—the material pleasures, comforts, beauties, powers of the world—can in no case secure the perfection which it craves; it may even become, with Plato, impatient of the distractions, by which the care of the body, the necessity of gaining all knowledge through the senses, and the clamour of the appetites, retard and confuse the growth of the spiritual life. Hardly less certainly it dissociates itself from any ultimate dependence on the world of persons. Our fellow-men may help the growth of the spirit in us; as (for instance) by the presentation to us of truth and beauty, by example and personal ascendency, by the educating power of love, and by the inspiring effect of sympathy. But ultimately the soul comes back to itself. In all the higher spiritual energies it is true that 'the heart knoweth its own bitterness, and a stranger doth not intermeddle with its joy.' Nature and humanity may help it to contemplate and rest on something higher. But in themselves they cannot satisfy. As Pascal has said, 'we must die alone;' all in some degree, and the leaders of mankind in a very high degree, must live alone, if they would live their true life.

Yet it is clear that this spiritual life, by its very nature, always catches something of the spirit of worship. It involves not only a cold perception, but an infinite reverence and love, of truth in the understanding, of righteousness in the conscience, of beauty in the imagination, of unity and self-sacrifice in the affections. It kindles the enthusiasm which bids men count life well lost in the service of these glorious principles; and the reverence which never 'counts itself to have attained or to be already perfect,' but, while it presses on higher and higher, always looks up to the pure mountain heights far above. Men call it, and rightly call it, a religion, an enthusiasm, a worship—using words which, in their proper sense, teach an all-important lesson. But to what, or rather to whom, is this worship paid?

The instinct of worship

I say 'to whom,' for I believe that worship must be paid not to a thing or an abstract principle, but to a person. Strikingly significant is the irresistible personification of forces, powers, ideas, principles, whenever they become to us the guiding influences of life. Even the creations of our own minds, as science, poetry, art, law—even the collections of individual men, families, nations, races, churches—we personify them all. We say, in words which are often strangely delusive, that they teach and guide us, rule and save us, speaking as though each was a real personal being, with a mind, a conscience, and a voice. There is in all human souls an instinct of loyalty, reverence, trustfulness, which issues in a kind of worship. If we have no personal object of unlimited trust and worship, we imagine personality in the things or ideas around us, in order that we may worship them.

<small>necessarily directed to a personal object.</small>

What shall then be the object contemplated in our spiritual life? If the world of things and persons be left behind, we must come to the old antithesis. It may be self; it may be the Supreme Power.

It may be self—the human nature as it exists in us and in our fellow-men, contemplated as the embodiment of these great principles of truth, right, beauty, and love. So it was, perhaps most openly, in the ancient Stoicism, which worshipped the humanity of the truly wise man, as self-contained and self-sufficient, insensible to appetites, closed rigidly against affections, denying to the Supreme Being (whether it was called the Universe or God) the power to give or take away anything more than those outer accidents of life, by which the true being within was essentially untouched. There was a grand strength and nobleness in the conception: the world might ridicule it, not without excuse, as transcendental and unreal; even those who had tried it might cry out, with the dying Brutus, that it was but the shadow of a shade. But it defied ridicule, and survived disappointment, because it had in it the true instinct of perfection. At all times it yielded stern but noble examples of greatness; in its last days, as in the writings of Seneca or the lives of Epictetus and Marcus Aurelius, it certainly became not a mere philosophy, but a religion—too aristocratic, too hard, too self-reliant, but a religion still.

<small>The worship of self.</small>

<small>Stoicism.</small>

So, again, the same idea appears, in a modern form, in

the doctrine of Self-culture, studying in wide experience all things and persons, constantly using them up in the process, and becoming in itself the one object of life. It is a doctrine larger and freer than the Stoicism of old, because it recognises and cultivates human nature in all its faculties. Yet in some sense it is less noble; for it hesitates about the supremacy of the moral sense in us, often dethroning it in favour of intellectual or even æsthetic refinement, sometimes admitting sensual enjoyment and high-coloured luxury far too near the throne. Certainly it is at least as arrogant and self-sufficient, as contemptuous of the common herd of men, as inhuman in its deliberate drying up of sympathy. We read its doom of dreary disappointment and failure in the soul's tragedy of the old book of Ecclesiastes. We can study in the 'Palace of Art' of a great living poet a terrible picture of its heartless magnificence and its ghastly collapse into ruin.

Self-culture.

Sometimes this self-worship assumes a softened form under the Agnosticism of the present day, which, without asserting that there is no Supreme Power to serve, and no Divine purpose to carry out, ignores both as unknown and unknowable. For many adherents of the Agnostic school content themselves with recognising the spiritual life, as a thing which we know to be real in us, although we do not know its relation to the Supreme Power, and urging the culture of that life in intellectual light, in moral purity and sweetness, or in study and creation of beauty, as the highest object attainable amidst the difficulties and ignorances of life. They will condescend to patronise, and in a measure to honour, the energy of moral beneficence and the aspirations of religious faith, provided they may regard these as subordinate to the higher purpose of self-culture, subserving, even as delusions, this one certain and real object of life.

Agnosticism.

Sometimes, again, in forms necessarily modified and diluted, it establishes itself even on religious ground. So it was, in the Christian Church, in that survival of pagan self-reliance which is known as Pelagianism, only half-recognising God, acknowledging His gifts of temporal blessing and spiritual opportunity, but making Him

Pelagianism.

(so to speak) only the helper, and not the originator, of spiritual life and salvation. For, under whatever forms and modifications, the essence of the Pelagian idea is the conception of the spiritual life as starting, at least in the main, from self. From time to time, as all Church history shows, this self-reliance has reappeared under other names, always cast down by a true instinct of its incompatibility with the very idea of Christianity, yet never so eradicated that it should not again appear.

It is one and the same spirit which shows itself in these and other forms—forms practically adopted by many who have never studied their true nature, and do not even know their names, so far as they live virtually self-reliant and self-contained lives, content to be totally or partially without God in the world. Under all its forms such a temper naturally inclines to ignore or gloss over evil in man and in the world. It holds it perhaps a simple ignorance which science will dispel; it trusts to remove it by better social and political machinery; perhaps it may even go so far as to deny that it is anything but a lower form of good, proscribed for the sake of convenience by antiquated laws and religions. But of sin as sin, even of blindness and weakness, as inherent in man, it has not, and indeed it cannot have, any deep conviction. For it has no Being to look to, whose purity may disclose to the soul its own blackness, and before whose light our little candles show pale and cast a dark shadow.

The extenuation of evil.

Yet certainly this element of the spiritual life, in its right place and order, has a reality and a truth in it. On it depend in great degree the sense of dignity, the spirit of freedom, the capacity of progress in all civilisation, the energy, which is as the salt of human society. It is true of the race, as of the individual, that the first condition of success is to believe in self. Where there is that belief—where each believes in himself and his fellow-men—there is the spirit which is the seedplot of victorious energy. In it is one secret of that power which has bidden the European outstrip the Asiatic mind in the career of progress, and enabled it, not least in us Englishmen, to exercise a lordship over the other races of the world.

The value of this self-consciousness.

CHAP. IV. CHRISTIANITY AS A SPIRITUAL LIFE.

III. But what if it breaks down—as, when forced into a place of supremacy, it must break down—before the fuller conception of the great laws and powers, under which our individuality is dwarfed into littleness—before the deeper consciousness of the gigantic power of evil, in suffering, in weakness, and in wickedness, against which, in ourselves or in others, we seem to strive in vain? *The reactions against it.*

It is notable in our days that both these causes are at work with singular power. For, in the first place, every discovery of physical and historical science shows us more of the actual power of the outer world of things and men on our own thought and character and will. Every advance of civilisation brings that power to bear more irresistibly on us, fettering and diluting individual originality. In the next, side by side with this, perhaps not unconnected with it, there is the growth of a dark sense of evil in the philosophies of Pessimism, replacing, even in the realm of nature, and much more in humanity, the shallow and cheerful optimism of days gone by. It is even instructive for those who occupy the unchanged position of Christianity to note how modern philosophy exaggerates those very conceptions of the unity of the race of mankind as a whole for evil and for good, and of the existence of a blight on man and on the world, which the earlier speculations of mere individualism and self-blinded optimism treated with so much scorn.

Hence, in our day, reaction leads towards the other extreme. Before the Supreme Power in the universe, whatever it be, inscrutable and infinite, men are tempted to sink all consciousness of their own personality, freedom, and energy—to find the true result of all thought in the absolute submission of the individual nature, if indeed it exists, to the spirit of the age, to the laws of nature and society—to despair of any ability to change the march of events, and by any original action of our own to turn darkness into light and evil into good. At any sudden call to action, indeed, we are apt to forget all these terrible theories. Taught, under the threat of philosophical condemnation, to believe our own individuality incapable of moving against the irresistible, we nevertheless mutter under our breath, 'Yet it does move, after all.' But, when the excite- *The practical denial of individuality.*

ment is over, the 'pale cast of thought' comes back, and 'the native hue of resolution is sicklied o'er,' till we despair of any firm individual purpose and aim in life; especially when we are assured that the very thought of such a thing is, philosophically considered, an obsolete superstition, and, from the point of view of what calls itself 'altruistic' morality, an unpardonable self-conceit or selfishness.

The most flagrant and terrible forms of this call to spiritual suicide, as they show themselves in the school of avowed Pessimism, seem to reproduce the strange dreams of Buddhism, that religion of despair. The human soul is not allowed to stand erect and look upwards, but is to bow down before a shrine where there is no God. They present to us the life of humanity, perhaps of the universe, as simply one continual flux and change, in which light and darkness alternate, in which life comes out of death, and death out of life. They bid us not only give up all ideas of an immortality, but all consciousness of will and personality, as a mere delusion. Like the Buddhist, they lead us to a *Nirvana* as the goal of this series of illusions which we call life. Sometimes, unlike him, they repeat the old Epicurean teaching: 'Let us eat and drink, for to-morrow we die.' Sometimes, on the other hand, the only attitude of the soul in this its fancied existence, which is regarded as reasonable, is the attitude of sad patience and absolute submission, in the sense of utter weakness, blindness, and misery—waiting, as in a fevered sleep, till dreams be over, not to wake to life, but to sink into the relief of unconsciousness—perhaps, as there is no eternal 'canon against self-slaughter,' hastening that wished-for hour by a wise and reasonable suicide.

The Pessimistic Nirvana.

But this extreme form, although it dominates some individual minds, and casts its cold shadow over any society which admits it even in theory, has little reality of power outside the philosophic schools. If life is to go on at all, and self-worship is impossible, there must be something to reverence besides the 'abysses, immensities, and eternities.' Self-annihilation before an empty shrine, whatever it may call itself, is not really worship.

The worship of the Universum.

Far more vital and powerful, therefore, is that worship

CHRISTIANITY AS A SPIRITUAL LIFE.

of a Supreme Power, unknown and dimly seen as pervading all the universe, of which the individual soul is but a reflection, fancying itself a light. We know it well in the enthusiastic worship of 'Nature'—whether in all the vastness and multiform variety of life, which science surveys with grave wonder, or in all the beauty and grandeur of mystery, which enthral the imagination of the artist and the poet. We observe that the two conceptions run into each other. Science itself rhapsodises, and is ready to colour the dry light of experimental investigation with the brilliant hues of imagination. Materialism, even if it retains its old name, is, by a change in the conception of the nature of matter, practically merged in Pantheism; and the 'loving study of Nature' loudly claims the right to be called a religion, appealing primarily, indeed, to the intellect, but secondarily to the feelings and the imagination, though it cannot bear directly on the conscience. To the worshipper of nature, the spiritual life presents itself as a complete forgetfulness of self or man—content to study and to gaze upon this world-pervading presence—content to yield ourselves up, as to some irresistible stream, to the power of an overwhelming and inscrutable majesty, and, like a drowning man, after the first struggle to sink into a dreamy peace, or at most to pay some vague and silent worship to a diffused presence, which is hardly a living God.

Then, again, if this worship of Nature be refused, there is offered to us the worship of Humanity, which yields up all individual originality to the rule of the spirit of the age, prostrates itself under the irresistible march of great laws of human nature and history, and proclaims its captivity under an absolute bondage of climate and circumstance, race and hereditary constitution. As distinguishing man from the universe, it may leave us some shadow of personality. But it denounces as an offence against the higher morality, and as a perversion of the higher life of the soul, all thought of our own perfection or happiness, and all craving for personal immortality. It is enough to have lived and seemed to act; then we are to be content if the bubble of our life bursts, and the stream which it has purified moves calmly on.

The worship of humanity.

Nay, when we turn from these vaguer worships to bow before a personal and living God, even then there is a not unfrequent tendency to lose all conscious personality in the sense of His infinite majesty, His all-pervading power, and His all-seeing love. There is a fascination in this religious self-abnegation. There is such a thing as the recognition of the Kismet of absolute sovereignty, in which the spiritual life is simply a dumb and patient submission, calm, but with the calm of death. There is such a thing as the mystic Quietism, which resigns the soul in perfect trust, without a thought, without an exertion, without even a prayer, into the everlasting arms of God's providence and His grace. In these there is not the same perfect sacrifice of personality, for in the consciousness of a living personal God we feel ourselves even while we resign ourselves. But still there is the same ignoring of freedom and responsibility; there is the same exaggeration of but one side of the spiritual life.

Religious mysticism.

Now, of all these forms of thought, it may seem strange, but it is most true, that they meet the opposite extreme in a very imperfect sense of sin as sin.

The acquiescence in evil.

No doubt the feeling of littleness and weakness, even of an indwelling corruption, is not merely strong but excessive. Men may accept it quietly, or groan and wail under it; but in either case they hold it to be a dark overwhelming power, from the chill shadow of which no man can escape. Yet for this very reason they cease to feel it as their own sin; to them it is rather a condition in which, for some inscrutable reason, they are placed; they hold it to be the fruit of law, and almost dare to call it the will of God. Like a painful disease or a physical scourge, they would think of it as little as possible, and bear it as quietly as they may. They fully understand St. Paul's terrible description of the bondage of evil. But they cannot enter into his struggles against it, or the cry, 'Wretched man that I am, who shall deliver me?'

IV. These, and such as these, are exemplifications of the two opposite conceptions of the spiritual life—the two extremes of self-assertion and self-abnegation, between which the soul of man oscillates to and fro. In the one the soul finds the secret of dignity, energy, progress, in the other the grandeur of mystery and the sense of peace. How shall these be harmonised, as in any complete view they must be harmonised, one with the other? Christianity claims, not without justification, to exercise a wonderful power as a spiritual life, into which all are called to enter. How does it unite these two elements, each obviously needful, yet each so apt to usurp over the other? *The Gospel harmony of both principles*

The answer is as before : 'Not by any elaborate balance of law and ritual, not by any subtle construction of philosophical theory, but by the manifestation and the reproduction of the life of Jesus Christ.' He (says St. Paul) is made to us ' sanctification '—the source of holiness. The holiness of the Gospel is a purity of heart, loving for their own sake all truth and righteousness and beauty and love, and so growing into their likeness, in that inner shrine of the heart where no created foot may tread. But it is a purity of heart which ' sees God,' and in the knowledge of Him, ' which is the life eternal,' is renewed day by day in His image; it has its true being hidden in Him, in the peace which none else can give or take away. This holiness is set forth to us in actual and visible reality in the life of Jesus Christ Himself. In that life we have both these elements set forth in perfect harmony. *in the life of Christ.*

It has its absolute freedom, self-concentration, dignity. He mixes, indeed, with men in perfect sympathy of beneficence, loving and being loved; He enters into men's thoughts as a teacher; He leads the great battle of life by constant work for good against evil. But all the while He has obviously an inner life, into which none can enter; in deepest thoughts, feelings, aspirations, always alone; needing for these the rest of solitude, although in these lies the strength of the outer life of communion with men. He moves even before God in perfect freedom, having life in Himself, working as God works, having power to lay down His life, and power to take it again, knowing what He came into the world to do, and when He could say ' It is finished.' There is no possibility here of any unreality, any stage-play of mere illusion; there is in Him an intense living personality, realising itself deeply in the inner spiritual life. *Its perfect individuality.*

Yet that life, at the same time, is hidden in God. Again and again He declares, with a holy earnestness, that what He does, what He says, what He knows, is simply the fruit of His communion with the Father, simply the carrying out of the Divine will, simply the manifestation of God in Him. What He thus declares in word is illustrated in deed, by those long hours of secret prayer on the mountain height, to which He returned after the work and intercourse of the day, as to the source of rest and peace. It was on one of these that there dawned the brightness of the Transfiguration, manifesting the glory which was always around Him through that Divine communion; among these stand out prominently His agonies of prayer in the great crises of His earthly life, in answer to which came now the voice from heaven, and now the message of God by the angel. There is here no life self-centred and self-contained. His is a life resting upon God, seeing by His light, and working in His grace.

Its absorption in God.

Such is the life of Christ in itself. Before it, in this marvellous union of spiritual majesty and profound religious humility, all minds bow down, confessing it an ideal of the true spiritual life, beyond human capacity to invent or perfectly to imitate. But here, as before, the great principle of Christianity is the reproduction of that life in Christian souls. In this, the most sacred sphere of human consciousness, more than even in the intellectual and moral aspects of our nature, the motto of the Christian is, 'I live, yet not I, but Christ liveth in me.'

Accordingly we note how singularly the union of the two elements of the spiritual life is marked, first and more simply, in the condition of the acceptance of it; next, and more profoundly, in the conception of its origin.

This harmony exemplified

The condition of acceptance, as everyone who glances at Christianity for a moment must avow, is simply faith. Now faith is, on one side, an act of perfect freedom in humanity; on the other, a surrender of all to God. It is a free act of the soul, calling out all its faculties of understanding, of conscience, and of love, for the contemplation and knowledge of God. It is an action passing

(a) in the principle of faith;

through various stages of personal consciousness : first believing that God is; then believing that His word is true; lastly, believing that in Him we live, and move, and have our spiritual being. It is an action which has to be repeated all the life long ; it is made energetic (says St. Paul) by love; it is made perfect (says St. James) by works. It is, therefore, an act in which humanity asserts itself. The capacity of faith, like all other human powers, must be the gift of God ; but actual faith involves eventually a free act of man.

But yet, on the other hand, faith is self-assertion simply in order to self-surrender. Because it differs from other spiritual actions of the soul in contemplating not an invisible truth or principle, but an invisible Person, it is capable of that absolute self-surrender, which cannot be made except to some personality. It gathers all the forces of our humanity together, in order to lay that humanity, in body, soul, and spirit, at the feet of God, to rest henceforward wholly on His love, His grace, His salvation. Thus it represents humanity as weak and finite, and teaches it to lose its weakness in the infinite strength of God. But, in its Christian form, faith does much more than this. It confesses, deeply and passionately, that sad reality from which both the partial forms of the spiritual life shrink—the reality of sin and its fruit of death. Its distinctive act is to commit man's sin to God's mercy, that in that mercy it may be done away. It is clear that in this primary condition of faith there meet together self-assertion and self-surrender, the sense of the divine in man, and the sense of his finiteness and his sin.

But we may go deeper still, to consider the conception of the source of the new life. Still we find the same true harmony of the two great ideas, although natu- rally here the greater consciousness of God rises dominant over the lower consciousness of self. (*b*) in the principle of religious life; Dealing with a condition of human thought in which self-reliance had assumed a morbid predominance, alike in the religion of the Jew and in the search of the Gentile after God, the New Testament pleads earnestly, and even passionately, that the source of the new life is in God, and not in us. If sin is to be done away, it is by the free initia-

T

tion of God's mercy: 'Not that we loved God, but that He loved us, and sent His Son to be the propitiation for our sins.' If the spirit is to grow into the Divine likeness, and attain to its true perfection thereby, it is in His grace, not coercing, but guiding and inspiring the spirit of man, that we find the secret of the very faith which turns to God, and of the love by which we learn to know Him. As truly as in the religions which abjure all individuality, God is the Alpha and Omega of the spiritual life. But yet, as an undertone never lost, we trace the accompanying consciousness, as of man's freedom to accept, so unhappily of his freedom to reject—of man's glorious privilege of fellow-working with God, and of the awful possibility that, being not with Him, we may be against Him. Man's part is insufficient in itself; it is merely secondary in the spiritual life. But it is still real. A Saviour may die for us, and may weep over us; but, if we will not, we cannot have life. The well-known paradox recurs again and again in different forms: 'Work out your own salvation,' just because 'it is God that worketh in you both to will and to do.'

The Gospel, indeed, does not profess to give the key to the reconcilement of these two principles. At most it opens, from time to time, an occasional glimpse into this mystery. In this respect it is like all true science, that it contents itself with bringing out two truths, both of which are clear in themselves, though it may not see the ultimate point where they meet behind the veil. Well indeed would it have been if all systems framed in the name of Christianity had been equally careful to resist the temptation to grasp at a comprehension of the incomprehensible, and to sacrifice to logical consistency plain but unmanageable truth. But that reconcilement it always holds to exist, and insists upon it as a fundamental condition of practical holiness. To all declarations that it is impossible, it simply answers by showing it actually embodied, perfectly in the life of Jesus Christ Himself, imperfectly, but truly, in thousands and thousands of human lives in which that life lives again.

For, like the moral force of Christianity, this spiritual life, in simple practical power, in universal scope, in detachment from all that is transitory and artificial, stands out unique in the history of the world.

Its characteristics are written broadly on the very ritual of Christian worship. There is represented the humility of conscious unworthiness, which bows the knee and the head before God. Yet there is also room for the standing erect, with face unveiled and eyes raised to heaven, which marks the confidence of sonship. There is the silent acceptance of God's pardon, of His word in Holy Scripture, and of His grace in the sacraments. Here He gives all, and we can but receive. But there answers to this the outburst of praise and thanksgiving—a thanksgiving always inseparably connected with promise of a free and willing obedience, in which we claim a right to offer something in return to the Lord. Perhaps most of all in prayer is this twofold conception most deeply marked. For prayer is, on the one side, a confession of absolute dependence on God; yet, on the other, in its strong desire and wrestling in supplication, it is an appointed means of 'fellow-working with God,' in accordance with His will. By every act of worship, the harmony of both elements of the spiritual life sinks into the soul. So only, perhaps, could it be realised by the mass of men, who have neither leisure nor capacity for pondering and learning it by abstract thought.

<small>Symbolized in Christian worship.</small>

For what we may see visibly expressed in worship is known also by experience as existing in life. There is unquestionably—even in the dull, the ignorant, the many workers, as distinguished from the few thinkers—a power of spiritual life in Christ, in which they rise to a higher and lovelier humanity than can be gained by culture and refinement, by high gifts and heroic energies, and in which they have a sense of God, and of the communion with God, which no depth of learning and no searching and originative ability can open to the soul. That beauty and exaltation of humanity is the image of the Christ in them. That insight into the Divine will and nature comes from the manifestation of God to them in the Saviour whom they know and love.

<small>Embodied in Christian practice.</small>

Such is Christianity as a spiritual life. Probably it is fully appreciated only by those who experience it in themselves, or who, by the insight of sympathy, can see it living and working in others. But, even if it be looked upon coldly and critically from without, it must be acknowledged to be a very great reality. It has stamped itself on modern literature; it has coloured modern thought; it has influenced largely even modern art; it has proved itself a potent factor in the manifold power which moulds modern society. The thoughtful enquirer has once more to face the consideration of the marvellous rise of that power from the little mustard-seed of one single humble life—planted in the hard barren soil of Judaism, and growing up without any of the aids, material, intellectual, social, which might have been thought needful for a world-wide growth—yet overshadowing already the choicest regions of the world, and every day rooting itself by a fresh attachment in the spiritual soil of humanity. Even in itself it is a phenomenon perhaps even more wonderful, and more imperiously demanding some adequate explanation, than the divine philosophy or the moral force of Christianity.

Conclusion.

But here, again, I must contend for the principles on which I laid stress in connexion with the witness of Natural Theology. In looking at the living force of Christianity as a witness for its truth, we must not confine ourselves to any one single aspect; the intellectual, the moral, the spiritual elements of that power must all be united in our consideration, as they are united in the Gospel itself, and in the human nature to which it appeals. Nor will their combined force be merely the sum of their forces taken separately. By the very law of convergence, the whole must be far greater than its parts. If the understanding, in its perplexity, finds a light great beyond all others in its brightness, and in its origin inexplicable by merely natural causes, the soul will even thus be in some degree prepared to believe that it comes from God. But if, in the same Gospel which enlightens the understanding, there is found a moral force, unique in its character and power, capable of being received and assimilated by all, even by those who can hardly appreciate the intellectual enlightenment, and proving itself able to pervade by its influence the actual fabric of human society, then the conviction already formed is far more than doubled in its

The convergence of these three forces in Christianity.

intensity. If, now, from this we go on to discover that what is a light to the understanding, and a never-failing spring of moral action, can at the same time disclose the secret of the spiritual life, solving there a hitherto insoluble problem, by revealing a communion with God, in which, nevertheless, our own personality is not absorbed, the result must rise rapidly, by the convergence of these three lines of witness, to something like moral certainty. We find ourselves face to face with a reality unique and unapproachable, combining in one the three great forces which dominate the world. Whence can a power come, which so entirely commands the whole of our complex human nature, except from Him who made it? It is not surprising that in the sense of this marvellous combination of intellectual, moral, and spiritual power, the mass of men are contented, and reasonably contented, to rest. But yet even now the whole case is not stated. How infinitely is our wonder enhanced, and the enthusiasm of adoration and allegiance quickened in us, when we discover that this extraordinary combination of power is concentrated in the manifestation of One Personal life—a life which can be apprehended in its concrete reality by every mind—a life which commands, as no abstraction can command, the homage of every heart! If once men come to believe that Jesus Christ is thus to them 'wisdom, righteousness, sanctification,' they mostly seek no further evidence that He is their Lord and Master.

But to the mind led by taste or necessity to further enquiry, there remains still that to which we must next turn—the consideration what the life of Christ, so fruitful of these world-wide spiritual results in the present, actually was in its historic manifestation on earth by deed and word. Yet, when we enter *Leading on to the study of the life of Christ itself.* upon this, it is most unreasonable to do so in forgetfulness of these signs of power, as though we ought to expect to find it a mere ordinary life. Whatever it is, the fact of its actual power shows it must at any rate be far more than this. Whatever records of unique and exceptional character present themselves to us must be considered in relation, not to the round of everyday experience, but to a life which undoubtedly has proved itself by its results to form an epoch absolutely unique in the experience of the world, and which claims to be the central point of all human history. In such connection, supernatural as they are, they become in some sense 'natural,' because they fall under a law of their own, distinct from the laws of ordinary experience. When we trace to its source a river which waters the whole world of humanity, we may well expect to find that source deep and high—deep in its strength and freshness, high in that position, far above the plain of ordinary life, which gives it force to flow thus wide and strong. If, therefore, our examination has shown us that for the mind, the conscience, and the spirit of all men, Christ has 'the word'— an 'engrafted word' growing into the soul—'of eternal life,' then, in contemplating His life on earth, we must see that all our ordinary principles of judgment cannot but be fundamentally modified. The very laws of probability and improbability are so inverted, that it ought rather to surprise us, if we failed to discover in that life extraordinary features of its own, extraordinary relations to the history of the world, and extraordinary demands on the faith of man. Strangely uncritical here is the negative criticism, fast bound in the prosaic traditions of ordinary experience, and accordingly opposing an obstinate incredulity to the strongest evidence of the supernatural. Clearly we are on sacred ground. What wonder if we find there visible traces of a presence of God?

CHAPTER V.

THE LIFE OF CHRIST MANIFESTED TO THE WORLD.

'Can any good thing come out of Nazareth? Philip saith unto him, Come and see.'—John i. 46.

IT was once said, boldly but truly, that 'we need not a dead Christ, but a living one.' In accordance with that principle (which comes home at once irresistibly to the hearts of all who hear it proclaimed), I have hitherto contended, that if we desire to understand what are the claims which Christianity has upon our allegiance, we must first survey it in its present actual power. If it be dead, or if it obviously carry in it the seeds of death, I do not see why it should be to us anything more than a matter of historical and critical interest, to ascertain by what process and by what power it arose. So we judge, and rightly judge, of all religions of the past. They are, indeed, of deep interest, as spiritual phenomena and as historic forces, to every student of humanity; but by the very fact that they are of the past, they confess that they are not religions for all humanity, because they are not ultimate revelations of the one living God. Accordingly, as the first preparatory step in the process of right study, we have to consider what Christianity actually is—first, as an intellectual system, a divine philosophy, solving the great problem of being; next, as a moral force, at once guarding the individuality and re-creating the unity of man; lastly, as a spiritual life, harmonising the consciousness of spiritual dignity within with the unreserved worship of the great Supreme Power above. In each and all, I have suggested that it stands out very much as the present reality of miracle and the fulfilment of time-honoured prophecy stood out to the first ages of the proclamation of the Gospel. It shows itself

Survey of previous argument.

a unique living power, challenging as its right, and obtaining in actual fact, a marvellous adhesion of faith and obedience. It shows itself, moreover, a power so absolutely dissociated from all that implies limitation or transitoriness—so extraordinary in the character and extent of its power over humanity—so absolutely inexplicable by any of the merely human conditions of its origination—that to many minds it carries its own evidence of divine origin, and that on all it must at least act, like any other miracle, to arrest attention, to command reverence, to prepare the way for faith.

But we have noted that in every aspect Christianity entirely refuses to allow the mind to rest upon its visible embodiment, in ritual law, in morality or theology. In a sense which is true of no other religion, 'Christianity is Christ Himself.' In all its aspects the Christian life in any soul claims to be the reproduction, by light and by grace, of the life of the Lord Jesus Christ. Hence, from the contemplation of the fabric of our actual Christianity we must go on to examine what is declared to be at once the foundation on which it rests, and the cornerstone by which its great lines are determined. We must study the life of Christ in itself, and gather from such consideration the secret of this transcendent spiritual empire over souls. Like St. Peter on the day of Pentecost, starting from the outpouring on earth of a spiritual life to regenerate humanity in mind, in conscience, and in heart, we go back to the life and word of Jesus Christ, who ' hath shed forth this which we see and know.' In other words, we have hitherto contemplated the life of Christ as it is reproduced imperfectly in others, shining through the veil of individual peculiarity and imperfection and sin; we now have to ask what it is in itself, undimmed and undistorted by the interposition of any earthly medium.

Study of the life of Christ.

But how shall we do this? It is notable, and it should increase our wonder at the universal power over man of the life of Jesus Christ, that, after all, we know but one small fragment of that life with any degree of clearness. Hence the glory, which has illuminated and regenerated the whole world, is really little more than a flash of the true light itself. From its power we

Our imperfect means of knowledge.

can understand the declaration that, if we could see Him as He is in the glory of His whole being, we should become perfectly like Him. If we consider the life of Christ as it is regarded by the Christian faith, through which it has actually told upon the world, we must remember that it is a necessary part of such faith to hold that, as Son of God, He existed through all the ages of an eternal past, and that, having taken upon Him our humanity, he lives still, as God and man, in heaven, to all eternity. But of all these ages, before and since His appearance on earth, we know nothing, save in brief and partial glimpses of mystery. It is only of the few years which He spent on earth that we have record; out of these, and these only, the whole living picture has to be drawn. If, again, without drawing on the insight of faith, we consider this historic manifestation, we find that of its few years at least nine-tenths were spent in a retirement, over which there hangs an almost impenetrable veil of secrecy. It is but of three years at the very most that we have any detailed records at all. These, moreover, profess themselves at every point memoirs and not histories, lighting up a few salient points, leaving in darkness 'many other things which Jesus did' and said. Even putting aside the difference between actual eye-witness and hearing at second hand, it is obvious that we can have but little idea of the power with which the life of Christ impressed itself on those who had known it as a whole, and who for that very reason were alone thought fit to be the apostolic missionaries of the new faith. Yet this brief imperfect knowledge is enough to enable us, in a very true sense, to enter into the secret of that marvellous life, which has (as I have said) actually stamped itself on the whole spiritual nature of mankind. Under all these limitations, its supernatural power manifests itself, as a force able to move the whole world.

Again, when through these records we consider the life of Christ, we must remember at the outset that this consideration is wholly independent of those questions which have been constantly raised, and which of late the author of 'Supernatural Religion' has revived— questions in themselves of the deepest interest and the greatest importance—whether the Gospel narratives, as we *Our study independent of minute criticism.*

have them, are really the work of eye-witnesses, as the ancient tradition declares, or are documents of the second century, derived from some older and simpler record, and therefore are in their details liable to suspicion of inaccuracy and of unauthorised addition. I cannot, indeed, affect to believe that all possible ingenuity of criticism and speculation is likely to shake either the strong external evidence on which their authenticity rests, or the still more powerful witness of the marvellous living reality and unity of the picture which they draw, utterly incompatible with the notion of mere secondhand tradition or of multifarious authorship. But, I repeat, our knowledge of the life of Jesus Christ in its broad outlines—as laid down, for instance, in the Apostles' Creed—is quite unaffected by these questions. If all the Gospels were lost, it could be reconstructed from the Epistles. If the whole New Testament were to pass away to-morrow, it could be drawn out, with no difficulty or precariousness of induction, from the writings, the ritual, and the history of Christianity itself. Hence whatever may be thought as to details, the life of Christ, in its main outlines, appears to stand out in indisputable historic reality. No man can believe that the life, which has thus left its traces upon history, is a mere ideal picture. No man who studies it in the Gospels, can fail to discern its general historic truth. No man, who knows anything of the Christian thought of the second century, can suppose it capable of creating the Christ of the New Testament. In whatever light we consider it, we need not doubt for a moment that we can discern the great features of the true life of Christ, and substantially reproduce the voice which issued from His lips so many centuries ago.

Now, if we consider our knowledge of any great human life, we shall find that mostly it consists of three elements, melting, of course, into each other. There is, first of all, that aspect of the life and character which can be discerned by the world at large, as it moves in the visible sphere of action. There is, next, the aspect under which a man's life presents itself to those who live in close familiar intercourse with him, watching his face, hearing his words, entering by sympathy into his soul, and thus

The various forms of knowledge of a life.

adding to the observation of visible fact the intuition of a closer knowledge. There is, lastly, that aspect of the life which can be revealed only by the man himself, in words or writings addressed to man, or the more sacred utterances heard only by himself and by God. Experience has made us familiar with the startling differences, which often exist between these aspects of the same life, especially if that life be a really great life. How often a man's friends, who know him in private intimacy, smile or sigh at the erroneous conceptions of him formed by the outside world! How often those who believe themselves to know his soul as they know their own, find by his self-revelation, perhaps when the grave has closed over him, that there were depths of good or evil in his nature of which they had never even dreamed! All these views may be true, as far as they go, and, moreover, each has its own peculiar value; just as in the picture of some great mountain there is a special and characteristic beauty in the breadth and comprehensive unity of the view from far away, in the fuller detail and richer colouring of the mid-distance, and in the overwhelming majesty of the view, which bursts upon us at the very base or on the mountain side. But clearly, for full knowledge of a life, we should combine all; and the right order of study is first to pass from the outer circle of the world to the closer familiarity of intimacy, and then to go on from this nearer observation to seek finally the inmost knowledge of all in the outpourings of the man's own soul.

Hence, if we are to gain any knowledge, so far as human knowledge is possible, of the life of Jesus Christ in itself, it seems clear that we should follow some such course as this. It appealed to the world in certain plain and obvious forms of manifestation; it contained much which, as He Himself declared, could be seen and heard only by the few; it had much also from which He Himself had to lift the veil, either before or after His ascension. It will be a wise accordance with a natural law, if we contemplate it in this order. *Application to the life of Christ.*

But, whatever order is followed, it is of infinite consequence to contemplate it at every step as a whole, the various parts of which explain and support one another. In studying the actual life of Christ, just as in considering the actual power of Christianity, I must still earnestly contend for the same principles, under which I have urged that the witness of Natural Theology to God should be estimated. It is surely, in the first place, a fatal error, contradicting all sound laws of induction and evidence, when any one element in that life is considered in itself, and when men attempt to weigh its evidence and its significance altogether apart from the rest. How can we rightly judge (for example) of the miracles of His life, if we altogether dissociate them from the prophecies of the Messiahship linking them to the history of the past, or from the teaching, up to which He Himself declared them to lead as a climax, and which they subserved, both as signs and as actual revelations? To do this is to commit the same fundamental error which gave colour to the Pharisaic declaration that they were wrought through Beelzebub. So also in respect of all the other signs of a superhuman authority which draw men to Him—the fulfilment of prophecy, the manifestation, acknowledged even by His enemies, of a perfect wisdom in teaching and a perfect moral beauty of life—it is a strange error to regard each separately; it is hardly less unreasonable simply to add their evidences together, instead of considering how, by the very law of convergence, the cumulative force of their combined evidences so increases by each separate coincidence, as to rise rapidly from mere surmise to moral certainty. We might as well judge of the beauty of a picture by looking at each feature separately, and adding up our isolated impressions, without considering the harmony of colour and composition in the whole. That whole is infinitely greater than its parts. The life of Jesus Christ tells its tale, not by the separate tones of a divine music, not by the accumulation of all, either in succession or in haphazard coincidence; but by their arrangement according to the laws of a full symphony, making a music at once manifold and one. Looking, then, at that life as a whole, let us consider how it manifested itself to the outer world.

I. At a period when undoubtedly, by conclusion from prophecy, and by observation of the signs of the times, the whole Eastern world was hushed in expectation of some great deliverer, and when, through the proclamation of a great ascetic preacher of righteousness, the expectant world had been roused to a glad conviction that the deliverer stood unknown among them, there appeared suddenly, no man knew how or whence, in the peasant life of a half-barbarous province, one who declared that 'the kingdom of heaven was at hand,' and not obscurely intimated that He Himself was the King. *The proclamation of the kingdom of heaven,*

It is easy to ascertain what this proclamation of a 'kingdom of heaven' to a Jewish audience unquestionably carried with it. It meant the kingdom of the Messiah, in the promise of whom every line of Jewish thought and life was firmly bound up. Putting all details aside, we can see broadly what that promise was. It had its three great stages in Abraham, in Moses, in David. In Abraham it told of the future birth of One in whom should centre a covenant of universal blessing to all families of the earth. In Moses it involved the conception of a Prophet above all other prophets, who should reveal the perfect will of God, bowing men's hearts by the free influence of divine truth and love. In David, it proclaimed a king of all nations, crowned with the glory of a kingdom never to pass away. These three great principles it had been the office of all after-prophecy to work out in transcendent clearness and beauty, not unchequered by some darker predictions of a predestined suffering and a mysterious sacrifice. Now it dwelt on the kingdom in its all-embracing scope, its spiritual law, its divine inspiration of the soul. Now it looked on to the King Himself, always a Son of Man, on whom were gradually accumulated attributes of glory and majesty far too high for mere humanity. But, in one or both of these ways, the promise was so worked out that, as a matter of fact, the conception of the Messiah became a commonplace in the knowledge of all the people of Israel, and had even by reflection become visible on the horizon of heathen thought. It is characteristic of the relation of the supernatural to the natural, that the proclamation of the kingdom of heaven was like the lesser events, which we call great in the world's history, in having its period of preparation. 'The hour' was made ready, that 'the Man' might come.

But this proclamation of the kingdom of heaven came in a form not only utterly unexpected, but directly contradictory to all natural inference and hope. There were two forms under which it was looked for. The one by the people at large, especially (it would seem) in Galilee—the form of temporal power, warlike daring, heroic appeal to the fierce hatred of patriotism against the heathen conqueror; the other by the learned of the schools, the Pharisees and the Scribes—the more spiritual form of a new mystic doctrine, a more perfect ritual, an ascetic purity, uniting itself perhaps, as in the old Maccabean times, with an inextinguishable resistance to Roman law and Roman idolatry. Both these forms of expectation existed in singular clearness and power. But this sudden manifestation of a Messiah accorded with neither, and even contradicted both. The new King was simply a Galilean craftsman, from a despised city and from an unknown home. He absolutely refused, and even rebuked, all use of physical force, all exclusive patriotism, all appeal to the fierce arbitrament of war. Not less utterly did He hold aloof from the learning of the schools, proclaiming it unnecessary for those who would enter His kingdom, and denouncing it as vain and artificial before the people, who heard Him gladly. It seemed as though of set purpose He threw away the only possible supports of His kingdom, and so reduced His proclamation of it to the level of a merely fanciful pretension, the dream of a pious imagination, out of all connexion with the realities and necessities of actual life. It might have appeared certain to any shrewd observer of the times, that the representatives of both these principles would turn away with equal disappointment, and almost equal contempt, from One who began the declaration of the law of the kingdom with the words, 'Blessed are the poor in spirit, for theirs is the kingdom of heaven.'

Yet that shrewd observer, like many of his class at all times, would have been strangely mistaken. The new teaching did make its way. Crowds hung upon the lips of this new Prophet, following Him from city to city. The delegates of the Scribes and Pharisees, sent down to watch Him, felt themselves in the presence of a power which they could not resist. When from time to time He appeared in Jerusalem itself, the very officers sent to take Him cried out, 'Never man spake like this man.' At His last entry into the holy city the confession was wrung from the disappointment of His enemies, that 'the world was gone after Him.'

What was the secret of this? How, in spite of a method of proclamation which disappointed alike the learned and the ignorant, did a sense of the reality of His mission stamp itself so unmistakably on the hearts of the people?

The answer must simply be: 'By what He did, by what He said, by what He was.' There are three great forces which dominate the souls of men—power, wisdom, and goodness. They must, if they exist in any nature, show themselves in combination at every point, in thought, and word, and deed. So certainly it was with Him; in His acts, His views, and His life, there is obviously a perfect unity. But yet it can hardly be wrong to consider as predominant, power in what He did, wisdom in what He said, goodness in what He was.

II. In the study of that manifestation of power in what He did, which would first startle the world, and which perhaps, even to the end, would most impress the multitude, who looked on from without, we are brought at once face to face with the recorded miracles of Christ; and accordingly we are forced to consider two questions—the question of the reality of those miracles, and the question of their function in setting forth the kingdom of heaven. Now on both these questions controversy has raged, and is raging still; but out of that controversy certain points emerge with absolute clearness. *The manifestation of power in miracle*

Thus it must be allowed that what is called the 'miraculous element' is an integral and ineradicable part of the life of Christ, however we read it—whether in the records of our Gospels, in the allusions of the undoubted Apostolic Epistles, or in the indirect testimonies of Christian literature.[1] Its existence does not turn on the interpretation of this or that wondrous *an essential part of the manifestation of Christ.*

[1] See, for example, the remarkable summary of the life of our Lord, drawn from the apologetic writings of Justin Martyr, in Mr. Sanday's *Gospels of the Second Century*, c. iv. pp. 91-98.

work, and the discussion to what extent it can be referred to natural causes. In its various manifestations it pervades the whole history. In the final miracle of miracles—the miracle of the resurrection and ascension—it so stamps the meaning of that history, that St. Paul declares the faith of Christians vain, and the preaching of the Gospel false, without it. Moreover, this case is one in which the strength of the chain is that of its strongest and not its weakest link. If we convince ourselves in any one instance—as in the great culminating example of the Resurrection—of the existence of this miraculous power, it is a small matter whether it was exercised more or less frequently; and, indeed, isolated cases of its exercise are taken out of the category of intrinsic improbability, and therefore need no extraordinary evidence. To get rid of the miraculous element from the Gospel history (as from the history of the Old Testament) is simply to tear that history to pieces, and to make it in many parts unintelligible. It is not too much to say that, looking at the life of Christ in its historical results, considering its immediate and ultimate influence upon men, it actually becomes incredible, if the miracles be disbelieved. That, except on the supposition of a belief in miracles, it is impossible to understand the acceptance of His mission; that this belief in His miracles, and, above all, in the final miracle of the resurrection, was a potent factor in the actual process of faith which drew men's souls to Him in the first age of Christianity, are things beyond all reasonable contradiction. The one question is, whether it was a groundless or a well-grounded belief.

Now this question has been answered loudly, and almost arrogantly, by the declaration that a miracle is *ipso facto* incredible, and that, accordingly, no examination of evidence as to the reality of miracles in any particular case can be necessary. But the next point, which, although it will not be as yet universally allowed, seems again to be emerging into clearness out of the smoke of controversy, is the conviction that the ordinary *à priori* objections to the possibility of miracle—on the ground of 'the invariability of law,' 'the contradiction of universal experience,' 'the unworthiness of the conception

The futility of à priori objections to miracle.

of interferences,' and the like—are philosophically untenable, wherever there is any belief in a personal Creator and Ruler of the universe exercising a moral government over men.

These objections have, indeed, done good service to the cause of truth by forcing us to consider more accurately what miracles really are. They are not, as has (*a*) The invariability of been loosely said, and as the first objection evi- law. dently implies, 'suspensions of the laws of nature,' 'interferences with physical forces,' and the like; for, so far as we can judge, physical laws and the action of physical forces are not for a moment suspended, or in any strict sense interfered with, in the working of miracles. In such working there may or may not be the introduction of forces of creation or rapid development, which are not continually in operation in the present system of things; but the essential point of miracle is the plain exhibition of will, working through visible forces, directing them to a declared purpose, intensifying, quickening, or modifying their action so as to produce results of a wholly exceptional character, which present themselves to us as instances now of creation, now of recovery from sickness or death, now of subjugation of great physical powers. Thus viewed, miracle is seen to be a supernatural exhibition of a power which we know that human will exerts every day when, although destitute of all power to create, it nevertheless modifies arbitrarily the disposition and combination of matter—when it directs the action of physical forces, or calls out latent force which otherwise would remain dormant into energetic action—and when, above all, it acts in the spiritual sphere, to set in motion spiritual forces, which in their turn work out physical results. In fact, miracle merely implies the removal of the limitations which encompass the exercise of that power by the simple will of a creature, but which, of course, cannot be conceived as attaching to the action of an exceptional power, delegated by express will of God. When this idea is clearly grasped, it is seen that the 'invariability of law' is simply an imposing phrase—valueless as an objection to miracle, if 'law' be used in its only strict sense, to signify the exhibition of a supreme governing power—untrue to fact if it is intended to assert the universal dominion of an iron law of physical necessity unmodified by the action of will.

Nor, with regard to the 'contradiction of experience,' which did so much service in the old Deistic controversy, is it difficult to see that if 'experience' be taken in the largest sense, it simply begs the question; for the contention of Christianity, for which it is prepared to advance positive evidence, is that the experience of our Lord's age actually led men to recognise miracle as unmistakably present. While, on the other hand, if by 'experience' is meant the experience of every day, then the very idea of miracle, and, indeed, its whole evidential value involves divergence from that experience; and it is also evident that the whole question of the probability of miracle is necessarily connected with the extraordinary character which by universal confession attaches to the life of Christ in itself, removing it, as a matter of course, from the domain of such ordinary experience.

(b) The contradiction of experience.

Still less substantial, if possible, is the notion that the conception of 'interference' with the ordinary course of nature is a clumsy conception, unworthy of any enlightened idea of the perfect wisdom of God. For these interferences, improperly so called, are simply parts of a fore-ordained dispensation, governed, as we cannot doubt, by laws not less real, though more subtle, than what we call 'laws of nature.' That dispensation is designed to manifest to man the reality of God's moral government of man and the attributes which it exhibits. Its miracles are simply for the sake of man, to aid him to grasp the invisible; and no man can reasonably doubt that it is by the union of the experience of general laws, with the exhibition by salient instances of miracle of the divine will, working behind and through those laws, that a singularly clear knowledge of that dispensation is actually given.

(c) The objection to 'interference.'

Hence, when these objections are attentively scrutinised, they cannot stand. They do their work in correction of superficial impressions, and, having done that work, they pass away. So, without prejudice, the enquiry is thrown back to the old ground, on which Christians need have no fear of joining battle—whether there is, or is not, sufficient evidence to convince us of the reality of our Lord's miracles. For extraordinary events it is confessed that evidence of extraordinary strength is needed; the question is whether it is not forthcoming.² The author of 'Supernatural Religion' has shown much sagacity in passing by the *à priori* argument with a rather perfunctory treatment, and devoting all his energies to the task of shaking the authenticity of the Gospels in which this evidence is so plainly advanced. Christianity cannot fear this test. Only let the objections, which preclude all examination of evidence, be put aside, and we need ask no more. The work which Paley once did, on a somewhat narrow basis, but with incomparable force and clearness, can be done again, only in accordance with the larger and keener historical criticism of our own days, and with a more discriminating stress on the one great miracle of the resurrection, to which almost alone the appeal of early Christianity was actually made. It is curious to note here a signal instance of that which occurs again and again along the whole line of conflict. Those who hold the ancient positions of Christianity see the attack, after assuming new and formidable phases, veer round again to the old quarters, and watch how the advocates of the *à priori* and *à posteriori* methods turn their weapons against each other, in respect both of the credibility and the evidential function of miracles.³

The enquiry into the evidence.

Again, in examining the positive evidence on which the belief in our Lord's miracles rests, it is an important step that we have now come to understand more clearly how intimately the credibility of these miracles is connected with a true idea of a certain meaning pervading them all, and of their actual function, as a part of His general manifestation of Himself. It is, indeed, singularly unfortunate (for all errors of name avenge

The true position of the Gospel miracles:

---

² The denial of this necessity, in the confusion of improbability before testimony and after testimony, is one of the very few defects which have been proved in Butler's argument (see *Analogy*, Part II. c. ii.)

³ On this subject I would refer to Mozley's *Lectures on Miracles*, to Mansel's Essays in *Aids to Faith*, and to a very able article on the *Rationale of Miracles* in the 'Church Quarterly Review' of April 1876.

themselves by introducing errors of thought) that the very word 'miracle,' which we commonly use, simply means a work exciting wonder—a strange, unaccountable phenomenon, merely arguing the existence of an unknown power not already tabulated and accounted for in our philosophy. Of such phenomena there are many, which have no moral purpose and may have little scientific significance; so that men engaged in the great moral and intellectual questions of life may reasonably pass them by, or, at most, bestow on them a very slight attention. Between these and the miracles of the Gospel specious analogies have been drawn, but drawn most unreasonably. For the miracles of our Lord unquestionably claim to be a part of a great spiritual work. It has been constantly remarked, though the remark seems to be forgotten, that the very names by which they are called raise them infinitely above the superficial idea of mere 'miracle.' They were 'signs,' to call attention to something greater than themselves; they were 'works,' that is, they were an integral part of the actual work of His divine life upon earth.

They were 'signs,' and of what? Clearly of a power—certainly superhuman, presumably Divine—to sway the forces of the universe, physical, animal, and spiritual, in order to fulfil His will, or rather the mission which He came to discharge. It has been already noticed that a certain share of this power over the world and man, bringing the force of individual will to bear on the system of the universe, belongs to every human being, and is exercised by each just in proportion to his largeness of knowledge and his loftiness and strength of character; for it is a part of our 'fellow-working with God.' A power over physical forces, a power to heal the sick, a power to cast out devils from the soul, belong in some sense to the daily life of humanity. They are strictly natural. But there are limits—often narrow, and always unyielding, limits —to this ordinary power. Where they are crossed, the inference is natural and irresistible, that we are face to face with a superhuman manifestation of this power over the world, exercised in virtue of a superhuman mission for Him, under whom alone man can thus work. It may amuse subtle

(*n*) As signs.

minds to question the logic of that inference; but the mass of men, for whom especially these more visible manifestations are designed, will impatiently put all such questions aside. Whether in the first century or the nineteenth, in the streets of Jerusalem or the streets of London, if a man, professing to come as a messenger of God, were seen and known to rule the winds and the sea, to feed the multitude with a few loaves, and by a word to heal the sick, to recover the maimed, to raise the dead, the popular mind would never refuse to draw the old conclusion: 'No man can do the things that he does, except God be with him.'

It is true that these first thoughts may be checked by the second thoughts of hesitation, perhaps of scepticism. If there be a superhuman power, is it necessarily divine? If there be an exceptional power, is it necessarily supernatural? The first takes the form of the old cavil against our Lord's miracles, uttered by the Pharisees, and often repeated by the ancient opponents of Christianity, that they were wrought by the power of the Evil One. The second issues in the modern suggestion that the belief in them, possibly even the claim to work them, was a hybrid production of imagination and imposture. But in this case, as in so many others, *dolus latet in generalibus*. The objections have force only so long as they are wrapped in the vagueness of an application to miracles in general; they vanish when closely scrutinised in relation to the actual case of the miracles of our Lord. *Objections to their significance.*

Thus, as to the first, we have but to follow out the thought implied in our Lord's recorded answer to its original utterance. His miracles are simply a means of setting forth a 'kingdom of God;' they are bound up with a teaching of wisdom and goodness and holiness, showing a perfect accordance with God's previous revelations, and yet going infinitely beyond them; they are themselves simple exhibitions of beneficence and mercy in the visible sphere, connected with higher exhibitions of the same attributes in the sphere invisible. Look at them in this light—unquestionably the actual light in which they shone upon the world—and the theory, which might be tenable so long as they were regarded as isolated works of wonder, or even as exhibitions of mere power, is seen to be preposterous. Were it not for the not infrequent revival of theories supposed to be exploded, we might assume at once that it need hardly be treated as having a substantial existence under the light of modern thought.

As to the last, so far as it deals with any claim by Jesus Christ Himself to miraculous power, it seems almost too monstrous to be seriously discussed, except by those—if any such there be—who, after studying His life as a whole, can bring themselves to believe with the Jews of old that He was either a madman or a blasphemer. But, in fact, it is hardly advanced seriously. If the question is pressed home, the objection is sure to change its ground, and to transfer itself to the attribution of delusion or imposture to the disciples, who are supposed to have misunderstood or misrepresented their Master. Looking at it, then, as it concerns the belief in the reality of His miracles, we may make all conceivable allowance for the credulity of the age, for its ignorance of physical forces, for the extraordinary power—half physical, half spiritual—of an enthusiastic or superstitious imagination ; but when we look at the actual facts of the case, examine the record of the actual miracles as given in the New Testament note the opportunities which both the curious opponents and the disciples, whose all was staked on faith, had of scrutinising their reality, and trace the effects produced on both classes, especially by the great miracle of the Resurrection, we must absolutely refuse to entertain any supposition of innocent delusion. Yet how can we even contemplate the moral monstrosity which is involved in the attribution to the teachers of such a faith as Christianity of a deliberate resolution to base it on a great imposture? It is idle, again, to use vague phrases here as to the different standard of veracity in ancient days and in the Oriental mind. Human nature, after all, is the same in essence in all ages. The notion that the belief in our Lord's miracles, which was unquestionably a wide-spread and deep-rooted belief, was a mere delusion or a mere imposture, is seen to be an impossible demand on our own credulity, whenever it is taken out of the haziness of general phrases, and looked at as it actually is. We have to come back to the conviction that they are real exhibitions of a superhuman power, and that, as such, they furnish the best means—possibly almost the only means —by which One who came forth with no support of any human authority or influence could have startled and impressed the souls of the mass of men—the poor, the simple, the unlearned—whom He especially loved.

But they are only means to an end. It is the office of a sign to call attention to something beyond itself. What that something was our Lord Himself taught when, before St. John Baptist's disciples, He appealed to His miracles as signs, and yet made all, by a glorious climax, lead up to the preaching of the Gospel to the poor as the ultimate purpose of the whole. Unlike the strange phenomena, the so-called miracles, which perplex men from time to time, they had a background of high spiritual teaching for which they commanded attention. When the soul was once brought to dwell on this, their function as 'signs' was gone. It is often asked whether the miracles prove the doctrine, or the doctrine the miracles. But the antithesis is a false one. The miracles, in themselves, show a superhuman force at work; whether that force has a moral and spiritual significance must be shown by association with doctrine; and whether, by its accordance with God's known revelations, and by its advance beyond them, that doctrine can maintain a claim to a special divine authority, must be judged by the examination of the doctrine itself. In the complex proof required, both the work and the word have their proper functions. *Their relation to the word.*

But the miracles of our Lord were not only signs, they were also 'works'—that is, they were visible parts of our Lord's great work of redemption, and, in virtue of the essential unity of that work, they were types of the character of the work as a whole, as it goes on for ever, whether by His hand or the hands of His servants. With but an exception here and there, they were always visible manifestations of deliverance, redemption, mercy. 'To heal the sick' showed forth that side of the divine work which ministers to suffering, hunger and weakness, sickness and death. 'To cast out devils,' that yet nobler side, which forgives and conquers the sin which is the source of suffering. *(b) As works.*

Both were always closely united together. As He Himself declared, it was all one to say, 'Thy sins are forgiven thee,' and to say, 'Arise and walk.' Hence they stood out as 'manifestations of His glory,' showing not merely whence He was, but who He was, and what He came to do. In them there was not only power, but a power directed to salvation —just that power which a world like this so ardently longs for, and so essentially needs. No wonder that men, especially the simple and the unlearned, turned to them so gladly and so thankfully. Perhaps even to the last, so far as concerned 'the multitude,' whether of Galilee or of Judæa, these manifestations of a wise and beneficent power contributed the chief element to that spell which bowed all men at His feet.

Such was the influence which our Lord's wonderful works exercised then on the world at large. Naturally the revelation of Him through them was not the highest and clearest; naturally the faith which could rest only on 'signs and wonders' was branded by Him as crude and imperfect. Yet still there was a revelation in them, and the faith based on them was a not unreasonable faith. On us, looking back on them through the dimness of centuries of antiquity, they cannot produce the vivid impression which startled the world of eye-witnesses. But if we seriously consider the matter even now—putting aside *à priori* objections of impossibility, and vague depreciation of the force of testimony, without considering what their testimony actually was—I cannot think that any reasonable historical criticism, undisturbed by untenable assumption, can refuse to recognise their reality, and if it recognises their reality, to acknowledge also their evidential force. We do not (as I have already contended) need their evidence so much as the observers of our Lord's own day. Yet still, less enthusiastically, but not less earnestly, we must hail them as signs, and draw nearer to examine who and what He is to whom they point.

III. But they cannot, as I have already urged, be looked upon, even for a moment, as dissociated from the word, which He invariably connected with them. From the power of what He did—itself wise and beneficent—we pass on to the wisdom of what He said, and the goodness of what He was. Both will have to be

The revelation of wisdom.

more fully considered hereafter, when from the distant point of view of the multitude we advance to the inner circle of discipleship; yet both must be glanced at here. From whatever point His life is contemplated, it must be considered as one.

In relation to wisdom, we cannot now refer to the inner and deeper wisdom, known only to His disciples. We must look simply to the more general teaching, known to the outer world, which, for example, was uttered from the Mount in Galilee, or which drew the common people to hang on His word in the Temple.

Wisdom, in the true sense, is the knowledge of the end and purpose of man's life, and of this as subserving the greater purpose of God's whole dispensation. Now of that knowledge He declared Himself to have the key. He spoke, 'not like the Scribes,' from mere secondhand learning, but 'with the authority' of One who sees and knows. Even of the law itself He declared, 'It was said otherwise to them of old time, but I say unto you.' In comparison with the proverbial type of an inspired wisdom, He declared that 'a greater than Solomon was there.' The people heard Him gladly; even His adversaries were put to silence.

But how was this profound impression produced by one of humble rank, unlearned in the wisdom of the schools? Partly, we cannot doubt, by the tone, partly by the substance, of His teaching.

There is always a great power in the tone and style of teaching. In Him that power must have been marvellous chiefly by its self-restrained and subdued force. In the tone There were times, indeed, when He could flash out ing. the lightning of a righteous indignation, or melt into the pleading persuasiveness of tears. But, as a rule, it was the calmness, the dignity, the unwavering certainty of His teaching, which bowed the souls of men before Him. And again, if from the tone we pass to the style of His teaching, we note that He spoke with that simplicity, born of profound knowledge, which came home to the unlearned, and the commonplace, and the ignorant, while yet it baffled the subtlest objections, and gave to the deepest reflection food for wondering thought; and which, moreover, while it spoke emphatically to Jewish thought and practice, yet was plainly universal in its application to man as man. It was clearly a teaching at once simpler and deeper than that of the scribe or the philosopher—a teaching which appealed to the whole world, and could move it at every point.

But we pass from considering how He spoke to examine what He said. We note at once that He spoke to human nature as it is, imperfect yet spiritual, fallen but not cast away. He offered to all the way to the higher life in God, in which all sins were forgiven, and the likeness of the Father renewed. The publicans and the sinners were addressed as children of God; the babes of unlearned simplicity could enter into His revelations. We note, again, that He revealed God in His choicest attribute of Fatherhood, especially in the mercy which, indeed, cannot condone sin, but is always ready to forgive the penitent, willing to accept and bless the first faint dawn of faith. The kingdom of heaven was open to all. How all this should be, He told not as yet to the people, but He promised that it should be, and they believed. No wonder that, although men turned gladly to His works of beneficent power, they hung even more on the words of this divine wisdom—this Gospel, so simple yet so deep, so lofty in its conception, yet so absolutely appropriate to this world as it is. The mind of man, though it be too dull or too hopeless to discover, yet leaps up gladly at the voice of Truth, and, as it catches the sound of an unhoped-for Gospel, knows itself to be listening to one who speaks for God.

In its substance.

It would be, of course, utterly futile to attempt any survey of His teaching to the multitude as a whole, even so far as it is recorded for us. Only by a thoughtful study of it in detail can its general character grow upon us in the fulness of its wonder and power. The whole, as usual, is greater than its parts.

But, if we would gain some conception of that power, we need only take any signal example of His direct popular teaching. We have but to consider (for example), in the Sermon on the Mount, the characteristic graciousness and wisdom of the Beatitudes, the bold and authoritative extension of the law from the letter

The Sermon on the Mount.

of old time to the higher spirit, the searching requirement of a consciousness of God, and of God alone, in all the duties of the religious life; we have but to study the perfect prayer which is the prayer of all humanity, the superhuman teaching of inexhaustible love to man, and the exquisite picture of a childlike faith in the goodness of Him who gives the necessaries of life to the fowls of the air, and clothes with splendid beauty the lilies of the field; we have but to learn those immortal proverbs of the Gospel, which close the whole with incisive impressiveness, and have stamped themselves on the whole mind of humanity. A greater than man is here. It is an extraordinary error, indeed, to believe that in its preparatory teaching we have the 'sum and substance of Christianity.' But we can well conceive how, even taken alone, it must have been to its hearers an all-sufficient evidence of a wisdom from above; and we ourselves can almost consent to stake on it alone the enquiry whether He has or has not 'the words of eternal life.'

We may turn again from His direct preaching to the great series of His parables, which must necessarily have impressed themselves, far more than any abstract doctrine or exhortation, on the minds of the multitude, and have spread by repetition from tongue to tongue. *The teaching by parables.* Teaching by parables is a universal form of teaching; it was specially familiar and congenial to Jewish thought; it is embodied in great variety of form in the Old Testament itself. But it is a simple fact of universal acknowledgment that the parables of Christ stand alone and unapproachable in beauty, in depth, in power, in their manifold unity of meaning, and in the unearthly wisdom underlying a perfect simplicity. They are a revelation through the earthly life of the kingdom of heaven, now in all the vicissitudes of earth, now in the crisis of the Judgment and the entrance on an unchangeable eternity; in the picture which they draw, no point which man needs to know is untouched, nor is there one which another hand will dare to retrace. In them, no doubt, there is more than wisdom: there is a pervading atmosphere of holiness and graciousness. But, again, simply as a manifestation of wisdom, intended for the world at large, we may well be content to bid men judge from them whether 'man ever spake like this man.'

These specimens alone would be sufficient to show how absolutely unique in its power is the wisdom of His teaching, in the region within which ordinary man can understand and judge. It is hardly necessary to remark how immeasurably it rises above all which early Christianity was capable of devising or inventing. But we may note how entirely different it is even from the apostolic teaching of a St. Peter, a St. Paul, or a St. John. There is stamped upon it a personality to which none other is like, according, indeed, with the impression of a supernatural power derived from the knowledge of His works, but far surpassing it in spiritual force, and throwing such light upon it as to dispel any shadow of doubt as to the origin of that supernatural power. By His works and by His words, coming forth in close connexion and harmony, we may well understand how He drew all men after Him.

Its characteristic peculiarity.

IV. But yet, even now, the conception of that extraordinary influence is not complete. Beyond the power of what He did, and the wisdom of what He said, is the consideration of what He was. The spell of His goodness, no doubt, told most on those who followed Him and knew Him close at hand. By the world at large the person of the Lord was seen only from afar in its vague outline, not in the subtler lineaments through which the real self is seen. Yet even so, who can doubt that it exercised a commanding power? After all, for impression on the common sense of humanity at large, there is no force like the force of goodness. A man like Balaam, who wields a superhuman power with a base and sordid heart, is despised even while he is feared. Another may speak with all the wisdom of men and angels, unlocking to us the secrets of knowledge, dazzling us by the light of genius, speaking as by intuition to all the faculties of our nature; but, if he is once known to speak with a double tongue or from a polluted heart, his wisdom turns to folly. A third may bring to bear on us the still greater force of a strong and daring will, such as befits the kings of men; but unless that will can clothe itself in at least the appearance of righteous-

The revelation of goodness.

ness, there will be a constant rebellion, or a murmuring discontent, under his sway. Even the cynical wisdom of the world has recognised in many a proverb the supreme value of a character for goodness, though it be only assumed. The power of the reality, in the trust which it creates, in the sympathy which it kindles, in the reverence which it commands, is strong and permanent beyond all other forces.

But the goodness of Jesus of Nazareth was such that, even from a distance, it could not be ignored or mistaken. It was like the ideal goodness of which speculation dreamed, in the perfection and harmony of all its various elements. But it was utterly unlike it in this, that it presented a vivid and intelligible reality to the eyes of men. *Its universal and supreme power.* It appealed to the understanding of the people. The very life in which it was manifested was the life of the many, appearing in that 'working class' in which the multitude in all ages is included, mixing with all the homeliest scenes of life, and entering into its commonest relations. The goodness of the great prophet itself was embodied in the humility, the soberness, the truthfulness, the charity, the purity, which all men can understand and appreciate. Yet it certainly rose above their understanding. There was in it a certain majesty, indicative of depths of moral and spiritual power, unfathomed by the eye of man. Even His enemies did not dare to question its commanding influence then, or to accept His challenge, never uttered before or since by any child of man, 'Which of you convinceth me of sin?' In succeeding ages, most of those who have turned away from the Gospel have yet acknowledged the moral perfection of Christ, only accusing Christianity of misrepresenting it and falling away from it. It has been reserved for our own generation, by a sagacious instinct of hatred against the Gospel, to seek to impair it by covert insinuation, and by a half-patronising forbearance of criticism, or by open blasphemy to attack in the character of the Christ the true centre of Christian faith. But the very attempt recoils on those who make it. The character of the Lord stands out unassailable and unapproachable, and its evidential force is surely beyond all other forces. To the challenge, 'Which of you convinceth me of sin?' it was natural to add the question, 'Why do ye not believe me?' For goodness, above all else, is necessarily 'born of God,' and sustained by God. He who rises above all men in such goodness gives the very surest sign, not only that God is with Him, but that, in a special and unique sense, God is in Him. Supernatural power may be from the power of evil; there is even a wisdom which is earthly, sensual, devilish; but goodness cannot be from beneath: it must be from above, from God, and from God alone.

Yet we must also observe that it was not merely the existence, but the combination in perfect harmony, of the three great ruling influences of power, wisdom, goodness, which drew men to Christ. For that harmony is the true image of God in humanity. It strikes us as something sad and unnatural—a mark that the world's course is out of joint—that they should be so often separated, that power should be unrighteous and unwise, wisdom impotent and immoral, goodness narrow-minded and weak. Even so they have a marvellous power. But, wherever they are united, the soul is bound by a triple cord of allegiance not lightly broken.

The harmony of these three revelations.

V. Such is the form in which the life of Christ presents itself to those who look upon it from a distance like the multitude, before that instinct of faith is awakened which makes men His disciples indeed. There is a singular beauty of natural development in the stages of the actual impression made on the people, as they are described in our Gospel narrative. Three chief epochs stand out as typical epochs in the progress of that impression.

The impression actually made on the people.

The first is the day at Cæsarea Philippi, when our Lord's special ministry at Capernaum was coming to an end, and He asked St. Peter the question of what its result had been: 'Who do men say that I am?' We notice a simple and striking candour in the narrative, disclosing the comparatively vague conception yet gained by the people. He was a Prophet, clothed, like those of old, in the twofold power of miracle and inspiration, one who came from God and spoke for God. So far they had advanced in knowledge; but beyond this they doubted. He might be (as

(*a*) His prophetic mission.

Herod thought) John the Baptist, risen from his bloody grave. He might be the Elijah who was to be the forerunner of the Messiah, or the Jeremiah who saw the destruction of the old Jerusalem, and who was believed to be reserved for the appearance of the new. The conception was true and natural; but it was utterly, and to our conception surprisingly, inadequate.

Another year passes by, and at the last Passover this hesitation had for one great moment of enthusiasm vanished, for Galileans and for the people of Jerusalem alike. (*b*) His Messiahship. Now they felt that He was greater than all prophets; He was the Son of David, the King of Israel, coming in the name of the Lord. It was a great step. Round the head of the Messiah the prophets had thrown a halo of divine glory, commanding homage for One who was 'wonderful in counsel, the mighty God, the Father of Eternity, the Prince of Peace.' Then it was that the Pharisees so bitterly said, 'The world is gone after Him,' and the disciples thought that ' the kingdom of God should immediately appear.'

But yet there still clung to their acceptance of His Messiahship too many of the lower conceptions of earthly majesty and glory. Hence there came an awful revulsion, (*c*) His spiritual when, after the disappointment of their eager expec- royalty. tations, suddenly the cruelty and craft of the enemies presented the hoped-for King of Israel before them as a degraded and helpless malefactor, crowned with thorns, and bleeding from the Roman scourge. It might have seemed as if in the shout ' Away with Him! crucify Him!' all the impression on the people of the life of Jesus Christ had passed away. It might have seemed so; but that it was not so we see in the third and final epoch of the day of Pentecost. The miracle of the outpouring of the Holy Spirit led up, as usual, to a declaration of the great fact of the resurrection—that miracle of miracles, in which all others were lost. Then, not for one brief hour only, but for all time, they accepted the inference, ' God has made Him whom ye crucified both Lord and Christ.' Then they began to understand the deeper things, of which they had yet seen only the outward exhibition in His earthly life. The conversion of that day was surely the fruit not of that one day only, but of the ministry which had manifested Him again and again, sowing seeds which were destined apparently to die, but really only to sleep in the spiritual soil till the springtide of Pentecost yielded the harvest of three thousand souls—themselves but the harbingers of the ' multitude that no man could number.'

In these salient portions of the Gospel narrative we trace the actual steps in the progress, by which the multitude, looking on the life of Jesus of Nazareth from afar, were gradually drawn towards the acceptance by faith of Him as their Saviour. I cannot but see in them also the representation of the successive impressions, which must always be made upon us, when from the consideration of Christianity as an actual power, intellectual, moral, and spiritual, we go back to contemplate in broad general outline the life from which it claims to spring. We can, I think, even trace the existence of these impressions upon modern thought in actual fact.

The corresponding stages in modern thought.

Thus, in relation to the first. That Jesus of Nazareth is a Prophet—a true speaker of the truth of God to man—a true teacher and leader of humanity—a Son of Man, such that the world's history cannot find His parallel—this is what the very slightest observation must show; and this, in all probability, is hardly doubted by any thoughtful student of His life, who believes in God at all, and recognises that there is such a thing as a prophetic mission from Heaven. How high that estimate may rise in one who does not call himself a Christian, has been shown in the remarkable declaration of Mr. John Stuart Mill.[4] In various degrees of clearness and decisiveness, this confession of Jesus as a Prophet—perhaps as the greatest of prophets—pervades all serious modern thought; and various philosophies, intellectual, social, and moral, even claim to reproduce, more truly than Christianity, the real spirit of Christ. If we could be content with this vague and tentative acknowledgment, the world might be held to have gone after Him.

His teaching.

[4] ' Religion cannot be said to have made a bad choice in pitching on this man as the ideal representative and guide of humanity; nor, even now, would it be easy, even for an unbeliever, to find a better translation of the rule of virtue from the abstract to the concrete than to endeavour so to live that Christ would approve our life.'—*Essay on Theism*, pt. v.

But it is impossible to study with any serious care the life of Christ without seeing that to advance only to this point is to advance either too far or not far enough. Evidently He claims—and without such a claim Christianity cannot stand—to be more than this. The next stage must soon be reached, corresponding to the Hosannas of His triumphal entry, by the acknowledgment in Him of a superhuman kingship over body and soul, actually exercised in part now, and promising a full perfection hereafter. To this stage belongs that profound and even enthusiastic admiration of Christian morality, Christian sentiment, Christian devotion, as the exhibitions of the truest humanity, even as reflections of the will of God, which nevertheless advances not to the fulness of Christian faith. Perhaps, like the enthusiasm of the shouting multitude of Jerusalem, it is apt to have its alternating fits of action and reaction, of half-adoring faith and half-blasphemous condescension. To this many attain who yet go no further.

His kingship,

Yet there is a stage beyond this still, when first the darker features of the Gospel are disclosed to us by the Cross, with its mystery of sin and suffering, and when next the truth of the Resurrection and Ascension swallows up that darkness in the light of salvation. On the threshold 'many go back and walk no more with Him.' Naturally the mind hesitates, for it is called upon to pass from the natural to the supernatural, from the Son of Man to the Mediator who is both God and man. But when the evidence and significance of the Resurrection dawn upon it, then, even if it will not at once accept Him in the light in which Christianity regards Him, yet at least there must be sufficient impression made to induce the enquirer to draw nearer into the inner circle of the disciples, to study closer at hand the inner teaching and life of Jesus Christ, to ponder thoughtfully the mysterious doctrines which cluster round the Resurrection, the Mediation, the Incarnation. The results of that closer study must, in the next place, be considered. But it is much to have stirred even the disposition to accept the invitation of the Gospel, 'Come and see.'

preparatory to full spiritual knowledge

CHAPTER VI.

CHRIST AS SEEN BY THE DISCIPLES.

'We have found the Messias, which is, being interpreted, the Christ.'—John i. 41.

'Lord, to whom shall we go? Thou hast the words of eternal life.'—John vi. 68.

'Thomas answered and said unto Him, My Lord and my God.'—John xx. 28.

AT a marked epoch (to which I have already alluded) in the Gospel history, our Lord, resting for a time at Cæsarea Philippi, is described to us as drawing forth from His disciples a statement of the results of His self-manifestation to the world by the simple question, 'Who do men say that I am?' The answer given is one which might well have seemed strangely vague and utterly unsatisfactory. He was (they said) some Prophet, marked out beyond others as a messenger from God—perhaps a risen John the Baptist, perhaps an Elijah or Jeremiah reappearing on earth. Thus much they knew: strangely enough, they knew no more. But in the Gospel narrative, which contains this candid avowal of what looked like a partial failure, the Lord Jesus expresses neither surprise nor disappointment. He goes on at once to the question, 'But who say ye that I am?' and draws out a clear unhesitating answer, 'Thou art the Christ, the Son of the living God.' On that answer He bestows an emphatic blessing; on the faith which it embodies He promises to lay the foundation of His Church. If His life had only produced a vague inadequate impression on the outer world, it had told its story with sufficient distinctness to those who stood near enough to understand and to love it. The preaching and manifestation to the multitude were but preparatory. Not through it, but through the knowledge gained and proclaimed by His apostles, was the Lord to be manifested, and the world to be won.

I. There is something striking and significant in the choice of this method of the manifestation of Himself, indirect as it is, and (as it might seem at first sight) at variance with the ordinary law of human nature, which places eye-witness far above ear-witness, and personal knowledge still farther above derived knowledge. Yet perhaps it is in this way that most teachings, destined to have deep and permanent influence, have been conveyed. Certainly it may be remarked—if the comparison may be ventured upon without derogation from the unique character of the Lord Jesus Christ—that this was the way in which the great teacher, who of all mere men has most profoundly affected abstract human thought, stamped his mark on the history of the world. Socrates left no writings, founded no school, during his lifetime hardly attained to anything like a world-wide fame; yet from his teaching—to say nothing of lesser intellectual and moral impulses—there went out the Cyrenaic, the Cynic, the Platonic, the Peripatetic philosophies, which have fairly divided among them the area of metaphysical and moral thought. For it would seem that the inner teaching and the true personality of one who is to be a leader of mankind —not in the outer dominion of the conqueror, the ruler, and the lawgiver, but in the spiritual dominion over the soul within—can be understood only by the few who are drawn to him in close familiar intimacy, and who, by the very fact of discipleship, show at once a greater receptivity and a greater energy of thought and resolution than the mass of men. Standing near the master, but on a lower level, they are fit to be the mediums through which his inspiration may be diffused (each perhaps transmitting but one or two rays of the perfect light), till it spreads over the length and breadth of the world. But it must be added that, since the mission of Jesus Christ necessitated that self-assertion of His own personality, which contrasts so remarkably with the self-effacement of such men as Socrates, the law in His case must exemplify itself with tenfold force. For, by the confession of all, it is just this true conception of a great personality which cannot be gained by the multitude, and which grows on the mind only by daily familiarity of reve-

The method of the manifestation of Christ to the world.

rent study and obedience. Hence the emphasis laid upon this familiarity by St. Peter, on the eve of the great day of Pentecost, as the chief qualification for apostolic leadership and authority. Hence the repeated references of St. Paul to his actual vision of the Lord on the road to Damascus, and that knowledge of Him by special revelation, which, as a knowledge of the spirit, compensated for the want of 'knowledge after the flesh.'

We may, therefore, be inclined to conclude that this was the only way in which the knowledge of Christianity, which is knowledge of Jesus Christ, could have struck root deep and wide in the faith of mankind. But whether this be so or not in the abstract, certainly this was the method actually adopted for its dissemination; and therefore, following as always the historic order, it must be our task to go on from the life of Christ, as it showed itself to the world, to the life of Christ, as it drew the souls of the disciples to Him, and through them asserted its dominion over mankind. Here perhaps, even more than before, we feel how impossible it is to do this with any approach to completeness. We have but brief and scanty records of His life, avowedly but a very small part of that knowledge of Him, which changed the whole character of the disciples, and lifted them above themselves to an exaltation from which they might move the world. Even what we have, we can but read. No effort of imagination and of faith can reproduce to us the effect of that living presence, which is infinitely greater in its power than any record of words and deeds. If much of all this was at the time but half understood, yet even then it must have been felt, and, when the hour of spiritual enlightenment came, it would, according to His own promise (John xiv. 26), flash back into their memory. All this is beyond our power; it was given only to those who were to be His chosen witnesses to the whole world. But what we have is all-sufficient; and in studying it we have at least this compensation, that we can read what is placed within our knowledge in the light of subsequent apostolic teaching, and of the Christian thought and the Church history of centuries. In that light much may be plain, which without it even an eye-witness could not see.

The life of Christ as seen by the disciples.

Therefore even on what we can reproduce to ourselves we need not be afraid to rest the conclusions, which a view of the life of Christ from the inner circle of discipleship may reasonably be expected to suggest.

Into the nature of the preparatory manifestation to the world we have already entered, and the remembrance of what it actually was must go with us in our further investigation. Without any adventitious aid, in direct contradiction to the cherished ideas both of the people and of the Schools, it gradually drew forth an acknowledgment of Him, first as a Prophet, next as a King, finally as 'the Son of God with power.' That victory was achieved by the threefold exhibition of power in what He did, of wisdom in what He said, of goodness in what He was. Clearly these three elements must still form the means of His revelation to those who gaze upon Him close at hand. How can it, indeed, be otherwise? Power, wisdom, and goodness combined constitute the ideal of our own highest humanity, and through it shadow out to us the revelation in man of God Himself. But certainly they will be combined in very different proportions of prominence, according as we stand near or far away. *The same three elements in different proportions.*

To the world at large (as I have already suggested) the chief influence would be the conviction of a Divine power, working through various miracles, and culminating in the great miracle of the Resurrection—serving, indeed, to lead up to His teaching, and serving also to manifest His character and office of beneficence and salvation, but yet in itself acting chiefly as a sign, and drawing out mainly the conviction, 'No man can do these things, except God be with him.' To the disciples, on the other hand, although this manifestation of a Divine power had its function—a function especially marked in the record of His first miracle (John ii. 11)—yet it would certainly have a somewhat different character and hold but a secondary place. Probably the miracles to them would be not so much signs as disclosures (ἐπιφάνειαι) of His inner nature and office. Instead of standing out in startling and exceptional prominence, they would be interwoven with the general texture of His action, His teaching, and His life. *The lower function of miracle.*

They would be (so to speak) acted parables, showing through visible action the greater realities of His spiritual redemption, and exhibit themselves rather as manifestations of a higher law than as suspensions or modifications of the lower. But certainly they would hold a much lower place in the thoughts of the disciples than in the mind of the wondering multitude. They would soon cease to be needed as signs. In fact, they would be seen to be 'natural' in one who was what they saw Him to be. So from the signs they would go at once to the things signified—to the teaching to which they were declared by Himself to lead up, and perhaps even more to the character, of which miracles were mere vivid flashes of manifestation, and which shone on them with a full calm light, quietly pervading their whole consciousness. In other words, they would mark what He did; but they would far more earnestly ponder what He said, and realise what He was. In fact, till the long line of His wonderful works culminated in the supreme miracle of the Resurrection—which was to them infinitely difficult to credit, but which, when once credited, threw a flood of light on the true nature of their Master, and simply transformed the whole character of their faith—it may well be that the significance of His lesser miracles was not fully understood. Till, in the light of the Resurrection, they had to preach Him to the world, it might not occur to them to speak of Him as one 'approved of God by miracles, and wonders, and signs.'

Not unlike this is our own experience when, having once recognised in the Lord Jesus Christ One who may be seen to stand out unique among the children of men, and who may be at least reasonably presumed to have God with Him, we draw nearer to study more thoughtfully His true nature. The one only miracle which is essential to our faith is the Resurrection, and it is all-sufficient. If it be true, the others are of little evidential necessity to us, while, at the same time, they become in the highest degree appropriate and natural. We study them rather as manifestations of His character and office, than as signs of His mission. What really concerns us henceforward is to ponder His teaching and His life, to see whether in them there is ground for the faith which is so boldly claimed by Him and for Him, and, if so, to go on wherever that faith leads.

Standing then (so to speak) with the disciples, we endeavour to be 'taught by Christ' what He says, and 'to learn Christ,' what He is.

Now in the record of this process of learning, in the case of the disciples, we are at once struck by the candid and repeated confession of its imperfection. Partly, as the Gospel story declares, they understood His teaching; so far as they understood it, it gave light to their minds, strength to their moral being, fire to their hearts. Partly they understood not; they found it soar into regions to which, at the moment at any rate, they could not follow. At times He spoke of this calmly: 'I have many things to say unto you; but ye cannot bear them now.' At times He even uttered complaint: 'Are ye also without understanding?' 'O fools and slow of heart to believe!' Nor was it otherwise in respect of His life. They saw it in the daily round of beneficence abroad, and in the familiar intercourse of their own home-circle. But there were phases of it, when He retired from all earthly companionship to the communion with the Father on the mountain-top or in the garden, passing into a region too high for them, coming back (so to speak) like Moses, with the light of that heavenly region upon His face, shining too bright to look upon. 'Do ye now believe?' He would say; 'Ye shall leave Me alone, yet I am not alone, because the Father is with Me;' 'Have I been so long time with you, and yet hast thou not known me, Philip?'

The higher manifestations to the disciples.

The imperfection of their understanding.

But it is not always remembered that in the consciousness of this incompleteness of understanding lay one part of the power with which the manifestation of their Master laid hold of their souls. Even in ordinary cases the teaching most impresses the soul which speaks to us obviously out of the store of an unexhausted, and to us unfathomable, wisdom; for it is just this teaching which at once gives us present understanding, and yet creates a continual thirst for deeper knowledge. Even in itself that life is fullest of instruction and inspiration which, while it comes down to our level, yet has a higher

This imperfection an element of faith.

level of its own, to which we trust that it will gradually draw us up. But, besides this, we have to remember that our Lord, in this respect unlike all other great teachers, had to call, not for mere understanding of His word, not for mere following of His example, but for a personal faith in Himself as the Revealer of God and of heaven. Such faith, it is clear, is the child neither of complete understanding nor of complete ignorance, but of partial knowledge, knowing enough to trust, and willing therefore to follow beyond that which it knows. It may seem a paradox, but to those who know human nature it will be obviously true, that, both by the reality and by the incompleteness of their understanding, this manifestation of their Master laid hold of their whole nature, and conformed it to His own.

Nor can I doubt that to this also there is a correspondence in our own experience. Thanks to the light of that which was then future, but which for us now pervades the whole history of the past, much is to us clear which was dark to them. But one great source of the actual power of the life of Christ upon the soul lies in the conviction that it is a reality which we could not have conceived, and which we but imperfectly comprehend. That it is a perfect humanity we see; but we feel at the same time that it would not be this, if it were not something more. The world has certainly looked up to it with a wholly different reverence from that which it bestows on a St. Paul or a St. John. In the very fact that it transcends even our admiration lies one great secret of its spiritual power.

But, in the knowledge of the disciples, the same Gospel narrative which so plainly discloses its imperfection, marks out certain epochs, embodied in the three great confessions which I have placed at the head of this chapter.

<small>Three epochs of progress.</small>

On these I need make only two brief prefatory remarks.

First, I have taken all from the fourth Gospel, which is so especially the Gospel of the inner teaching of Christ to His disciples. Nor can I feel a moment's doubt that, in spite of all the attacks naturally made on the Gospel, which is the very stronghold of a full Christology, the overwhelming evidence, external and internal, for the genuineness of the Gospel is such as to dispense with all hesitation in quoting from it even in evidential argument.[1] But it must be noted that the principles which they represent are entirely independent of all critical questions upon the fourth Gospel itself. Even putting it aside, they are written broadly on the whole of the apostolic teaching; they are impressed on the whole system of Christian doctrine and life, as it afterwards developed itself in the world; they unquestionably embody the phases of faith through which they who knew our Lord actually passed.

Next, being chosen from the beginning, the middle, and the end of our Lord's ministry, these passages may well represent the actual order of development of new ideas in the conception of His nature. But, of course, these ideas in no sense supersede one another; on the contrary, they naturally and necessarily coexist in Christian faith; each adds, as it were, a new strain of its own, but the older ideas still remain, and still contribute to the full harmony.

II. In the first we note at once the expression by the first disciples of that which was the popular conception of the Lord Jesus Christ in the outer world: 'We have found Him of whom Moses in the law and the prophets did write. We have found the Messias.' Fresh from the teaching of St. John the Baptist, they started from that belief to which the multitude attained only by slow degrees, and which indeed, at Jerusalem, was not fully accepted till the day of His triumphal entry. That belief went with them through the whole period of their familiar intercourse with their Master, at times perhaps discouraged by the hope long deferred, at others deepened by some special manifestation of His true nature, and stirred to the eagerness of immediate expectation. We can see in St. Peter's words (next to be quoted), after the discourse at Capernaum, or in Martha's confession in her sorrow over the grave of Lazarus, how they fell back on

The ackowledgment of Messiahship.

---

[1] It may be sufficient here to refer to Mr. Sanday's 'Authorship and Historical Character of the Fourth Gospel;' to Mr. Hutton's remarkable Essay in his 'Essays Theological and Literary' (Vol. i. Essay vi.); and to Professor Westcott's 'Introduction to the Gospel of St. John in the Speaker's Commentary' (New Testament, vol. ii.)

this belief as a sure ground of refuge, in the face of declarations of our Lord which were to them wholly or largely mysterious (John vi. 69, xi. 27). It is obvious that in their case the belief was, in definiteness, in fixity, and in comprehensiveness, a very different thing from the vaguer faith of the multitude.

Probably it flowed chiefly from a different source. For we gather from their own teaching that in their case the predominant position which miracles seem to have held in the eyes of the multitude as a sign of His Messiahship was transferred to the other great sign—the sign of the fulfilment of prophecy. It is, of course, to be understood that these two signs were interwoven with each other, as we see in Christ's own appeal to His miracles before the disciples of St. John the Baptist, embodying as it does an obvious reference to the Messianic prophecy of Isaiah. But in the two cases they may be fairly considered to have held different degrees of prominence. To the multitude, perhaps, the remembrance of prophecy rather illustrated the present greatness of miracle; to the disciples the miracle simply threw light on some striking feature in the great picture drawn by prophecy.

Based on the witness of prophecy.

Now I have endeavoured already to show how the great prevision of the Messiah pervaded the whole of the Old Testament in all its various elements, as implied in history, in law, in religious thought and aspiration, as explicit in a constantly increasing degree in what we especially call prophecy.[2] Hence the conception of Messiahship so gained, whether bright or dim, was always large and comprehensive; it was not merely an impression of divine power, as in the sight of miracle, but of the perfect and harmonious union of power, wisdom, and goodness. The notion just possible to the multitude, when it was suggested by the malicious subtlety of the Pharisees, that His wonders were wrought through Beelzebub, would to the disciples be obviously and even monstrously incredible. To them the argument that the 'kingdom of Satan could not be so divided against itself' as to subserve the kingdom of God, would come home with irresistible force.

Therefore comprehensive in idea.

[2] See Part I., c. vi.

That this 'argument from prophecy' (as it is commonly called) strongly possessed the minds of the disciples, we see clearly. In the Messiah they especially found 'Him of whom Moses in the Law and the prophets did write.' To His miracles, always excepting the great miracle of the Resurrection, they refer in their preaching, unhesitatingly indeed, but so rarely that the very rarity of such reference has been actually made a ground of difficulty and question. But on the fulfilment of prophecy they dwell again and again: sometimes in the broad lines of general fulfilment, which more strikingly impress us who look on from a distance; sometimes in the vivid details, which came home most strikingly to men constantly in the habit of dwelling on those ancient prophecies, to whom in every point they were familiar in thought, and bright with fresh and living hope. It is especially notable that, in the first preaching of Christ risen, they urged this sign of His Messiahship fearlessly on Jewish hearers, who knew the predictions of the prophets in every line and letter, and had watched the life and death of Him for whom now these predictions were claimed. In the very first sermons of St. Peter the three great epochs of Messianic prophecy—to David, to Moses, and to Abraham—were at once seized upon as finding their fulfilment in Christ.[3] In the Gospel record the detailed applications of prophecy to His birth, His preaching, His miracles, His death, and His resurrection, are brought out with a confident and affectionate particularity. Those Epistles, which are addressed to Churches Jewish in birth or in origin, literally teem with appeals, implicit and explicit, to the 'sure witness of prophecy.' The conviction that he was the 'hope of Israel,' the heir of all the ages of God's revelation, for whose coming all the past had by different methods been a preparation, was to them an unquestionable truth, of which they expected to find indications everywhere, significant not only to themselves, but to all who had drunk in the true idea of ancient prophecy. They did not, therefore, in the spirit of some modern criticism, enquire jealously, and with a kind of negative presumption in their minds, whether this point might be

[3] See Acts ii. 25-34; iii. 22-25.

one of mere coincidence, or that point one of deliberate and intentional fulfilment of the predicted sign by Christ Himself. The great reality they knew to be there. That it should crop out in what might seem to the ignorant mere casual emergences, was to them a thing expected and therefore at once understood.

There is a striking significance in the existence of this deeply rooted conviction in their minds, and its acceptance by so many Jewish converts—a ready acceptance, so long as it seemed to promise a simple completion of Jewish hope and privilege—a reluctant and yet undoubting acceptance by those who, like St. Paul, longing for 'the hope of Israel,' yet came to see that its fulfilment involved the downfall of exclusive Jewish supremacy. To account for it by imagination and superstition is a sweeping, but an improbable, almost an impossible, theory. This is, indeed, a case in which we can see more clearly through the eyes of the first Christian preachers and converts than through our own. The very fact of their deliberate belief, which was obviously far from being in the first instance unhesitating or uncritical, and which was maintained in the face of natural prejudice and fierce denunciation, is a thing which has to be accounted for. It is most unreasonable to ignore its interpretative force in the consideration of the application of prophecy to Jesus Christ; for all such ignoring of history is manifestly unphilosophical. But even if we thus unreasonably put it aside, and study the prophecies as if we had nothing but present criticism to guide us, still I cannot doubt that this great sign of prophecy will in degree, though perhaps in less degree, be living to us. When sceptical criticism has done all that it can do in referring detailed fulfilments, of which earlier ages never doubted, to mere coincidence, in finding fulfilments in the earlier history of what Jewish tradition invariably held to be Messianic promises, and in tracing others to the intentional assumption by Jesus of Nazareth of the Messianic character, still the great general tendency of prophecy remains substantially undisturbed. It is our wisdom to take a broad comprehensive view, starting with the universal promise to Abraham, examining the unques-

The 'argument from prophecy' to us.

tionable expectation of the Prophet of prophets from the time of Moses downwards, marking the declaration of the 'sure mercies of David;' then examining the roll of prophecy, and tracing out, under the immediate messages of God to the people, a constant undercurrent of prevision—now of the spiritual kingdom over all the world, now of the personal Messiah, the Son of David in true humanity, and yet 'Lord of David' in attributes of superhuman majesty constantly brightening around His presence; lastly, studying, in the Psalms and Books of Wisdom, the growing consciousness of the significance of this prophetic promise, gradually working itself into mind and heart, as the truth of truths. Then, when we turn from this great prophetic conception to the actual manifestation of Jesus Christ, we can hardly fail to be struck with two convictions.

The first, that in it and its world-wide consequences there is a fulfilment of the whole conception itself, which cannot be misunderstood as a mere pious imagination or vague coincidence. It cannot be reasonably doubted that the Old Testament, especially in its prophetic element, starts into new life and clearness when it is completed by the full revelation of the New Testament; that when that connexion is denied the older revelation remains simply as a magnificent fragment, crying out in vain for its right completion; and that no other expectation, either of a personal Messiah, or (as in some modern Jewish thought) of a Christ in the race, has ever yet taken any substantial form, or established any pretensions to appropriateness. It is no slight matter that every thread of the Old Testament revelation fastens itself naturally and firmly to the life of Jesus Christ. *Christ the fulfilment of prophecy.*

Yet there is a second conviction, hardly less significant, that the historic manifestation of Christ contains elements which could never have been evolved from prophecy, either by imitation in His own actual life, or in an ideal picture drawn by Christian faith and hope—elements which sometimes transcended the prophetic picture, sometimes, as in the whole doctrine of the Cross, utterly contradicted the popular conceptions of it. The Jesus of history is plainly the Christ of prophecy, but *Christ greater than all prophecy.*

He is as plainly very much more. We may find Him as the Messiah 'of whom Moses and the prophets did write;' but we come hereafter to know Him as He is, and to acknowledge in Him a greatness which no thought of man, even of inspired man, was able to conceive.

But with this higher element in the knowledge of Christ we are not yet concerned. At present we have to refer to the belief in His Messiahship, as it grew upon His disciples day by day in their following of their Master, largely, as it appears, through their increasing conviction of the fulfilment in Him of all that prophecy had taught; although there were depths in that conviction which He Himself, as we are told, needed to disclose to them after the Resurrection, and into which they could not enter, till His glorification threw back light on His life in great humility.[4] But, however imperfectly, it was firmly grasped. Whatever else was true of their Master beyond the highest conception of the office of the Messiah, His Messiahship, with all that it implied, was a thing absolutely known, almost taken for granted as a sure basis for larger and deeper inference.

The effect on the disciples.

But this faith in them, as it was infinitely stronger and more comprehensive, so also tended naturally to rise to a higher character than the common belief of the multitude. In all cases the conception of the Messiah, as we have seen,[5] implied a superhuman nature. He was, indeed, a true Son of Man—the 'seed of Abraham,' the 'Son of David'—yet in Him was to be concentrated an absolutely universal Royalty, ruling and blessing all nations of the earth; and, as a natural consequence, since such sway could belong to no mere creature, round His head were gathered attributes virtually divine. Satisfying the craving of which idolatry was a diseased perversion, and the whole Jewish system a half-satisfaction, He was to be an 'Emmanuel'—a God with us.

Their belief higher in character than that of the people.

But that conception of His kingdom might yet be content to dwell on the characteristics of mere earthly royalty—on power, splendour, beneficence, merely raised to an unexampled degree. In that light they who simply

[4] See Luke xxiv. 27; John ii. 22, xii. 16. [5] See Part I. c. vi.

saw His miracles looked on Him. After that miracle of the feeding of the five thousand, which was performed on the largest scale, they would have 'taken Him by force to make Him a King;' after the crowning miracle of the raising of Lazarus it was as the King of Israel that they welcomed Him. Their souls were filled with visions of triumph over the enemies of Israel, to be followed by peace and happiness, prosperity and dignity—which are, indeed, real gifts, but which at least seem as if they could be received without any spiritual preparation in the recipient— differing in infinite degree, but still only in degree, from those which a beneficent earthly despot scatters with open hand. Possibly this was not all that they conceived. The very barest conception of the Messiah had in it so much obviously spiritual that it could not be absolutely carnalised. But these lower elements filled up the foreground of their hope; the higher were thrown back into an obscurity which was at least half-oblivion.

_{not in the earthly kingdom,}

For, indeed, the subtler and nobler lineaments of the prophetic picture could not be realised adequately without some deeper insight. To such insight it would gradually become clear that the Messianic kingdom was to be a spiritual kingdom, ruling by the influence of God, not over the lives of men, but in their hearts, and hence in its chief blessings incapable of being enjoyed, except by those who were prepared to receive what, without the spiritual answer of the soul, is

_{but the spiritual royalty and the Cross.}

> not to be given
> By all the blended powers of earth and heaven.

Not obscurely, also, was it suggested that the King Himself, and they who should be His, must—the world being what it is—win their way to glory through sufferings, 'despised and rejected of men,' every one in his degree 'a man of sorrows and acquainted with grief.' These things, lost to the multitude in the blaze of expected glory, naturally grew on the disciples. It is of course true that, as the Gospels candidly confess, carnal prejudice clung to them very long; it is still more true that, for very love, they could not and would not dream of suffering and shame and death for their Master. But His teaching, especially in its later stages, after the great confession at Cæsarea Philippi and the Transfiguration which followed, gradually deepened to them both truths—of a kingdom not of this world, and of a kingdom won by suffering. What His teaching unfolded, His life at the same time realised. The power which He actually did wield was a spiritual power over faith and love; and the tone of His life had in it undoubtedly much of the seriousness and sadness of one who bears the burden of humanity, united though they were with calm, gracious, unhesitating sovereignty. In spite of prejudice and reluctance, the deeper and truer conception gradually sank into their hearts. It is notable that the confession of Him as the Messiah, both in the first declaration of St. Andrew, and in the celebrated answer of St. Peter, was called out not by the sight of miracle, but by simple communion of familiar intercourse and of spiritual teaching. Gradually and imperfectly, but yet really, it must have grown upon them, though not till His death and resurrection had completed His self-manifestation, did it flash out in complete and full comprehension. They knew the Messiah, not by what He did, but by what He said and by what He was. Therefore, unlike the multitude, ever varying from day to day, and hesitating between this opinion and that, they 'found Him' once for all; and even if their hold at times faltered, yet they never let Him go.

III. The fruit of this growth in knowledge is seen in the second great confession of St. Peter, recorded in the sixth chapter of the fourth Gospel. In the interval which had elapsed since the first declaration of St. Andrew is included the chief part of the Galilean ministry, manifesting the Christ both in teaching and in miracle—not to speak of the visit to Samaria, and some brief but instructive sojourns at Jerusalem. Clearly it had not passed in vain: the daily experience of the disciples, watching both His life itself, and its effect on the people, had wrought out into explicitness much which had but been implied before. The confession of St. Peter still embodies the older declaration, only with more incisive emphasis: 'We believe and are sure that Thou art the

The confession of St. Peter.

Christ, the Son of the living God.' But it ushers in that old confession by a new preface of explanation: 'Lord, to whom shall we go? Thou hast the words of eternal life.' In these few words very much is implied, tending at once to define and to exalt the simple belief in the Messiah. We may notice how, with singular truth to nature, they are described as following, indeed, not long after that display of miraculous power which so greatly impressed the multitude, but as immediately dependent on certain strange and mysterious teaching to which it was made the introduction—a teaching to some the cause of apostasy, to none, not even to the twelve, a clear light of truth. For, indeed, they express that mingling of partial knowledge with partial ignorance, out of which a true faith naturally springs.

Each phrase in the answer is full of meaning. First, the disciples had learned the reality of an eternal life for man—that is, both in the present and in the future, a life of the spirit, far higher than the mere animal life of the body, incapable of decay or death. *The eternal life.* Not only in this special passage, but everywhere, the belief in this eternal life is a commonplace in Christian teaching, having passed from the region of mere speculation and hope to the firm ground of certainty. No sense of the power of material laws and forces over the body—no consciousness of the sin which seems to laugh to scorn the very idea of a high spiritual life in man—no sight of the death in which the body moulders to corruption, and the soul disappears in darkness—could shake it for a moment. Whence came this confident decision by a few fishermen of Galilee of the great problem, before which all human thought from the beginning had stood at least half bewildered? The answer is simple, and in Christian teaching it is given again and again. They had been with their Master; they had learned from His lips; and, what was even more, they had actually seen in Him, through its threefold manifestation of a power, wisdom, and goodness above this world, the eternal spiritual life which is the image of God. They knew, simply because they had thus seen, what true humanity is. Therefore they had no room left for speculation, no further need for mere hope. They were as sure that there was for man an

Y

eternal life which should endure, as that there was an animal life which must die. Others might 'labour only for the meat that perishes,' not unreasonably, if the present life were all that they knew. Others might start and turn away, when the Master spoke strangely of the means by which the eternal life was to be given and sustained. But not they; for they doubted not that for man there was an eternal life. It was nothing to them if the way to it was not yet wholly clear; in the certainty on the main point they could well afford to wait.

For these words also express the conviction that the Lord Jesus Christ had 'the words of eternal life.' Now this phrase denotes not a vague instinct or incomplete idea, but a clear, definite revelation of what eternal life is, and how it shall be ours. Of what it is—that is, of the nature of God, who is necessarily the one true source of this eternal life, and of the nature of man, as capable of receiving it and growing into it. Of the means by which it may be ours, by which we may rise above the earthly life, doomed to die and, in fact, dying already every day, and by which, moreover, we may throw off the weakness, the blindness, the sin, which mar and deaden even our higher nature. These 'words' they firmly believed that He had, in a sense in which no other ever had them or could have them, drawn from the depths of a perfect knowledge of the great mystery of all being. And they knew, moreover, that from His mouth they were not dead words, but living and powerful—not merely spoken, but what are called, in one of the earliest forms of Christian teaching, 'engrafted words,' striking root in the nature, growing into it, yielding by a spiritual necessity the fruits of an actual new life, and the promise of a higher life in the hereafter.

The words of eternal life.

All this, and more, is implied in the simple declaration: 'Thou hast the words of eternal life'—the more notable because it is clear that as yet they knew not at all fully what these words actually were. Even the teaching which drew out this declaration, so full of beauty and light to us, seems to have been dark to them. There was an eternal life; that was certain. He had, and could declare, the words of that eternal life; that was equally

The conviction a conviction of faith,

certain. This was all which as yet they had; and this was all that they needed.

How could that conviction have been produced? There is but one possible answer. By the simple presence of Jesus Christ with them. Not any longer mainly by the consciousness of the fulfilment of all prophecy in Him; still less by mere sight of His miracles of divine power and divine mercy. These had largely contributed to bring them to Him; these, no doubt, still clothed His presence with a royal vesture of solemnity and glory. But the supreme power which ultimately conquered their allegiance to Him belonged not to the physical, but to the moral and spiritual sphere. It was the spell of His presence, the consciousness of a wisdom above all human wisdom in His words, and of a goodness beyond all human goodness in His life. Even in the case of great earthly teachers and leaders of men, we know how, in the power of their actual presence, in the atmosphere which surrounds their life, and in the spirit which pervades their every word and deed, there is a deep inner knowledge of them, which in no other way can be gained, out of which rises the faith, believing in them against all difficulties and perplexities, and willing to live and die for them. This is a shadow—a faint shadow—of what drew the disciples to Christ, and wrought in them that conviction—which goes far beyond even the allegiance to His spiritual kingdom—that He held the key to that mystery of mysteries, the spiritual life of humanity; that He could actually give them the words of a revelation which should make it clear to mankind, so far as it can be known to man; and that, when the time should come, they should know plainly what now they could only grasp in an implicit faith. It was a great self-surrender indeed. To what mere man could it be rightly made?

wrought by the presence of Christ.

IV. But we pass on to the third great utterance; and note that between it and the last there had passed another year. That year had been a time of still further experience in the knowledge of Christ, of fuller and deeper teaching from Him, especially of a clearer revelation of His own nature. Even thus the souls of the disciples might be prepared to advance further in the

The confession of St. Thomas.

course of faith, using the knowledge of Him as the Messiah, and the acceptance of His words as the words of eternal life, as stepping-stones towards the conception of the higher truth which was implied in these. But the all-important matter is that this year had been closed by two events of unspeakable significance—His death and resurrection. It is a simple fact—let it be accounted for how it may—that the knowledge of these two events wrought a profound and permanent change in the whole tone and attitude of the souls of the disciples. There was a power of revelation in them, greater even than the teaching of word and deed in our Lord's earthly life; confirming His own words, that only when 'lifted up' would He 'draw all men unto Him.'

I have spoken of His death and resurrection; but it is on the latter almost alone that our attention must as yet be fixed. For till the meaning of that death should be revealed hereafter, it was in itself inevitably the great and terrible stumbling-block to the disciples. Before it actually occurred, they could not and would not believe it possible. After it had come upon them, the language of the disciples at Emmaus tells plainly the story of its natural effect: 'We trusted that it had been He who should have redeemed Israel.' 'But now what shall we say?' Perhaps even then, by the very sight of His calm submission to death, and His patient endurance of all that the cross implied, they might understand something of the moral sublimity of a perfect self-sacrifice, absolutely unconquered by physical agony, by hatred and contempt of man, and by spiritual desolation. Perhaps through this they might see some faint glimmerings of a mysterious meaning underlying it all. But that there should have been this death, and that too the death of the cross—that the Power of Evil should have been allowed so signal and horrible a triumph—that the thunders of God's righteous wrath should have slept, while His dear Son was thus ruthlessly trampled on, and all the work of His life apparently swept away in disappointment and ignominy—this was to them the great inexplicable perplexity. How it overcame their faith and love we see in the desertion of their Master at the Passion itself; we can conceive how it must have spread a dull

The cross a stumbling-block.

gloom of despondency over the silence of the first Easter eve.

Clearly it was the Resurrection, and it alone, which at once dispelled all this darkness and lighted up the whole life and nature of Jesus Christ with a new brightness of meaning. From that time it is evident that there passed over the whole spiritual character of the disciples a change, from cowardice to boldness, from hesitation and doubt to faith, from narrow earthly hopes to a sure and certain grasp of heavenly realities—perfectly intelligible if the Resurrection be true, entirely inexplicable on any one of the theories of delusion, imposture, mythical imagination, which explain it away as false. We have seen already that the fact of the Resurrection was everywhere the very centre of all the first Christian preaching, till even a clear-sighted heathen like Festus discerned plainly enough that the one question was whether Jesus was dead, or whether He was alive for evermore. Certainly an apostle, who of all others grasped most firmly the essential spirituality of the Gospel, knew well and declared emphatically that, if Christ was not risen, all Christian faith was a vain delusion, and all Christian preaching a lie told in the name of God. The religion which is sometimes offered to us in the name of Christianity, surrendering all belief in the reality of the Resurrection, and yet proposing to retain a faith in Christ as the Son of God, is in no sense the actual Christianity which once conquered the world.

The power of the Resurrection

Now the effect of the belief in the Resurrection as a sure and certain fact, forced on the mind in spite of many difficulties of conception and earnest doubts of the strength of testimony, is most powerfully represented in the great confession of St. Thomas. With marvellous truth to nature we are told that it was the doubting apostle, who at last pronounced the most striking and absolute profession of faith: 'My Lord and my God.' The words themselves have naturally startled every thoughtful reader. For they are words which, as in a sudden flash of anticipation, give us a glimpse of a great truth, at the clear knowledge of which Christian thought only arrived by degrees hereafter. They are words of which it might be

shown in the confession of St. Thomas.

easy to show that they far outrun in their bold inference all hard logical conclusions from the facts on which they were based; they are words on the exact scope and meaning of which men may dispute. But, after all, they simply describe what the first intelligent heathen testimony as to Christian worship describes as a thing of course at the close of the apostolic age.[6] They are an outpouring of worship to the risen 'Christ as God.'

How were they drawn forth? There is again but one answer: By the sudden realisation at once of the fact and *Its manifold power:* of the infinite spiritual meaning of the Resurrection (implying, of course, the Ascension) as a manifestation of Jesus Christ.

It was not merely that He had always staked His truth upon it, as the only worthy conclusion of His earthly life, *as a seal of His truth;* and the explanation of the true meaning of His death—that it proved Him to have power to lay down His life, because it visibly manifested His power to take it again— that without it His life would but have been the noblest of human lives, and His death the greatest of all human martyrdoms.

It was not merely that it was the completion of the manifestation of Him by power — the great miracle of *as the miracle of miracles;* miracles, at once crowning all others, and manifesting a power in Him to which the working of them was but a little thing, and in which He rose infinitely above all servants of God who had worked miracles in days gone by.

Nor, again, was it only the completion of His manifestation in teaching, opening, both in itself and in the doctrine *as crowning His teaching;* grounded upon it, a glimpse for all mankind of the future life, not in the vague glorious haze of speculation, but the calm clear light of fact—so that the hopes which were the deepest mysteries of the schools, became a commonplace of every day for the whole race of man.

But it was, above all else, the final manifestation of what He was. It told out at last unmistakably the true

---

[6] See Pliny's letter to Trajan: 'Carmen Christo, *quasi Deo*, dicere.'

nature of Jesus Christ Himself. It showed visibly the existence in Him of that inherent life, superior to all material laws, untouched by the corruption of sin and death, which is the special attribute of God and of God alone. It pointed naturally to a further inference that, as He rose from earth to heaven, so He had come from heaven to earth, and that His true home was in the bosom of the Godhead. These truths were hereafter to be pondered in their profounder theological expression and meaning, and finally expressed in the great doctrine of 'the Word of God.' But their simplest and most vivid expression was certainly in the words of St. Thomas. 'My Lord' they had long called Him, as the long-expected Messiah, and as a King actually ruling over their souls, moving among them on a higher level of being, speaking what they knew but in part, and yet felt to be the very truth of heaven. But now that phrase was found insufficient without the addition, so startling in itself, so infinitely strange from Jewish lips, 'My Lord and my God.' That addition, like so many exclamations from the fulness of the heart, outstripping the slower pace of the understanding, simply meant that God was not only with Him, but in Him—that in reality, and not in metaphor or paradox, He was the Emmanuel, 'God with us.' How that truth was related to the nature of the Godhead in itself—how its two parts were represented in the name of the Son and the name of the Word—all this no sign, however marvellous, could possibly show. If it was to be known at all, it must be known through faith in our Lord's own explicit teaching, of which I shall speak hereafter. But the truth itself in its broad simple outline was forced on the soul by the sight of the risen Lord on earth, or the vision, such as St. Paul saw afterwards, of Him in heaven. It was none other than that which is so plainly stated in the Epistle to the Romans (Rom. i. 3): 'Jesus Christ was of the seed of David according to the flesh, but was declared to be the Son of God with power by the resurrection from the dead.'

V. Such is the general outline of the actual progress in the mastery, which the sight of the life, death, and resurrection of the Lord Jesus Christ gained over the disciples who were to be the actual preachers of the Gospel to the world. I have confined myself strictly to the accounts of this given in the actual Gospel narrative. It would be easy to extend the view by dwelling (as indeed I have dwelt already) [7] on a similar evolution of the faith in Christ, starting with the Resurrection, passing on to the Mediation, ending in the clear conception of Godhead, which showed itself in the subsequent teaching of Christianity. There is, indeed, in the comparison of the two forms of development, similar yet not identical, a strong evidence of the substantial accuracy and independence of the record of the Fourth Gospel, not wholly unlike that which Paley worked out so ably in the comparison of the Acts and the Epistles in his 'Horæ Paulinæ.' But the examination of the development of Christian doctrine in the Epistles belongs more properly to the consideration of the results of definite faith in the word of the Lord Jesus, of which I do not yet speak. It is in the Gospels that we can most clearly understand that preparatory stage of faith with which we are now concerned. It is best to see the life of Christ through the eyes of the disciples themselves.

The method of progress in faith.

What is the impression which these considerations should make on us?

We have first to consider the significance of the great fact of this gradual conversion of the disciples to an absolute allegiance, of the extraordinary change which that conversion wrought on them, and the still more extraordinary power which, thus converted and changed in their whole character, they were able to exercise over the world at large, laying firm hold on the three great elements of the ancient civilisation—the Hebrew, the Greek, and the Roman—and subjecting them all to the name of Christ. The fact is unquestionable in its reality, and in its importance it transcends all that the world has yet seen. How is it to be accounted for? As has been urged again and again, the account which the New Testament gives of it is a simple and adequate account. If Jesus Christ be what Christianity supposes Him to be, if the

The significance of the faith of the disciples in itself.

[7] See Part I. cc. vii. viii. ix.

manifestation of Him in life was crowned by the facts of the Resurrection and Ascension, we can well explain the faith which He actually inspired, and the power of such a faith, at once to lift His apostles above themselves into a new spiritual and heavenly life, and to make their witness go forth from one end of the world to the other, with a sound which has continued unbroken, and has spread wider and wider through eighteen centuries. But, without this supposition, how can the facts be probably or even possibly accounted for? The supposition of delusion and imposture, or the mixture of delusion and imposture which is more common and more powerful than either separately, will surely not bear examination in the face of the actual facts of the case. How could their long discipleship of close familiar intercourse, gradually overcoming all prejudice, all hesitation, all doubt, and inducing them to stake life and death on the service of Christ, be compatible with mere delusion? When they so simply pleaded that what they told they had 'seen with their eyes, and their hands had handled,' so that it could not be a 'cunningly devised fable,' or the fancy of a blind fanaticism, the common-sense of the world rightly accepted the plea. How, on the other hand, could a deliberate imposture be morally compatible with the extraordinary loftiness and spirituality of their teaching, with the enthusiasm which raised them above all earthly things, and nerved them to face laborious life and ignominious death without a moment's hesitation, and with the marvellous power exercised through their witness over Jew and Gentile, in the teeth of every possible influence of opposition? What sign is there anywhere, either in their life or their teaching, of the mingling of the incongruous elements of honest enthusiasm and self-deceiving imposture, with the inevitable inconsistencies and discomfitures which it must bring with it? Yet it must be remembered that their own faith, and their claim of allegiance from the world, were not for an idea or a principle, but for a Person; that their preaching was not brilliant argument or eloquent exhortation, but simple witness of the great facts of His manifestation; and in such a work, if there be delusion or imposture, it is infinitely difficult for it to escape the detection, which might be evaded in the hazier atmosphere of abstract argument or heated moral enthusiasm. It is not (I think) too much to say that, if the Gospels were lost to us, so that we could not trace out for ourselves the records of His self-revelation—if the actual teaching of the Apostles were unknown to us, so that we could not through it know what the preaching of the word was—yet that the very fact of the faith of the Apostles and their conversion of the world would remain as a fact which must be explained, and which yet is inexplicable, except on the supposition embodied in the belief of Christianity. If there is one thing which modern historical criticism has taught us, it is to refuse to ascribe great results, and especially great spiritual results, to petty, base, unsubstantial causes; we claim the application of that sound canon to the confessedly unique phenomenon of historic Christianity. The day is past when Gibbon's famous discussion of 'the causes of the growth of Christianity' could be accepted, as either superseding, or indeed contradicting, the claim which Christianity makes for itself. The choice is really between a miraculous origin which is adequate to the result, and a non-miraculous origin so inadequate as to be incredible; and a sound criticism, unbiassed by foregone conclusions, will hardly hesitate between the two alternatives.

But, if we ourselves endeavour to take our place among the disciples, and to consider the life of Christ as it reveals itself to us now in broad outline, what should the result be?

The contemplation of its grounds.

It cannot, from the nature of the case, reveal itself with the same freshness and vividness to us as to those who were eye-witnesses, or who heard from eye-witnesses what 'they had seen with their eyes and their hands had handled.' Yet, on the other hand, here also we have some compensation. The very fact that we stand far away enables us perhaps to see that divine life in greater unity and more perfect proportion; the lapse of ages has given us, in the treasure of thought and experience gathered by many generations, some new means of insight into this great mystery; and the very growth of Christianity in that threefold power— intellectual, moral, and spiritual—at which we have glanced already, throws light back on the life out of which it sprang.

Accordingly, however we consider the life of Christ, I cannot but believe that this progress of the disciples in faith must justify itself. We may, with the Synoptic narrative, work out our consideration inductively, dwelling on the record of His actual words and deeds, following Him from His baptism to His passion, without any prepossession of faith, and at last asking what conclusion we must form of His nature. We may trace in the Acts of the Apostles and the Epistles what the life of Christ was in its great leading lines, which, although too well known to be recorded, are there implied as the ground of actual Christian preaching. We may, with St. John, proceed deductively, starting with the full conception of Christian faith, and drawing out deliberately, from stores of our Lord's history yet untouched, whatever may illustrate the substance and the growth of that faith. But, whatever way we choose, and whatever allowances we may claim to make for supposed imperfections or excrescences in the record, still, if we calmly estimate His acts, His words, and His personality in life, and if we convince ourselves that the Resurrection is a reality, and no fable or deceit, I cannot see how we can very well refuse to follow the steps of the disciples, or to take steps somewhat similar to those by which they advanced in faith. Our first conception corresponds to the acceptance of Him as the Messiah; for it must accept Him as the great Founder of a spiritual kingdom, absolutely unique, over the souls of men, and so as being in a peculiar sense the true 'Son of Man.' The next is the acknowledgment of Him as One who has, as no other man ever had, the words of 'eternal life,' spoken out of the depths of an unsurpassed and unapproached knowledge. But neither of these steps can be final; they must imply more than they express—a confession like that of St. Thomas, that He rises above all humanity, even above all created being, that He is in some very real and true sense an incarnation of God.

This is not indeed all; beyond this there is still very much to learn, before we can enter into the whole doctrine of Christianity. For, beyond this manifestation of Himself,

<small>The same result on all methods.</small>

there is still a self-revelation in explicit words, accepted in faith, without which His true self cannot be known.

But I contend that the contemplation of the life of Christ from the inner circle of discipleship must irresistibly draw us on to this ultimate confession. Either we must pause sooner, refusing Him even that vague reverence and faith which all the world has hitherto conceded; or we must go on far beyond it, convincing ourselves that He is One who speaks for God, who cannot be deceived and cannot lie, and therefore One at whose feet we may sit in perfect confidence, to learn from Him that which yet remains to be learned, and which, without His direct teaching, we cannot learn.

<small>The exact scope of that result.</small>

Beyond this there opens upon us the true function of faith, in which lies the whole difference between a religion and a philosophy. Doubtless we must first 'know in whom we believe;' else faith is but credulity and superstition. But when we have known this, then begins that condition of soul—which in words seems a mere paradox, but in experience is proved to be profoundly natural and true—when, by having 'Christ dwell in our hearts by faith,' we come to 'know what passes knowledge,' and, weak and finite as we are, to be 'filled up to the fulness of God.' What is the province of that faith in the system of Christianity, and what truths essentially belong to it rather than to the sphere of reason, must now be considered.

<small>The province of faith.</small>

CHAPTER VII.

THE PROVINCE OF FAITH.

'If I have told you earthly things, and ye believe not, how shall ye believe if I tell you of heavenly things? And no man hath ascended up to heaven, but he that came down from heaven, even the Son of Man, which is in heaven.'—John iii. 12, 13.

I. THESE words of Christ, under the form of reproach, are at once a striking demand of faith, and a still more striking enunciation of the ground on which such faith is claimed. The demand itself is striking in its boldness and its extent. For the faith here claimed is a faith in His power to declare what certainly it is beyond the capacity of any mere man either to discover or even to comprehend—not 'the earthly things,' that is (as the context shows), the manifestations of God's power and grace on earth, but 'the heavenly things,' the realities of the divine will and nature, underlying all these visible manifestations. Yet the ground on which such faith is claimed is more remarkable still. It is the asserted possession by Him of a knowledge of the secrets of heaven—an actual presence, by Divine insight and communion with the Godhead, in heaven itself. 'No man hath ascended into heaven but He which came down from heaven, even the Son of Man, which is in heaven.' The passage itself is a part of the deeper and more mysterious teaching, which only the Fourth Gospel records to us. But it is obvious to any careful student of the New Testament that in no sense can it be thought to stand alone. If, in accordance with the general tone and character of St. John's writings, it is more striking, because more explicit, than any other; yet it is simply the fullest embodiment of an assertion of authority and a claim of faith, which implicitly or explicitly pervade the New Testament. Thus, for example, if we glance at the simpler picture of the

_{The claim of faith in Christ.}

ministry given to us in the Synoptic narrative, we find, in the one great passage which opens to us a glimpse of the inner teaching of our Lord, the express declaration: 'All things are delivered to Me of My Father. . . . Neither knoweth any man the Father but the Son, and he to whomsoever the Son will reveal Him. . . . Take My yoke upon you and learn of Me' (Matt. xi. 27, 29; Luke x. 22). If we look at the ordinary tone of apostolic teaching, we note the contrast which St. Paul draws between 'the wisdom of this world' and 'the wisdom of God.' He answers the question of bewilderment, 'Who hath known the mind of the Lord?' by the glad rejoinder, 'We have the mind of Christ' (1 Cor. ii. 16). Accordingly it follows that this claim for faith, and the reason assigned for it, are essential elements of the teaching of the Gospel; they must be carefully weighed by all who would understand what true Christianity is, and who would form a full conception of the nature and mission of the Lord Jesus Christ. They have peculiar value as an ultimate and crucial exhibition of principle; for clearly they rise infinitely above what can be rightly advanced for any prophet or teacher or king, who is merely the greatest of men.

At this point of the argument we now stand. Hitherto our consideration has been of the life of Christ, in its threefold manifestation of power, wisdom, and goodness, as it presented itself, first to the world at large, viewing it from afar, and next to the inner circle of the disciples close at hand. The contention advanced on such consideration is that, as crowned by the great miracle of the Resurrection—known clearly to the disciples, and by them testified to the world with power—it carries with it overwhelming evidence of a divine mission, and of a superhuman wisdom and goodness, claiming for Him the hearing of an implicit faith. It might well justify the assertion, 'We have found the Messias,' or the confession, 'Thou hast the words of eternal life.' Beyond this it cannot go in strict cogency of reasoning, although, as in all pursuit of knowledge, swift intuitions of a deeper truth still may flash out, in anticipation of the slower process of reason, as in the enthusiastic cry of St. Thomas, 'My Lord and my God!'

The preparation for this claim.

At this point, therefore, comes in the function of faith; and the claim of that faith is written on the very forefront of Christianity. The Gospel claims to be accordant with reason in itself, and consents to be judged by reason in respect of its evidence. So far it is a divine philosophy. But it claims to go beyond reason at those points, so familiar to all thinkers, where advance along each line of thought is met by black impenetrable mystery. There it becomes a religion, resting on the knowledge and the revelation of One who has entered into the eternal light hidden behind these clouds of blackness—'the Son of Man, who came down from heaven, who went back to heaven, and who is in heaven now.' Here, indeed, lies—and it is well that this be clearly understood— the crucial test of a real Christianity. Here we reach the point of divergence, at which the Christian has to part company with those, hitherto his companions in the defiance of Atheism or Pantheism, who simply reason up to God, whether by the theoretical examination of the various lines of Natural Theology, or by the historical study of the philosophies, the institutions, and the religions of the world. For he believes, and they cannot believe, in a full revelation of the mysteries of God in the Lord Jesus Christ.

Now, in considering this claim of faith, those two characteristics impress themselves on the mind, which are (as I have tried to show) evident in the substance of Christian doctrine. Here also the Gospel is at once natural and supernatural. Its claim is, on the one hand, accordant with an unquestionable law of human life. It is, on the other, a unique and ultimate manifestation of that law; to which others hardly approach, and beyond which no other can conceivably go. *The Gospel in this claim natural and supernatural.*

II. The law of faith is certainly a fundamental law of human nature and life. By faith I here mean the accepting on the word of another what we do not, perhaps cannot, discover for ourselves. This is not, indeed, the whole of faith. Faith is distinguished from all the other higher actions of the soul, in reason, conscience, imagination, as having a distinctly personal object. Being thus directed to a person, faith is the result of the action of the whole of our personal being. It is an action partly of *The law of faith natural.*

the understanding, partly of the conscience, partly of the heart; for not through one of these faculties, but through all, we know one another. It is called out by the existence or the appearance in its object not of wisdom only, but of the threefold exhibition of power, wisdom, and goodness, which denotes a perfect personality. The cord of faith (like that of knowledge) is 'a threefold cord not quickly broken.' Hence it has always been noticed that faith, having in it a moral element, must necessarily be a practical power, obeying the categorical imperative of the conscience, and, having in it an emotional element, must necessarily grow and be made perfect by love. It has in itself the seeds of action and affection; it is assumed, as a matter of course, that, if it is not dead, they must grow.

This characteristic, I may note in passing, emphatically marks faith in the highest sphere, where it rests upon God. Reason, conscience, imagination may all be described as the 'realisation of the invisible.' They all rise from the visible to the invisible sphere—from concrete objects, from formal rules, from embodiments of beauty, to the abstract principles imperfectly exhibited in these, and in themselves contemplated by the eye of the soul alone. By so doing, indeed, they take the great step which advances the human mind beyond the narrow limits of brute instinct. In this action faith in God is like them. But its especial characteristic is that it 'sees Him who is invisible;' it rests not upon a principle or a law, but on a Divine Person, and accordingly it cleaves to Him, not simply by the cold adhesion of the understanding, but with the warm and living grasp of duty and love.

But, since we are speaking here of the revelation of truth, it is clear that, although the production of faith is thus a complex process, and its results equally complex in their effects on human nature and life, yet the special exhibition of faith with which we have to do is what may be termed its intellectual aspect—the acceptance, on the declaration of another, known to be in wisdom and goodness superior to ourselves, of truths which we ourselves have not discovered, to which we can at most imperfectly approach in investigation, and which perhaps we may not be able thoroughly to test, even when they are put before us by his word.

In this sense, therefore, I assert that, both for the deepest and the most ordinary knowledge, both for the daily needs of practical life and for the great critical periods in which life seems summed up, the exercise of faith is a fundamental law of human nature. I believe that this law makes itself evident to any man who thinks or observes at all. It is so true for the individual, that, without faith in others, no man can know and do what he must know and do in order to live. It is so true for the race, that, as a matter of fact, it is faith, even more than understanding, that moves humanity.

It is hardly possible to exaggerate the function of faith in relation to the individual soul. Life is, we truly say, an 'education;' the development of humanity depends on the right harmony of that capacity which is drawn out from within, and of the forces which play upon it from without. Now of these forces some are merely physical, acting chiefly by impressions conveyed through the senses—secondarily, perhaps, by subtler influences, felt rather than consciously perceived. But far greater and more powerful are the forces of human influence, acting, almost invariably, in great part through the medium of faith. Every one allows that in the earlier days of the human existence the child lives, naturally and necessarily, the life of faith. Parents, teachers, masters—all must, not by choice, but by necessity, require it at his hands. 'Do, and thou shalt know,' not 'Know, and so shalt thou do,' is the very principle of natural growth in body and mind and heart. It is, of course, not a mere thoughtless faith which is thus required; at every step a right faith is the offspring, not of ignorance, but of partial knowledge. The child fully understands, by observation and experience, that those whom he trusts are wiser, stronger, better than himself, knowing what he cannot know, and doing what he cannot do. Nor is this childish faith permanent. Gradually the power to know and to judge, and so to think and resolve for himself, grows as the mind unfolds; till he comes to the ripeness of manhood, stands in this respect on a level with those who

(*a*) Its application to the individual

have hitherto been his guides, and, so far as they are concerned, begins to walk not by faith but by sight.

But it is to be noted that, as soon as this early phase of faith vanishes, another and a larger phase succeeds. Not for an hour, not for a moment, does the law of faith cease to operate through the course of life. We have only to ask ourselves whence come, at any moment, the actual stores of our knowledge, our ordinary principles of thought, even our ordinary laws of morality. If we consider the accumulated knowledge of outer facts—of the geography which describes the visible world; of the science which unveils its laws; of the history, past or present, of the actions of men—we see that it is largely taken on faith. Even our commonest knowledge on which we have to act—our notion of the map of England, or our acquaintance with the events of everyday life—we gain by faith in others; we do not trace these things out or observe them for ourselves: we cannot, in many cases, even test for ourselves the truth of the information given to us. We understand that there are those whose business in life it is to know these things; we have no reason to think that they err or deceive, and every reason to conceive that, with perhaps considerable inaccuracy, they yet speak the truth. Therefore we rest on their testimony; and, if we did not so rest, we could hardly live, certainly we could not do our own work in life.

in respect of knowledge;

But let us pass from the accumulated observations of fact to principles of thought. How stands the case as to the laws of physical science, the laws of human society, the laws of individual human nature, which we recognise and act upon every day? There is no one who, considering these as a whole, does not live largely by faith: there are very many, among those who must work rather than think, who have to accept on trust almost every single principle. What is here our wisdom, and, indeed, our necessity? We know that there are those who have studied these principles deeply, and searched them out; we know that there is a common sense of mankind which has tried these discoveries by long experience. On faith in these things we act. In some degree, as before, we can

in respect of thought;

understand these things when they are explained to us by the learned; in some degree we can verify them more or less by our own actual experience, proceeding still, however, on the old principle, 'Do, and thou shalt know.' But we do not, as a matter of fact, discover these things for ourselves. No doubt here, as in all else, it is 'blessed to give,' to add our little particle to the great sum of human knowledge; but many of us absolutely, and all in great degree, must be content with the lower position of receiving.

The same great law is again visible in respect of the moral rules which guide our life. It is true that here our individual action starts into a greater prominence and greater vigour. The conscience imperatively asserts that to act against it, even through faith in others, is always wrong. But to act according to conscience is not necessarily right. Conscience needs to be guided and enlightened; as a matter of fact, it is trained and developed by constant influences without, of law and social system, of personal guidance, teaching, and encouragement. Perhaps this is most strikingly exemplified in the social and political action, which is so closely akin to the moral. For here we inevitably follow leaders, partly knowing them and understanding their policy, partly trusting them in much which the mass of men do not and cannot know. Yet what is seen most clearly in the political life is true also in some degree in the moral. Even here there is much room for faith; there is much in which we need, and for which we accept, a guide. *in respect of morality.*

All this refers simply to our individual experience; but it is easy to see that what is true of the individual is true of every class in a nation, of every nation in the great commonwealth of mankind, of every generation in the long succession of ages. A little consideration shows us that in this fact lies the secret of human progress, as well as the happiness of human life. The great work of civilisation moves on under the same laws as the education of the individual. It is no mere metaphor by which we trace out in the race, or in any single member of the great body of humanity, the stages of childhood, of youth, and of maturity, through which the law of faith works in different *(h) Its application to the race.*

degrees. Some nations and ages seem born to teaching and leadership, some to discipleship and obedience. But even the first in some degree, as the last in a far higher degree, have to advance by faith. In every sphere of human existence the plausible saying, 'I will believe only what I can understand,' unless it can be justified by an equivocal sense of the word 'understanding,' is a delusion and a snare.

But if we look more closely at the working out of this law of faith, we shall notice that, except in its simpler and ruder phases, this educating faith is not primarily placed in society itself, but in individual leaders of humanity. The great forward steps made by humanity seldom, if ever, originate with the world at large. There is a curious felicity in the old saying, *Vox populi vox Dei*, if it be rightly understood. For the *vox populi* is not the *vox plebis*, the verdict of the mere majority, in which all voices are equal. The *vox populi* is the expression of the public opinion of men in their right orders and degrees, prepared by the consultation of the few, the true senate of wisdom, and accepted by the whole people—their opinions being weighed as well as counted, all having votes, yet not necessarily having equal votes. It is only this which can even pretend to be *vox Dei*.

<small>Faith in leaders of humanity;</small>

So it certainly is in the growth of the collective wisdom of humanity in all phases. We have but to study the advance of science, of civilisation, or of religion, in order to see that every original step is made by individuals, often in defiance, always in independence, of the common notions of the world around them. There is, indeed, a wave of preparation which heaves, as it were, through the great mass, but the impulse which directs each movement, and gives it a definite character, is from the individual. There rise up men of what we term 'genius,' distinct from mere talent in the spontaneousness of its action, in the sense of inspiration and mission, and perhaps in the rapid intuition which supersedes the long process of reasoning. Who can estimate the effects produced on the knowledge and culture of humanity by a Socrates, a Plato, or an Aristotle, by a Bacon or a Newton, by a Dante, a Shakespeare, or a Goethe, by a Raffaelle or a Beethoven? These are the men

<small>in thought;</small>

who give the great impulses to the course of thought, and take the great forward steps in the advance of science. The mass of men have merely the office of accepting or rejecting; they judge in part, and generally in that part wisely, by what is called common-sense. But then they have to act on the faith, which is here again the child of partial knowledge—their knowledge of the true greatness of the teacher, and their power to verify his teaching by trial. The old saying that a proverb is 'the wisdom of many'—that is, the unformed, half-conscious thought of the many, illuminated and fixed by the original 'wit of one'—is true of all steps in knowledge. It is indeed the recognised characteristic of genius to bring out into clear and vivid life what lay 'without form and void' in the mind of humanity at large. When this has been done, men become, (so to speak) fully conscious of what they had unconsciously, or half-consciously, held.

Nor is this prerogative of the royalty of genius confined to the world of thought; it has its counterpart in the world of moral, social, political activity. There is a 'hero-worship,' indeed, which is idolatry, but there *in action;* is a hero-worship which is a necessity of life. Men always must follow some great leaders of their age, and leave it to them to make the onward steps; and it has been said wittily that a nation or a party is in an unsound state when it moves like a serpent, not by the head which represents it, but by the tail which propels it. The very idea that democracy tends to prevent the emergence of these leaders of mankind, or to impair the loyalty which is their due, has been contemplated by sagacious thinkers as one of the most serious dangers to true human progress.

But this universal law of faith in individuals has its most extraordinary exemplification in the religious sphere of thought—perhaps the sphere in which it might have seemed likely that the soul would most resent *in religion.* all interference with the individuality of its existence before God. Putting for the moment Christianity (with Judaism as included in it) out of the question, how marvellously does the spiritual life of millions rest on faith in revelations of God, accepted on the testimony of prophets and more or less enshrined in sacred books! It is impossible to measure the effect thus produced on the actual religious life of the world by faith in the Vedas or the Koran, in Confucius or Gautama or Mohammed. In spite of themselves, against their own deliberate doctrine, these accepted prophets of humanity are almost deified, and their utterances accepted as permanent embodiments of a divine wisdom. Yet, as if this were not enough, there is no great religion in the world—the Christian, unhappily, not excepted—which is not divided into sects tracing their origin to leaders, whose very names they often perpetuate, and to whose inspiration they defer. In all this there is surely a deep significance. To brand it as pure superstition is a mere evasion of that significance. If ever there was evidence of the necessary working of a natural force of transcendent power, it is certainly here.

But whence comes this natural leadership of humanity? It may be accepted, but it is certainly not conferred, by the will or the wisdom of mankind. The common language of men answers the question by calling them 'inspired men,' and by attributing to them a 'mission' to their own generation and to all time. That answer is at least an adequate and intelligible answer in the ordinary sense, in which it implies the ineradicable belief in a God who inspires, a God who sends. We gain nothing, and lose much, by the substitution for it of an appeal to the law of 'natural selection,' or 'the dominion of the fittest.' For this answer cannot claim either adequacy or intelligibility, unless the 'nature' to which we attribute the personal act of selection be really a person—that is, a god—and unless we explain 'fitness' by that reference to design which properly belongs to the word. Yet in that case the new answer is simply a dilution and mystification of the old simplicity. But, whatever form we give to the answer, it is clear that these teachers of humanity gain their leadership in virtue of a clearer understanding of the Supreme Power, whatever it is, and, as a consequence of this, a greater ability to wield the forces and work with the laws which rule the world. Nothing can be more historically certain than that, in fact, the great leaders of humanity

This leadership from inspiration and mission.

have gained the allegiance of men through a faith in their inspiration and mission, based simply on these grounds. Such faith, in some form or other, they have held vividly and unhesitatingly for themselves, and have impressed it on the mind of humanity, mostly through the impression made directly on the souls of immediate disciples, and by them transmitted to the world at large. Faith has been the lever to move the world, simply because that on which it rests has been held to be not of the world.

Most emphatically, of course, has this been exemplified in the avowed prophets of the religions of the world; but not in them alone. The 'inspiration' of genius in a poet or philosopher implies a special and unique power in him; yet it is the power of a spirit ruling, in different degrees of lower energy, through the whole of that humanity which can recognise and enter into his inspiration. The 'mission' of the statesman, the lawgiver, the conqueror, is the declaration of a like special and unique example of the purpose and work, for which all men are made, and in which their happiness lies. Most of such men, just in proportion as they feel that they are dealing with the actual life of men, and so with the moral and spiritual issues involved in it, understand the meaning of the prophetic declaration: 'I said, I will not speak any more. . . . But the word was in my heart like a burning fire shut up in my bones, and I was weary with forbearing, and I could not stay.' All, even if they are not conscious of this internal conflict, yet feel the truth of the calmer apostolic declaration: 'Though I preach the word that is in me, I have nothing to glory of. Necessity is laid upon me. Yea! woe is unto me if I preach it not.' Everywhere, in different degrees of clearness, we hear from the true leaders of mankind these avowals of a call, a mission, a power which is not their own, nor solely the property of the humanity for which it is used. It is through this that they speak and act, in this that they live and die. It is for this that they claim, and for this that they receive, the faith of mankind at large. If, moreover, we look more closely into the history of their actual work in the world, and see how the hour and the man harmonise with each other, though neither produces the other—how, in fact, the visible course of the world and the appearance of these exceptional types of human nature converge to one great end—then it is difficult not to feel that there is one will ruling both by different powers, and fulfilling itself, although in different ways.

III. Such I believe to be a true outline of the actual working of faith as a great law of human nature, proving itself the most potent of all forces in the working out of human history. Gathering up the results of the whole, we find that such faith operates under three chief aspects.

<small>The phases of faith.</small>

In the lowest and most ordinary phase, concerned with the common knowledge of every day, it simply accepts from individuals or from the world at large what we could, if we had time and opportunity, discover for ourselves. Here it has little, if any, moral significance. In the child it belongs only to the early crudeness of his nature; in the man it may be looked upon simply as a division of intellectual labour, through which alone the race of man can advance as a whole. Yet it is a sheer necessity. Every day reveals to us the imperfections and uncertainties which attend it, but we keep to it as a condition of life. It has its limits, and those limits we may in any special case be called to pass. Within limits, however, we use it. Cynical proverbs scorn it, and scorn us for using it; we smile at them, and go on using it still.

<small>(a) Faith in things which we might know fully.</small>

Next—and here it rises to a higher region—it accepts from others that which we could not discover for ourselves, but which, when disclosed to us, we can, wholly or partially, understand. On this half-provisional exercise of faith depends the whole possibility of teaching and learning. By it the great mass of men live and act in all the spheres of life. Such faith is placed to some extent in the world at large. The wisdom of old gradually accumulating in tradition, the spirit of the age expressing itself in public opinion, the watchwords even of any great school or party to which, after mature thought, we have given allegiance—all claim some measure of this faith, and often punish heavily any refusal of it. But all the grander and deeper exemplifications of this faith rest on individuals. In political, social, or ecclesiastical

<small>(b) Faith in things which we may understand partly.</small>

action, men have to choose their leader, and to trust him with a not unintelligent trust. In respect of all profounder science, higher art, nobler poetry, they have to sit at the feet of the great masters of human thought, partly seeing, partly believing, that there is truth and beauty in what they cannot fully understand. Perhaps there is no more striking characteristic of the criticism of our own days, as compared with the criticism of a century and a half ago, than the importance which it rightly assigns to this principle of faith in genius. What but this is the secret of the change which has passed on the modern criticism of Shakespeare, by which it stands out always in contradistinction, and mostly in infinite superiority, to the older criticism of the school of Pope and Johnson? What is that hero-worship of Carlyle—which, whatever may be its exaggeration, has produced so powerful and radical an effect on the whole tone of modern historical judgment—but simply an emphatic proclamation of this law of faith?

This is a far higher exercise of faith. It approaches at least to the character of a moral action; it is certainly ennobled by the force of affection and enthusiasm. Yet it also has its limits. No man can wholly abdicate his right and duty to think, resolve, and act for himself, especially in the great crises of his life in which he is alone before God. It matters not whether an individual leader claims his allegiance, or whether he is called upon to trust in the *vox populi* —that is (as has been said), the accumulated and concentrated wisdom of humanity—speaking perhaps in the spirit of the age, perhaps in the thought and institutions of days gone by. In some respects this wisdom of the world is greater, in others less, than the wisdom of the great individual thinker. But in no case can either be perfect; hence in neither can there be full and absolute trust.

Now comes the question: Can the law of faith anywhere attain to perfection in that third phase, in which we shall believe what we cannot discover, and what in many points we cannot, even if it is disclosed to us, understand at all in itself, though we may see that it is the goal towards which human thought is tending? All lines of that thought (it is said) end in mystery. Can we

(c) Faith in mystery.

accept mystery in the New Testament sense of the word, as a thing hidden from ages and generations, impenetrable to the understanding, but now revealed and accepted in faith? It is obvious that we can do so only from the voice of God. Is that voice anywhere to be found, speaking distinctly, perfectly, authoritatively in and to man?

Now it is at this point that the Christian's claim of faith for his Master comes in, as I have said, taking up the law of faith, which all must acknowledge as true in its lower phases, and carrying it on to a unique and supernatural completion. Here, therefore, it comes in collision with the wisdom of the world. That wisdom very naturally denies that any such completion is possible; for how, except on the Christian hypothesis, which it rejects, should it be even conceivable? If men do not believe in God, they hold that all intelligence comes from an Eternal Mind pervading the universe, and 'becoming in humanity conscious of itself;' or, in the refusal of all theory whatever, they present us the concrete humanity as the one known and reasonable object of intellectual worship. On neither supposition can they possibly hold that there is anywhere to be found a final and absolute declaration of truth, such as should command an unqualified faith. If they believe in a God, holding of necessity that He 'has not left Himself without a witness,' tracing His voice in the voice of reason and conscience, accepting the natural leadership of inspired men, and studying respectfully the religions of the world, yet they reasonably insist that the voice of God can never be heard perfectly in any utterance either of the individual or the race. They may perhaps hold that, as the law of gravitation was established once for all by Newton, or the law of the circulation of the blood by Harvey, so certain great moral and spiritual truths have been ascertained for all men by great spiritual teachers, and, above all, by the supreme wisdom of Jesus of Nazareth; but the claim of an absolute faith, the notion of an absolute finality of revelation, they must reject. Why should not the future be greater than the past?

This faith supernatural.

> Not in vain the distance beacons. Forward, forward let us range;
> Let the great world spin for ever down the ringing grooves of change.

All their creeds are provisional; they are simply modest attempts at chronicling the stages arrived at in the discovery of scientific, moral, or religious truth, for the benefit of a posterity which may well amend or enlarge them. The Gospel stands out in bold and direct contradiction to this view. The *vox Dei* it is not content to hear in the *vox populi*, though it never denies that there it may, in various degrees, be heard. It claims to find its ultimate expression, for all times and for all men, in the *vox Christi*. Its motto is simply this : 'God, who at sundry times and in divers manners spake in times past to our fathers by the prophets' (I take the word in its largest sense), 'has in these last days spoken to us by His Son, who is the brightness of His glory, and the express image of His person.'

Now in this claim the Gospel stands, strictly speaking, alone. It is, indeed, true that the other great religions of the world practically recognise in their founders something like an absolute authority; but it is remarkable that these founders, with but a single exception, claimed no such place for themselves. The impulse, for example, which, against their own express declarations, and against the theories of the religion which they taught, has practically deified a Confucius or a Buddha, is profoundly instructive as to the spiritual craving for an absolute faith, and the inferences which such a craving suggests. But these men themselves no more dreamt of such a claim than Socrates or Moses themselves. Confucius declared himself but a transmitter of the wisdom of old; Gautama foretold the extinction of Buddhism when it had served its time. If Mohammed seem to be an exception, in claiming for all times and places to be the Prophet of God, I can hardly doubt that he felt this forced upon him by the necessity of meeting the claims of Christianity, and accepted it in spite of the main principle of his absolute monotheism. For, indeed, if these prophets be mere men, although they may be the holiest, the wisest, and the best of men, they cannot claim a unique and absolute supremacy over their fellows, a unique and perfect power of revelation of the Infinite God. The more they conceive His majesty, the more they will hold that the speaker is nothing, and that the truth, infinitely greater than his conception of it, is everything. 'Care nothing for Socrates; care much for the truth. He will die and pass away; the truth will live for ever.'

Now the Gospel, thoroughly acknowledging, as all reason bids, this limitation of faith in all mere men, and, in the case of all the greatest servants of God before and after its Master, readily acknowledging such limitation, and candidly revealing in the Bible the imperfections which showed them weak and fallible men, yet treats Christ Himself as holding a position different not in degree, but in kind. It calls for a faith in Him, absolute, universal, permanent; but, with perfect consistency, it refuses to believe Him a mere man—to hold Him anything less than the only begotten Son of God.

but claimed for Christ.

IV. If it be asked on what ground does it make that claim, the answer of Christians is, that it is Christ who makes it for Himself.

Our Lord's own advance of this claim.

It has been said, and confidently said, by men of great name, in times past and present, that here, like the other religions above noticed, it advances for Christ a claim of which He Himself never dreamt. But I cannot think that this assertion will bear any critical examination, in relation either to the historic records of the Gospel or to the actual growth and perpetuation of Christianity itself. The question does not turn upon the criticism of this or that passage in the New Testament. Study the record of our Lord's teaching in whatever form you will, or listen to the actual preaching, which took up His word, from the lips of any apostle you may choose; still the fact remains that—in this point unlike all other great teachers—He preaches Himself, and that, inverting the common order of teaching, He makes faith in Him not the preparation for contemplation of the truth or acceptance of the law which He declares, but, on the contrary, the end to which these things lead gradually up in the later stages of His revelation. It matters only in degree how we study His teaching. We may follow it in the earlier Gospels inductively, gradually observing His self-manifestation in miracle, His teaching with an authority above the scribe or even the prophet, His rebukes and judgments of all whom the world reverenced,

His words of superhuman authority to His own disciples, till we end in that marvellous climax: 'All power is given Me in heaven and earth. Go and make all nations My disciples. Teach them to observe all things whatsoever I have commanded you; and lo! I am with you alway, even to the end of the world.' We may study it, as it is reflected in the apostolic teaching, in that remarkable order which has been traced out already, and which bears, alike in its unity and its variety, the most obvious signs of being drawn from a divine original in His own Word. We may note how St. Peter expands this last charge of Christ to His disciples into a constant exhibition of the divine majesty of the risen Lord; how St. Paul makes the great declaration at the Last Supper of the 'blood shed for the remission of sins' the keynote of his preaching of the universal mediation; how St. John draws out the solemn words spoken to the disciples on the eve of the Ascension into a full explicit declaration of His divine nature. Everywhere, with a unanimity which it would be in the highest degree uncritical to refer to any origin except His own teaching, they make in His name the same absolute claim for faith—a faith always one in essence, yet varying in depth and wearing a peculiar phase of meaning, according to the especial form of the preaching of Christ with which it is associated. We may turn to the Fourth Gospel, and we shall find an additional proof of its genuineness, beyond all those which a sound criticism has brought forth to an enquiring world, in that simple record of deeper sayings of our Lord, in which we trace the greater original of all the great apostolic preaching, and in which the claim for faith in Him as alone able to 'reveal the Father,' from 'whom He came and to whom He went,' and whom, indeed, they 'saw in seeing Him,' is set forth with the most startling emphasis. It is true that here, in this respect as in others, St. John's Gospel 'goes on to perfection,' and without it we should feel that we had not the crowning completeness of the revelation. But, wherever we follow out His teaching, however we narrow the area of our study, still the fact remains: He does put forward His claim to an absolute faith as the true Revealer of God, the true Mediator between God and man, and the true Lord and

Judge of all creatures to the end of time. It is a startling claim, before which we cannot be surprised that men have recoiled, even those who, like the hearers described to us in the Gospel, have up to a certain point followed Him as a King, listened to Him as a Prophet, even believed in Him as a Saviour. Like those half-disciples of His time, they cry, 'It is a hard saying. Who can hear it?' But they betake themselves to an expedient impossible in those earlier days, and against irresistible evidence persist that He never uttered it.

Yet it is certainly a claim which He made, in a sense in which no other son of man ever dared to make it. It has been said truly that the picture of the Christ of the Gospels proves its truth to life by its unspeakable superiority to all of which the imagination of the early Christians—we might add the imagination of men of any age—could be capable. Is not the remark equally true of the inconceivable boldness of this demand of absolute faith, and the marvellous depth and universality of the doctrine to which it is made the introduction? None but the Jesus of Nazareth, whose person stands out in living majesty in the Gospel history, could have conceived and justified so magnificent a demand. That He made it again and again for Himself it seems impossible that the most jealous criticism can doubt, if only it resists the hasty incredulity, which turns away at once from anything that is unexpected and mysterious, without caring to examine its claims to acceptance.

But if He did make it, then we are obliged, however reluctantly, to consider the alternative presented to us. We cannot ignore the claim, and continue in the same attitude towards Him which we held before. For if the claim be not true, so that it is the very life of our souls to accept it with an unreserved devotion, it must be what we hardly dare to name—the wildest dream of infatuation or the presumption of an almost blasphemous imposture. Yet can any one who, looking on even from without—following that path of observation which the author of 'Ecce Homo' paints to us with such marvellous felicity—surveys the life of Jesus of Nazareth, entertain for a moment either of these alternatives?

The alternatives presented to us.

The singular calmness and simplicity of its whole tone, the perfect personal humility which accompanies the very highest of these self-assertions, the profound wisdom of its teaching, and the insight into the nature of God and of man which it manifests at every point—all these are absolutely inconsistent with the supposition of fanatic infatuation. Such infatuations the world has often seen in religious teachers, but has always, after a short time, seen through them and rejected them utterly, leaving their effects to die out by their own intrinsic hollowness. Such infatuations have betrayed themselves as mere excrescences or perversions, by their want of connection or even consistency with the great principles of the teaching itself; they have proved their fantastic unreality by breaking down under the test of criticism from opponents, and the stress of trial of faith in the believer. But here there is something wholly different in kind. These superhuman claims present themselves as a natural climax of the teaching and the life of Him who makes them; they are the only appropriate completion of His mission; they supplied to Christianity the only adequate fulcrum from which to move the world. Whenever any bodies of men calling themselves Christians have put them aside or explained them away, their Christianity has gradually faded away into a kind of religious Deism, or perhaps a religion not unlike Judaism or Mohammedanism, except that it has Jesus Christ as its prophet. The reference of this claim of the Lord for absolute faith to a noble infatuation will not stand before the examination, either of the life of Christ, or of the Christianity which has been derived from it.

(a) The notion of infatuation.

As for the other alternative—the idea that these claims originated in what (in spite of loose talk about ancient standards of truthfulness and 'the Oriental mind') must be characterised as a distinct imposture, doing evil perhaps that good might come, forced upon Him by the necessities of His position, and accepted in a halfwilful self-delusion—the very mention of it seems almost to need apology. In a Jew, brought up under the shadow of an awful Monotheism, which by the time of Jesus Christ had so worked itself into the whole texture of Jewish

(b) The notion of imposture.

thought as to expel all tendencies to idolatry, such pretensions as His would be absolutely indefensible, incapable of the excuses and palliations which modern thought has invented for them, on any supposition except that they were plainly and solemnly true. Yet to any one who contemplates His life, as recorded in the Gospels and stamped on the Christianity of the world, the very notion of referring the great climax of His teaching to an imposture will appear so monstrous, that to entertain it even for a moment must argue either an extraordinary moral obtuseness, or a resolution to maintain a preconceived theory against the obvious witness of fact. It must be remembered that for it He lived and died. How can we study the truthfulness, the humility, the reverence of His life, or the calm self-devotion of a death which voluntarily endured the cross, and all that the cross implied, in witness of a mission from God, and yet allow ourselves to ask whether such a life and such a death were devoted to the establishment of a lie, and a lie, moreover, of which it might well be said that it was not only against men, but against God? Nor, in relation to this subject, must we omit the consideration that, on evidence which, coming from eye-witness of the apostles, convinced the world then, and challenges the test of criticism now, the life of Jesus Christ was marked by a power of miracle which argued a mission from God, and His death crowned by a resurrection and ascension into heaven. Yet who can conceive it possible that One who thus visibly manifested a divine mission could dare to arrogate to Himself what no prophet before and no apostle after Him ever dreamed of claiming, assuming what is ultimately due to God alone, and yet being permitted to seal such assumption by resurrection from the dead?

It is not too much to say that either supposition is impossible. We are thrown back again on the alternative of faith. The demand upon that faith is great; and the very greatness of that demand is acknowledged to be a 'trial of faith'—at once a test of its reality and a means of developing its strength. But to what else can we turn? If, first with the multitude and then with the disciples, we have pondered the manifestation of power,

(c) The acceptance of faith.

wisdom, and goodness, which declares Him the true Son of Man, and shows in Him a mission from God, we cannot refuse to take the last step—to sit at His feet in absolute faith, and accept His declaration even of 'heavenly things.' So only can we hope to enter into the depths of Christian doctrine; so only to catch the right spirit which animates a Christian life!

The act is an act of faith; yet, like almost all other acts of reasonable faith in men, it has its preparation by previous process of reason, and its verification by subsequent experience. By the former it is obvious that the effort of faith is made easier to us; by the latter its power over the soul is deepened. *The preparation for faith.*

There is that preparation of reason in the conviction, which I have already endeavoured to establish, that the mystery of the word of Christ, however inconceivable beforehand, however imperfectly comprehensible to us even now, is yet marvellously in harmony with all the higher thoughts of men in searching after God, and adapted especially to meet that great moral perplexity, which those thoughts indicate, but cannot dispel. Surely it must help us in that supreme act of faith, which ultimately rests on our knowledge of Christ Himself, to find that what His teaching presents to us does thus satisfy all the cravings and needs of humanity, for a solution of the great problem of being, for a moral force able to conquer the world, for a spiritual life which shall unite in perfect harmony the consciousness of self and the consciousness of God. In accepting the revelations of even the highest human inspiration, we find every day that our faith is prepared and aided by the conviction: 'Yes! There is the truth, clear and bright, which I have been half-blindly groping for. Never could I have found it; but now it finds me, and I know, in heart as well as mind, that it is true.' Increase all that experience a hundredfold, and it is but a faint expression of that drawing to Christ which they have felt, who, laying hold on His word by faith, know in it what at once confirms and yet passes knowledge.

So also, as it has its preparation in previous thought, it has its verification in actual experience. How wonderfully has experience again and again justified the great act of faith, by finding it a new spring of spiritual life for understanding, and conscience, and heart, in which it is no metaphor, but a simple truth, to declare that men become new creatures, and pass from death to life! They have (to use the expressive language of Scripture) 'tasted that the Lord is gracious:' they find that Christ has fulfilled His promise to be to them light, strength, holiness; and so they know that they have not 'believed in vain.' How irresistibly that verification proved itself, not only to those who felt it, but to the world at large, in the first days of the Gospel preaching, all history tells us. It even became in itself a sign of the reality of a spiritual life of faith, which, as much as any other, served to preach Christ to the heathen; and 'faith working by love' could be appealed to as a visible seal of discipleship of Christ, compared with which 'circumcision was nothing.' Nor has that verification ceased. Even now, with whatever falling off from the simplicity and fervour of early days, there is, as I have already urged, a sign, which Christians themselves know well, and which even the world cannot refuse to read, in the intellectual light, the moral power, the spiritual regeneration, which they enjoy who have learned Christ by the obedience of faith. There are few men whose experience, either without or within, has not disclosed to them the power of faith in Christ to inspire even the weakest and dullest soul, and to convert the sinner, from whom the stern moralist would turn as hopeless, to a life really spiritual, raised above the power of the world and the flesh simply by 'being hid with Christ in God.' This great enthusiasm stands out from all the other enthusiasms of personal faith which, as has been said, have written themselves so emphatically on history, in respect of its permanence, its universality, and its moral fruitfulness. They have done good service in their day, in certain ages and peoples, in certain directions of moral energy. This has for eighteen centuries proclaimed and proved itself Catholic, both in its universal sway over all ages, races, and characters of men, and in its power to regenerate not one faculty, but all the many and varied faculties of the spiritual life.

In some sense the working out of this law of faith seems to stand in no distant analogy to the well-known process by which great physical laws are established. There we find, first, a preparation in thought or experiment, which suggests the rudimentary idea of the law. Then comes, next, the step which is usually the work of original genius—the conception of the great law itself in full clearness and generality. There is, lastly, the verification of that conception, by comparing what should be its results with the results of independent observation. Then, and not till then, does the law stand out to us, still not in demonstrative certainty, but in the moral certainty which in such cases is all that is attainable, and all that is necessary. So is it here—only that here the all-important intermediate step is due not to the concentrated thought and imagination of human genius, but to the direct revelation of God in the Lord Jesus Christ; and the acceptance of that step by the many is an act not simply of an intelligent common-sense, but of a faith combining the intellectual, moral, and emotional elements of human nature in the attachment to His Divine Person.

Analogy to discovery of natural law.

Still, however prepared for, however verified, the main act which the Gospel demands is an act of faith. Once more it claims to take up a great natural law, and carry it on to a supernatural culmination, which in itself it may constantly approach, but can never reach. It seems to survey all mankind with the eyes of thoughtful sympathy, noting the inextinguishable craving of faith, noting the strange objects on which, in an earnestness half ludicrous and half pathetic, it lavishes all the wealth of its allegiance, noting the indignant reactions, in which it casts down these idols as their hollowness is discovered, sometimes merely to seek new ones, sometimes to sink down in a blank despondency of utter unbelief. Then, in the spirit of St. Paul at Athens, it presents to that ignorant worship One who, as at once God and Man, is its only worthy object; and, while it denies not to lower objects the degrees and measures of faith which are their due, fixes on Him at last the absolute perfection of an unqualified trust. Whatever may be learned by human reason and experience of the 'earthly things' of God, still for the 'heavenly things' themselves it rests on the word of Jesus Christ, spoken by Himself on earth to the few, spoken by them

The completion of the law of faith.

under the special inspiration of the Holy Spirit to the many, and drawn out under the inspiration of ordinary grace to the Christian and to the Church in the living teaching of Christianity, even to the end of time.

Here, therefore, lie the two great questions between the Church and the world. Is this completion of the law of faith true or false? Has Jesus Christ a right to claim it for Himself? Christian evidence, in whatever form, direct or indirect, it presents itself, has its office, not in giving to the reason an absolute proof of the deepest mysteries of the Gospel, but in establishing an affirmative answer to these great questions, and then, both for ultimate knowledge and for spiritual life, leaving each soul to the obedience of faith in the Lord Jesus Christ Himself.

Faith the crucial test.

In that claim of faith there is no antagonism to human progress. The Gospel leaves the freest possible scope to human reason and energy in all the three great spheres of thought and experience. In nature it bids the reason go on boldly, studying all forms of law, learning to discern the nature and correlation of all physical forces, tracing out the evolutions in a wonderful order of all forms of being, striving to go back from the organised *Kosmos* to the first original condition, without form and void—now gazing on the vastness of the universe,' now peering into the infinite minuteness of perfection in each separate thing. But it claims that in all this search there should go with us the belief in the one God and Creator of all, whom Christ has revealed all but visibly to us, and who under all these laws is fulfilling Himself in many ways. In the contemplation of humanity it encourages the reason to study in each human being the secret of the bodily and spiritual life, to discern the subtle laws which rule the little world within, to mark the links of connection between man and other animate beings, to note the strange action and reaction ever going on between individual freedom and universal law, and between the bodily and the spiritual natures. Nor does it leave the reason less free for wide historical survey, going back by direct or indirect study to the dim ages of antiquity, tracing out from first begin-

Faith and progress

in knowledge of nature;

in knowledge of man;

nings the civilisation, material, intellectual, moral, spiritual, which is the heritage of the present time, and watching here also the power of universal laws and forces, underlying the rich and turbulent play of individual energies. Moreover, in both forms of search the Gospel never bids, never even allows, men to shut their eyes to the great perplexity of all thought—the contradiction by the power of evil, whether in decay, or in sorrow and pain, or in blind ignorance and wilful sin, of all that tells of power, and wisdom, and beneficence in nature and in man. But again it asks that throughout, alike in the brightness of knowledge and hope, and in the gloom of despondency and ignorance, there shall be cherished that truth which the Lord Jesus Christ taught by His word and by His life—that man is really the child of God, having in him a divine image, which cannot be obscured by close connexion with the material universe, and must prove itself victorious even over sin and death. So, also, in the search after God Himself, Christianity encourages the confident hope that, as the ages roll on, we may know more and more of Him as the Creator of all things and the Father of all men in knowledge of God. —outgrowing some superstitions, putting aside some forms of thought which satisfied earlier ages—perhaps learning, here as elsewhere, that lesson of greater simplicity which belongs to the more advanced stages of knowledge, and better distinguishing what we know from what we can only approach in speculation and hope. But it still teaches us under all changes to lay firm hold on the knowledge of the Father, in the Son and by the Spirit, which Christ has set forth to us, and in that knowledge to have the life spiritual and eternal. Everywhere, just as much as in the life of unbelief, there is bold progress, launching out from the shore of present knowledge, and 'bursting into the silent sea' of discovery. But in this case there is always with us, pointing to the one unchangeable presence of God, a compass which no darkness of the sky above us can hide, and no blasts or waves below can disturb; and they who have this, even if they know not how they move, or whither at any moment they are going, can go on, sure of their course, to the appointed haven where they would be.

CHAPTER VIII.

THE DOCTRINES OF FAITH.

'This is the victory that overcometh the world, even our faith.'—1 John v. 4.

The mysteries of faith.

THE claim of faith advanced for the Lord Jesus Christ is, as has been already seen, emphatically asserted in relation to the declaration of the 'heavenly things.' The 'earthly things,' indeed, may also need to be declared by Him, for there is much in them which mankind generally could not for themselves discover; but if declared, they can be, at least in great degree, tested by human judgment, and it is the function of Christian evidence to show how they meet the test. But the 'heavenly things' are those ultimate truths, which are called the 'mysteries' of the Gospel. Now the Scriptural use of the word 'mystery' denotes a secret, once hidden, and now revealed to man; the more usual modern use of the word adds to this original sense the further idea that, when revealed, they are capable of being apprehended rather than comprehended, so that we may understand that the truth revealed actually is, but how it is, and how it is reconciled with other truth, we know not, and probably cannot know. In both senses the name of 'mysteries' may well be applied to the 'heavenly things'— the fundamental realities of the Gospel—as opposed to 'the earthly things,' which are the manifestations of those realities upon earth. They can be accepted by us only on the ground of faith. For that faith in Christ we hold that amply sufficient reasons can be given; and we also note that, in respect of the substance of that which He discloses to our faith, we have both antecedent preparation of reason, and subsequent verification of experience. But the act of acceptance is still an act of faith, crowning in a supernatural perfection all the imperfect natural exemplifications of the law of faith as a necessary law of human life. It is this supreme act which distinguishes a religion from a philosophy, and which gives Christianity 'the victory that overcometh the world.'

But, for a fuller conception of the true relation of evidence to faith, it will be well to distinguish those elements in the creed of Christendom which rest on the one from those which appeal to the other. The characteristic tenets of Christianity, as such, are embodied or implied in the various steps of the manifestation of Christ. Hence the question, in other words, is this: What parts of that manifestation are within the cognisance of reason and observation, and what parts lie altogether beyond the sphere of their operation—to be accepted, if accepted at all, by faith in the word of our Master Himself? *The preparation for faith.*

In describing the function of Christian evidence, I have already endeavoured to show that the first step in the study of that evidence is the consideration of the actual power, intellectual, moral, and spiritual, which Christianity exercises at the present moment, and the inference of a divine origin to be derived from the acknowledged fact that this threefold power is unique in the history of man, in its origin, its method, and its actual scope. Holding it to be, in fact, a virtually 'miraculous' power, I have also contended that, like all other miracles, it should be to us a sign, to lead to the contemplation of the Worker Himself, as He was seen by man in His manifestation upon earth. Then, on considering that manifestation, we see at once that the main features of His life, His death, His resurrection and ascension, lie open before the eyes of men; and Christian evidence offers reasons first for believing these great facts themselves, next for entering, at least in great degree, into their significance, and lastly for seeing in them manifestations of superhuman power, wisdom, and goodness, amply sufficient to lead to the conclusion that He 'has the words of eternal life,' and has therefore a right to claim the adhesion of an unreserved faith.

But beyond these we discern other articles of the Christian creed which are simply doctrines of faith— accordant, indeed, with all that reason and conscience, imagination and hope would suggest, but going so infinitely beyond this as to be incapable of being *The doctrines resting on faith alone.*

established by appeal to them. These articles are, first, the doctrine of the Atonement, next, the doctrine of the eternal existence of the Lord Jesus Christ after His ascension and before His incarnation; and finally those truths as to the nature of the Godhead, to which we are 'compelled by this Christian verity.' All these are 'heavenly things,' belonging to the Divine counsels, capable of being known only by entering into 'the mind of God.'

I. It has been observed, accordingly, that the first preaching of the Gospel naturally started with that part of the Christian creed on which appeal could be made to the reason and knowledge of the hearers. The witnesses of Christ dwelt before all things on the life of Jesus Christ, as crowned by the all-important fact of the Resurrection; they claimed for it, when thus crowned, the well-known signs of Messiahship, in the visible power of miracle and the fulfilment of prophecy. The life itself, with these acknowledged signs, had been before the eyes of their hearers. The Resurrection and Ascension they declared that they had seen, and gave visible tokens of a power shed down by the ascended Lord. This was the natural order. The deeper doctrines were to be preached hereafter; but, since they were to be understood only by faith in the word of Christ, it was but reasonable to give grounds for claiming that faith, and to 'let the house of Israel know assuredly that God had made that same Jesus, whom they had crucified, both Lord and Christ.'

The Atonement.

From this first phase of Christian preaching, we have again seen that the next step was to dwell on the doctrine of the Atonement, in which was contained the meaning both of His death and His resurrection. That this doctrine is, in a very unique and peculiar sense, the characteristic doctrine of Christianity, is clear from the prominence which it at once assumed in the preaching of the Gospel, so that St. Paul in his conversion of the Gentile world declares that he cared not to 'know anything save Jesus Christ and Him as crucified,' and is testified to us every day by the simple fact that the chosen symbol of Christianity is not the cradle of Bethlehem or the broken tomb, but the sign of the cross. But whence came that doctrine, and how was it taught?

The answer is simple enough. It came from the word of the Lord Jesus Christ, whether spoken during His life on earth, or (as St. Paul so often urges) taught after His exaltation by the Holy Spirit, whose very office it was 'to bring to the remembrance' and understanding of the disciples 'whatever He Himself had said.' From Him alone the truth could be known. To some extent, indeed, the very contemplation of the Passion might have told its tale. We can well understand how one, who simply gazed in awe and wonder on the victorious majesty of the great Sufferer, and the signs which marked the supreme moment of His death, might discover in the Passion a certain unique and mysterious significance, and cry out 'Truly this man was the Son of God.' When the dimness of that significance had been illuminated by the light of the Resurrection, we can still better conceive how, especially on a Jewish mind, the idea might gradually dawn that in it He was suffering for the sins of others, and in some sense offering a sacrifice such as no other had ever offered. But, on the other hand, to the disciples themselves before the event, and to the Jewish hearers who listened to them after it, the Cross was, at first sight, the great stumbling-block, because apparently the sign of the utter failure of all the hopes which they had conceived of the reality of His Messiahship. Even if they pierced below this first superficial impression to discern such meanings as have been referred to above, their ideas would be at best vague and doubtful, stronger in hope than in reason, and cherished not so much in the mind as in the heart. If, as was necessary for the conquest of the world, they were to turn these hopes into certainties, they could only do this just so far as He Himself taught them. The knowledge was one of those 'words of eternal life' which they were convinced that He had, and which they accepted from Him in faith.

Its foundation in the word of Christ.

That He did teach them this truth is certain. We do not, indeed, find it in the earlier and more popular teaching addressed to the multitude. In the Sermon on the Mount, for example, there is no shadow of the cross. Even when He began to disclose the darker features of His service, the cross was declared not as a symbol of

His actual teaching

atonement, but simply as a type of self-sacrifice in Him and in those who would follow Him. The teaching of the Atonement was an inner teaching addressed to His disciples, who had already been taught by the Baptist to look upon Him as 'the Lamb of God, taking away the sins of the world,' or to the 'Master in Israel' (perhaps in their hearing) who could understand the lifting up of the brazen serpent, as the type of the lifting up of the Son of Man, that 'whoso believed in Him should not perish.'[1] The earliest Gospel records tell us that from a critical time in His ministry—succeeding the great retrospective question at Cæsarea Philippi, and coincident with the glorious vision of the Transfiguration—He began to teach them continually that the Son of Man must suffer, and to press that sad teaching upon them, when for very love's sake they would hardly consent to listen.[2] It is difficult to suppose that this reiterated and emphatic teaching could have been confined merely to the enunciation of the fact, without some exposition of its meaning, in relation to His Messiahship, such as that which He is represented as giving hereafter on the road to Emmaus. We note that, on one occasion at any rate, He referred—in one of those *obiter dicta* which cannot be used except of a familiar truth—to the certainty that He was to crown His ministry to men by 'giving His life a ransom for many.'[3] But we are not left to mere speculation or forced to dwell on glimpses of His occasional teaching. There was unquestionably one rite, which He ordained on the eve of His passion to be the new and characteristic rite of His kingdom. The object of that rite—whatever else it signified and conveyed—was to 'show forth His death,' not only in its reality, but in its meaning. It stamped for ever on the very forefront of Christian teaching those immortal words: 'This is My body broken—this is My blood shed—for the remission of sins.' That teaching even in itself is too plain to be mistaken. But we can read in the apostolic doctrine of the hereafter how it was understood by St. Peter, St. Paul, and St. John under the illuminating power of the Holy Spirit. In their

---

[1] See John i. 29; iii. 14, 15.   [2] See Matt. xvi. 21; xx. 17, &c.
[3] See Matt. xx. 28.

teaching we see that from the fruitful germ of our Lord's great declaration there grew out various developments of the doctrine itself, and various applications of it to the souls of men. Yet still, taken simply in itself, it really sums up all that we need to know, and almost all that we can know. His death was an atoning death for the remission of the sins of the world. Therefore (as even His forerunner declared) was it ordained for Him, the true 'Lamb of God;' therefore, in spite of the weakness of the flesh, to be conquered only by agony, did He bow His head to it. This whole truth, so emphatically the characteristic truth of Christianity, rests ultimately on His word and on it alone.

For what can reason say concerning it? It has been the object of an earlier lecture[4] to examine what preparation reason can make, and has made, for the acceptance of the mystery of the Cross, and how, in this way as in so many others, Natural Theology leads up to supernatural Revelation. The various steps are obvious and important enough. *The preparation of Natural Theology.*

First, reason can recognise the terrible reality of sin, as being a disobedience to the supreme law, as involving a real guilt, and as bringing with it a real spiritual bondage. It can see that, if there be any supreme law whatever, retribution must necessarily wait on sin; and the inference of reason will be confirmed (though not without some imperfections and contradictions) by experience of that which actually does go on under God's moral government to punish sin as such, and to give reason for expecting fuller retribution in the future.[5] It must confess, however unwillingly, that man in himself has no power to atone for sin even by repentance, and little power to break for himself the fetters of evil habit, in which past sins invariably bind the soul. *(a) The sense of sin and retribution.*

Next, if it acknowledges a God all-righteous and all-loving, reason will necessarily, in spite of this consciousness of sin, refuse to believe that sin can be allowed to stand up for ever in rebellion against His righteous *(b) The hope of pardon.*

---

[4] See Part I. c. viii.
[5] On this subject see Butler's celebrated chapter on the 'Moral Government of God' (*Analogy*, Part I. c. iii.).

will; and will still less acquiesce in the horrible idea that His love can have left His creatures hopelessly bound in the chains of sin, and thus hopelessly doomed to the death which is its fruit. So in its perplexity the mind will take counsel with the heart. Man knows how to forgive freely, not seven times, but seventy times seven. A true father, imperfect and sinful as he himself is, will always receive back a prodigal son, or will even go out to seek him, strive to awaken penitence in him, and invite him back to his home. There will always, therefore, arise a sure and certain hope that the Heavenly Father will in some way show mercy, as far above the highest human love as the heaven is above the earth. That this trust is ineradicable from the human heart all the religions of the world very plainly testify.

Then comes the next step. The idea that there must be, and that there will be, some atonement for sin, is undoubtedly (c) The idea embodied in the universal rite of sacrifice. It is easy of sacrifice. to brand this rite as a mere superstition; it is still easier to trace out and gather up a mass of instances of what is grotesque and puerile, or repulsive and horrible, in the actual sacrifices of the world, and to use these for the purpose of pouring contempt on the whole idea. But, after all, this is surely a shallow and arbitrary mode of reasoning. Universality must prove accordance with human nature; survival, in spite of all these hideous perversions, must be some proof of vitality. Nor is the idea, when examined, incapable of giving an account of itself. For in it lies the reconcilement of justice with mercy—a reconcilement which we must believe to exist, however hard it may be to draw it out in theory, however hard it may be (as everyone placed in authority knows) to carry it out in practice.

Nor is this all. Beyond this point reason may take one last step. It can certainly be shown, as great thinkers have (d) The principle of mediation. proved, that mediation, by which I mean the power of altering the spiritual condition and prospects of others before God, is a fundamental law of human life—that is, a law of God—dependent on unity between man and man, carried out under limits, but in a thousand varying forms, every day of our life. It may be shown that such mediation, when applied for the help of sinners in a world like this, generally, if not always, involves some amount of suffering; and that, if a man would in any degree save others from the punishment of their sins, it must be at the price of bearing that burden for them, though to him who so bears it it ceases to be punishment. These things reason can show as the results of all thoughtful observation; and so showing them it may naturally conceive the idea that, if the hope of atonement is to be fulfilled, it would be, under the ordinance of God, fulfilled by man for man, in some supreme exhibition of this law of mediation, in some great voluntary self-sacrifice for others.

So far as this the moral reason may go, and, as I have already urged, this is no slight advance in the suggestion of thought, and in the kindling of hope beyond that which reason can establish, as a preparation for faith.

But here must come in the function of faith itself; and where shall that faith be placed? In some measure it had been demanded for all who under the old covenant spoke the 'word of the Lord.' The Old Testament, on all the points above referred to, had certainly clenched with authority the inference of reason. In virtue of the fundamental notion of the covenant with God, as a covenant emphatically made with sacrifice, the idea of atonement pervaded the whole of the teaching and thought of the chosen people. In virtue of the equally fundamental Messianic idea, the fulfilment of the promise of atonement, as of all other promises of God, pointed continually to the Messiah. Every declaration of law, every prediction of prophecy, every development of spiritual teaching, and every corresponding growth of spiritual consciousness, must necessarily have at once developed and deepened these great fundamental beliefs. Nor can it be doubted that the appeal was invariably made not only to understanding and to conscience, but to faith—faith ultimately in God Himself, but secondarily in those who declared His mysteries. In this point, as in others, the new covenant justly claims to be the perfection of that which existed in germ and promise from the old times.

The preparation in the Old Testament.

But for absolute faith there can be only one claim—the

claim made by Jesus Christ Himself. We have convinced ourselves that He alone 'has the words of eternal life.' Now, if we are to pass from what may be to what is—if we are to ascend from limited and imperfect forms of mediation to the absolute and universal mediation, which they can but suggest, and which the salvation of a world requires—it can be only by accepting the word of Christ Himself. None before He speaks can unfold the mystery itself, even if they can catch some glimpses of its manifestation through earthly things. For to know it is to know the mind of God. Only One can do this. He who knows the secrets of heaven can alone tell how the sins of men can be remitted, what atonement is needed, what atonement is sufficient. After He has spoken, not even apostle or prophet can do more than draw out the consequences of His divine word. How this has been done we have already seen. Under the two great figures of redemption and propitiation, the 'remission of sins in His blood,' which He Himself declared and perpetuated in the new rite of His kingdom, is shown to be a deliverance from the bondage of sin, and an atonement to take away its guilt and its penalty. In the one is seen the action of the love of God, in the other the mediation of the Son of Man. In the union of the two is represented the inseparability of justification and sanctification in the salvation of man. All this is the work of a true Christian theology, at every step addressing itself to the thought and conscience of man, and at every step appealing to the revelation of God in Christ. But the foundation on which all rests is still the word of the Lord Himself.

The ultimate root in faith.

It is true that here also is exemplified the process of verification already described. There is a verification in thought. When that word is revealed to us, we can see the fulness of its moral truth and beauty; we can view it as an accordance with Divine righteousness, and as a consequence of perfect unity and sympathy with man; we may venture to examine how the sacrifice of Christ, and it alone, can meet the universal need. All this has been done with infinite advantage.[6] There is a

The verification of experience.

---

[6] It is hardly necessary to refer on this point to Dr. Macleod Campbell's *Doctrine of the Atonement.*

still more striking verification in experience. For thousands and tens of thousands, accepting that truth in faith, have found in it a light in darkness, a consciousness of Divine forgiveness, and a spring of newness of life. Both verifications have their value; both may do much to strengthen the conviction of faith.

Yet still we must come back to the remembrance that in its essence the doctrine of the Atonement is a doctrine of faith. Christian evidence may suggest it, prove that it is not unnatural, and show that it is effective as a moral and spiritual force in the soul. *The practical results from this rest on faith.* Christian evidence may give us reasons for coming to Christ in faith, and enquiring on this matter at His lips. But it can do no more, and any attempt to make it do more will necessarily break down, and, by the usual judgment on exaggeration, will throw discredit upon it even in its own proper sphere. It is well that this should be clearly understood in the presentation of this doctrine to the ignorant or unbelieving, that we may know how to make our appeal rightly. It is well also for our conception and study of the doctrine, that we may learn to shrink from those elaborate reasonings, claiming to prove it by logical or moral necessity, which have in practice become derogatory to the righteousness and mercy of God, and so become hindrances instead of helps to true Christian faith and knowledge. It is right to follow apostolic example, and speak of its meaning as a 'redemption,' a 'propitiation,' a 'satisfaction' (although this last is not strictly a Scriptural phrase); for of these each illustrates one side of the mysterious truth. But, after all, what can we know more than is contained in the simple words, 'My life is a ransom for the many;' 'My blood is shed for the remission of sins'? If we be asked how we know it, how we have gained light on the dark inscrutable mystery of sin and death, it is better to go at once to the only ultimate answer—that we rest on the word of the Saviour Himself.

So accepted, we see how the revelation throws back a new light on the life of Christ as visibly set forth to us. It shows us His life on earth as not only a manifestation of perfect humanity and a revelation of God's mercy, but as being itself a preparation for the end, and in strict truth containing the first stages of the great self-sacrifice—alike in the joy of mediation and in the sorrow by which that joy is bought. A thousand things, before obscure, start into light. We understand now why there was so much of conflict and suffering in His life, why 'He was despised and rejected of men;' we see the meaning of His daily struggle against the contradiction of sinners, His sigh in the act of healing, and His tears over the grave which He was about to open. For the end teaches us that all these things were part of the work of mediation in a sinful world; they were the beginnings of His conflict against the powers of evil; in every act and word and thought we trace the first workings of that obedience made perfect by suffering which is the essence of sacrifice, and of which the Passion was the awful completion.

The light thrown back on His life.

But as the doctrine of the Cross throws light back on His life, so also it throws light forward upon His Resurrection. In itself that Resurrection is the great miracle of miracles, the seal of His Messiahship, the visible manifestation of an inherent and eternal life in Him. But, in the light of His teaching of the Atonement, the Resurrection is seen as the proof of the acceptance of the Atonement, and thus of the justification of all men in the blood of Christ. Therefore it is that it assumes the deeper senses which are assigned to it in Scripture, as the seal of our spiritual resurrection here, and the certain earnest of the resurrection of our whole nature hereafter. For these senses, which might indeed be inferred from the knowledge of Him as the true Son of Man, were raised from inference into plain certainty by the knowledge not only of the Resurrection itself, but of the true meaning of the Passion.

The light thrown on His Resurrection.

II. Such is the first of those great doctrines of the Gospel which lie entirely within the province of faith. For this reason, as for other and deeper reasons, one chief action of faith is the acceptance of our free justification in the blood of Christ, and Faith personified is represented symbolically as the bearer of the cross. But it is at the same time clear that the teaching of the Cross is not the ultimate teaching of the Gospel.

The connection of atonement with mediation.

It necessarily leads on to larger and deeper revelations still. For the Passion, while it is the completion of Redemption and Propitiation, is but a part of the great Mediatorial work. Indeed we observe that generally, in all human mediation, suffering and death for others are not essential to the idea of mediation in itself, but are rather a price which has to be paid for the exercise of mediatorial power, and which, but for the existence and power of evil in the world, need not be paid at all.[7] Thus the doctrine of the Cross, thoughtfully pondered, leads on to further inquiry as to the nature of the mediatorial office, to which the Atonement of the Cross belongs. In pursuing that inquiry we note at once that the most prominent feature in all conceptions of the doctrine of the Atonement is its universality. It was for 'the world;' and for the world in all ages from the beginning to the end of time; when it was studied deeply, it was seen to have been 'ordained before the foundation of the world,' and in the efficacy of His death Christ Himself was said to have been 'slain from the foundation of the world.' But in man it has been already shown that the power of mediation for others, while it obviously varies in degree with the closeness of unity, in blood, in actual life, and in spirit, between us and them, yet is in all cases limited—often incapable of touching more than their circumstances—always incapable of changing their spiritual state except by their consent. For, of course, no unity between man and man can be perfect: there is, and it is well that there should be, much in each individual soul which no other soul can touch. If so, how is it that in the Atonement, and therefore in the mediatorial power of Christ, there is no limitation—that it can touch all alike, that it can change, even before the consent of the will, the spiritual condition of man, and so open a way for return to the love of God? To this inquiry an answer can be given only by the knowledge of the nature of Christ Himself, and therefore of His whole life, before He came and since He departed from the earth. Who, again, can give this but He Himself?

Now here, again, it is clear that such teaching was

[7] See Part I. c. viii.

largely given by Him. But we may confine our attention to one special instance of it, not only because of its terse and unmistakable clearness, but because it marks plainly that connection of ideas which has been here suggested. It forms a part of the record by St. John of the farewell discourses to the apostles on the eve of the Passion, which, it will be noticed, with singular truth to nature, say little or nothing of the death itself, but carry the thoughts away, mostly to an illimitable future, sometimes to an illimitable past. For of His coming death there was no need to speak; at last their unwilling souls had received it; they knew well that it was to be, and was to be for them. But the very thought of the mysterious meaning of that death absolutely compelled the inquiring mind to go beyond it, before and after. If this was true, much more must also be true. It is always through the great practical truth of an atonement for sin and a salvation from sin that the still deeper mysteries of the divine nature are pressed closely on the faith of man. Accordingly, of those mysteries it was His pleasure to open at least glimpses in the last teaching of His dying hours. Not till then had the time come; hitherto much had been implied, now all was to be explicit. 'I came forth,' He said, 'from the Father, and am come into the world; again I leave the world and go to the Father.'

<small>Christ's declaration of His own nature.</small>

Of these two declarations it is obvious that, as indeed was natural, the latter was first taken up. For in preaching Christ, the one point of immediate importance was to know, not what He had been in the eternal past, but what He actually was at the very moment when His apostles came out to proclaim Him as a living Saviour to the world. The whole claim of allegiance for Him depended on the fact that He 'had been dead, but was alive for evermore,' and held accordingly for all mankind 'the keys of death and hell.' Moreover, on this side of the doctrine of His true nature they could be led some stages towards the whole truth by a twofold evidence—an evidence in the past and an evidence in the present. There was an evidence in the past. They could declare that they had seen Him with their own eyes not only rise from the dead, but ascend up through the everlasting doors, in fulfilment of the great

<small>The Ascension and session in glory.</small>

Messianic promise of the 110th Psalm, there to 'sit on the right hand of God.' From the very first, in their witness of what they had seen and heard, they were never weary of dwelling, principally indeed on the Resurrection, but secondarily on the Ascension, as inseparable from it, and as indeed the only conceivable completion of the new life of their Master. We even note that, as the teaching of the Gospel became more fully developed, the proportion (so to speak) of the prominence of these two inseparable truths was reversed, and the Ascension and the life in heaven which it began were strongly emphasised, while the Resurrection was taken for granted.[8] For the Ascension at least had been seen by the eyes of men, and the reality of the life of Christ in heaven followed necessarily from it. To this evidence in the past, moreover, there was added a fresh evidence in the present. They believed that in vision their glorified Master had actually revealed Himself from heaven—to St. Stephen in the hour of martyrdom, to St. Paul in the great crisis of conversion, above all to St. John in the revelation at Patmos, which entirely centres round Christ as exalted to the right hand of God. But over and above these visions they realised in the present gift of grace and of miraculous power a continual and convincing sign of the exaltation of their Master in heaven, and a means by which He was then actually exercising His spiritual royalty and completing His mediatorial work. The rule over the Churches, which the Apocalypse pictured in vivid detail, they realised broadly in daily experience. 'Being exalted at the right hand of God, He shed forth this,' which both they and the world could 'see and know.' Hence they felt that in declaring that 'He had left the world and gone to the Father,' they could appeal to strong and tangible evidence. Therefore it was plainly natural that of the two eternities between which the earthly life of Jesus Christ was held to be the link, the preaching of Christianity should first dwell on the latter.

But here also, as of the actual exaltation of Christ in heaven, so more especially of the future judgment which was to be its close, and to which, while content to paint the

[8] This is notably the case in the Epistles to the Philippians, Ephesians, and Colossians, and the Epistle to the Hebrews.

present glory of His kingdom in dim majestic outline, they constantly recurred with the greatest plainness and vividness of certainty, the doctrine is ultimately a doctrine of faith. From the time that the cloud received Him out of their sight, they knew nothing, except in occasional visions and continual spiritual effect, of His mediatorial work. Of a judgment to come they might share with all others who believe in righteousness and in God that universal anticipation, so strong that it rises to moral certainty, which has stamped itself on human consciousness in all ages; and, in proportion as they had learnt beyond all others to know righteousness and to see God in the face of Jesus Christ, that anticipation would assume in their minds an unusual vividness and solidity. They might enter into the moral beauty and comfort of the declaration which He had made to them—that the judgment of man is rightly committed to the Son of Man. They might also see clearly that the final judgment in perfect righteousness was the only adequate completion of the universal royalty and mediation which they had learnt to ascribe to their Master. But again, in order to rise from vague conceptions to definite knowledge of the work of Christ in heaven, from anticipations that judgment might be and ought to be, to a certainty that it shall be, they had but one means then, as we have but one means now. That means is simple faith in the word of Him who said: 'I ascend to My Father and your Father,' 'The Son of Man shall come to judge both the quick and the dead.' No doubt, as in all such cases, they went on, under the teaching of thought and experience, to draw out in various aspects the full meaning of that declaration. The whole belief in His Intercession in its largest sense, the conception of the mediatorial kingdom as lasting till all enemies are subdued, and then to be surrendered to the Father, the character and principles of the final judgment and its relation to the judgment constantly going on in this life—all this would grow upon them under the guidance of the Holy Spirit, and constantly yield fresh lights of spiritual significance. But the foundation was still the same; whatever was built up could rest only on the word of Jesus Christ.

III. But what is true of this part of the doctrine of Christ's true nature is still more true of that other eternity of the past, which preceded the incarnation at Bethlehem. For of that no glimpse could reach human sight; no sign, except the angelic vision to the shepherds at Bethlehem and the previous annunciations from heaven, marked out the birth of the Lord as anything essentially different from the birth of any mere human child. How could man know whether He was or what He was from the beginning, except from His own word? That He is now very man, like us in all things except sin, the first preachers of Christ might declare of their own knowledge. They knew this by the experience of His life on earth, by what they had seen and heard and their hands had handled; they knew it by a different experience, yet still a tangible experience, of His life after He rose again; they had seen how in a true humanity He had passed into heaven, and they concluded without doubt that in that humanity He was living then, and should come at the last day. All the early fancies of a merely phantasmal humanity in Him, as one of many emanations from the divine nature, and the more elaborate conceptions, which finally took form in Arian heresy, of an intermediate nature in Him neither divine nor human, could not stand thoughtful examination of the meaning of this undoubted experience. Certainly He was true man, and on his true humanity depended His power to save. But was He before the incarnation in this human flesh, and if He was, what was He from the beginning?

The pre-existence of Christ

These deep questions, perhaps, hardly forced themselves explicitly upon Christianity at the first; yet at all times their substance was implied. I have already sketched out briefly the actual order of the manifestation of Christ. In St. Peter's teaching, as has been shown, alike in the Acts and in the first Epistle which bears his name, the great central idea is Christ risen and ascended into heaven, still, in glory as in humiliation, the Mediator between God and man even to the end of time. The same thought, with the clearer vision of future judgment, runs clothed in sublime imagery through all the manifold glory of the visions of the Apocalypse. Yet it is significant that

implied in the teaching of the Ascension.

in these very books of Scripture the idea of Him as 'foreordained before the foundation of the world,' as 'slain' in God's foreknowledge 'from the foundation of the world,' as being not only the Omega but the Alpha, the beginning and the end, the first and the last, comes out by necessity, not as yet in the foreground, but in the solemn background of thought.[9]

So, again, in St. Paul's teaching, the same principle is more strikingly exemplified. In all the earlier Epistles it is *implied in the mediation;* (as he himself says) on Christ crucified, and on all the unspeakable preciousness of His Atonement, that he delights to dwell. Yet from that standing-ground in the present he has to look backward as well as forward, to the eternal predestination of God as well as to the final accomplishment of His will in Christ. Accordingly, as time goes on, and as the faith in the Atonement victoriously asserts itself against all doubts and limitations, we see how, in his later Epistles, both the past and the future assume a more decided prominence. On the one hand (as has already been said) Christ in heaven, our life hid in Him, His headship over His Church and over all created beings even to the end, are brought out again and again.[1] But on the other hand we hear now of Christ as 'the first-born before all creation,' 'the Creator of all things,' 'the image of the invisible God,' in whom 'the fulness of the Godhead existed' before all time.[2] These great ideas are now necessarily brought out, and always through faith in that universal Mediation, of which His atoning death is the great visible act.

Finally, in St. John, the process, here seen in its growth, comes to maturity. In the preface to his Gospel, as less *set forth in itself.* distinctly in his First Epistle, his revelation is emphatically of Christ as in eternal being before the world. The very name the 'Word of God,' inseparable from the Father, marks out (as we have seen) that eternal unity with God which 'Sonship of God' might not make unmistakably clear. The attributes ascribed to 'the Word,' being manifestly Divine, bring out explicitly what that name

---

[9] See 1 Pet. i. 20; Rev. xiii. 8.
[1] See Eph. i. 20-23; Phil. ii. 9-11; Col. ii. 9-15; iii. 1-4.
[2] See Col. i. 15-17; ii. 9; Phil. ii. 5, 6.

implies. The answer to the question whether He was and that He was before the incarnation, stands forth at last in startling clearness: 'He was in the beginning; He was with God, and was God.'

But what was the foundation of this declaration, either in the earlier or later forms?

It is true, indeed, as I have already endeavoured to show, that it is an inevitable conclusion from acceptance of the other great doctrines of Christ, —His universal royalty and His universal Mediation. But the idea that this deduction was drawn simply by one or other of the apostles for himself—that (to use the old phrase), it is the teaching of 'Paul or John, not Jesus'—if it can be held by any one who studies any apostolic writing in itself, is scattered to the winds by the mingled variety and unity of the whole apostolic testimony. There could be but one ultimate foundation on which all alike would be content to build—the word of Christ Himself. In respect of that word Scripture draws no hard and fast line between what He actually spoke on earth with His own lips, and what He revealed to the apostles by the Holy Spirit. But if we ask, as in this inquiry we must ask, for His own word, we shall not ask in vain. The declaration 'I came from the Father' is no isolated or exceptional declaration.

The founda- tion of all in His word.

Of His teaching on earth, be it remembered, we know but a part, and the Evangelist who has recorded most declares expressly that it is but a small part. That unrecorded teaching is not, indeed, absolutely lost to us; for we must trace its effect in the varied fulness of the apostolic teaching in the hereafter, when, having perhaps been ill-understood and easily forgotten at the time, it flashed back again on the mind under the grace of the Holy Spirit. But in St. John's Gospel there is, as he himself declared, fully sufficient of the word of Christ on which to rest our faith. I know, indeed, that the genuineness of that record is questioned, and that on its substance contempt has been poured by some who venerate the Christ of the Gospel history. But independently of the strong external evidence which has been so abundantly adduced—independently even of the internal evidence of the narrative part of

The Gospel of St. John.

the Gospel, which is at least as strong—I must confess that, looking at these sayings themselves in their substance, it is to me fairly inconceivable how any one can fancy them to be utterances of the theology of the second century, or to be philosophic teachings of St. John himself, audaciously put into the mouth of His Divine Master—how any one, studying them deeply, can fail to recognise a marvellous unity of profound truth running through them, which is, as truly as the recorded life of Christ, utterly above the power of human speculation to devise. They carry their own evidence with them. In them we find explicitly brought out what the whole tenour of the apostolic teaching implies to have existed—a self-revelation of the Lord Jesus Christ, not as in the older Synoptic narratives, by action and life, but by distinct and unambiguous words.

What that self-revelation is, the slightest study of the Fourth Gospel declares plainly. To estimate it adequately the Gospel must be regarded as a whole; to choose out great passages and isolate them, as if they could rightly stand alone, is to sin against the pervading unity of conception of which they are but salient points. Still, if for the sake of brevity we confine our thoughts to a few notable utterances, the character of the self-revelation of the Lord stands out with unequivocal and even startling distinctness.

The main points of His teaching.

In the early stages of the ministry the emphasis is laid on His peculiar Sonship of God; as the 'only-begotten Son,' infinitely above all mere created beings, into whose 'hands all things are given,' and to believe on whom is ' to have everlasting life.'[3] Next follows the declaration of His unceasing work, paralleled with the sleepless beneficence of God's Providence, of His possession of the Divine attribute of inherent life, and of His power to give life in the present and resurrection in the future to all who hear His voice.[4] Then, after the feeding of the five thousand and the promise of a spiritual communion with Him to all who shall eat His flesh and drink His blood, which is an eternal life,[5] the self-revelation rises to a climax at the Feast of Tabernacles at

[3] John iii. 16–18, 35, 36. [4] John v. 17–29.
[5] John vi. 53, 54.

Jerusalem. It is not enough that He is set forth as the giver of the Holy Spirit and the Light of the whole world, as One who is 'from above,' exalted not in degree of dignity, but in nature, over the great lawgiver and the great father of Israel. At last the incommunicable name of Godhead is claimed by Him, 'Before Abraham was born, I AM.'[6] Beyond this nothing could go; henceforth His teaching seems rather designed to guard against all conceptions of Ditheism, by emphasising His subordination to the Father and His unity with the Father, and His perfect unity with all men as being to them the resurrection and the life.[7] Only at the last to His disciples on the eve of the Passion, all that was brought out in startling and vivid distinctness by that one great declaration is wrought out in calm beauty and solemnity of detail. His Mediation, as 'the Way, the Truth, and the Life,' His perfect unity with the Father, through which 'they who had seen Him had seen the Father,' through which (as is reiterated again and again in varying tones) He 'is in the Father and the Father in Him,' glorified with the Divine glory before the foundation of the world, able to gather up all men into Himself, and so into the very communion of the Godhead[8]—these are the thoughts which seem to grow one out of the other in the outpouring of His love to them at the time of farewell, and roll on and on, as in the fulness of a divine music, exalting and inspiring their souls with conceptions which belong to the secrets of heaven.

All this is not only clear beyond all possibility of doubt and error, but it bears upon it, in the sublimity of the whole conception, in the calmness of its authoritative certainty, in the fundamental unity of ultimate truth, which comes out in the unsystematic and inartificial variety of the successive utterances, in the spiritual force which tells in every word, not upon the mind only, but on all the higher faculties of our nature—what (but for objection and cavil) we might have thought irresistible evidence of the genuineness of a Divine utterance. Let it be compared—I will not say with any utterances of the Chris-

Their character and signification.

[6] John vii. viii.   [7] John x. 15-18, 30; xi. 25, 26.
[8] John xiv.-xvii.

tianity of the second century, but even with the apostolic teaching itself in all its various forms of conscious inspiration. It will be seen to be absolutely different in kind. Impatience might stop the ears of men at so startling a declaration, and bid them take up stones to cast at the blasphemer. But if it were once listened to with that reverent attention which the character of the speaker demands, the old saying must be uttered again and again: 'Never man spake like this man.' 'These are the words of eternal life;' 'Who can speak them but the Son of the living God?'

Moreover, in these words, and in these only, can we find the ultimate foundation of that great fabric of thought which the apostolic teaching undoubtedly raised. It is not hard to understand how such words should have lain, at most but half-understood, in the silent recesses of memory, till the light of the Holy Spirit, under long experience of Christian thought and life, should flash upon them, and kindle them to a living reality and a significance before unknown. It is not strange to us to notice how the style of the sayings themselves indicates that they had passed through the mind of the Evangelist, perhaps in form affected by it, perhaps having themselves stamped upon it its characteristic impress. But when the time came for the declaration of the ultimate truth, it is inconceivable that St. John should have gone back to anything else than the word of his Master—the word which had all along been the inspiration of the whole apostolic teaching, but which had treasures yet to be yielded to the demand of a critical time, and to the necessity for completion of the Christian revelation.

Their ultimate authority.

Here, again, the same law meets us. This ultimate truth has its preparation and verification. It is plain to all thoughtful consideration that up to this declaration all the teaching of the Gospel has been gradually leading, and that in the doctrine thus declared all the various inductions of our natural theology find their only adequate satisfaction. Experience has proved that only by a firm grasp of it is Christianity able to maintain a permanent vitality, as a divine philosophy, a moral force, and a spiritual life. But still the truth itself is a doctrine of faith. It is absolutely impossible to find any firm basis for it, except in the word of the Lord Himself.

IV. Nor, even now, is the whole cycle complete. For in this revelation of the nature of Christ is implied also that declaration of the ultimate nature of Godhead which Christians call the mystery of the Holy Trinity. I have already quoted the striking passage in the creed called 'Athanasian,' which declares that, while the belief in one God belongs to 'the Catholic religion'—the true religion of all places and all times—yet that the profounder doctrine of a Trinity, from which some turn away as if it were far removed from all practical religion, is forced upon us by 'the Christian verity'—that is, by the declaration of the true nature of the Lord Jesus Christ. This saying is obviously true. We should search in vain through Scripture for any such formal and systematic declaration on the nature of the Godhead as that which the creed puts forth with such masterly grasp and precision. Perhaps, when we study the disputes and strifes of which that creed is the final issue, we are startled and almost shocked by subtle refinements of metaphysical theory, advanced unhesitatingly and fought for as matters of life or death, on that dim mysterious ground. But in Scripture, as in the earliest creeds, the Christian verity necessarily brings out substantially, and as it were in separation, the elements of that great doctrine.

The doctrine of the Trinity.

For, first, as we have seen, it manifests clearly the nature of the Son of God. What can be the nature of One who was, and is, and is to come, dwelling with God and in God—drawing to Himself as Mediator all the countless millions of human souls, of which no one can absolutely know or rule another? Whatever terms are used, substantially there can be but one answer, 'It is and must be Divine.' Arianism, the last refuge of dying paganism, sought to find another answer, adorned its answer with all the grandest titles of honour which could be heaped upon a created being, and urged it as the escape from a mystery which no man can penetrate. But yet that answer was sought, adorned, and urged in vain. Backed by all the power and the philosophy of the world, it yet died of its own

The doctrine of the Son.

hollowness; the truth which it impugned stood alone against the world and triumphed by its own solidity. Forced to a clear expression of its own meaning, it declared that the nature of Him who was thus Universal and the Eternal, must be 'of one substance with the Father,' 'very God of very God.'

But side by side with this doctrine, we observe that another also gradually emerges in Scripture into full distinctness. In the form of baptism traced up to the apostolic times,[9] in the blessing which St. Paul,[1] in an Epistle universally accepted as genuine, has taught the Church, in the natural evolution of Christian thought which manifests itself again and again, now in practical exhortation, now in teaching of the relation of the soul to God, now in the doxologies of adoration[2]—we discern clearly the doctrine of the Holy Ghost. Whence could that doctrine in its fulness come?

The doctrine of the Holy Ghost

It is perfectly true, as has been already suggested, that the conception of the action of a Divine Spirit upon human spirits belongs to the advanced stages of all religions. For it bridges over the gulf between the *Non ego* and the *Ego*, the great world without and the little world within. Thus it affords the only adequate conception of the universal sovereignty of God; for it extends His sway over the inner as over the outer life of His creatures. Yet it is the only suggestion of a possible reconcilement between the freedom of human will and this supreme will of God; for we are familiar with the power of will over will, exercised by spiritual influence in substantial reality, and yet absolutely different from an iron law of compulsion. It gives a complete explanation of those laws of human life and history, which show that, amidst all the infinite variations of human natures and wills, there is a great unity in the action of humanity as a whole. Yet, again, it is certainly the only explanation of that individual consciousness which the 139th Psalm so grandly describes, of a Divine presence acting with personal power upon the soul, searching, guiding, teaching, rebuking it, as it were face to face. Necessarily,

(a) in natural theology;

---

[9] Matt. xxviii. 19.   [1] 2 Cor. xiii. 14.
[2] Rom. viii. 26, 27; 1 Cor. xii. 3, 4; Eph. ii. 18; iv. 3, 4, 30.

therefore, the belief in the influence of a Divine Spirit on the soul establishes itself as a part of all vital religion.

It is clear, again, to every one who reads the Old Testament, that here, as in other cases, the ancient revelation to Israel brings out clearly and with certainty, as a well-known religious truth, all, and more than all, which thus gradually suggested itself to the deeper thoughts and aspirations of man. No one can read the declarations of Prophecy, or the responsive outpouring of devotion in the Psalms, or the meditative recognition of a Spirit of God in man, which runs through the Sapiential books,[3] without seeing this so plainly written there that he who runs may read it.

(b) in the Old Testament.

In all this there is, as before, a preparation for the conception of the full truth. But it is still very far from expressing it in the Christian sense. For in the Christian exposition of that truth is implied, as we know, not only a far clearer and more universal notion of this Divine action, but the conception of a Divine Personality—the belief in the Holy Ghost as a Divine Person proceeding from the Father, co-equal and co-eternal with the Father and the Son. In that doctrine we ascend (to use the distinction already referred to) from the 'earthly things'—the manifestations of the action of a Divine Spirit in the soul—to the 'heavenly things' of the actual nature of the Godhead. Certainly not less than this is involved in the time-honoured form of Christian baptism, which is obviously an absurdity on a mere Sabellian hypothesis. As the other great sacrament stamped on Christianity the doctrine of the Atonement, which involves the true conception of the nature of the Lord Jesus Christ, so this proclaims on the very threshold of the Christian covenant the belief in the Holy Ghost. On what could such a belief be based? The only possible answer, as in the other case, is that it rests on the word of the Lord Himself. The very idea that so profound a doctrine could have been made by any lower

(c) in the word of Christ;

---

[3] The conception of the Divine Wisdom, as a personal manifestation of Godhead, leads up to the doctrine of the Word; the conception of the Divine Wisdom, as inspiring the soul with the notion of true wisdom in man, prepares for the doctrine of the Holy Spirit.

authority the key of entrance into His kingdom is incompatible with the most rudimentary ideas of the nature of Christianity. The Gospel narrative of St. Matthew gives us, therefore, the only account of the origin of that baptismal formula which it is possible to accept, when it makes it a part of His last charge to His disciples on the eve of His departure from them—the charter in all main points of the kingdom of the future. But even so the account is still imperfect. For so profound a formula, so startling to Jewish minds trained from childhood in the all-absorbing sense of the unity of the Godhead, must have needed some explanation from the same voice which ordained it as a perpetual heirloom for the Church even to the end of time. Yet in the Synoptic narratives we find none. Here, accordingly, as so often in other cases, the 'supplemental Gospel' of St. John comes in to supply the missing link in the chain of teaching. To the farewell discourses of his Master on the eve of the Passion he went back in memory under the light of a fuller inspiration; in them he found, and in them he preserved for the Church, the only adequate foundation of the truth thus impressed on Christianity. For in these discourses it is not only the grace of the Holy Ghost which is described. In every word a distinct personality is disclosed, as real and living as the personality of Him who spoke. The revelation is of the Paraclete, 'who proceedeth from the Father,' 'whom I will send you from the Father, who shall testify of me,' and by whose coming 'I will come to you' again, and 'leave you not orphaned' in the world.[4] The doctrine so revealed is again a doctrine of faith. We see how marvellously it completes and establishes all the earlier teachings, whether of human consciousness or ancient revelation; we cannot but feel how it supplies that which is needed for the full harmony of Christian truth; accepting it as true, we can by spiritual experience assure ourselves of the fulfilment of our Lord's promise of the Paraclete. But still it is by faith that we accept it. For it comes out of the mystery of that heavenly region to which no power of human reason or aspiration can ascend; and therefore it

[4] See John xiv.–xvi.

can be known only through One to whom that region is a familiar home.

In these two great declarations of divine personality in the Son and in the Holy Spirit, taken in conjunction with the constant manifestation of the Father—accepted always under the fundamental truth of the unity of the Godhead which is the soul of all true religion, and which pervades the Old Testament in every line—is implied the whole doctrine of the Holy Trinity. It is most instructive to notice that in Scripture the doctrine is conveyed only in this implicit form—emphasising the truth of the reality of the three divine Persons, and taking for granted the truth of unity of Godhead, rather than placing the two truths in formal systematic antithesis and explicitly declaring the mystery of their coexistence.[5] We see without surprise that in this all the earliest creeds follow the line of the first Scriptural teaching, and in no case adopt the systematic explicitness which rules in the later document called the 'Athanasian Creed.' For, indeed, it is only in this form that it could subdue the world to itself; only thus can it come home to every man, through his own actual spiritual experience of the divine Fatherhood, the divine Salvation, and the divine Inspiration, in all of which he lives day by day. In this department of truth, as in all others, formal scientific exposition is for the few; the informal substance of truth and its practical results are for the many. Still the truth in its elements is there, and the doctrine itself is simply the comprehensive exhibition of all that has been implied in those lesser doctrines of faith which have been already described. The truth of the Atonement, the eternal existence of the Christ before and after His brief manifestation on earth, the divine personality of the Comforter—all lead up to this ultimate mystery of faith.

It is, indeed, interesting and not difficult to show how the three great ideas of religion are: God over man as the

---

[5] The well-known passage (1 John v. 7), 'There are three that bear record in Heaven, the Father, the Word, and the Holy Ghost; and these Three are One,' independently of all MS. authority, is condemned as spurious by the systematic explicitness of its form.

Creator and the Father of all; God in man by a divine image stamped upon man's nature, giving him the spirit of sonship and the power of communion with God; God in man, again, as working by His Spirit on the individual spirits so made in His likeness, to develope in them the seed of the divine nature, and to harmonise them freely with the divine will. It is profoundly interesting to trace out accordingly shadows of some divine Trinity in Platonic philosophy or in Eastern religion, which are, so to speak, the gatherings into more definite shape of these great ideas latent in the souls of men. All this can be done, and not unprofitably done. It brings out —to modify a well-known saying—the *testimonium mentis naturaliter Christianæ*. It shows us how it is that the great Christian mystery, just because it is complex, as contrasted with the naked simplicity of bare Monotheism, lays hold of human nature and human life in all the richness of their manifold energy. Perhaps still more interesting, and certainly less vague and difficult, it is to trace out in the Old Testament, under the shadow of the divine unity which pervades the whole in every line, some indications (perhaps only visible after the event) of the doctrine of the Son and the Spirit. For this, again, shows how in all lines of development, Christianity is really from the beginning, and how all lesser revelations work up towards the final and absolute revelation in Jesus Christ.

The witness of Natural Religion.

The witness of the Old Testament.

But when all this has been done, still it is more and more obviously true that, if we would know on what we have to rest at last, we must come back to the word of Jesus Christ, and trace the inevitable development from it of this ultimate mystery. From the first teaching of the Atonement all follows in necessary order. I do not, of course, mean that in every soul which believes the word of Christ and trusts in His Cross, the whole process of religious thought must be gone through. It is a characteristic of faith, and indeed it is the characteristic which gives it power to overcome the world, that wherever it is real, even if it be theoretically imperfect, it can supply the strength of action and kindle the fire of love. But in the Church as a whole, the thoughtfulness of faith ought not to stop half-way. It

The word of Christ

must draw out all that is implied. Certainly it is notable that, wherever faith has entered deeply into the mystery of the Atonement, it has always gone on till it rested at last on the final belief in the Holy Trinity; and that whenever that final belief has been ignored or rejected, then, slowly but surely, all faith in the Atonement has crumbled away, till the Passion becomes only the noblest of martyrdoms, and He who endured it only the greatest of the sons of men. Thus, indeed, history itself justifies that scientific process of theology which is so often unwisely decried, and of which the Athanasian Creed is the most famous embodiment. It is well to hold the truth in unsystematic and living reality for our own spiritual life; but, if its meaning be challenged from without—if its relation to other truth, religious or metaphysical, be scrutinised—if rationalistic attempts be made to pare off this or that element of it, in order to compress it within the limits of logical system—then it is the duty of the Church to face all these requirements in dependence simply and solely on the word of her Master, and, having drawn out that word in full precision of meaning, to declare 'this is the Catholic faith.' *drawn out by Christian theology.*

V. In these great doctrines, up to which all Christian teaching leads, and which indirectly all Christian morality implies, we see clearly the function of faith. Nowhere is it disconnected with reason, and with the conclusions as to the nature of God and man, at which, with more or less of certitude, it arrives. Nowhere does it refuse the verification of spiritual experience in mind and conscience and heart, by those who have accepted its great principles, and tried how they will bear the difficulties and satisfy the needs of human life. But yet it claims to go far beyond the farthest point to which reason can hope to advance, simply by a personal trust in the word of One whom we know to be of God by manifest proofs; and equally it declares that even the verification of experience will be but partial, true as far as it goes, but utterly incapable of sounding all the depths of that which is revealed to faith. It is absolutely necessary that we should understand this in declaring to questioners what is the real foundation of our Christianity. It is not less necessary to understand it *Conclusion.*

for our own guidance, when we are pondering the deeper things of our theology; in order to know where we may hope to draw our scientific conclusions by appeal to reason and conscience, to experience and history, and where we must be content with the simplicity of faith, not comprehending fully the truth, although we know deeply Him who declares it, and therefore resisting the temptation of claiming already to grasp in perfect systematic knowledge what we can never know fully, unless perhaps on the other side of the grave.

At this point it is obvious that Christianity stands out in antagonism to the exclusive and unbounded claims of science as the one sole guide to truth, even while it looks gladly and thankfully on its accumulation of knowledge along the various lines of thought. If science declares that it can find no proof of the universal Atonement and the universal Judgment, of the true nature of the Godhead and its relation to humanity in Jesus Christ, Christianity will feel neither surprise nor apprehension. For on these things it appeals to a power which every student of human nature must acknowledge to be one of the truest and greatest in the world—the power of faith. In the contemplation of the life of Jesus Christ it is content to find the grounds of an absolute faith in Him, crowning all the lesser developments of faith of which human history is full. When it surveys the actual effects which that faith has wrought, not for the few but for the many—teaching the mind to know what passes knowledge, inspiring the moral nature with a strength made perfect in weakness, raising the spirit to a communion with God which it feels to be a life eternal,—it is not ashamed of blazoning faith upon its banner, and doubts not to find in it 'the victory which overcomes the world.'

CHAPTER IX.

CONCLUSION.

IT remains now once more to recapitulate the various points of the argument presented in these pages, and to bring out through them the leading idea, for which I venture to claim attention.

The main point on which throughout I desire to lay stress is the consideration of the right principle and order of the study of Christian evidence, and of the relation which it holds to actual Christian faith.

In the examination of the nature and force of Christian evidences, I have endeavoured to pursue that which appears to me to be a 'natural method,' as contradistinguished from the more artificial and abstract systems, under which they are perhaps more commonly viewed. For, in accordance with the apparent intention of the founder of this lectureship, I have had in these lectures a practical object—to offer, if it may be, some aid to the inquiring mind, as it ponders on the all-important issue between faith and unbelief. Now to such a mind the great question presents itself in one of two forms. Either it is strictly individual—the question, 'Why am I, or why should I be, a Christian?' Or perhaps, in form somewhat more general—'In what light does Christianity present itself to this nineteenth century, and on what grounds does it now claim allegiance for its Master?' It is (I think) our wisdom to examine the question in these forms, in which it presses forcibly upon us, rather than to treat it in the abstract, throwing off all connection with our own actual life and history, as if we were examining it *de novo* in the first century, or studying a purely scientific and theological conception, independent of all associations of time or place. The

The 'natural method' of study.

substitution of natural for artificial systems, of historical examination for abstract theory, is in many directions one special lesson of modern thought. I venture to plead for it as specially appropriate to this all-important study. For here we have to do with what is, by the nature of the case, a practical and personal question. The very protest of Christianity against a merely agnostic scepticism depends on its claiming to be not a theory, but a life.

I. Now, in looking at the question under this form, the first consideration which should present itself to us is the historical existence of the Scripture and the Church of Christ for eighteen centuries, in virtue of which we inherit our Christianity from the past, and receive it in each generation by traditional teaching. This is the process by which all the most precious treasures of humanity, in science and art, law and civilisation, become ours; it would be strange if in religion alone there were a contradiction to the universal law. The very fact of an unbroken vitality and a dominant power for so many centuries gives a first prescriptive claim to attention, which it is in no true sense prejudice to acknowledge. From this we must, of course, go on to ponder it and test it ourselves by all the various faculties of our nature. Yet all that is necessary, perhaps all that is possible, for the mass of men, is simply to try by experience, whether, as a religion, Christianity exercises such a power as it professes to exercise, over mind and heart and spirit, exalting whatever is good and noble in us, conquering whatever is base and sensual, and opening a way to a living knowledge of self, of man, and of God. By such practical knowledge alone do all great truths come home to the minds of men generally. On such practical knowledge, therefore, they need not be ashamed to rest their religious belief. It is not reasonable, in this case alone, to call upon every man to solve all difficulties, to examine for himself the ground of all doctrines, to regard all second-hand knowledge as necessarily valueless, and all deference to authority as a superstition. No Christianity is worth the name, which does not bring its religious inheritance to a practical test of reality. But a Christianity may be perfectly real and perfectly reasonable, which goes no further

[margin: Tradition and practical experience.]

than this in the path of investigation, content with this personal experience of a real light and grace in the Gospel, and, for the rest, living by simple faith.

II. But if, by necessity or by choice, we inquire further into the grounds of belief, proceeding accordingly to a more scientific and abstract examination of Christianity— with a view to give to ourselves or to others a distinct reason for the hope which is already ours by inheritance and practical appropriation—the next consideration which ordinarily suggests itself is the relation between Christianity and the 'natural religion' which, under various forms, unquestionably asserts itself as a universal consciousness in man. What is the relation between the Gospel, as a revelation, and the various conclusions to which we are led with more or less of definiteness, by intellect and imagination, conscience and affection, when we search into the true nature of the world and of man, and ask whether we can ascend to the knowledge of the Supreme Power which is over both? If we conclude that this power is a mere law, or a diffused presence, or a power unknown and unknowable—if (that is) we embrace the Materialistic or Pantheistic hypothesis, or fall back in despair on Agnosticism—we can, of course, have nothing to do with Christianity, except, perhaps (though even this should properly be doubtful), with its morality. The Gospel must destroy such hypotheses before it can win a hearing. Perhaps, in fact, when such hypotheses are overthrown, their overthrow is due much oftener to the concrete power of Christianity, embraced at once and as a whole, than to abstract Theistic reasoning. But if, working out into definiteness the universal religious instinct of man, we believe that Supreme Power to be a living and personal God, we have taken the first step towards establishing an accordance between our belief and Christianity.[1] From this, consciously or unconsciously, we are apt to pursue something like the train of thought which I have endeavoured to sketch out in the First Part of this volume. In this, our natural belief, we are sensible at once of truth and of imperfection. Our life passes through

The harmony of Christianity with natural religion.

[1] On this subject see the Boyle Lectures for 1876. 'What is Natural Theology?'

alternations of light and darkness, of knowledge and ignorance, of communion with God and alienation from Him. Most of all, we feel painfully the mystery of evil in all its forms, and cry out for deliverance from it. We ask accordingly, What can Christianity do to help us here? If it be what it professes to be, it must at once confirm and perfect what we know, and give us light on what we need to know, and yet cannot know for ourselves. Does it actually do this? We study its Scriptures, with these questions ever present to our minds, and watch how they gradually unfold to us the great principles of Christian doctrine. If, as we do so, we come to the conclusion, which I have ventured to urge, that Christianity clenches by authority the great convictions of natural theology as to the personality of God and the spirituality of man, and at the same time throws a light sufficient for all practical purposes on the mystery of evil,—if it thus shows itself both 'natural and supernatural,' agreeing perfectly with all that we know or probably conclude, and yet boldly declaring to us what we do not know, opening to us the deeper mysteries of this life, and leading us on to the heavenly regions of communion with God, where the slow and cautious foot of reason dares not tread—then a second great step has been taken, which to many minds is again all-sufficient. To them 'Christianity is its own evidence,' by its accordance with the voice of God in the soul, and its power to go infinitely beyond what that voice declares; and they do not care to search any further.

III. But it is obvious that Christianity is not content with a place of mere superiority of degree to the authority of reason or the various religions of men. We find that it claims for its Master a dignity absolutely unique and divine, and an authority differing from all others not in degree, but in kind. This is, no doubt, a 'hard saying,' which many refuse to hear altogether, and which must necessarily establish some strong grounds for acceptance by the thoughtful mind. It may, therefore, be necessary to go further by asking what those grounds are. I do not think it reasonable in such further advance to put aside altogether the results of previous consideration—the significance of the historical existence and dominance of Christianity, the

The actual power of Christianity.

reality of its practical power to ennoble and purify life, and its accordance, as supernatural, with all natural truth. These convictions must go with us; they necessarily affect the examination of the positive evidences which the Gospel presents to our investigation and judgment; for they unquestionably tell us beforehand that we are dealing with no phenomenon of ordinary experience, but with something which we may expect to lie beyond the sphere of such experience in itself, as, in its effects, it is certainly unique in the history of the world. But still we go on to consider these positive evidences. How do they present themselves to us? In what order should we examine them?

Now, in taking this next step, I deprecate[2] the not unfrequent attempt to go back at once in thought for eighteen centuries, and to endeavour vainly to reproduce to ourselves the impression which the Christianity of the first century made on the world, by its signs of visible miracle, by its argument from fulfilment of prophecy, and by its presentation to the eyes of men of the actual life of Jesus Christ, as seen by themselves or testified by living eye-witnesses. It is not only that the attempt must necessarily be vain, but the method seems to involve a kind of anachronism in idea, and to be directly at variance with the principles of the first preaching itself, which invariably started from the present, and then proceeded to claim for Christ both the past and the future. Our point of view is necessarily changed. What was then present is now past; what was then future is now past or present. It seems equally unreasonable to seek in that which is to us past the vivid power of conviction which it naturally exercised on those for whom it was present, and to neglect all consideration of the historic growth and existence of Christianity, which then could but be anticipated in a vague future, but which to us is known as a past and present reality. Hence I would contend that we should start with the consideration of the actual power of Christianity over the world of our own generation. The sense of the unique character of that power is to us what the sight or witness of miracle was to the early Christians; the con-

[2] See Part II. chap. i.

tinual outpouring of the light and grace of Christ upon the Church holds to us the place of the great miracle of Pentecost, which was indeed its first beginning. The contemplation of the actual historical power of Christianity, ruling over all races and through all generations, has for us much the same significance which the recognition of the fulfilment of prophecy had for older times; for it shows the manifestation of Jesus Christ to be the central point of God's dispensation to man, to which all led up beforehand, and from which all is now derived. We should start with what is thus actually our own now, and so go back to the great manifestation in the past.

Accordingly, the first of positive Christian evidences is the actual power of Christianity—as a divine philosophy, as a moral force, and as a spiritual life.[3] I contend that these phases of its power should first be contemplated separately. In each we see how Christianity recognises the great antithesis of all human consciousness between the *Ego* and the *Non Ego*: first, in respect of the great problem of being, in the reconcilement of individual personality with the unity of the great world without; next, in the moral recognition of individual freedom, responsibility, and rights, in harmony with the unity which binds all creatures in one; lastly, in the spiritual consciousness of a true individuality of being before the presence of the infinite and eternal God. I venture to challenge comparison with rival systems of thought, morality, and religion, in respect of the completeness of this recognition of the whole conditions of the problem. Christianity absolutely declines, for the sake of logical coherency, to sacrifice the consciousness either of the *Ego* or the *Non Ego*—to ignore our own individual being, on the one hand, or, on the other, to forget in our self-consciousness the great realities of nature, man, and God. But next I would urge that we should duly weigh the convergent evidence of truth, which arises from union of all these powers in the one great simple conception of the life of Jesus Christ, as made to us at once 'wisdom and righteousness and sanctification.' We notice how other conceptions which claim our allegiance as having

[3] See Part II. chaps. ii. iii. iv.

the key of life, are in this respect fatally defective. One has a philosophic grandeur of idea, but is destitute of moral and spiritual power. Another confines itself to the moral region of conduct, and steadily refuses all intellectual theory or spiritual enthusiasm. A third would dismiss all religion to an honourable banishment in the shadowy realm of sentiment, disconnecting it entirely from all scientific search into truth, and largely from the moral and social action of life. But if Christianity unites all the three elements in one single fundamental idea, the evidence of truth which arises from this union is necessarily far greater than the more aggregate sum of the evidence derived from each. By the natural law of convergence in evidence it rises to a moral certainty, that we have in the life of Jesus Christ a reality which is absolutely unique in its sovereignty over man's whole life, and which therefore, like all manifestations which are in the largest and truest sense of the word 'miraculous,' impresses at once on the mind a strong presumption that it comes from God.

This consideration comes in natural sequence to those already dwelt upon. It is, indeed, simply an elaboration by deliberate thought of that practical experience of the living power of the Gospel, which is the first condition of a vital Christianity, and at the same time an extension of it from the individual experience within to the collective experience of the world in the ages past and present. It is, moreover, closely connected with the consideration of the relation of the Gospel, as at once natural and supernatural, to all the conclusions of natural religion as drawn by the mind, the conscience, and the spirit. Again, it seems to me that many pause, and not unreasonably pause, here in their examination of the evidence of the authority of Christianity, holding that its vital power is in itself a sufficient proof of a divine origin, and therefore a sufficient ground for faith.

IV. But it must be observed, in the course of this investigation, that under all its aspects, intellectual, moral, and spiritual, Christianity fixes our whole thought on the life of Jesus Christ, as manifested in Himself on earth, and as reproduced in His followers. It is in that we are bidden to find the key to the problem of

The study of the life of Jesus Christ.

being, the moral force of regeneration, and the secret of spiritual communion with God. Under all circumstances, and for all necessities of life, the one thing needful is to 'learn Christ.' Hence in the next stage of thought [4] we simply contemplate the life of Christ, as it is recorded in the Gospels, as it is implied in all apostolic teaching, and as it is embodied in all subsequent Christian life. Again, if we seek to follow a natural order, we should look upon that life, first, as it was seen, and may be seen now, by the world at large, outside the circle of discipleship ; and then as it discloses itself to those who have been wrought upon to take the first step of faith, and join the inner circle, where Christ is seen face to face. But in either case we must look upon it as a whole. Once more applying the same law as before, we must recognise the power in what He did, the wisdom in what He said, and the goodness in what He was, not separately or successively, but in that union by which each illustrates the others, and all together tell on the soul by the irresistible force of convergence.

It is, for example, in the view from a distance that we find the chief function of His miracles as 'signs' and 'works.' Vainly, as it seems to me, is their evidential force set aside by vague *à priori* assumptions of the impossibility of miracles. Nor need we fear the closest scrutiny of the positive evidences of their actual reality. But to understand the true function of miracles we must consider His miracles as simply a part—an effective part, but not the principal part —of His self-manifestation. Even from a distance they are seen to be inseparably connected with the wisdom of His teaching and the holiness of His life. Only in the unity of the threefold manifestation could that life have exercised the actual power over the world, which is shown in the answer of St. Peter at Cæsarea Philippi, and the acclamations of His triumphal entry. Only when that manifestation had been crowned by the supreme miracle of the Resurrection did it show power really to overcome the world.

So, again, it is to the closer view of His life from the circle of discipleship that the 'argument from prophecy' especially

[4] See chaps. v. vi.

belongs. It seems to me fairly impossible, even after the most jealous criticism, to doubt that in Jesus Christ there was the only adequate fulfilment of ancient prophecy, and yet a reality so far transcending its highest utterances that it could not have been evolved from them. So the disciples undoubtedly judged, living in greater nearness to that fulfilment, and therefore recognising it far more vividly, even in its details; so we also, looking at it from a distance, and therefore seeing it chiefly in its great outlines, may judge still. But as the Messianic idea in the Old Testament spread beyond the prophetic element, and pervaded the whole along every line of thought, so the fulfilment of that idea to the disciples depended not only on isolated points of accordance with prophecy, but on the impression which the life of Christ, as a whole, made upon their souls. The stages of that great impression we can distinctly trace, from the conviction that in Him they had 'found the Messias,' to the belief that He had in certainty and fulness 'the words of eternal life;' from this, again, to the magnificent confession wrung from the doubting apostle by the certainty of the Resurrection and all it signified—'My Lord and my God.' We can weigh the significance of that gradually perfected faith in itself and in its power over the world; we can place ourselves in thought with the disciples, and let the presence of Christ gradually tell upon our own souls. So only can we, I think, expect to be able rightly to weigh the evidence of Christianity.

Thus the ultimate step in the examination of the grounds of faith is the study of the life of Jesus Christ in all that He did, in all that He taught, and in all that He was. On this very fact depends, I think, an instructive universality in Christian evidence. For the study of a life is exactly that which is at once the simplest and deepest of studies, open to some knowledge even of the child, and yet involving depths which may try the intuitions of the maturest philosophy. It is the only study, moreover, which enlists all the faculties of our nature in its service—full of interest to the mind, full of inspiration to the conscience, full of satisfaction to the heart. It is the only study which is never obsolete, living on, while forms of thought, systems of law, and even records of collective history, change and pass away. Clearly it is the evidence which befits a religion claiming to embrace every phase of character and knowledge, to include in its allegiance the whole nature of man, and to endure through all vicissitudes till time shall be no more. We give up its real strength and permanence, if we dissect it (so to speak) into various elements, necessarily destroying vitality in the process, and then take any one of them in the abstract, or all of them separately one after another, as if we could thus arrive at the true basis of faith. When we consider it as a living whole, the same contemplation, which is to the believer the continual sustenance of spiritual life, supplies to the inquirer or doubter the only sufficient ground on which to lay the foundations of belief.

V. It is, therefore, on the result of our study of the life of Jesus Christ, directly for ourselves in the records of the small portion of that life which are preserved to us, and indirectly in the effect which the fuller knowledge of that life produced on the minds of the apostolic teachers of the world, that the question of faith or unbelief in Christ must ultimately depend. This is, indeed, the true form in which to put the ultimate question of the truth or falsehood of Christianity.[5] Christian evidence, of whatever kind it be, does not profess to demonstrate the doctrines of the Gospel. Its work is done, if it produces on our mind the conviction that Jesus Christ is one in whose word and grace we may place an absolute confidence. The results of philosophic investigation are rightly called theories; the summaries of Christian doctrine are creeds. At whatever stage we pause in the investigation here described—whether we rest contented with the testimony of practical experience of the light and grace of Christ, or with the sense of a marvellous harmony of the supernatural teaching of the Gospel with the great principles of natural religion, or with the contemplation of the actual power of Christianity, intellectual, moral, and spiritual, to rule the world—whether in contemplating Christ Himself we satisfy ourselves with the general aspect of the life of Christ seen from afar, or more reasonably go on to that closer

The function of faith.

[5] See Part II. c. vii.

knowledge of Him, which belongs to the reverent contemplation of true discipleship—still the final advance to full knowledge of Christianity is always by the way of faith in Jesus Christ. The only difference is that some arrive sooner and some later at this faith. All alike, if they would be Christians, must advance by it to the fulness and maturity of Christian knowledge.

The law of faith should, therefore, be attentively considered, to see whether it is not a universal law of human nature and life, by which the individual soul grows to its perfection, and by which the whole world is guided to the great steps of collective progress; manifesting itself in various phases, all involving more or less of moral action; placed now in mankind at large, now, especially in its highest phases, in individuals; always implying some acknowledgment of mission and inspiration in those to whom it is given. The study of that law as it is written broadly on human history, and the comparison of these continual exemplifications of it with the kind of faith which is claimed for Christ, because unquestionably He claimed it for Himself, will, if I mistake not, bring out again the principle that Christianity is supernatural, yet not preternatural. For the claim of faith for Him is simply a supernatural culmination of this great natural law. The question between Christian and non-Christian is the question whether this culmination can be rightly acknowledged. The function of Christian evidence is discharged when it has led us, with the apostles, to confess that He has the 'words of eternal life,' not only in 'the earthly things' which we can understand and test, but in 'the heavenly things'—the mysterious realities— which no mere man can know.

From this acceptance alone can we go on to the deeper and grander doctrines of Christianity.[6] At every point His revelation has its preparation in reason, and its veri- The doctrines refication by experience; but at every point it appeals vealed to ultimately to faith. So only it is that we can know faith. the full meaning of the Atonement, the mystery of Christ in heaven in these two eternities, which stretch backward

[6] See Part II. c. viii.

from the Incarnation and forward from the Ascension, the ultimate truths of the Godhead itself in the Holy Trinity. That they rest on His word cannot well be doubted; that by faith in that word alone they can be realised is hardly less certain. Such faith is in every sense a universal power. Unlike the more abstract speculations of reason, it is within the reach of all men, and is sufficient for all. By its very nature it lays hold in each of the whole human being—in thought, in moral sense, in affection, and in spiritual aspiration—and brings it to its only natural rest in God. When it has so laid hold of our humanity, it cannot remain inactive; it developes itself in work, and is inspired by the enthusiasm of love. Hence in it, and in it only, lies 'the victory that overcomes the world.' We fall away from the true Christianity, which has achieved world-wide dominion, whenever we seek such victory in abstract reasoning or in practical morality, in the beauty which enthrals the imagination, or in simple sentiment, whether of brotherhood or of adoration.

VI. Such I believe to be the natural method by which Christianity actually grows in the soul and in the world. It is for the method itself, which I believe to be true, rather than for the exhibition of it, in which I know that many defects will be found, that I desire to claim attention. It may not unfairly ask for careful consideration from those who stand aloof from Christianity, or even in opposition to it. For such alienation and antagonism constantly arise from mistakes as to the true nature of Christianity, perhaps not unfrequently excused by the perverted representations of it put forth by men speaking in its name. It may not be without interest to the believer, if it gives him a clearer idea of the process which has actually moulded his thought and life, and if it shows him in what light he may declare to the world his reason for the hope on which he rests. But perhaps it may speak especially to the intermediate class—always large, never larger than in these days —composed of those, on the one hand, who believe, and yet hold only by a vague and feeble grasp to a faith which they hear daily decried as obsolete; and of those who, on the other, long to believe, even go so far as to honour Chris-

Conclusion.

tianity and to reverence Christ, but yet hesitate as to the reasonableness of faith, and the possibility of reconciling it with the real achievements and the sanguine pretensions of science.

Perhaps we have been too apt to forget that all right witness for Christ to the world should move along the lines so clearly drawn in His own manifestation on earth. He took His stand then on the vantage ground won by the past— appealing to all the signs of God's presence in the old dispensation under which Israel had grown up, and claiming them as preparations for the manifestation of God in Him— appealing to all previous knowledge of God, whether written on the heart of all humanity, or visibly embodied in the oracles entrusted to the chosen people, as similarly preparations for the word of God spoken by Himself. Like all new things which are really true, His Gospel grew out of the old, and yet showed a power as yet unknown and unconceived. From that vantage ground of the past, He advanced next to the present. His manifestation was of a present royalty, combining in one the various elements of intellectual and moral and spiritual power; and that royalty was based on nothing else than the manifestation of Himself and of God in Him, by His works, by His word, and by His life. Such manifestation was made to the world, imperfectly and generally, rather as a preparation for the future than a thing sufficient in itself. The true manifestation was to the disciples alone, and through them hereafter, under inspiration of God, to the whole world; and their all-sufficient preparation and credentials for the great work consisted simply in their knowledge of Christ Himself. Finally, for the future, for the development of His kingdom of grace and salvation on earth and in heaven, His appeal was simply to faith. That faith was not a mere credulity, without basis on sufficient proofs, without preparation in reason, and without verification in experience; but yet it was really and truly faith, leading up to mysteries, which had to be known, yet which passed all knowledge unless they could be seen through the mind of Christ. What His manifestation of Himself was, that, in principle, must all witness of Him be even to the end of time. It must take into account the past and the present, while it looks on to the future. Its main principle must be the study of the life and person of Christ Himself. It must acknowledge and glory in the law of faith. So only can it be rightly put forward in His name, and hope for that blessing, whether of conversion or establishment in the truth, which is promised only to such witness as draws its inspiration from the word of Christ Himself.

www.ingramcontent.com/pod-product-compliance
Lightning Source LLC
Chambersburg PA
CBHW020122020526
44111CB00049B/991